CRITICAL INSIGHTS

Saul Bellow

CRITICAL INSIGHTS

Saul Bellow

Editor
Allan Chavkin
Texas State University-San Marcos

Salem Press
Pasadena, California   Hackensack, New Jersey

Library of Congress Cataloging-in-Publication Data
Saul Bellow / editor, Allan Chavkin.
    p. cm. — (Critical insights)
Includes four new essays commissioned especially for this volume as well
as fourteen previously published essays.
Includes bibliographical references and index.
ISBN 978-1-58765-824-2 (alk. paper)
    1. Bellow, Saul—Criticism and interpretation. I. Chavkin, Allan Richard,
1950-
    PS3503.E4488Z8453 2012
    813'.52—dc22

                                                                2011018806

PRINTED IN CANADA

Contents_____

Resources

About This Volume_____

Allan Chavkin

This volume presents a wide-ranging selection of essays on Saul Bellow's fiction. The essays employ a variety of literary approaches, and all of Bellow's full-length novels and two of his most important novellas, *Seize the Day* and *The Bellarosa Connection*, are discussed at length. In addition, Bellow's best collection of shorter works, *Him with His Foot in His Mouth, and Other Stories*, which includes three novellas and two short stories, is the focus of one essay. Other essays examine Bellow's most anthologized early story, "Looking for Mr. Green" (1951), and one of his best stories of the latter part of his career, the elegiac "Something to Remember Me By" (1990).

This volume is divided into four sections. The first consists of my introductory essay on Bellow's work, a short biographical sketch of Bellow's life, and an essay providing the perspective of *The Paris Review* on Bellow's work. The second section presents four new essays commissioned specifically for this book by distinguished Bellow critics Andrew M. Gordon, Judie Newman, Daniel Fuchs, and Gloria L. Cronin. The third section offers fourteen reprinted essays that not only offer provocative and thoughtful readings of the major texts but also collectively reflect the history of criticism on Bellow's work. These essays are organized chronologically by the novels they examine, from *Dangling Man* (1944) to *Ravelstein* (2000), with essays on two of Bellow's short stories concluding the section. Finally, the fourth section provides a chronology of Bellow's life, a list of his published works, and a selected bibliography of literary criticism on his work.

In "On Saul Bellow," I survey the author's career and explain how his writing developed over almost six decades. Victoria Aarons provides a brief biography of Bellow in which she not only summarizes the major events of his life but also presents her view on the connection between Bellow's life and his art. She recounts how from the dispiriting conditions of a childhood marked by poverty he eventually became "one of the major figures of twentieth-century American letters." In her *Paris Review* perspective, Natalie Jacoby allows the reader to hear Bellow's point of view, in which, among other things, he confesses that he dislikes being pigeonholed with various categorizations such as "Jewish writer," "immigrant writer," and "midwestern writer." Jacoby argues that Bellow's sickness during his childhood, which resulted in an extended separation from his family when he was hospitalized at one point, transformed him into a voracious reader and also made him sensitive to mortality and "the struggle for life."

Andrew M. Gordon discusses the paradoxical situation in which critics present psychological readings of Bellow's novels even though the author himself disdains psychology. Gordon analyzes Bellow's deep understanding of modern psychology and his ambivalent attitude toward it. He describes Bellow's personal involvement with different psychiatrists and his initial interest in and eventual rejection of the theories of Sigmund Freud, Wilhelm Reich, and Heinz Kohut. Gordon uses *Seize the Day* (1956) as a case study to show how critics have employed a variety of psychological theories to interpret the neurotic protagonist Tommy Wilhelm, who is on the verge of a nervous breakdown.

In her essay on the cultural and historical context of Bellow's work, Judie Newman presents a provocative argument in which she concludes that "the dominant feature of Saul Bellow's relation to his cultural and historical context is his absolute refusal to be defined by it." Although his fiction reflects the intellectual currents of the day, Bellow's independence from cultural fashions is clear from the opening of his first novel, when he rejected the hard-boiled code of the 1940s, and this independence can be seen throughout his career. Newman notes that in *Herzog* (1964), a novel that did much to establish Bellow's stature as one of America's premier writers, Bellow depicts "his great theme: the need to come to terms with the past without being defined by it." Bellow's Jewish immigrant background and his early education in social anthropology helped shape his attitudes toward culture and history and profoundly influenced his fiction.

Focusing on Bellow's *The Bellarosa Connection* (1989) and several short stories of Bernard Malamud, Daniel Fuchs contrasts differing responses to the Holocaust and history in the two writers. Haunted by guilt over his freedom after he moved away from his father and his brother, Malamud portrays with great pathos Holocaust survivors and Jewish ethics, with an emphasis on the importance of generosity. Whereas typically Malamud writes about the Holocaust at a remove through the refugee experience, Bellow's more direct rendering of the event is saturated in history.

Gloria L. Cronin examines the critical reception of Bellow's fiction. She explains how Bellow "dominated American literature from the late 1950s to the early 1980s," but his novels and novellas after the early 1980s to the publication of *Ravelstein* in 2000 often received mixed reviews. Cronin not only discusses the critical reception of Bellow's works but also summarizes the variety of critical interpretations each of the works prompted. Her essay concludes with a thoughtful analysis of the critical eulogies that appeared on the death of Bellow in April 2005 and explains what critics see as his literary achievement and his place in world literature.

Jean-François Leroux investigates the subject of boredom as a major concern of Bellow's fiction and considers Bellow's treatment of this topic in his fiction in relationship to the "vast literature of ennui." Leroux focuses his discussion on *Dangling Man*, a novel with important connections to Jean-Paul Sartre's *Nausea* (1938) and Fyodor Dostoevsky's *Notes from Underground* (1864). The essay reconsiders Bellow's ambivalent relationship to Dostoevsky and the influence the nineteenth-century Russian writer might have had on the work of the Jewish American author. Leroux notes that there are substantial differences between the two novelists. From the interminable debate of the mind with itself, "Dostoevsky escapes in the direction of religious asceticism, Bellow in that of gnosis and silence."

Jonathan Baumbach begins his discussion of *The Victim* (1947) by analyzing *Dangling Man*, which "chronicles Joseph's deteriorating state of soul." Both of the protagonists of Bellow's first two novels are dangling men and victims, who feel persecuted and guilty. Baumbach explains the complex psychology of persecutor and victim in the confrontation between Asa Leventhal and his double, Kirby Allbee. The truth of the novel is complicated and ultimately ambiguous. The primary "moral dilemma of the novel" can be posed with this question that Bellow suggests cannot be answered with any certainty: "How far can a man be held responsible for the unintentional consequences of his acts?" Much of the effectiveness of the novel is a consequence of the reader's seeing the events of the work through the point of view of Leventhal, "making the reader a sympathetic participant in his nightmare experience."

Donald Pizer sees *The Adventures of Augie March* (1953) as extending the tradition of American literary naturalism in its presentation of the difficult balance between the conditioning forces of life and the individual's search for positive values and affirmation despite these forces. The novel is about the "rough forces" that shape the individual, especially other human wills that would control the individual. Pizer examines how other people seek to control Augie, and he puts these people into the categories of the "adopters," whose power over Augie derives from Augie's material needs, and the "theoreticians," who would impose their ideology on Augie and satisfy the need for unquestioning belief.

Using an unpublished draft of *Seize the Day* (1956) from the Harry Ransom Center at the University of Texas at Austin, I reveal Bellow's intentions in this complicated novel, which has prompted contradictory interpretations. This early draft, titled "One of Those Days," is especially helpful for an understanding of the complicated characters, who are "like the faces on a playing card, upside down either way," to use the protagonist's language. I also find support in this early unpublished draft for an interpretation of the final scene of the novel as one that suggests Wilhelm's spiritual rebirth and not his final defeat and existential despair.

Malcolm Bradbury offers an intriguing argument that Bellow's novels of the 1950s, *The Adventures of Augie March*, *Seize the Day*, and *Henderson the Rain King* (1959), are written in a new style that can be regarded as a departure from the author's tight, angst-ridden novels of the 1940s. In his novels of the 1950s, Bellow creates a new form and a new type of hero. These new heroes are "self-creators" who "command large dimensions of their own fate" and achieve spiritual growth. *The Adventures of Augie March* presents a narrator who is extravagant morally, intellectually, and emotionally. Seize the Day is a comedy, with a protagonist who is a schlemiel, a suffering joker torn between the everyday world and "a larger world of being." *Henderson the Rain King* is a novel with another extravagant narrator, but unlike *The Adventures of Augie March*, this novel owes a debt to the form of romance. The adventures of Henderson occur in a mythic Africa where "all travel is mental."

M. Gilbert Porter explores a neglected topic in the study of Bellow's fiction, the complicated point of view in *Herzog*, which is "directly reflective of the emotional and intellectual condition of the protagonist." In fact, Porter investigates the functioning of narrative technique in the book as it contributes to the formation of Herzog's character. He observes that most of what occurs in the novel are images re-created and relived by the suffering consciousness of the protagonist. He argues that Herzog's wish for transcendence manifests itself in imaginative reflection, and he analyzes key images (such as mirrors, water, and eyes) and suggests that the "reflections of the self are symbolic" of Herzog's troubled soul, his keen sensitivity, and his obsessive inclination to recall his painful past. Porter's central thesis is that Bellow employs "strategic shifts in person and time" to embody the protagonist's divided self, "torn as he is between the realm of thought and the realm of feeling, between the evidence for despair in the world and the desire for affirmation in himself, between the active man and the reflective consciousness."

S. Lillian Kremer addresses the issue of the Holocaust in *Mr.*

Sammler's Planet (1970). She observes that Bellow chooses to avoid dramatizing Nazi atrocities and instead focuses on the effects of the Holocaust on the survivors, especially on the termination or disruption of the creative impulse, the damage to the "capacity to love," and "religious confusion." Bellow reveals the deplorable consequences of the long-term effects of Nazi persecution on Sammler and other survivor-victims, including Eisen, a disturbed artist; Shula-Slawa, Sammler's religiously confused daughter; and Bruch, a tormented man who re-lives his wartime horrors. Bellow also investigates other aspects of the Nazi genocide in the novel. He offers an intriguing interpretation of the career of Chaim Rumkowski, the deranged Jewish dictator of the Lodz ghetto. He also presents Sammler's scathing indictment of Hannah Arendt's "banality of evil" argument, in which Sammler insists that banality is a ploy to trick the gullible and that individuals must be held accountable for their actions.

With the use of unpublished drafts of *Humboldt's Gift* (1975) from the Special Collections at the University of Chicago Library, Nancy Feyl Chavkin and I offer a reading that concentrates on the extensive references to automobiles and drivers in the published novel. We contend that the automotive references and the driving habits reveal the central theme of the novel, add to its satiric perspective on society, and help disclose the status and the social ambitions of the primary characters, whose real selves are hidden beneath their social masks. Bellow's focus in the novel is on the comically incongruous situation of the idealistic writer in a society full of cynical "realists" who are satisfied to see artists fail and become "farcical martyrs," as Humboldt did. These cynical realists, or "deeper thieves," view such failures as verification of their nihilistic outlook.

In his close reading of *The Dean's December* (1982), Robert F. Kiernan provides a thorough overview of the novel's themes and major characters. He disentangles the complicated strands of the divided character of Dean Albert Corde, the protagonist of the novel, and suggests that the reader cannot always accept the dean's self-evaluation. In disagreement with some critics on this issue, Kiernan argues that the self-righteous crusading Corde possesses a philanderer's disdain for women and fails to admit that "they accomplish the ordinary business of life while he spins theories and devises categories." Moreover, Corde patronizes his sister Elfrida and misunderstands and misjudges his self-contained wife, Minna, who is more sensitive and astute than he realizes. Kiernan suggests that at the end of the novel, Corde's decision to help Beech in only a limited way indicates that Corde "has clearly broken his commitment to undivided truth in favor of the unresolved, the problematic, and the contingent." Corde will remain a divided man but now will feel less compelled to resolve the tensions associated with being conflicted; in short, his decision to retreat from the social and political controversies that consumed him should be seen as "a necessary adjustment" and "not a death of mind and spirit."

Daniel Fuchs argues that the unifying theme of Bellow's *Him with His Foot in His Mouth, and Other Stories* (1984) is aging. Only "Zetland: By a Character Witness," a fragment from a novel about Isaac Rosenfeld that Bellow abandoned, does not reveal this preoccupation with aging. Fuchs suggests that the most distinguished work in the volume is the novella *What Kind of Day Did You Have?*, and he examines the complexities of the characters of Katrina Goliger and Victor Wulpy. By the end of the story Katrina is disillusioned and Wulpy, the hardboiled Marxist intellectual, who is dying, is unsettled by lucid spiritual impressions that contradict his materialist ideology. Another remarkable story in the volume is "A Silver Dish," in which the narrator, a man in his sixties, reflects upon the recent death of his father, whose theft decades earlier transformed the son's life. "Him with His Foot in His Mouth" also presents the reflections of another narrator who is in his sixties, but the tone is comical as he explains the witty insults that created immense difficulties for him throughout his life. Fuchs argues that in "Cousins" "character sketch does the work of plot," and he discusses the characters and Bellow's thematic concerns in this work.

Ellen Pifer regards *More Die of Heartbreak* (1987) as a novel that continues what *Humboldt's Gift* initiated. She argues that Charlie Citrine's interest in certain occult ideas, especially the assumption that there is a "hidden design" behind the appearances of contemporary existence, is at the center of *More Die of Heartbreak*. Benn Crader, an internationally famous botanist, is both a scientist and a "plant clairvoyant" who has the intuitive power to see behind appearances. The narrator, Ken Trachtenberg, has a similar relationship to his uncle Benn as Citrine does to Humboldt. Both narrators deeply admire their spiritual fathers, who possess visionary powers but who squander them in the distractions of contemporary existence; both narrators feel compelled to tell the stories of these great men and explain their relationships with them.

Sarah Blacher Cohen discusses the various comic characteristics of Bellow's final novel *Ravelstein*. In this roman à clef, in which Bellow (fictionalized as the narrator Chick) pays homage to his dear friend Allan Bloom, the eponymous hero, Abe Ravelstein, serves as a spokesman for Bellow's comedy of ideas. This manic intellectual, who can play the clown at times, functions as the spiritual conscience of the work. The novel reveals a "Jewish sense of humor, with its mockery of mortality," which "energizes the dying Ravelstein and the frail" narrator. Cohen explains how the comic quality of this novel enhances and clarifies the thematic concerns.

Eusebio L. Rodrigues considers "Looking for Mr. Green," calling it "one of the great short stories of our time"; he analyzes how Bellow transforms a "simple, Dreiserian piece into a metaphysical parable." He argues that the story is a "modern dramatization of Ecclesiastes." George Grebe, the protagonist, is a modern *Koheleth* (Hebrew for the Greek Ecclesiastes or "the preacher"), who is searching for the elusive Mr. Green and for the meaning of the human condition. Grebe's search to deliver a relief check to Mr. Green is also an archetypal quest. It is important for the reader to understand that this story "consists of two planes," the realistic and the symbolic, "that constantly dissolve, merge and fuse into one another without either plane insisting on its own supremacy."

In his essay on "Something to Remember Me By," Andrew Gordon employs a psychoanalytic approach to analyze why Louie, the elderly narrator and protagonist, reveals a humiliating story about himself to his son instead of a story that presents him in a positive light. Gordon suggests that the pattern of ritual degradation in the story can be seen in Bellow's other heroes and that Bellow's comedy is largely "the comedy of shame." In this instance the source of the shame is in Louie's neurotic character. He copes with his shame by confession and judges himself harshly. Gordon suggests, however, that shame is a humanizing emotion with penitential, reparative, and pedagogical functions and can lead to love, as it does in this story.

It is my expectation that the essays in this book will help readers understand aspects of Bellow's fiction that they have previously ignored or neglected. It is my hope that these essays will inspire readers to explore Bellow's works again and to look at them from fresh perspectives.

CAREER, LIFE, AND INFLUENCE

On Saul Bellow_____

Allan Chavkin

I

Saul Bellow published his first book, *Dangling Man*, in 1944 and his final book, *Collected Stories*, in 2001, four years before his death. His *Letters*, edited by Benjamin Taylor, appeared posthumously in 2010. During his long career, Bellow's writing, which included plays and nonfiction as well as novels and short stories, attracted enormous attention from the literary establishment as well as the public. He received lavish recognition, including a Pulitzer Prize, three National Book Awards, and the Nobel Prize in Literature "for the human understanding and subtle analysis of contemporary culture that are combined in his works" ("Nobel Prize").

Frequently mentioned by critics and scholars of American literature as one of the premier writers of the second half of the twentieth century, Bellow attracted a large readership, and publication of each new novel usually meant lead book reviews in magazines and newspapers. A great comic writer, he achieved this popularity despite the fact that many readers considered some of his novels difficult because of their erudite allusions. Unlike best-selling novels with an emphasis on suspense, mystery, and graphic violence, Bellow's fiction sometimes subordinates plot to an exploration of complicated issues and the rendering of the interior life of the protagonist. Bellow's troubled protagonists, whether they are intellectuals or college dropouts, devote much of their time to pondering the mistakes and misadventures of their own lives and those of their culture. Evident throughout Bellow's work is "his belief that fiction ought to address the great moral questions of human existence and 'account for the mysterious circumstance of being'" (Kakutani, "Dispatches" C1).

II

In his first novel, *Dangling Man*, Bellow reveals that he had no apprehension of going against the grain of the dominant orthodoxies of his time, a feature that would become characteristic of his fiction. In the opening of the novel, the narrator, Joseph, repudiates Ernest Hemingway's hard-boiled code of the tough guy who keeps his emotions bottled up and his interior life hidden.[1] Joseph suggests that those who abide by this widely accepted code are "unpracticed in introspection, and therefore badly equipped to deal with opponents whom they cannot shoot like big game or outdo in daring" (9). In fact, Bellow's narrator Joseph is the antithesis of Hemingway's stoic hard-boiled hero; he is highly emotional, introspective, and guilt-ridden. His alienation is reminiscent of that of Fyodor Dostoevsky's narrator of *Notes from Underground* (1864). Bellow's first novel consists of Joseph's diary from December 1942 to April 1943, as he waits to be inducted into the army. Joseph recounts his quarrels with family members and others during this difficult time in limbo. His marriage is deteriorating, and he has ambivalent feelings toward his wife, Iva, who is modeled on Bellow's first wife, Anita Goshkin (Meyers 164). The novel lacks a plot and instead focuses on Joseph's intense self-scrutiny; at times he converses with his alter ego as he strives to know himself.

Not only is Bellow's first novel similar to Dostoevsky's *Notes from Underground*, but it also resembles Jean-Paul Sartre's *Nausea* (1938), in which the narrator, Antoine Roquentin, experiences an existential crisis as he seeks a way out of his spiritual death-in-life. Also written in the form of journal entries, *Nausea* is really plotless and focuses on the self-hatred and alienation of the narrator. Like Antoine Roquentin, Joseph's "dangling" refers not just to his state of limbo as he waits to be inducted into the army but also to a metaphysical problem of suddenly finding oneself a stranger in a world indifferent to all human concerns.

Like Joseph in *Dangling Man*, Asa Leventhal, the protagonist of *The Victim* (1947), is an introspective man with a vague sense of guilt. With his wife temporarily absent, the insecure Leventhal is dangling, and his situation suddenly becomes much worse when Kirby Allbee, an acquaintance from his past, emerges to accuse Leventhal of ruining Allbee's life. Allbee states that years ago Leventhal, angry at anti-Semitic remarks that Allbee had made, acted rudely during an interview with Allbee's boss, Rudiger, that Allbee had arranged for him. Allbee maintains that Leventhal wanted Allbee to be fired. After Rudiger fired Allbee, the unemployed man drank excessively, his wife left him, and he became a bum. Now the anti-Semitic Allbee has returned to insist that Leventhal is responsible for this dramatic change of fortune.

The novel with great precision depicts the complex psychology of the interaction of persecutor and victim, anti-Semite and Jew. On another level, however, the novel explores the problem of unnecessary suffering, as it is most poignantly seen in the instance of children. The two epigraphs of the novel indicate that Bellow was concerned not only with social prejudice but also with the philosophical problem of suffering and the question of responsibility for it. "Who runs things?" wonders Leventhal (294). The subplot of the novel evokes the problem of unjust suffering by recounting the illness of Leventhal's nephew, who eventually dies of a rare disease. It is likely that the source for this subplot of *The Victim* is in Dostoevsky's *The Eternal Husband* (1870), but *The Brothers Karamazov* (1880) might also have influenced this subplot.[2] A third possible source is the Holocaust, in which multitudes of Jewish children perished. Published only two years after the end of World War II, *The Victim*, though it does not refer directly to the Holocaust, examines the psychology of anti-Semitism and prompts one to consider the philosophical issues associated with that catastrophic event.

As Robert Penn Warren pointed out, Bellow's first two novels were in "the Flaubert-James tradition," with strict forms (22). With his third novel, Bellow took a new direction. By the time he came to write his third novel, Bellow had become disenchanted with the depressive temperament of restrictive formal standards, with their rigid structures, detached tones, and restrained emotions. The author himself explained to fellow writer Bernard Malamud: "I can't allow myself to forget that I took a position in writing this book. . . . A novel, like a letter, should be loose, cover much ground, run swiftly, take risk of mortality and decay. I backed away from Flaubert, in the direction of Walter Scott, Balzac, and Dickens" (*Letters* 128). Bellow's *The Adventures of Augie March* (1953) differs radically from his first novels in style and theme. This picaresque novel, with its larky protagonist, opens in language reminiscent of Whitman. "I am an American, Chicago born—Chicago, that somber city—"and go at things as I have taught myself, freestyle" (1). Augie March is freewheeling, impulsive, and optimistic despite growing up in poverty without a father. Good natured and easygoing, he continually encounters Machiavellian characters who seek in various ways to control him as he moves from one adventure to the next. The novel is in part a bildungsroman in which he narrates the story of his life growing up in the 1920s and 1930s. By the end of the novel he finds himself in postwar Europe, where he is now married and involved in the black market. By the end of the novel his optimism and insouciance have been replaced by a darker awareness. Robert F. Kiernan observes, "One must have a taste for the large scale to fully appreciate *Augie March*, perhaps, but few novels of its kind have articulated so powerfully the drift into bitterness of a spirit resolutely blithe" (56).

The Adventures of Augie March was in part a response to Bellow's attempt to move away from his victim protagonists in the first two novels. It is likely that after his third novel, he decided that he had gone too far in the opposite direction. *Seize the Day* (1956) seems closer in mood to his first two novels than it does to *The Adventures of Augie March*, but Bellow does not return to the victim protagonists of his first two novels. Tommy Wilhelm does suffer greatly, but his suffering leads to his spiritual rebirth.

Seize the Day presents one day in the life of a down-and-out salesman of children's furniture; this novella portrays a day of reckoning for the protagonist, Tommy Wilhelm, who believes that he is in a desperate situation. He is separated from his wife, who is harassing him for financial support. Unemployed and with very little money, he hopes that his father will be sympathetic to his plight and help him financially, but his father considers him a failure and refuses to provide financial or emotional support. Despite his father's warnings, Wilhelm turns to the mysterious Dr. Tamkin for help. Claiming to be a psychologist, Tamkin is a charlatan who steals the remainder of Wilhelm's money by convincing the unemployed salesman to allow Tamkin to invest his money in the market. In the final scene of the novel, Wilhelm finds himself weeping in front of the corpse of a stranger. He is not crying out of self-pity here but for all humankind. Early in the novel Wilhelm quotes from John Milton's *Lycidas*, which provides the key metaphor of drowning and water imagery that are used in the novel to suggest Wilhelm's spiritual struggle and final rebirth. In a lyrical passage at the conclusion of the work, Bellow suggests that Wilhelm symbolically drowns and is then resurrected. The novella is a brilliant rendering of the process by which he achieves his spiritual breakthrough despite all the turmoil and frustrations that the world seems to heap upon him.

The eponymous protagonist of Bellow's next novel, *Henderson the Rain King* (1959), suffers immensely. He is a middle-aged white Anglo-Saxon Protestant millionaire who is profoundly dissatisfied with his life and desperate to satisfy the inner voice of "I want, I want" and to "burst the spirit's sleep," as he phrases it by quoting from Percy Bysshe Shelley's dedication to *The Revolt of Islam*. Henderson leaves his family in America and goes on a quest in Africa, where he has many adventures. With its comic hero, *Henderson the Rain King* is part fantasy, part farce, part fable, and part realistic novel. It can also be regarded as a transformation of the nineteenth-century English romantic quest-romance to which Bellow has added comic and ironic elements. The novel has an English romantic sensibility and includes quotations from the works of Shelley, William Blake, Samuel Taylor Coleridge, and

William Wordsworth. Disenchanted with the modernist devaluing of the ordinary individual and everyday life, Bellow is attracted to the affirmative outlook of the English romantic poets, with their faith in the power of the imagination to achieve spiritual regeneration and overcome anxiety over death. Henderson's progress from spiritual crisis to spiritual rebirth parallels the progress in Wordsworth's "Intimations of Immortality from Recollections of Early Childhood," which is quoted in part at the end of the novel. In his quest to "burst the spirit's sleep," he encounters Dahfu, who becomes his spiritual guide and romantic prophet, instructing him that he possesses the potential for spiritual regeneration if he recognizes the powers of the human imagination.[3]

Henderson the Rain King should also be considered Bellow's critique of Joseph Conrad's *Heart of Darkness* (1902), in which the British novelist's first-person narrator, Marlow, encounters his prophet Kurtz, who teaches him about humankind's capacity for total depravity. When Marlow returns to civilization after his disillusioning experience in the heart of darkness of Africa, he possesses a bleak view of the human condition. In contrast to Kurtz is Dahfu, who presents Henderson with a different worldview. Henderson concludes "that chaos doesn't run the whole show. That this is not a sick and hasty ride, helpless, through a dream into oblivion" (175). In contrast to Marlow's disillusionment, Henderson has gained a new faith in life and in the power of art. On his way home from Africa, he befriends an orphan, revealing his new capacity for love, and reflects: "As for this kid resting against me . . . why, he was still trailing his cloud of glory. God knows, I dragged mine on as long as I could till it got dingy, mere tatters of gray fog. However, I always knew what it was" (339). Borrowing Wordsworth's metaphor, Henderson believes in the English poet's view of spiritual development and now can cope with his anxiety over death, which in the past threatened to overwhelm him. He recognizes and accepts that with aging comes loss but understands, too, that by the power of imagination one can capture the child's sense of awe and wonder.

Bellow's allegiance to the values of nineteenth-century English romanticism can be seen in works published after *Henderson the Rain King*, especially his next novel, *Herzog* (1964), in which the eponymous hero, who teaches a course on "The Roots of Romanticism," finds repugnant the cynical realism that is ubiquitous in modern society. He sardonically observes that even people "who had never even read a book of metaphysics, were touting the Void as if it were so much salable real estate" (93). These people, "reality instructors," pride themselves on being tough-minded and realistic and consider Herzog a naive cuckolded professor. Herzog does realize that there is truth in their perception of him as "a chump, a failed intellectual, and at bottom a sentimentalist," but he rejects their conclusion that he must become like them and adopt their cynical kind of "realism" (*Letters* 540). Such an insidious outlook undermines traditional humanist values.

Herzog is one of Bellow's most challenging novels; it is in the form of a retrospective meditation in which the hero struggles to come to terms with the personal chaos of his domestic life and the cultural disorder that he sees as one of the contributing factors for the chaos in his own life. The novel opens with Herzog remarking that some people thought he was "cracked," and he too considers that he might be out of his mind (1). The discovery of his wife's adultery with his best friend and the end of his marriage cause intense emotional turmoil and prompt him to review his life and the ideas by which has he lived. He needs to understand how he has mismanaged everything and "ruined" his life. He obsessively remembers and meditates upon the past and writes letters to the living and to the dead. He feels compelled to write letters not only to friends and acquaintances but also to thinkers, such as Friedrich Nietzsche and Martin Heidegger, whose ideas have had a profound impact on contemporary culture. He "has been overcome by the need to explain, to have it out, to justify, to put in perspective, to clarify, to make amends" (2).

Herzog is a highly sophisticated work that does not fit into any of the traditional genres but owes a debt to the epistolary novel, the nineteenth-century English romantic crisis meditation, the novel of ideas, and the psychological novel. The work brilliantly captures the interior life of its protagonist, and the reader can observe how the process of Herzog's mind reflects associatively over a range of issues and over a variety of events and people. The novel is remarkable not only for its psychological acuity and its precision in capturing Herzog's complex consciousness but also for its analysis of the history of ideas and for its critique of contemporary culture.

Like *Herzog, Mr. Sammler's Planet* (1970) is a novel in which the protagonist recollects the recent past, and interspersed within these recollections of the recent past are recollections of a more distant past. Once again, as with Herzog, the mental stability of the protagonist is a concern. Sammler is a Holocaust survivor whose painful memories of the horrors of the war intrude upon his consciousness despite his attempts to suppress them. The Nazis blinded one of Sammler's eyes, and he also suffers in the present because his nervous system has been damaged, for which he receives an indemnity from the Bonn government.

Sammler's meditative bent is prompted by his desire to try to reconcile and to make some sense of three radically different worlds or "planets" where he has resided at different periods of his life. Before World War II, he lived in Great Britain, where he was one of the circle of H. G. Wells's progressive thinkers. This was an exciting time for him and his wife, Antonina, when they engaged in "the most distinguished intimacy with the finest people in Britain" (28). They were optimistic, idealistic, and complacent. When Sammler, Antonina, and their daughter Shula were surprised by the Nazi invasion of Poland at the outbreak of World War II, they were shocked to discover the barbarism on this new "planet" of wartime Poland. After the Nazis arrested them and other Jews, Sammler and his wife were shot at in a mass execution. Antonina died with the other victims, but by some fluke of fate Sammler was able to crawl out of the pit in which the corpses were piled and survive. Shula also suffered greatly during the war years. Separated from her parents and hiding in a convent, Shula survived the war, but like so many children during the Holocaust, she endured psychological trauma that shaped her personality.

After the war Sammler and Shula were brought from a camp for displaced persons to the United States by a sympathetic relative, Dr. Elya Gruner, who continued to help them financially. Yet in the postwar years, from 1945 to 1969, neither completely adjusted to life in the United States. Now in 1969, the present time of the novel, both Sammler and Shula suffer from post-traumatic stress disorder, though the disorder takes different forms in father and daughter. The cultural disorder of the 1960s seems to have a negative impact on both of them. Shula's chaotic lifestyle is exacerbated by the current social disorder, while Sammler associates the revolutionary impulse within the counterculture with Hitler's attempt to destroy civilization, and, paradoxically, angry at the intolerance of the counterculture radicals, Sammler becomes intolerant in his attitudes, with evidence of misanthropy, misogyny, and racism.

Sammler wants only to be left alone to think about the past and the present and the meaning of the different "planets" on which he has resided, but distractions in the present prevent him from doing so. His patron, Dr. Gruner, is dying in the hospital of a brain aneurysm, and Sammler's attempts to visit him during his last days are frustrated by the "degraded clowning" in contemporary culture. Sammler is distracted by Shula's stealing an Indian scientist's manuscript and by the antics of many others, including Dr. Gruner's grown children.

Humboldt's Gift attracted much attention when it was published in 1975, including a cover magazine profile in *Newsweek* in which the authors observed that Bellow was now "the most honored American novelist of his age" (Clemons and Kroll 40). This novel was awarded a Pulitzer Prize and no doubt played a role in Bellow's being awarded the Nobel Prize in Literature in 1976. With the publication of this book, some claimed that Bellow was now America's greatest contemporary writer and that he "consolidates the place assigned to him by Philip Roth, who identified 'the great inventors of narrative detail and masters of narrative voice and perspective' as 'James, Conrad, Dostoevski and Bellow'" (Clemons and Kroll 32). Bellow's attaining this success was not an easy achievement, and in *Humboldt's Gift* he explores the difficult role of the artist in American society, where many people believe in a hard-nosed realism and smugly view the failure or even the self-destruction of the artist concerned with spiritual matters as proof of the importance of maintaining their "realistic outlook."

A writer preoccupied with the failure and premature death of the idealistic poet Humboldt, Charlie Citrine feels frustrated by the distractions of contemporary society that prevent him, a longtime enthusiast of Rudolf Steiner's occult philosophy, from meditating on the metaphysical questions that fascinate him and from focusing on his spiritual growth.[4] One of the comic aspects of the novel is Charlie's continual difficulty in focusing on his spiritual concerns because of interruptions from a variety of people. With the help of ferocious lawyers such as "cannibal Pinsker," Denise, his ex-wife, plagues him with lawsuits. His voluptuous mistress, Renata, worries him, for occasionally she dallies with Flonzaley, and she may abandon him for this well-to-do mortician or another suitor. His friend and collaborator on a new journal, Pierre Thaxter, is charming but is probably conning Charlie and stealing his money. Ronald Cantabile, a small-time gangster, destroys Charlie's prized Mercedes-Benz by beating it with a baseball bat and then continues to harass him in a variety of ways, even after Charlie has paid him a gambling debt and apologized for his initial failure to pay it. The IRS, judges, and Denise's lawyers pose threats to Charlie's comfortable lifestyle.

The person who finally enables Charlie to overcome all of these distractions is Von Humboldt Fleisher, once a famous poet and Charlie's good friend, now dead, but who speaks to Charlie from the grave by way of a posthumously delivered letter accompanied by two film scenarios. The film scenarios can bring some economic relief to Charlie, but Humboldt's real contribution is the message in his letter that enables Charlie to understand that he must change his life and commit himself to the higher values of the romantic poet with faith in the power of the imagination to redeem the world. Apparently with Blake in mind, Humboldt tells Charlie that "we are not natural beings, but supernatural beings" (347). He warns Charlie not to make the same mistake he made when he became "a farcical martyr" instead of a visionary poet. When Humboldt became absorbed with material distractions and neglected the life of the imagination, he descended into self-destructive paranoia. By the end of the novel, Charlie decides that he will probably spend a month at the Swiss Steiner Center and then "take up a different kind of life" (483). The implication is that he will not follow the self-destructive path but will focus on his spiritual growth and become a serious writer.

Albert Corde, the protagonist of *The Dean's December* (1982), is similar to Charlie Citrine in his inclination to continually ponder the big questions, though he lacks Charlie's sense of humor. This is a much more somber book than Bellow's previous novels. Corde, a dean at an unnamed Chicago college, travels to Bucharest, where his mother-in-law is dying. In this Eastern bloc Communist country, Corde compares the quality of life in the West with that in the East and concludes that the individual's freedom has been lost in the penitentiary East and is threatened in the anarchic culture of the West. More than in any of his previous novels, Bellow in this work explores intractable social and political problems. Initially he had planned on writing a nonfiction book about Chicago (Eugene Kennedy 16). Parts of that abandoned book appear in this novel in Corde's controversial articles for *Harper's*, which focus on the problems of the African American underclass in Chicago. Bellow's most important motivation for writing the novel was to speak up for those who lack a strong voice and to suggest to the American public that the dire situation of the African American underclass has not been handled properly (William Kennedy 50). While the subplot in Bucharest does reveal Bellow's indictment of the nihilistic totalitarianism of the Communist bloc countries, the key focus of this novel is on racism and the evils associated with it.

Bellow's decision to see this issue through the lens of fiction instead of a nonfiction book as he originally planned was a consequence of his belief that fiction provides the freedom necessary to explore all of the intricacies of the problems addressed. Bellow believed that the novelist can be an "imaginative historian, who is able to get closer to contemporary facts than social scientists possibly can" (Kakutani, "Talk" 28). The objective approach, which must stick to the facts, fails to reveal the reality of the urban underclass, including the emotional and spiritual lives of the masses of people mired in poverty. Bellow explained to Michiko Kakutani: "It became clear to me that no imagination whatsoever had been applied to the problems of demoralized cities. All the approaches have been technical, financial, and bureaucratic, and no one has been able to take into account the sense of these lives" ("Talk" 28).

In *More Die of Heartbreak* (1987) Bellow returned to the comic mode. The novel explores a number of topics, but it focuses most intently on dysfunctional families, the war between the sexes, and the potential to see with a visionary power that defies the scientific worldview. The form of the novel is that of a monologue by its bachelor narrator, Kenneth Trachtenberg. After growing up in France with his expatriate parents, Kenneth accepted a position as a Russian literature instructor at the same university where his uncle Benn Crader teaches. Kenneth's preoccupation with his maternal uncle is partially a consequence of his disengagement from his divorced parents. Kenneth, awkward around women, has nothing in common with his father, a ladies' man. Kenneth and his uncle are perplexed by women and have immense trouble in their romantic relationships. Kenneth fervidly hopes that Treckie, the woman with whom he has had a child, will marry him and is furious when his hopes are dashed. Kenneth is particularly disturbed to see bruises on his ex-girlfriend Treckie. She has a boyfriend and the bruises are the consequences of their lovemaking, a fetish that prompts Kenneth to contact his father for his supposed knowledge of the desires of women.

After Uncle Benn escapes from his wedding and his fiancée, Caroline, he becomes involved with Matilda Layamon, and soon against his better judgment marries this woman who is young enough to be his daughter. Her father, a gynecologist who wants his daughter to be married to a rich man, pressures Uncle Benn to take legal action against Harold Vilitzer, a political racketeer who years earlier had cheated Kenneth's mother and Benn in a corrupt real estate deal. Benn desires to appease his father-in-law and to make his bride happy but is reluctant to pursue the plan to pressure Vilitzer, who is in very poor health. Kenneth believes that his uncle is a person who should be pursuing "higher meanings." At the end of the novel this renowned botanist escapes the Layamons to go to the North Pole to do his research and presumably to pursue these "higher meanings."

His "most overtly Jewish book," Bellow's *Ravelstein*, was published in 2000, only five years before his death at the age of eighty-nine (Safer 131). This novel is a roman à clef that centers on the relationship between the narrator, Chick (Bellow), and his pal Abe Ravelstein (Allan Bloom, author of *The Closing of the American Mind*). As in *Herzog* and some of Bellow's other novels, plot is subordinated to the narrator's discursive recollections and reimaginings of the past. Chick is preoccupied with portraying the grandeur of his friend, a great-souled man, and pondering nihilism. Ravelstein is dying of AIDS, and this Jewish professor, who was intrigued by the nihilistic books of the anti-Semitic Louis-Ferdinand Céline, is now absorbed by Scripture. Chick seems to see his friend as his mentor, who in his final days embodies the Jewish outlook, with its emphasis on the value of human life. This Jewish outlook is contrasted implicitly to the fascist nihilism that culminated in the Holocaust. The novel ends with a moment of revelation, a Wordsworthian "spot of time" that Chick recalls when he and Ravelstein encountered one winter day a huge flock of escaped parrots feeding on red berries. Ravelstein laughed with pleasure and astonishment at this surprising occurrence in the winter landscape. This book, in which death is ubiquitous, concludes with an epiphany that symbolizes the miracle of Jewish survival in a mysterious universe that transcends human explanation.

Bellow's final published book is his *Collected Stories*, which appeared in 2001. The title of the collection is somewhat of a misnomer; a more accurate title would be *Selected Stories and Novellas*. Of the four novellas in the volume, two are especially impressive. The novella *What Kind of Day Did You Have?* is a poignant story told primarily from the point of view of Katrina Goliger, who has abandoned her husband for her aging lover, a world-class intellectual. Full of pathos and comedy, this brilliant work reveals the process by which Katrina comes to call into question her understanding of her lover and their affair; her disillusionment threatens to shatter her fragile emotional state. *The Bellarosa Connection* is narrated by a highly assimilated Jewish American who contemplates the meanings of the strange story of Harry Fonstein, who survived the Holocaust with the help of the Broadway producer Billy Rose. This distinguished story is an exploration of the complex connections among memory, history, and identity. Other remarkable works in the collection are the short stories "Something to Remember Me By," "A Silver Dish," and "Looking for Mr. Green," all of which evoke Depression-era Chicago with striking verisimilitude; the stories are multidimensional and rich in social, psychological, and philosophical implications.

III

Bellow's fiction has often been praised for its profound psychological acumen, its vivid language, and its unique comic vision. One of the aspects of Bellow's work that separates it from the work of so many of his contemporaries is his ability to grapple with complex ideas and to examine metaphysical assumptions that many intellectuals regard as unscientific, obscure, and irrelevant. In defiance of the widely agreed upon skeptical modern worldview, Bellow believed in the existence of "natural knowledge" that cannot be verified by rational means. Influenced by Rudolf Steiner and Johann Wolfgang von Goethe, he suggested that there are some intangible truths that are not "merely human constructions" (Clements 77).

Bellow criticized the anti-intellectualism that came naturally to some writers and argued that literary artists would not be taken seriously if they refused to confront the difficult issues in the modern world. When he received the National Book Award for *Herzog* in 1965, he warned: "There is nothing left for us novelists to do but think. For unless we think, unless we make a clearer estimate of our condition, we will continue to write kid stuff, to fail in our function; we will lack serious interests and become truly irrelevant" ("Thinking Man's" 20). He did not believe, however, that the writer should be a prophet dictating to humanity or proclaiming absolute truths. A work of fiction "sets up the hypotheses and tests them in various ways, and it gives answers, but these are not definitive" (*Letters* 28). Although Bellow's novels were written in many forms, including picaresque narrative, comic fantasy, and naturalistic realism, throughout his career this master of narrative voice, who could move with ease from the language of the street to eloquent rhetoric, continually pondered in his work the big questions and explored human consciousness as it grappled with the irremediable conditions of modern life.

Notes

1. For discussions of Bellow's complex relationship to Hemingway, see Chavkin, "Fathers and Sons"; and Rovit.

2. For critical assessments of some of the connections between Bellow and Dostoevsky, see Fuchs (chapter 2); Chavkin, "The Problem of Suffering" and "Ivan Karamazov's Rebellion"; and Leroux (in this volume).

3. Bellow's debt to nineteenth-century English romanticism has been examined by

a number of critics—see especially Campbell; Chavkin, "Bellow's Alternative," "*Humboldt's Gift*," and "Bellow and English Romanticism"; Majdiak; Sandy; and Yetman.

4. The extent of the impact of Steiner's ideas on Bellow's novels has been discussed by critics—see especially Atlas (436-37); Clements; McSweeney; Pifer (431-36); and Smith.

Works Cited

Atlas, James. *Bellow: A Biography*. New York: Random House, 2000.

Bellow, Saul. *The Adventures of Augie March*. New York: Viking Press, 1953.

_____. *Collected Stories*. New York: Viking Press, 2001.

_____. *Dangling Man*. New York: Vanguard Press, 1944.

_____. *The Dean's December*. New York: Harper & Row, 1982.

_____. *Henderson the Rain King*. New York: Viking Press, 1959.

_____. *Herzog*. New York: Viking Press, 1964.

_____. *Humboldt's Gift*. New York: Viking Press, 1975.

_____. *Letters*. Ed. Benjamin Taylor. New York: Viking Press, 2010.

_____. *More Die of Heartbreak*. New York: William Morrow, 1987.

_____. *Mr. Sammler's Planet*. New York: Viking Press, 1970.

_____. *Ravelstein*. New York: Viking Press, 2000.

_____. *Seize the Day*. New York: Viking Press, 1956.

_____. "The Thinking Man's Waste Land." *Saturday Review* 3 Apr. 1965: 20.

_____. *The Victim*. New York: Vanguard Press, 1947.

Campbell, Jeff H. "Bellow's Intimations of Immortality: *Henderson the Rain King*." *Studies in the Novel* 1.3 (1969): 323-33.

Chavkin, Allan. "Bellow and English Romanticism." *Saul Bellow in the 1980s: A Collection of Critical Essays*. Ed. Gloria L. Cronin and L. H. Goldman. East Lansing: Michigan State UP, 1989. 67-79.

_____. "Bellow's Alternative to the Wasteland: Romantic Theme and Form in *Herzog*." *Studies in the Novel* 11.3 (1979): 326-37.

_____. "Fathers and Sons: 'Papa' Hemingway and Saul Bellow." *Papers on Language and Literature* 19.4 (1983): 449-60.

_____. "*Humboldt's Gift* and the Romantic Imagination." *Philological Quarterly* 62.1 (1983): 1-19.

_____. "Ivan Karamazov's Rebellion and Bellow's *The Victim*." *Papers on Language and Literature* 16.3 (1980): 316-20.

_____. "The Problem of Suffering in the Fiction of Saul Bellow." *Comparative Literature Studies* 21.2 (1984): 161-74.

Clements, James. "Bottomless Surfaces: Saul Bellow's 'Refreshed Phrenology.'" *Journal of Modern Literature* 33.1 (2009): 75-91.

Clemons, Walter, and Jack Kroll. "America's Master Novelist." *Newsweek* 1 Sept. 1975: 32-34, 39-40.

Fuchs, Daniel. *Saul Bellow: Vision and Revision*. Durham, NC: Duke UP, 1984.

Kakutani, Michiko. "Dispatches and Details from a Life in Literature." *New York Times Book Review* 9 Nov. 2010: C1, C6.

_____. "A Talk with Saul Bellow: On His Work and Himself." *New York Times* 13 Dec. 1981: 1, 28-31.

Kennedy, Eugene. "A Different Saul Bellow." *Boston Globe Magazine* 10 Jan. 1982: 16.

Kennedy, William. "If Saul Bellow Doesn't Have a True Word to Say, He Keeps His Mouth Shut." *Esquire* Feb. 1982: 48-54.

Kiernan, Robert F. *Saul Bellow*. New York: Continuum, 1988.

McSweeney, Kerry. "Saul Bellow and the Life to Come." *Critical Quarterly* 18.1 (1976): 67-72.

Majdiak, Daniel. "The Romantic Self and *Henderson the Rain King*." *Bucknell Review* 19.2 (1971): 125-46.

Meyers, Jeffrey. "Bluebeard Bellow." *Kenyon Review* 31.2 (2009): 160-85.

"The Nobel Prize in Literature 1976." Nobelprize.org. 2 Aug. 2010. http://nobelprize .org/nobel_prizes/literature/laureates/1976.

Pifer, Ellen. *Saul Bellow Against the Grain*. Philadelphia: U of Pennsylvania P, 1990.

Rovit, Earl. "Saul Bellow and the Concept of the Survivor." *Saul Bellow and His Work*. Ed. Edmond Schraepen. Brussels: Centruum voor Taal-en Literatuurwetenschap Vrije Universiteit, 1978. 89-101.

Safer, Elaine. "Saul Bellow, Master of the Comic." *Critique* 51.2 (2010): 126-34.

Sandy, Mark. "Webbed with Golden Lines: Saul Bellow's Romanticism." *Romanticism: The Journal of Romantic Culture and Criticism* 14.1 (2008): 57-67.

Smith, Herbert J. "*Humboldt's Gift* and Rudolf Steiner." *Centennial Review* 22.4 (1978): 479-89.

Warren, Robert Penn. "The Man with No Commitments." *New Republic* 2 Nov. 1953: 22-23.

Yetman, Michael G. "Who Would Not Sing for Humboldt?" *ELH* 48.4 (1981): 935-51.

Biography of Saul Bellow _____

Victoria Aarons

Solomon (Saul) Bellow was born on June 10, 1915, in Lachine, Quebec, Canada. He was the fourth child, and the first North American-
born, of Abraham and Lescha Gordin Belo, Jewish immigrants from
St. Petersburg, Russia, who set sail for Canada in November 1913. The
name "Belo" became "Bellow" through the careless transliteration of a
Canadian customs agent (Atlas 7). Like other Russian Jews living ille-
gally outside of the Imperial Russian Pale of Settlement (the area designated for Jews, from the Black Sea to the Baltic), Abraham Belo, an
importer of Turkish figs and Egyptian onions, and Lescha, the daughter of a rabbi, with their three small children, were smuggled out of St.
Petersburg, escaping the escalating restrictions and deplorable conditions imposed on Russian Jews. This was a time of anticipated self-
reinvention for Jewish immigrants; thus Abraham and Lescha Belo
(the surname derived from *byelo*, the Russian word for "white") became Abraham and Liza Bellow, resettling in Lachine, an impoverished, working-class town outside Montreal, where their fourth child,
Solomon, was born and spent the early years of his childhood. From
such dispiriting conditions—as the writer later described it, the "Jewish
slums of Montreal during my childhood . . . not too far removed from
the ghettos of Poland and Russia" (*Great Jewish Short Stories* 13)—
Saul Bellow would become one of the major figures of twentieth-
century American letters, a Nobel laureate whose distinctive, influential literary voice defined post-World War II American culture and
thought.

Bellow was in many ways a product of the immigrant upbringing that defined his early years, becoming a Jewish intellectual whose
verbal acuity was accented by highly textured descriptions of the
changing American urban landscape. Bellow's childhood milieu—the
sounds and daily life of Jewish immigrant existence in Lachine and
Montreal, where the Bellows moved in 1918, their new lodgings "in

the heart of the Jewish ghetto, the city's poorest neighborhood," and later in 1924, the family's move to Chicago's Jewish immigrant neighborhood Humboldt Park—provided the rich linguistic landscape, a mixture of idiomatic English, Hebrew, Yiddish, French, Russian, and other European languages, that informed Bellow's highly nuanced ear for the character and shape of language that enliven his novels and short stories (Atlas 11). Bellow grew up amid the stories and narratives of people for whom storytelling contained within it a communal memory and a link to a particularly Jewish history of struggle and survival, stories that defined individual identity and its place in history. As Bellow put it: "There is power in a story. It testifies to the worth, the significance of an individual. For a short while all the strength and all the radiance of the world are brought to bear upon a few human figures. . . . For the last generation of East European Jews, daily life without stories would have been inconceivable" (*Great Jewish Short Stories* 10-11).

It was from this deeply entrenched verbal tradition that Bellow created some of the most introspective, well-defined, and ironically self-evaluating characters in American literature, in a voice of brilliant wit and exactitude. Bellow's characters are drawn with a keen eye for the nuances of self-discovery, self-exposure, and comically tragic self-assessment. The way Bellow's characters define and construct the world in which they live is determined largely by how they talk—to themselves and others—about living in that world, a world shaped by the habits and constraints of human consciousness. "Intellectual man," according to Bellow's Mr. Sammler, is "an explaining creature. Fathers to children, wives to husbands, lecturers to listeners, experts to laymen, colleagues to colleagues, doctors to patients, man to his own soul, explained" (*Mr. Sammler's Planet* 3). A cerebral, analytical, and philosophical writer, Bellow unflinchingly describes twentieth-century America and its urban landscapes with unsentimental honesty and intelligence.

Life's Work

In 1933, Bellow began his academic career at the University of Chicago; he graduated with honors in sociology and anthropology from Northwestern University in 1937. At around this time, he publicly became Saul Bellow (Atlas 52-53). In 1938 Bellow married Anita Goshkin, his first of five wives, a marriage that produced one son, Gregory Bellow, born in 1944. Bellow received a scholarship from the University of Wisconsin to study anthropology, but by the end of the first semester he left graduate school to become a writer.

His first novel, *Dangling Man*, published in 1944, is a study of a man suffering from self-imposed existential alienation. *Dangling Man* was met with high acclaim, and Bellow's half-century career was launched. Nathan Rothman, writing for the *Saturday Review of Literature* in 1944, called Bellow a writer of "great original powers ... with a sharp cutting to the quick of language, with a brilliance of thought"; he stated that *Dangling Man* was "the herald of a fine literary career" (27). The publication of *Dangling Man* marked the beginning of a prolific and celebrated literary career for Bellow, unleashing, in the words of writer Delmore Schwartz, "the experience of a new generation ... seized and recorded" (348). From this propitious beginning Bellow would go on to become the voice of a generation of American Jewish intellectuals whose influence on American thought and cultural attitudes would span half a century. Increasingly, the Bellovian voice not only defined a place for an emerging American Jewish literary presence but also contributed to a newly defined American literary posture. As critic S. Lillian Kremer has noted, Bellow quickly became "an American cultural icon," both a product and creator of American culture at a critical time in history (130).

Dangling Man was followed in 1947 by *The Victim*, a novel that grippingly exposes the gradual unraveling of Asa Leventhal, a man plagued by his own fears as well as by the anti-Semitism of his time. Published only two years after the liberation of the Nazi concentration camps and the end of World War II, *The Victim* is a stunning portrait of postwar America set against the menacing specter of the Holocaust. The claustrophobic New York environs, the "sweltering . . . acres of cement," entrap Bellow's unhinged protagonist Leventhal, who, attempting to navigate the suffocating streets of Manhattan, riding the subway, crossing Staten Island on the ferry, "felt empty and unstable. The sun was too strong, the swirling traffic too loud, too swift . . . everywhere . . . choking crowds" (14, 96-97). *The Victim* metaphorically moves the Holocaust to America to show an inside view of the abiding menace of anti-Semitism.

In 1948 Bellow was awarded a Guggenheim Fellowship, which allowed him to spend two years in Paris working on his third novel, *The Adventures of Augie March*, which was published in 1953 and received the National Book Award for fiction in 1954. This work, set in Depression-era Chicago, established, as Gloria L. Cronin affirms, Bellow's "uniquely Chicagoan voice" (Cronin and Berger 27). Bellow's urban Chicago settings underwrite a landscape of existentialist self-containment that parallels the familiar New York cityscapes of Bernard Malamud and Philip Roth, with whom Bellow formed an emerging generation of ascendant American Jewish intellectuals.

In 1952 Bellow received the National Institute of Arts and Letters Award and became a Creative Writing Fellow at Princeton University. Bellow's first marriage ended in 1955, and in 1956, he published his fourth novel, *Seize the Day*, and married his second wife, Alexandra Tsachacbasov, who gave birth to their son Adam Bellow in 1957. In 1958 Bellow received a Ford Foundation Grant, and in 1959 his novel *Henderson the Rain King* was published. In 1960 his second marriage ended, and in 1961 he married Susan Alexandra Glassman, with whom he would have a son, Daniel Bellow, in 1964. In 1962 Bellow joined the faculty at the University of Chicago as a professor at the Committee on Social Thought, a position he would hold until 1993.

Henderson the Rain King, a novel about an American millionaire's adventures in Africa, was followed by the novel *Herzog* in 1964. *Herzog* received the National Book Award for fiction as well as the International Literary Prize in 1965. This novel, narrated largely through the unmailed letters of the cuckolded Moses Herzog, a middle-aged university professor in the midst of an existential midlife crisis, begins with the famous comic and self-parodic line, "If I am out of my mind, it's all right with me." In 1965 Bellow also received the James L. Dow Award and the Fomentor Award for his increasingly celebrated fiction.

Bellow's thwarted attempt at playwriting, *The Last Analysis*, a play about an ex-comedian's hard-won attempts at self-discovery, had a limited showing on Broadway in 1964 and received less-than-enthusiastic reviews. In 1967 Bellow traveled to Israel as a journalist for *Newsday* magazine to report on the Six-Day War, and in 1968 his collection *Mosby's Memoirs, and Other Stories* was published. Among the honors Bellow received in 1968 were the French Croix de Chevalier des Arts et Lettres (1968), the highest literary distinction awarded by that nation to noncitizens, and the B'nai B'rith Jewish Heritage Award. Also in 1968, his third marriage ended.

Mr. Sammler's Planet, which received the National Book Award for fiction, was published to wide anticipation in 1970. Bellow married his fourth wife, the Romanian theoretical physicist Alexandra Ionescu Tulcea, in 1974. *Humboldt's Gift*, for which Bellow received the Pulitzer Prize, came out in 1975; for this novel, Bellow drew from his experiences at Princeton and based his protagonist, Von Humboldt Fleisher, on the poet and short-story writer Delmore Schwartz.

Bellow's enormously productive and active years of the 1960s and early 1970s secured the author's place as, in Harold Bloom's words, "the strongest American novelist of his generation" (1). In 1976 Bellow published his first work of nonfiction, *To Jerusalem and Back: A Personal Account*, a description of his travels in Israel during 1975. Bellow received the Democratic Legacy Award of the Anti-Defamation League of B'nai B'rith in 1976, the same year in which he was awarded the Nobel Prize in Literature, "for the human understanding and subtle analysis of contemporary culture that are combined in his work" ("Nobel Prize").

Bellow continued a high level of productivity in the 1980s. In 1982 he published *The Dean's December*, followed by *Him with His Foot in his Mouth, and Other Stories* in 1984 and *More Die of Heartbreak* in 1987; two novellas, *The Bellarosa Connection* and *A Theft*, were published in 1989, and *Something to Remember Me By: Three Tales*, in 1991. His fourth marriage ended in 1985, and he was married for the fifth time, to Janis Freedman, in 1989. Bellow left the University of Chicago in 1993 and settled in Boston, where he began teaching at Boston University. In 1994 he published a nonfiction collection of previously published essays, *It All Adds Up: From the Dim Past to the Uncertain Future*, and in 1997 he published the novella *The Actual*, a love story. In addition to his posts at the University of Chicago and Boston University, where he ended his academic career, Bellow held an impressive number of other academic appointments, including teaching positions at Yale University, the University of Minnesota, New York University, Princeton University, the University of Puerto Rico, the University of Chicago, and Bard College. At the time of his death on April 5, 2005, in Brookline, Massachusetts, Bellow remained married to Janis Freedman Bellow, whom he had fictionalized as Rosamund, wife of the narrator, Chick, in his last novel, *Ravelstein*, published in 2000, an encomium to his late friend and University of Chicago colleague, the political philosopher Allan Bloom. Saul and Janis Bellow had one child, a daughter, Naomi Rose Bellow, born in 1999, when Bellow was eighty-four years old.

In his Nobel Prize acceptance speech, Bellow argued that the novel

> is a sort of latter-day lean-to, a hovel in which the spirit takes shelter. A novel is balanced between a few true impressions and the multitude of false ones that make up most of what we call life. It tells us that for every human being there is a diversity of existences, that the single existence is itself an illusion in part, that these many existences signify something, tend to something, fulfill something; it promises us meaning, harmony and even justice. ("Nobel Lecture" 325)

Indeed, it was through the novel, a genre he helped redefine and that gave shape to his brilliance and candor, that Bellow flourished as a writer of formidable honesty and intellectual integrity.

Works Cited

Atlas, James. *Bellow: A Biography*. New York: Random House, 2000.

Bellow, Saul. *Herzog*. 1964. New York: Penguin, 1996.

_____. *Mr. Sammler's Planet*. 1970. New York: Penguin, 1984.

_____."The Nobel Lecture." *American Scholar* 46.3 (1997): 316-25.

_____. *The Victim*. 1947. New York: Signet, 1965.

_____, ed. *Great Jewish Short Stories*. New York: Dell, 1963.

Bloom, Harold, ed. *Saul Bellow*. New York: Chelsea House, 1986.

Cronin, Gloria L., and Alan L. Berger, eds. *Encyclopedia of Jewish-American Literature*. New York: Facts On File, 2009.

Kremer, S. Lillian. "Saul Bellow." *Holocaust Literature*. Vol. 1. New York: Routledge, 2003.

"The Nobel Prize in Literature 1976." Nobelprize.org. 2 Aug. 2010. http://nobelprize .org/nobel_prizes/literature/laureates/1976

Rothman, Nathan. "Introducing an Important New Writer." *Saturday Review of Literature* 15 Apr. 1944.

Schwartz, Delmore. "A Man in His Time." *Partisan Review* 11.3 (1944).

The *Paris Review* Perspective

Natalie Jacoby for *The Paris Review*

Saul Bellow was meticulous in his craft—revising frequently, abandoning works, and devoting years to each of his novels. In 1966, he approached his *Paris Review* interview with a similar vigor and concentration. Carefully reviewing his answers and spending weeks working with his interviewer, Gordon Lloyd Harper, he explained that this was "an opportunity . . . to say some things which were important but which weren't being said." Bellow reflected on his desire to write freely and honestly: "A writer should be able to express himself easily, naturally, copiously in a form that frees his mind, his energies. Why should he hobble himself with formalities? With a borrowed sensibility? With the desire to be 'correct'?" At the time of the interview Bellow had already published six novels, but he was hesitant to discuss his earliest works—explaining that he felt repressed while working on *Dangling Man* and *The Victim*. It was not until his third novel, *The Adventures of Augie March*, that Bellow felt that any earlier restraints and formal anxieties had subsided; this novel was an "excitement of discovery."

Bellow would publish fourteen novels and novellas in his lifetime, as well as numerous short stories, and become one of the most decorated American writers ever—he received the Pulitzer Prize, the Nobel Prize, and three National Book Awards. For literary critic Harold Bloom, he was "the strongest American novelist of his generation." Still, even amid all of his critical and commercial praise, Bellow would never conform to any specific standard, technique, or tradition. He believed strongly that "the novelist should trust his own sense of life.

Less ambitious. More likely to tell the truth." He remained true to his own sensibilities as a writer and emerged a piercingly honest, thoughtful observer of modern civilization.

Saul Bellow was born in Lachine, Quebec, the son of Russian Jewish immigrant parents, but when he was nine the family moved to Chicago—a city that Bellow would immortalize in elaborate detail in many of his stories. When Bellow spoke of his youth, it was with great reverence and with a respect for how it ultimately contributed to his development as a writer. He believed that there was something of an interior voice, or "prompter," within himself—that in everyone there exists "that observing instrument in us—in childhood at any rate. At the sight of a man's face, his shoes, the color of light, a woman's mouth or perhaps her ear, one receives a word, a phrase, at times nothing but a nonsense syllable from the primitive commentator." Certainly, he grew up well positioned for observation as an outsider looking in, socially alienated as a member of a Jewish immigrant family and surrounded by the overwhelming multicultural landscape in the cities of Montreal and Chicago. Yet above all, Bellow's experiences with illness were what enhanced his already attentive nature with an intense sensitivity to the human condition. He suffered from respiratory problems as a boy and was hospitalized and separated from his family and friends for months. It was in this isolation that Bellow became a voracious reader, but his illness also afforded him a premature glimpse of death and an early intimacy with the struggle for life. An awareness of mortality and the disorientation of modernity permeates the minds of his characters.

Bellow's characters are the great strength of his stories; his fiction is never driven by plot. Literary critic James Wood, a former coprofessor with Bellow, described him as the "great portraitist of the human form." From the exploration of identity in *The Adventures of Augie March* to the struggle and desperation in *Seize the Day*, the tragicomedy of *Herzog*, and the "dark mortality" of *Humboldt's Gift*, Bellow's characters demonstrate an exuberance and humor even in the midst of their melancholy preoccupations. "If I am out of my mind, it's all right with me," believes his character Moses Herzog. For Bellow, "In the greatest confusion, there is still an open channel to the soul."

Focusing on this "channel to the soul" made Bellow into a quintessentially American author, renowned for his depiction of humankind's struggle with modern life and urban experience. Even amid the chaos of the city in Times Square, Tommy Wilhelm in *Seize the Day* feels "connected to humanity"—Bellow does not allow his protagonist to pessimistically disconnect from society, and he searches instead for a sense of solidarity with those around him. This universal resonance of his work becomes even more impressive in light of Bellow's heightened level of "otherness" in America, socially, and in American literature, aesthetically. He admitted that he never had "the right feeling for Anglo-Saxon traditions, for English words." He reinterpreted realism and injected it with a more human quality, condemning the literalization and factualism that "smothered" imagination and praising more personal representations of environments. The literature he grew up with—Shakespeare, the Old and New Testaments, nineteenth-century Russian novels—informed his opinion that fiction should raise great moral questions, and he was skeptical of the aestheticism, the complicated prose and postmodern techniques, that many of his contemporaries employed. He shied from categorization as a "Jewish writer," "immigrant writer," or "midwestern writer"—and these were all labels that cannot encompass his strength as an author. Bellow wrote to express what it meant to be human, to be—as he says in *Herzog*—"a man. In a city. In a century. In transition. In a mass. Transformed by science. Under organized power. Subject to tremendous controls. In a condition caused by mechanization. After the late failure of radical hopes." Who in America today—amid globalization, multiculturalism, consumerism, the increasingly data-centric and technology-centric landscapes—can remain unmoved by Bellow's soul-searching?

Works Consulted

Bellow, Saul. "The Art of Fiction No. 37." Interview with Gordon Lloyd Harper. *The Paris Review* 36 (1966).

_____. *Collected Stories*. New York: Penguin, 2001.

Bloom, Harold, ed. *Saul Bellow*. New York: Chelsea House, 1986.

CRITICAL
CONTEXTS

Psychology and the Fiction of Saul Bellow_____

Andrew M. Gordon

In the memorable opening sentence of Saul Bellow's *The Adventures of Augie March* (1953), Augie announces, "I am an American, Chicago born—Chicago, that somber city—and go at things as I have taught myself, free-style, and will make the record in my own way" (1). This opening constitutes both Augie's and Bellow's declaration of independence. Like his hero, Bellow is declaring his bona fides as an American and a Chicagoan, a son of the heartland, free and fiercely independent, self-reliant, an autodidact, determined to write things down his own way, unblushing, just as he sees them. Bellow is the same way about psychoanalysis: self-taught and stubbornly independent. As he told an interviewer: "I'm not a great friend of modern psychology on the whole. I've read a lot of Freud and I've read a lot of Jung. I'm not strong on it. I try to apprehend my characters in my own way" (Dommergues 15).

Throughout his writing career, Bellow carried on a love/hate affair with psychoanalysis, about which he was extremely sophisticated but also contemptuous and mocking. As Jonathan Wilson has noted, "His play, *The Last Analysis*, is a full-length parody of the analytic process, and his central characters have resisted one aspect or another of Freud's ideas since *The Adventures of Augie March*" (51). Daniel Fuchs observes that "though Bellow rejects Freudian thought in . . . fundamental respects, he is nonetheless sympathetic to and sometimes indebted to it in others" ("Bellow and Freud" 43).

As a novelist, Bellow was from the beginning a psychological realist, and his heroes are fully rounded characters, quirky and often deeply neurotic, fascinating case studies that have brought out the amateur psychoanalyst in many literary critics. Most of his protagonists need a therapeutic catharsis; some—such as Tommy Wilhelm in *Seize the Day*, Herzog in *Herzog*, Bummidge in *The Last Analysis*, Charlie

Citrine in *Humboldt's Gift*, and Clara Velde in *A Theft*—actually undergo psychoanalysis, and Henderson in *Henderson the Rain King* places himself in the hands of King Dahfu, who attempts to cure Henderson and transform him into a lion man by putting him through a kind of radical existential therapy.

Fuchs notes: "To say that Bellow knows his Freud very well is no exaggeration. There was a period when Freud was his nightly bedtime reading" ("Bellow and Freud" 27). Many Bellow heroes also know their Freud and quote him. Manuscript versions of *Herzog* refer to Freud's "Mourning and Melancholia," and Herzog, who is suffering intense divorce grief, even writes a letter to "Dear Dr. Freud" taking issue with the essay (Fuchs, "Bellow and Freud" 45). Yet Bellow tries to maintain his intuitive understanding of human psychology by adopting a skeptical, satirical attitude toward Sigmund Freud, Carl Jung, and Wilhelm Reich. All the psychoanalysts in Bellow's fiction are comic characters. Even if they impart some partial wisdom to the heroes, the analysts are physically caricatured and mocked as quacks or frauds. Freud, Jung, Reich, and many other psychologists and psychoanalysts Bellow knows quite well as part of the foundations of modernism, but he ultimately rejects their systems because as a novelist he wants to hold onto the mysterious nature of human behavior and the human soul.

Bellow's method in creating a character was to work from the outside in, taking his cues from the face and body of the character and then using the details of facial expression, posture, and gesture to guide him to the inner life. Because of that, he resisted the ready-made labels of modern psychology, which he felt had deteriorated into clichés or stereotypes inhibiting thought. He told an interviewer:

> What it means to me to encounter another human being. First in physical and sensory terms and then in some effort to interpret just what these impressions tell me about the deeper life I am not very much in favor of these ready-made perceptions and I resist them. As a matter of fact I do think

they've come to dominate modern literature perniciously. When you mention a child and his mother, then you know exactly what to think. The Oedipus conflict is at work and so on. I don't mind acknowledging the existence of a powerful sexual attraction between mother and son, but I'm against the automatic application of the measure, which by now has become habitual. Or if you speak of a woman who is chaste, then it simply follows that she suffers the harmful effects of repression and all the rest of that bullshit which I never buy for a minute. (Dommergues 15)

Bellow was willing to grant that there may be an unconscious, but not necessarily that it is a Freudian unconscious (Fuchs, "Bellow and Freud" 29). He stated: "I'm not thinking of any Freudian or Jungian unconscious, but of a much-neglected metaphysical unconscious. . . . The human understructure is much larger than any measure our culture gives us. Our meager measures get us nowhere" (Simmons 167). He told another interviewer:

The unconscious is anything that human beings don't know. . . . Is it possible that what we don't know has a metaphysical character and not a Freudian, naturalistic character? I think that the unconscious is a concept that begs the question and simply returns us to our ignorance with an arrogant attitude of confidence, and that is why I am against it. (Boyers 19)

In yet another interview, he said:

Do you believe the psychoanalytic explanation of your deeper motives? Or do you simply say, "These are my deeper motives, I don't care what psychoanalysis has to say about them." . . . What a woman does for her children, what a man does for his family, what people most tenaciously cling to, these things are not adequately explained by Oedipus complexes, libidos. . . . I don't believe that we go and dig in the unconscious and come back with new truffles from the libidinous unknown. That's not the way it really is. (Brans 142-43)

Elsewhere Bellow stated: "I experienced a violent reaction against Freud. Was it not possible to experience beauty or pity without thinking of your mother, or without the Oedipus complex? The rigidity of this repels me. I felt it was coarse and cruel. It's this sort of thing that I think of when I think of Freud" (Boyers 19).

Rather than the psyche, Bellow preferred to believe in the soul. He said: "I've become aware of a conflict between the modern university education I received and those things that I really feel in my soul most deeply. I've trusted those more and more.—You see, I'm not even supposed to have a soul" (Brans 142). According to Fuchs, "Comparing Bellow and Freud as thinkers points up perhaps more clearly than anything else can the religious tendency of Bellow's humanism" ("Bellow and Freud" 32).

However, Bellow's biographer James Atlas asserts that Bellow rejected Freud not so much on metaphysical grounds but because "Freud posed a threat to the artist's independence" (295). Bellow said in an interview:

Freud is one of our conquerors. In many branches of thought his authority is supreme. . . . Taken together, the body of "thought" created by these "intellectuals" is a huge affliction. Its effects are deadly. Few are strong enough to ward them off. Writers can't afford to draw their premises from this stock of "ideas"–*idées reçues* is a more suitable expression. (Gray, White, and Nemanic 204)

Even in his early adolescence in Chicago, said Bellow, "we were passing Freud from hand to hand at school. And Marx and Lenin" (*Bostonia*, "Half Life" 259). He felt he struggled for decades to free himself from the powerful grip of these thinkers. "Revising my life, I see with satisfaction the escape from certain tyrants: Marx, Lenin, Freud. These philosophers and writers are the source of powerful metaphors which took a grip on one. It took decades to escape" (Botsford 242). Moreover, these modernist thinkers did not help him to live his life: "You discover, in other words, the inapplicability of your higher learning, the absurdity of your spray-can culture" (*Bostonia* "Second Half Life" 287). Thus, throughout his writing career, Bellow flirted with many systems but eventually mocked and rejected all of them, ultimately preferring as an artist to think for himself.

Yet despite Bellow's skepticism toward psychoanalysis expressed in interviews and in his fiction, he went through two decades of exploring various forms of psychotherapy and being analyzed by therapists of different persuasions. He kept looking for help and put himself in the hands of analysts on four occasions when a marriage was disintegrating or he was suffering through a divorce (Bellow was married five times; he had great difficulty living with women or without them).

In 1951, when he was unhappy in his first marriage, he was treated by Dr. Chester Raphael, a Reichian analyst. Wilhelm Reich was a leftist post-Freudian who tried to merge Freud and Marx. His best-known writings are *The Function of the Orgasm, Character Analysis*, and *The Mass Psychology of Fascism*. Reich believed that the key to health is full orgasm and that neurosis manifests itself in the body through what he called "character armor," so that to dissolve the neurosis and attain full genitality one must break down bodily resistance. He also invented the "orgone box," which was said to concentrate something he called "orgone energy"; the user sat in the box naked, supposedly to achieve better orgasms. Reichianism attracted many New York City bohemians, intellectuals, and writers during the late 1940s and 1950s, including Paul Goodman, Norman Mailer, and the Beat writers William Burroughs, Allen Ginsberg, and Jack Kerouac, because Reich was more socially and politically radical than Freud. Bellow's good friend Isaac Rosenfeld was being treated by a Reichian and introduced him to the therapy. As Atlas describes, "Lying naked on a couch, the patient was exhorted to purge the body of its defenses by acting out rage and sexual tension, shouting, gagging, grimacing, pounding the couch" (163). Bellow also sat naked in an orgone box in his apartment in Queens, "reading beneath a bare lightbulb strung from its ceiling. At odd moments, he stuffed a handkerchief in his mouth and screamed—one of the methods Reich had supposedly prescribed for reaching emotional release" (Atlas 164).

Bellow said that he "enjoyed it as a game then being played," but he soon rejected Reichianism as a cult and even blamed it for destroying his marriage (Atlas 165). Atlas claims that "no system commanded his allegiance for long. To him, Reichianism was like Trotskyism and every other ism: an effort to rein in his autonomy. . . . He saw Dr. Raphael as another person intent on interfering in his life, another threat to his independence" (164-65). Bellow nevertheless made use of Reichianism in his fiction as a system of metaphor to describe character via the body, especially neurotic "character armor," and he mined Reichian therapy for both its comic and its serious potential in his fiction of the 1950s—*Seize the Day, Henderson the Rain King*, and a one-act play titled *The Wrecker*—and in a later story, "Zetland: By a Character Witness," part of an unfinished novel about Isaac Rosenfeld.

Discussing the influence of Reich on Bellow, the critic Mark Shechner says:

> What Reich provided the postwar writer, Bellow and Mailer in particular, was a modern version of a medieval craft, physiognomy, the craft of reading the character of a man from the features of the body. . . . Bellow is an acute observer of necks, throats, chests, mouths, teeth, and the inflected corners of the eyes, tiny fortresses in which the defenses of the entire system may be read. (122-23)

Shechner reads Bellow as "a diagnostic novelist specializing in the diseases of civilization and the distortions of the emotional life that underlie them. And although the terms of the diagnosis vary, the Reichian has been the most enduring." But he says that Bellow rejects Reich's revolutionary politics, preferring personal transformation—"and even that was normally rendered as comedy. The Reich we meet in his books is a vaudeville physician" (123).

Bellow's second visit to the analyst's couch came in 1958, when his second marriage was falling apart. He saw Dr. Paul Meehl, a clinical psychologist at the University of Minnesota who was an "eclectic therapist. A 'calm Protestant Nordic Anglo-Celtic,' as Bellow described him in the person of Dr. Edvig" in his novel *Herzog* (Atlas 264). Bellow's wife Sondra soon became a patient of Meehl too, posing a potential conflict of interest. In *Herzog*, a novel about a disastrous marriage and divorce, prior to the breakup Herzog and his wife Madeleine separately see Dr. Edvig. Says Dr. Meehl, "The book is a description of reality" (Atlas 264). According to Atlas, Bellow's treatment was unsuccessful because Bellow "made no secret of his contempt for therapists and therapy, even when he was in treatment. . . . Like many artists . . . he was reluctant to tamper with the source of his inspiration, believing it be . . . beyond the reach of prying analysts" (265). In *Herzog*, Edvig is portrayed not only comically but also as a villain who sides with Madeleine, one of the many supposed friends who betray Herzog by helping to hide Madeleine's adultery with Herzog's best friend.

Bellow's third experience with psychotherapy occurred in the spring of 1960, when he was under the care of Dr. Albert Ellis, one of the most influential American psychotherapists. "A famous figure in his day, Ellis shared with Bellow a Jewish-immigrant background and a reputation as a ladies' man" (Atlas 295). Ellis had earned a Ph.D. in clinical psychology and had begun practicing classical Freudian psychoanalysis but eventually developed the first cognitive behavioral therapy, "rational therapy," which aimed to replace a patient's irrational beliefs with more rational constructs—or, as Ellis put it, "I talk people out of their bullshit" (Atlas 295). Ellis was also a famous sexologist who had worked with Alfred Kinsey, the pioneering American sex researcher, and spoke across the country. In 1958 Ellis published the best seller *Sex Without Guilt*, which helped start the sexual revolution of the 1960s. "The goal of therapy, Ellis claimed, was sexual pleasure, pure and simple" (Atlas 295).

This time Bellow sought treatment to overcome his rage at his second wife after their divorce. According to Atlas: "He went into therapy when he was desperate and left as soon as he could tolerate the level of pain. . . . Bellow went through the therapeutic process but never engaged with it—instead he found material for satire" (296). Dr. Albert Ellis is mocked as Dr. Ellenbogen, Charlie Citrine's analyst in *Humboldt's Gift* (1975), described in the novel as "a celebrity himself, appearing on many talk shows, the author of liberating books on sex. . . . He hit a patient hard in order to free him. The rationality of pleasure was his ideological hammer" (163-64).

Bellow's fourth stint at being analyzed came in the spring of 1969, when he was divorced and bouncing from woman to woman. He consulted another famous psychoanalyst, Dr. Heinz Kohut, the founder of self psychology. According to Atlas, "Bellow himself later minimized the extent of his treatment with Kohut, insisting he had gone to see him only a few times during 'a period of turmoil' in his life" (384). Atlas speculates that Bellow may have been the patient Kohut wrote about who developed a "Don Juan syndrome" in order to provide "'an insecurely established self with a continuous flow of self-esteem.' His patient's avidity for women, according to Kohut, was 'motivated not by libidinal but by narcissistic needs'" (385).

After eighteen years of searching for a cure, Bellow apparently gave up on psychotherapy for himself. He dismissed it as a racket, as counterproductive. As Ithiel Regler says in Bellow's novella *A Theft* (1989), "'That's my argument with psychiatry: it encourages you to build on abuses and keeps you infantile'" (15). And Ithiel wisecracks about shrinks, "'Those guys! . . . If a millipede came into the office, he'd leave with an infinitesimal crutch for each leg'" (42-43). Nevertheless, despite Bellow's hostility (which some might see as defensive), his many years of reading Freud, Jung, Reich, Kohut, and other psychologists affected his thinking, and his sessions with different analysts provided him dramatic and comic material that he used in his fiction. After 1964, however, the year in which both the novel *Herzog* and the play *The Last Analysis* were published, Bellow's fiction was never again as heavily psychoanalytic.

Seize the Day (1956) is one of the most psychoanalytic of Bellow's novels, so I want to use it as a case study to consider the range of ways in which Bellow's works have been analyzed by various psychological literary critics: Freudians, Reichians, Jungians, and Kohutians. As the literary critic Bernard J. Paris writes: "Different psychological theories focus upon different kinds of phenomena and appeal to different kinds of people. . . . Each theory is better at explaining some things than others and is best used by those who have a genuine feeling for it in the study of phenomena with which it is highly congruent" (13). Bear in mind that psychological critics may attend to different areas of the text—plot, characters, relationships, symbolism, mood, language, or narrative point of view—or to the responses of readers or other critics of the text, or even to the psychology of the author him- or herself, as evidenced in biography, autobiography, interviews, or essays by the author.

Seize the Day seems to invite psychological readings because Bellow makes his hero so neurotic and troubled, in a crisis state, close to a nervous breakdown, and because Bellow playfully names many of the characters after famous psychologists and psychiatrists: Wilhelm Adler, suggesting Dr. Wilhelm Reich; Dr. Adler, suggesting Dr. Alfred Adler, a psychologist who split from Freud to found the school of individual psychology; Mr. Perls, suggesting Dr. Fritz Perls, founder of Gestalt psychology; and Mr. Rappaport, suggesting Dr. David Rapaport, an influential clinical psychologist and ego psychologist. Such in-jokes seem like clues scattered by the author, designed deliberately both to tempt and to mock psychoanalytic readings of the novel.

Psychological critics have focused on Tommy Wilhelm's self-punishing, self-destructive behavior, his conflicted relationship with his father, his attachment to the strange quack psychologist Dr. Tamkin, and the novel's concluding scene, which has inspired diametrically opposed readings as positive or negative, breakthrough or breakdown, baptism or drowning, redemption and rebirth or psychic dissolution and death, or as no real resolution because none is possible for the hero.

Seize the Day is short, intense, concentrated, and extremely well wrought. The plot of the novel concerns a day in the life of Tommy Wilhelm, a middle-aged, unemployed salesman, a sad sack who is down on his luck and desperate. Born Wilhelm Adler to a prosperous Jewish family—his father was the son of immigrants but became a successful physician—he adopted the stage name Tommy Wilhelm when he dropped out of college and went to Hollywood, seeking a career as a movie actor that never materialized. Now Wilhelm has quit his sales job because he felt mistreated by the company, has separated from his wife Margaret, and loves Olive, a Catholic he cannot marry because his unforgiving wife will not grant him a divorce and keeps asking for more money. He also loves his two sons but rarely gets to see them; he struggles to support them and to make alimony payments. Although only forty-four years old, Wilhelm has moved into a retirement hotel in Manhattan's upper West Side, an area filled with retired Jews, to be close to his aged father, Dr. Adler, a cold, rejecting man who refuses on principle to help his son financially. Foolishly, Wilhelm has invested the last of his money in a get-rich-quick stock market scheme with a shady doctor named Tamkin, who lives in the hotel, befriends Wilhelm, and claims he is treating him psychoanalytically. As the day proceeds, Wilhelm's troubles increase until everything comes to a head, overwhelming him: Tamkin loses all of Wilhelm's money in the stock market and then vanishes; his father won't give him money and rejects him cruelly, saying he can't stand the sight of him; and his wife hounds him for money and shows no sympathy. Thinking he spots Tamkin in the crowd entering a Jewish funeral home, Wilhelm joins the funeral party inside. He does not find Tamkin but ends the story crying his heart out over the body of a dead man who is a total stranger to him.

Seize the Day is narrated from a third-person, limited omniscient point of view. We have continuous access to the consciousness of Tommy Wilhelm as filtered through the omniscient narrator but also occasionally see him through the eyes of his father or his wife. We never have access to the consciousness of Tamkin, who remains a mysterious figure. The third-person narrator is largely sympathetic to Wilhelm but can also remain detached and see both his virtues and his failings with a far clearer eye than can Wilhelm.

The earliest important essay to use a psychoanalytic perspective on *Seize the Day* is Daniel Weiss's "Caliban on Prospero: A Psychoanalytic Study on the Novel *Seize the Day*, by Saul Bellow," which first appeared in the psychoanalytic journal of literary studies *American Imago* in 1962. Weiss claims that Tommy Wilhelm is a "moral masochist," a term developed by the post-Freudian Bernhard Berliner in his 1947 essay "On Some Psychodynamics of Masochism." The moral masochist is "the victim, for whom suffering is a *modus vivendi*, a means of self-justification" (Weiss 121). Berliner calls moral masochism "a pathological way of loving," a character neurosis that develops from an unhappy childhood where a parent was cruel and rejecting (460). The moral masochist exhibits "the servility of the beaten dog"; he "makes himself the whipping boy for the benefit of a sadistic parent" (Berliner 463-64). Tommy Wilhelm represses his hatred of his father, wills himself to fail, and feels that his suffering means he is worthy of love. His relationships with a series of authority figures and older men—the head of his company, Dr. Tamkin, and Mr. Rappaport (a rich old man at the stock office)—repeat or are attempts to work out the conflict with his father. In the ending, "The dead man in his coffin is the symbolic fulfillment of two alternatives—the wish to destroy the father and the wish to be destroyed." Yet Weiss sees this ending as a catharsis in which Wilhelm gives up his hatred and "no longer wishes for his father's death" (137). Weiss sees Dr. Tamkin as a problematic figure who gives Wilhelm some sound psychological advice and yet is also a "palpable fraud" who cheats Wilhelm and is "a figure of fun" (138-39).

Weiss's essay helps to account for Wilhelm's self-destructive behavior, but that ending remains puzzling, as it is difficult to see Wilhelm's purgation as anything more than a temporary emotional relief, not a change of character. The satiric portrait of Tamkin as both shaman and comic fraud I would suggest perhaps reflects Bellow's own ambivalence about the theory and practice of psychoanalysis.

In my essay "The Hero as Sucker in Saul Bellow's Early Fiction," I develop an idea from Weiss's essay that Tommy Wilhelm is an "oral" character, always stuffing his face with food, even eating off his father's plate, swallowing pills, or sucking on a Coke bottle, retreating to the state of a nursing infant, seeking the love and nourishment he craved but never received from his father. Rather than look at *Seize the Day* in isolation, I see this pattern of "oral" characters also in Bellow's first novel, *Dangling Man*, and in two of his short stories of the 1950s, "A Father-to-Be" and "Leaving the Yellow House." I argue that the Bellow hero's emotional dilemma "revolves around problems of oral passivity and dependency. His heroes seek total mothering yet at the same time fear being mothered because it renders them passive, dependent, and powerless. . . . Almost every Bellow hero is seeking 'succor' and yet is potentially a 'sucker,' in the dual sense of parasite and fool" (48).

John J. Clayton, in *Saul Bellow: In Defense of Man*, builds on Weiss's interpretation of Tommy Wilhelm as masochist. Clayton, looking at the psychic pattern of Bellow's fiction, says that "Bellow's characters are lonely, despairing, cut off not only from society but from friends and wives. Moreover, they are pathological social masochists, filled with guilt and self-hatred, needing to suffer and to fail" (53). Clayton distinguishes between Bellow and his heroes, however, saying *Seize the Day* "is not a novel expressing the author's masochism but a novel about a masochist" (70). Tommy Wilhelm is "a *self*-persecuted individual, created with the full awareness of the author" (71). Tommy Wilhelm punishes himself to remove Oedipal guilt. He "luxuriates in his suffering" and has "married suffering" (72-73). The novel is filled with "images of death by being devoured and death by water," so that the ending is the logical climax of "Tommy's self-pity and his drive toward self-destruction and even death" (73-74).

Yet Clayton reads the ending scene as hopeful. According to Clayton, Tommy suffers from Reich's "character armor," such as a persistent knot in his chest and a feeling of choking. When Wilhelm tries to rip the phone from the wall in a rage after his conversation with his estranged wife, Margaret, and when he bursts out sobbing at the funeral, he is trying to break down his character armor, behaving like the patient of a Reichian analyst (132-33). Moreover, Dr. Tamkin had told him about the battle between the real soul and the parasitic, pretender soul, so that at the funeral Wilhelm kills off his pretender soul, symbolically dying so that he can be reborn (132). Clayton's approach is one way to account for both the positive and the negative reverberations of the ending scene, with its intimations of both death and rebirth.

The most detailed Reichian reading of *Seize the Day* is found in Eusebio L. Rodrigues's *Quest for the Human: An Exploration of Saul Bellow's Fiction*. According to Reich, writes Rodrigues, "Human character structure . . . consists of three layers: the outer one with a mask of politeness and artificial sociality; the second layer, which consists of all the inhibited impulses of greed, lust, envy, and sadism; and finally, the deepest layer, where the natural orgone energy vibrates" (87). Character armor traps the energy within. "The denizens of the Hotel Gloriana and the gamblers at the stock exchange, all consummate actors, wear perfect masks that hide the second layer" (87). But Tommy Wilhelm is not a good actor and cannot mask his deeper feelings. Moreover, he periodically receives "mysterious promptings" from the third and deepest layer, but "he will not and cannot allow his pent-up energy to discharge itself" (88).

Reich had his own theory of masochism as the effects of social repression on the mind and body. Rodrigues notes that, "according to Reich, masochism is the result and the expression of an inner tension which cannot be discharged" (88). Thus Wilhelm's bundle of nervous tics and physical symptoms. "His present disfigured and armored condition needs to be treated and dissolved" (91). Wilhelm's teaching by Dr. Tamkin and his ordeal throughout the day constitute his therapy, the breakdown of his character armor so that he can reach the deepest level of the self in the climactic scene. Tamkin's talk of the real versus the pretender soul and his poem are both Reichian. The telephone booth in which he acts out his rage resembles Reich's orgone box (102). His sobbing at the funeral parlor is "the final stage in the dissolution of his armor" (104). *Seize the Day*, according to Rodrigues, is "a Reichian parable of hope for sick humanity" (106).

Mark Shechner, who does a modified Reichian reading of *Seize the Day*, does not see the same hope in the novel as do Clayton and Rodrigues. He considers Tommy Wilhelm simply a loser "who is dead set on being gulled." Shechner writes, "With his massive aggressions, his secret guilt, his will to failure, his nervous feet and constricted chest, he is a walking nosology, a compendium of symptoms from Reich's *Character Analysis*" (132). Shechner considers Dr. Tamkin not a Reichian but "a shyster Fritz Perls. . . . a champion of Gestalt 'here-and-now' therapy. . . . But Tommy is in no position to enter the here and now, since his reality is an actual hell. . . . A release of passion would be a release of violence, and Tommy is not prepared, any more than is Bellow, for blood" (133). His crying at the funeral "does nothing for his real problems. . . . It is also unclear what Tommy has learned, for the therapeutic doesn't traffic in education but contents itself with epiphanies" (133).

In contrast, the French critic Claude Lévy, in *Les Romans de Saul Bellow*, chooses a purely Oedipal reading of *Seize the Day*, providing the most detailed analysis by any critic of the father-son relationship in the novel. According to Lévy, Wilhelm returns to live near his father out of a sense of guilt for unconsciously harboring Oedipal desires. The death of Wilhelm's mother only exacerbated his guilt, so he tries to blame his father for the death, implying that his father never cared for her and was freed by her death. At the same time, Wilhelm must deny his hatred of his father, repeatedly stating that he loves his father and even wants Dr. Adler to outlive him (Lévy 128). By his immature behavior, Wilhelm is unconsciously trying to exculpate himself and make it seem that he could never be a sexual rival or threat to his father because he is not a real man but an overgrown infant. His father even accuses Wilhelm of having homosexual affairs (126-27). Wilhelm's self-destructive behavior—overindulgence in alcohol, food, and pills, poor driving, and foolish decision making—and seeming desire for death are his ultimate form of denial for wishing for his father's death (129). Yet Lévy reads the final scene as ambivalent, combining imagery of death and rebirth (140-41).

Julius R. Raper does a Jungian analysis in "Running Contrary Ways: Saul Bellow's *Seize the Day*." Jung is best known for his concepts of the archetypes and the collective unconscious; he appeals to myth critics. Wilhelm's powerful feelings at several points in the novel of being united with all of humanity suggest Jung's collective unconscious. Raper argues that "Tommy must undergo what Jung called *enantiodromia*, the psychological process of 'being torn asunder into pairs of opposites' ([Jung] *Essays* 83). Dr. Tamkin, in most things the opposite of Dr. Adler, represents to Tommy the Spirit of Alternatives holding out to him an alternative self. But to reach this new self the old must die" (77). In a Jungian sense, Tamkin represents "the unacknowledged contents" of Tommy Wilhelm's psyche. "The archetype Tommy projects on Tamkin is the important figure of the magician" (77). Tamkin is an archetype emerging from the unconscious, a surrogate father and spiritual guide who prepares Wilhelm for a new life. "In the language of Jung," he develops Wilhelm's "suppressed capacity for feeling" (79). The novel is filled with powerful mythic imagery as Wilhelm appears to take a trip into the underworld. "But as guru, Tamkin can neither tell nor show Wilhelm what he needs to know—only lead him to the threshold and hope he will take the final step" (81). That final stage in Wilhelm's enlightenment takes place at the funeral, when Tamkin has disappeared. "Then, like Tammuz or Osiris, ancient son-gods and sacrificial quickeners of new life, he feels the sea of lamentation pour into him as he sinks 'deeper than sorrow,' where he must await rebirth" (81).

Raper's Jungian analysis of the novel helps to account for certain mythical and mystical elements of the story that a strictly Freudian interpretation might overlook, and it also provides a better explanation of the function of Tamkin. Moreover, Bellow said he did not believe in a Freudian unconscious but in a more "metaphysical unconscious" and preferred the concept of a "soul." Because such spiritual concerns were also those of Jung, a Jungian analysis of Bellow's fiction seems apropos.

J. Brooks Bouson does a Kohutian reading in "Empathy and Self-Validation in *Seize the Day.*" One could argue that such a reading is justified since Bellow was briefly Kohut's patient, although thirteen years after Bellow wrote *Seize the Day.* Heinz Kohut was an Austrian psychoanalyst who fled Nazi Germany for the United States and founded psychoanalytic self psychology. Self psychology is described as follows on the online Self Psychology Page:

> While rejecting the primary importance of innate Freudian sexual drives in the organization of the human psyche, self psychology was the first major psychoanalytic movement in the United States to recognize the critical role of *empathy* in explaining human development and psychoanalytic change. . . . Kohut's work has developed into the study of *selfobject experiences*, experiences (usually with other people) that nourish the self and which define the experience of the self and self-esteem. *Healthy narcissism* is the appearance of a strong, vital, cohesive self striving with ambition and ideals toward the full realization of a person's skills and talents. *Narcissism* is the appearance of a weak, vulnerable self attempting to maintain self-cohesion and bolster self-esteem.

Bouson interprets Wilhelm as a weak, vulnerable narcissist and focuses on the role of the reader and the vexed question of the ambivalence of *Seize the Day.* According to Bouson, "Installed as an empathic listener and observer, the reader, as the narrative unfolds, becomes aware of Wilhelm's entrapment in his own stifling, interior hell." We see Wilhelm's many faults, but "we are also urged to feel sorry for him" and to wish for his rescue. But the "conscious project of this text" is contradicted by what the text backgrounds, which is "Wilhelm's split-off anger." This division poses "unanswerable questions" for critics or readers who want traditional "narrative closure, character development, and resolution of conflict" (86). "Drawn into Wilhelm's interior world, readers are urged, in effect, to enact the 'good father' role by sympathetically responding to Wilhelm's need for understanding and rescue" (90). This, however, is to ignore the fact that Wilhelm is a "shame-prone narcissist" who "protects himself through boasts and lies" and that he alternates in his behavior toward his father between helplessness and hostility, which are guaranteed to further alienate and anger his father (89).

Bouson sees Dr. Tamkin as both "a father surrogate" and "a complex self-representation," for, just like Wilhelm, Tamkin is grandiose, boastful, and dishonest (91). And Bouson reads the ending scene completely negatively, as "both a loss of self-cohesion and a regressive retreat into the world of earliest childhood" (95). "His self defective, Wilhelm inhabits not the glorious here-and-now fantasied by Tamkin but the bleak here-and-now of his own crippled self" (98).

Finally, Daniel Fuchs, in *Saul Bellow: Vision and Revision*, claims that the psychoanalytic critics do not do justice to *Seize the Day* because it is a novel of spiritual and moral affirmation. Fuchs admits that "neurosis, sickness is at the center" of the novel; "Wilhelm is to the oral-fixation what his father, Dr. Adler, is to the anal" (80). He notes, "The psychoanalytic explanation attributes Wilhelm's failure to weakness, and there is much truth to this" (81). Nevertheless, Fuchs finds strength in Wilhelm's capacity for love.

Fuchs objects to Weiss's characterization of Wilhelm as a "moral masochist":

Like most good psychoanalytic explanations this one is illuminating as far as it goes, but it does not—particularly in a writer like Bellow, schooled in psychoanalysis but finally critical of its assumptions—go far enough. Wilhelm's love is not merely a function of his neuroticism; it is a motive as good as, indeed, better than gold. . . . It is one thing to be a masochist and another to be transfigured by suffering. Despite its psychological orientation, the central perspective of *Seize the Day* is closer to the religious. (82)

Fuchs finds a nobility in Wilhelm that "resides in his resistance to nihilism" (92). "He loves not only out of neuroticism, but also out of love itself" (82). "Wilhelm's only weapon is love, and this is why he is in such a bad way among the money men; it may also be why much informed literary opinion treats him primarily in terms of pathology" (97). Fuchs reads that much-debated ending as positive, a "transfiguration through suffering" (96).

"Transfiguration through suffering" is how Fuchs reads *Seize the Day*, although Bellow has said, "I can sympathize with Wilhelm but I can't respect him. He is a sufferer by vocation. I'm a resister by vocation" (Roudané 246). Nevertheless, writers may put unresolved or contradictory ideas and feelings into their work, even unawares, and there is no way of controlling reader responses. "Never trust the artist. Trust the tale," said D. H. Lawrence (2), and *Seize the Day* has aroused diametrically opposed readings.

Bellow's fiction has attracted many psychological readings because he is a psychologically sophisticated novelist and because his heroes are usually neurotics swamped with troubles, in the midst of crises, apparently headed for nervous breakdowns. Bellow seems to invite psychological readings at the same time that he disdains psychoanalysis and turns fictional analytic sessions into comedy. Bellow's ambivalence—his deep knowledge of psychology combined with his aversion to it and his insistence that his concerns are more metaphysical than psychological—makes his fiction slippery, difficult to get a bead on. The many psychological critics have all provided worthwhile perspectives on his fiction. Each theoretical framework—Freudian, Reichian, Jungian, or Kohutian—highlights certain aspects of the work, although none fully accounts for everything in the text. As Bellow once said: "We haven't gotten to the pith and nucleus yet. . . . The *real* thing is unfathomable. You *can't* get it down to distinct meaning or clear opinion" (Atlas 464-65). Or as the character Harkavy puts it in Bellow's novel *The Victim* (1947): "'The truth is hard to get at. . . . This one says this, and that one says that. Y says oats, and Z says hay, and chances are . . . it's buckwheat. Nobody can tell you except the fellow that harvested it. To the rest it's all theory'" (77).

Works Cited

Atlas, James. *Bellow: A Biography*. New York: Random House, 2000.

Bellow, Saul. *The Adventures of Augie March*. New York: Viking Press, 1953.

_____. *Humboldt's Gift*. New York: Viking Press, 1975.

_____. *Seize the Day*. New York: Viking Press, 1956.

_____. *A Theft*. New York: Penguin Books, 1989.

_____. *The Victim*. New York: Vanguard Press, 1947.

Berliner, Bernhard. "On Some Psychodynamics of Masochism." *Psychoanalytic Quarterly* 16.4 (1947): 459-71.

Bostonia. "A Half Life: An Autobiography in Ideas." *Conversations with Saul Bellow*. Ed. Gloria L. Cronin and Ben Siegel. Jackson: UP of Mississippi, 1994. 248-77.

_____. "A Second Half Life: An Autobiography in Ideas." *Conversations with Saul Bellow*. Ed. Gloria L. Cronin and Ben Siegel. Jackson: UP of Mississippi, 1994. 278-92.

Botsford, Keith. "Saul Bellow: Made in America." *Conversations with Saul Bellow*. Ed. Gloria L. Cronin and Ben Siegel. Jackson: UP of Mississippi, 1994. 241-47.

Bouson, J. Brooks. "Empathy and Self-Validation in *Seize the Day*." *The Critical Response to Saul Bellow*. Ed. Gerhard Bach. Westport, CT: Greenwood Press, 1995. 83-99.

Boyers, Robert T. "Literature and Culture: An Interview with Saul Bellow." *Salmagundi* 30 (Summer 1975): 6-23.

Brans, Jo. "Common Needs, Common Preoccupations: An Interview with Saul Bellow." *Conversations with Saul Bellow*. Ed. Gloria L. Cronin and Ben Siegel. Jackson: UP of Mississippi, 1994. 140-60.

Clayton, John J. *Saul Bellow: In Defense of Man*. 2d ed. Bloomington: Indiana UP, 1979.

Dommergues, Pierre. "An Interview with Saul Bellow." *Delta* (Université Paul Valery, Montpellier, France) 19 (October 1984): 1-27.

Fuchs, Daniel. "Bellow and Freud." *Saul Bellow in the 1980s*. Ed. Gloria L. Cronin and L. H. Goldman. East Lansing: Michigan State UP, 1989. 27-50.

_____. *Saul Bellow: Vision and Revision*. Durham, NC: Duke UP, 1984.

Gordon, Andrew. "The Hero as Sucker in Saul Bellow's Early Fiction." *Saul Bellow Journal* 6.2 (Summer 1987): 47-63.

Gray, Rockwell, Harry White, and Gerald Nemanic. "Interview with Saul Bellow." *Conversations with Saul Bellow*. Ed. Gloria L. Cronin and Ben Siegel. Jackson: UP of Mississippi, 1994. 199-222.

Jung, Carl. *Two Essays on Analytic Psychology*. Trans. R. C. F. Hull. New York: Pantheon, 1956.

Lawrence, D. H. *Studies in Classic American Literature*. 1923. New York: Viking Press, 1966.

Lévy, Claude. *Les Romans de Saul Bellow: Tactiques Narratives et Strategies Oedipiennes*. Paris: Klinksieck, 1983.

Paris, Bernard J. "Introduction." *Third Force Psychology and the Study of Literature*. Ed. Bernard J. Paris. Cranbury, NJ: Fairleigh Dickinson UP/Associated University Presses, 1986.

Raper, Julius R. "Running Contrary Ways: Saul Bellow's *Seize the Day*." *The Critical Response to Saul Bellow*. Ed. Gerhard Bach. Westport, CT: Greenwood Press, 1995. 73-83.

Rodrigues, Eusebio L. *Quest for the Human: An Exploration of Saul Bellow's Fiction*. Lewisburg, PA: Bucknell UP/Associated University Presses, 1981.

Roudané, Matthew C. "An Interview with Saul Bellow." *The Critical Response to Saul Bellow*. Ed. Gerhard Bach. Westport, CT: Greenwood Press, 1995. 234-47.

Self Psychology Page. "What Is Self Psychology?" http://www.selfpsychology.com/whatis.htm.

Shechner, Mark. *After the Revolution: Studies in the Contemporary Jewish-American Imagination*. Bloomington: Indiana UP, 1987.

Simmons, Maggie. "Free to Feel: Conversation with Saul Bellow." *Conversations with Saul Bellow*. Ed. Gloria L. Cronin and Ben Siegel. Jackson: UP of Mississippi, 1994. 161-70.

Weiss, Daniel. "Caliban on Prospero: A Psychoanalytic Study on the Novel *Seize the Day*, by Saul Bellow." *Saul Bellow and the Critics*. Ed. Irving Malin. New York: New York UP, 1967. 114-41.

Wilson, Jonathan. *"Herzog": The Limits of Ideas*. Boston: Twayne/G. K. Hall, 1990.

Saul Bellow:
The Cultural and Historical Context _____
Judie Newman

Paradoxically, the dominant feature of Saul Bellow's relation to his cultural and historical context is his absolute refusal to be defined by it. Bellow's first published novel, *Dangling Man*, opens with a manifesto that declares his formal rejection of the Hemingway "tough guy" masculine model of American fiction and openly espouses the powers of feeling and intelligence. For Bellow's narrator, transgressing the current code to keep a personal diary of his alienation, the forties are an era of hard-boileddom, of the code of the tough guy and the athlete:

> Do you have feelings? There are correct and incorrect ways of indicating them. Do you have an inner life? It is nobody's business but your own. Do you have emotions? Strangle them (9).

With the introspective, self-questioning, urban heroes of *Dangling Man* and *The Victim*, Bellow rerouted the American novel away from its pastoral, romance form and atemporal engagement with American dreams toward a renewed engagement with ideas and an organic connection with Europe. Strongly influenced at the beginning of his career by Trotskyism and the *Partisan Review* group of intellectuals, Bellow continued to demonstrate as his distinctive qualities an intimate awareness of the intellectual currents of the day, a persistent engagement with the movement of history, and an eclectic gathering together of a wide range of polyglot cultural fields and traditions (Hyland). Something of this eclecticism is indicated in the variety of responses to his work. John J. Clayton discovers within the works a psychic pattern based on Oedipal conflicts and the fear of deserved death; Judie Newman reads Bellow as deeply engaged with Nietzsche's "sixth sense," the sense of history, whereas Ellen Pifer's essential thesis is that each of Bellow's protagonists is polarized between the alternative claims of reason (in the loser's corner) and faith (emerging triumphant) and that Bellow's development reflects a deepening commitment to articulating the reality of the soul. Psyche, History and Soul continue to be identified as central to Bellow's fiction, though they are variously weighted in different critical readings.

Voice (and particularly monologue) was identified almost immediately as the unifying characteristic of Bellow's fiction, from the early stories ("Two Morning Monologues," "A Sermon by Dr. Pep") to the rhetorical, declamatory protagonists of such later works as *Herzog*, *Humboldt's Gift*, *The Dean's December*, and *More Die of Heartbreak*, protagonists often misread as mere mouthpieces for their creator rather than as ironically conceived unreliable narrators. Sharp, ironic effects are fostered by the problematic relation of author-character-narrator, while the characteristically rich mixture of high seriousness, low comedy, esoteric reference, street slang, lyrical power, and savage wit speed the reader through a thickly textured realist world, densely populated with memorable characters. Drawing upon his Russian Jewish heritage and his American immigrant upbringing, Bellow uniquely brings together the worlds of high and popular culture, demonstrating that the material plurality of the world can be expressed and given meaning (Hyland 131) and that in the modern soup of signs the individual can still avoid submersion and maintain selfdom.

Two key factors in Bellow's cultural context are his Jewish immigrant background and his early education in social anthropology. The two are intimately related. Although Bellow began his undergraduate career at the University of Chicago, studying English, he transferred to Northwestern University, graduating in 1937 with honors in anthropology and sociology. One of his tutors was Melville J. Herskovits, whose studies of cattle cultures provided the material for Bellow's African tribes in *Henderson the Rain King* (Rodrigues). Bellow went on to do graduate work at the University of Wisconsin but dropped out after only a few months to become a full-time writer. As he explained, "Every time I worked on my thesis, it turned out to be a story" (Breit

272). He has described his decision to study anthropology in terms that suggest a conscious identification with universalism and demystification in the cause of freedom:

> Anthropology students were the farthest out in the 1930s. They seemed to be preparing to criticize society from its roots. Radicalism was implied by the study of anthropology. . . . It indicated that human life was much broader than the present. It gave young Jews a greater sense of freedom from the surrounding restrictions. (Steers 36)

Many of the founders of the field were Jewish: Émile Durkheim, Lucien Lévy-Bruhl, Marcel Mauss, Franz Boas, Edward Sapir, and Robert Lowie. Bellow's own choice of topic for research fieldwork, as he revealed in *To Jerusalem and Back*, was to investigate bands of Eskimos who were reported to have chosen to starve rather than eat foods that were under taboo. How much, he wondered, did people conform to culture, and at what point would the animal need to survive break through the restraints of custom and belief? Bellow suspected that so-called primitive peoples had the edge over the "civilized":

> I'm not at all certain now that civilized minds are more flexible and capable of grasping reality, or that they have livelier, more intelligent reactions to the threat of extinction. I have read writers on the Holocaust who made the most grave criticisms of European Jewry, arguing that they doomed themselves by their unwillingness to surrender their comfortable ways, their property, their passive habits, their acceptance of bureaucracy, and were led to slaughter unresisting. (*To Jerusalem* 130-31)

Although Bellow does not endorse this latter, tendentious argument, the development of his thought in this paragraph—from Eskimo taboos to the Holocaust—suggests that questions of cultural change and adaptation have a special relevance for him as an immigrant Jew. It is, of course, precisely this issue—obedience to custom versus adaptive plasticity—on which Henderson and the Arnewi part company. The Arnewi prefer their cows to die of thirst rather than drink water polluted by taboo frogs. Henderson blows up custom, frogs, and water source all together in a scene of wholesale destruction.

For Bellow his immigrant status was also relevant to the choice of anthropology. Describing himself as "an exotic among other exotics," he pointed to the lack of stability available to the children of immigrants, who therefore needed to adapt as speedily as possible to their new environment. "The word for this was 'Americanization'. The masses that came from Europe in the great wave of immigration between 1870 and 1930 wanted to be as American as possible" (Gray, White, and Nemanic 21). Bellow cited Augie March's desire for fraternity, for example, as common to adolescent Americans of immigrant background. Augie's refusal to be conditioned by a time and place, whether as the result of his Jewish background or his American present, was also shared with his creator. In an interview Bellow commented:

> As a Middle-Westerner, the son of immigrant parents, I recognized at an early age that I was called upon to decide for myself to what extent my Jewish origins, my surroundings . . . were to be allowed to determine the course of my life. . . . The commonest teaching of the civilized world in our time can be stated simply: "Tell me where you come from and I will tell you what you are." . . . I would not allow myself to become the product of an environment. ("Civilized Barbarian" 1)

In juxtaposing these autobiographical statements with Bellow's comments on anthropology, a common thread can be discerned: a concern with the influence of, and the resistance to, environment and with the degree to which human adaptation in customs and in culture is desirable, or even possible. Breaking with custom may involve the permanent loss of valuable traditions. On the other hand, new opportunities may be generated. In the same interview Bellow expressed his belief that the weakening of the older, traditional branches of civilization might open fresh opportunities, forcing an independent reassessment of what culture is. Later in his career Bellow became identified, falsely in many respects, with neoconservatives such as his friend Allan Bloom, author of *The Closing of the American Mind*, a key text in what became known as the "culture wars" between scholars defending the classical canon of humanist and literary works and others advancing the claims of those marginalized from culture, particularly as a result of race or gender. (Bloom features as the model for Bellow's eponymous hero in *Ravelstein*.) Arguably, however, Bellow had no quarrel with his supposed opponents; he had been writing about cultural change and culture wars from the start.

Bellow's early training in social anthropology allowed him to present his vision of society something in the manner of a participant-observer, simultaneously engaged and critically detached. Motifs from social anthropology provide structural pivots in the plots of *Seize the Day* (the trickster figure), *Henderson the Rain King* (East African cattle cultures), *Humboldt's Gift* (gift exchange), "Mosby's Memoirs" (death customs), and "Cousins" (shamanism), among others. Bellow's associated reading in psychoanalytic theory is also mined for scorching attacks on naive Freudianism in *The Last Analysis* and *Herzog*. Bellow's intertextuality is creative, multifarious, and something of a challenge to most of his readers, but it appeals to the autodidactic strand in the American popular mind. Unusually for such an erudite and allusive writer, Bellow featured repeatedly on the best-seller lists.

Though a remarkably unified achievement, Bellow's oeuvre nonetheless falls into several phases of development, beginning with an initial period marked by victim literature and featuring tightly controlled, short, and spatially ordered forms. A major change in style occurred with the publication of *The Adventures of Augie March*, a loose and baggy monster of a novel, which made explicit homage in its title to Mark Twain, declared itself as defiantly American, and prepared readers for the comic invention of its equally picaresque successor, *Henderson the Rain King*. The change in style may be linked to the way in which *The Victim* exorcised the guilt of Bellow's own background. In an interview in 1990 Bellow was asked about the relative absence of the Holocaust in his writing. He agreed that "there were lots of things I hadn't been able to incorporate. Things that got away from me. The Holocaust for one" (*It All Adds Up* 312).

According to Bellow, it was only in 1959, when he visited Auschwitz, that the Holocaust "landed its whole weight on me" (*It All Adds Up* 313). He admitted to finding it odd that he had not been moved to write about it; he had lost close relatives. Bellow's reluctance to confront the topic—understandable as it is—becomes potentially more comprehensible in the description offered, in the same interview, of his childhood. At the age of eight, Bellow spent six months seriously ill in the hospital. Already a good reader, he could read his chart at the end of the bed and knew, even at that age, that his diagnosis was very unpromising. In the ward he was constantly exposed to the deaths of children. As a result, Bellow felt forever after that he had been in some fashion excused from death, "that it was a triumph, that I had gotten away with it." There was, he concluded, "a duty that came with survival." "I owed something to some entity for the privilege of surviving" (*It All Adds Up* 289). Bellow, in short, was already possessed of that complex of emotions termed "survivor syndrome" (Epstein 100-103). In his childish narcissism, Bellow describes his survival as a triumph.

In *The Victim*, Leventhal, recalling his narrow escape from indigence in the 1930s, often says that "I was lucky. I got away with it" (22). He never forgets the hotel on Lower Broadway, and "the part that did not get away with it—the lost, the outcast, the overcome, the effaced, the ruined" (23). Leventhal's imagery here draws upon the notion of economic disaster, but his guilt is clearly that of a survivor, who did not particularly deserve to survive but was luckier than the rest. The slippage here between economic and historical frames of reference has a special relevance to Bellow's reaction to the Holocaust. In an interview, Bellow was asked about the intellectual impact of World War II. He replied that he had completely misunderstood the war because he was under the influence of Marxism. Although Kristallnacht gave him pause, Bellow, as a Trotskyite, stood by the belief that a workers' state, however degenerate, could not wage an imperialist war. "I was still at that time officially sold on Marxism and revolution, but I sobered up when France fell" (307). Earlier, Bellow had been scheduled to meet Trotsky in Mexico, but arrived immediately after his assassination when Trotsky was in the morgue (the material of "The Mexican General"). In short, Bellow's initial understanding of the events in Europe in terms of the primacy of economic forces in history was impelled to yield to a sharper awareness of the nature of anti-Semitism. He promptly joined up:

> I had recognized Hitler for "what he was." I knew most of the story, and not only did I feel that my Jewish Marxist friends were wrong in theory, but I was horrified by the positions they—we—had taken. (*It All Adds Up* 310)

The Victim is Bellow's examination of both the guilt and the responsibilities of the survivor. It is, in a sense, about the Holocaust, because it is not, ostensibly, about the Holocaust. Significantly, the novel alternates between two plots, Leventhal's persecution by anti-Semitic Allbee and the sickness and death of Mickey, Leventhal's nephew. A precise correlation exists between the death of the child and the emergence of Allbee as persecuting double, a connection that draws upon psychoanalysis. Otto Rank understands the double as originally an insurance against the destruction of the ego, an energetic denial of the power of death, so that the "immortal soul" may be considered as the first double of the body. Doubling is preservation against extinction on the part of the self, in its narcissistic self-love. Rank notes, however, that the initially reassuring figure is capable of reversing its aspect and from being an assurance of immortality becomes the uncanny harbinger of death: the dead person becomes the enemy of the survivor and seeks to carry him off to share his new life with him.

Dreams are particularly interesting in connection with doubles. Rank argues that man may have taken the proof of his belief that the ego might exist after death from the experience of dreaming. In Bellow's novel Allbee's uncanny nature is dramatized in his mysterious appearance. Leventhal hears a bell ring—but there is nobody at the door, nor has the super seen anyone enter or leave. Yet Allbee's letter is in Leventhal's box. Against a background featuring a revivalist band, Allbee appears and remarks, "Now you've found out that I still exist . . ." and Leventhal instantly responds, "Why should I doubt that you exist? Is there any reason why you shouldn't?" (28). When Leventhal tries to grip Allbee's arm he feels no resistance, as if his hand were going through Allbee as easily as Allbee apparently goes through doors. After dismissing Allbee, Leventhal recalls him only when Mickey's condition worsens: "what a time it was to have thought of him!" he reacts. (46). But as later events demonstrate, it was absolutely the right time to have thought of him. Allbee appears as a ghostly harbinger of death and a persecuting double in direct response to the threat to Mickey. Just as the Holocaust reactivated Bellow's childhood experience, reviving repressed material in sharpened, guilty form, so in the novel a Jewish child is threatened by death, and in guilt and fear Leventhal allows a double to emerge to persecute him.

The connections to the Holocaust emerge most clearly in relation to two structural elements: acting and dreams. Acting offers an exceptionally good metaphor for the narcissistic splitting and reduplication of the ego. Allbee is repeatedly characterized by Leventhal as a bad actor, a poor imitation of the genuine article, himself. The horror film that Leventhal sees in the novel also highlights the uncanny double. Discussions among the characters about acting (in the dual senses of role play and moral behavior) center on acting as duplication, the modern inability to face death, and survival guilt. (Mrs. Harkavy feels "wicked still to be here at my age while the children die"; 200.) Schlossberg draws the moral:

I have to be myself in full. Which is somebody who dies, isn't it? . . . I'm not three people, four people. I was born once and I will die once. You want to be two people? More than human? Maybe it's because you don't know how to be one. (208)

The images of acting and the Holocaust also come together in two dreams. In the first dream Leventhal is quite overtly split into two selves:

He had an unclear dream in which he held himself off like an unwilling spectator; yet it was he that did everything. (138)

The situation, a railway station hung with flags, in which crowds controlled by guards are being loaded onto trains, is instantly recognizable as an image of the Holocaust (Kremer). Leventhal, however, is eager to board the train, running in an attempt to catch it, but before he can reach the tracks, a man in a business suit pushes him out into an alley. The dream suggests that Leventhal has made every effort, in his double dream self, to get on the train, to share the fate of the crowd around him, but has been thwarted despite himself. Waking, Leventhal has "a sense of marvellous relief . . . a rare pure feeling of happiness" (139). His dream double has assuaged his guilt, sought out his own destruction, and been excused from death by a mysterious authority figure.

Leventhal's other dream returns to the business representative of the first, not as a savior but as complicit in the horror. In the dream a salesgirl in a store demonstrates shades of rouge to Leventhal by drawing spots on her face, wiping each off on a smelly towel, and then bending back to the mirror to repeat the process. In making herself up the woman is "putting on a face"—many faces, multiplied in the mirror. Leventhal's mind, semiconscious, moves from the smell of the towel to an uneasy awareness that although steam is audibly hissing in the pipes, his room is cold. He rouses himself to the smell of hissing gas: Allbee is attempting to gas them both. The reference to the Holocaust could hardly be more explicit. Where Leventhal's first dream potentially suggests the saving force of capitalist America (the businessman), the second dream indicts big business, recalling its crucial role in the Holocaust. Bellow's Marxism was not lightly abandoned. The colors (in German, *Farben*) of the woman's paint recall I.G. Farben, the German business conglomerate that began by making dyestuffs and paints, then went on to build both its own plant and a concentration camp at Auschwitz, and manufactured Zyklon B, the gas for the camp's extermination block, a gas deliberately manufactured without the indicator of smell (Borkin, Hayes). Leventhal's life is saved by the dream of a smelly woman. The dream expresses Leventhal's renewed openness to sexual love and signals the disappearance of the deathly double.

The Victim was therapeutic for Bellow, who himself noted a change after it from gloom to holiday (*It All Adds Up* 318). Critics have also been swift to see the subsequent novel, *The Adventures of Augie March*, as marking a breakthrough. Bellow's first epigraph to *The Victim* is from "The Tale of the Trader and the Jinni," an example of the "ransom frame" in which the act of storytelling serves to redeem a human life (Caracciolo), much as Scheherazade distracts Shahriar in the frame tale of *The Thousand and One Nights* from his intention to kill her. As the multiple plot structures of *The Thousand and One Nights* demonstrate, storytelling is a better defense against the powers of death than any other, for it doubles reader, author, and character by sympathetic identification—a form of love. *The Victim* is a narrative of trauma that becomes a narrative of reparation, the first of a long, reparative career. Arguably, it is also highly suggestive in the paradigm offered for the importance of the theme of death in Bellow's novels, and for the treatment thereof. Double plots are a common feature of Bellow's writing, with one half of the pair often associated with the "Other": America and Mexico in *The Adventures of Augie March*, America and Africa in *Henderson the Rain King*, America and Eastern Europe in *The Dean's December*, Dr. Lal and the pickpocket in *Mr.*

Sammler's Planet, Dahfu and Henderson in *Henderson the Rain King*, Mosby and Lustgarten (in a story set in Mitla, the mythic center of the Zapotec world of the dead). In *Humboldt's Gift* Cantabile emerges as a persecuting double when Citrine learns of the death of Humboldt; Henderson sets off for Africa in immediate response to the death of Miss Lenox; the death of Valeria haunts *The Dean's December*; *Seize the Day* ends with Tommy Wilhelm absorbed into the crowd at a funeral. Herzog writes letters to the dead but is brought back to emotional health after watching the trial of a woman accused of causing the death of a small child.

It was *Herzog* that established Bellow's reputation on a permanent basis and that delineated his great theme: the need to come to terms with the past without being defined by it. If amnesia is, as Gore Vidal reputedly remarked, America's middle name, memory is Bellow's. Mr. Sammler, Willis Mosby, Dean Corde, the unnamed narrator of *The Bellarosa Connection* (and founder of the Mnemosyne Institute), the central figures of "Cousins" and "A Silver Dish"—all are memory-driven, deeply and imaginatively engaged with coming to terms with the past. Even Bellow's nonfiction *To Jerusalem and Back*, a personal account of a visit to Israel (from a decidedly pro-Israeli perspective) is conceived as a journey back into his own past. "It is my childhood revisited," he declares in the opening paragraph, contemplating a group of Hasidim. When *Herzog* first appeared in 1964, it was immediately heralded as a masterpiece, becoming a best seller and going on to win the National Book Award for fiction in 1965. Readers responded to Bellow's scorching attack on fashionable literary pessimism and his renewed emphasis on the duties and responsibilities, rather than much-clamored-for rights and freedoms, of the human being. When his hero derided the "cheap mental stimulants of Alienation" (75), there were cheers from readers ready for the more politically activist 1960s. The novel struck a popular chord. Herzog's wife throws him out in October 1963, a month before the assassination of John F. Kennedy, and Herzog's postdivorce grief focused the grief and betrayal of a nation.

In rejecting the therapeutic emphasis of American culture, Bellow mounted a thoroughgoing attack on popular Freudianism. Herzog begins and ends on the couch ("If I am out of my mind, it's all right with me" is his opening statement), with the hero going over the past repetitively and in ever-receding terms, from the recent to the not so recent, with flashbacks to the events of childhood, in a fashion that suggests the flight into neurosis and the escape into the deepest recesses of the psyche. Bellow thus targets the core idea of psychoanalysis as the attempt to emancipate the patient from the burden of history, underlining the extent to which popular psychoanalysis offers an attractive possibility of avoiding responsibility.

In the major formal device of the novel, a series of unsent letters addressed to such public figures as Martin Luther King, Dwight D. Eisenhower, Hegel, Nietzsche, and Nehru, Bellow offers an image of an alternative flight away from the psyche into history, portrayed as massively dwarfing the individual under its sway. Where the psychoanalytic structure enacts the flight out of time into the determining realm of the psyche, the letters engage with world historical concerns. In both flights the individual is absolved from responsibility for himself and for his own particular history, surrendering to the determinism of either personal psychological time or all-encompassing historical movements. In the outcome, Herzog sees that history is neither curse nor supreme value, but the medium in which he (and implicitly the reader) must make difficult moral judgments. As Herzog remarks, "You must start with injustices that are obvious to everybody, not with big historical perspectives" (48). A crucial example is offered in the climactic scene of the novel, in which Herzog witnesses a trial. Prophetically, given the late-twentieth-century furor over false memory syndrome and moral panic over the welfare of children, the case concerns child abuse. As master narratives collapsed, American society in this period retreated increasingly toward the child as moral touchstone and the victim as the norm. Herzog's wife Madeleine was abused as a child, as was Herzog himself, but where she allows her victim status to control her life, he refuses to embrace the victim role, insisting on the need for individual responsibility. Though real suffering is firmly fore-grounded, the novel mounts a strenuous resistance to the therapeutic model of the permanently traumatized individual.

Madeleine is perhaps the least sympathetic of Bellow's female char-acters. Indeed, his portrayals of women have been lambasted as tend-ing to create images of sadistic brutes, compliant slaves, sex god-desses, or pseudointellectuals. Gloria L. Cronin, however, offers a persuasive argument that Bellow's male protagonists are almost all in search of an absent mother, lover, sister, female friend, psyche, or anima. For Cronin there emerges from the singularly masculine scopic economy of the novels a profoundly ambivalent representation of his-torical American masculinity (147). While the constant staging of mi-sogyny remains a problem for some readers, even allowing for the ironic unreliability of the narrator-protagonists, it is worth noting that there is a difference between earlier and later Bellow in this respect. A final didactic phase (*The Dean's December, More Die of Heartbreak, A Theft, Ravelstein*) demonstrates a deepening debate and engagement with the writings of Jung, and a focus on women as centers of value. In all these works, in contradistinction to his previous male-centered practice, Bellow focuses attention on aspects of the feminine, particu-larly the relation to the mother and to matriarchal mythology. *The Dean's December* establishes an entire "love community" (72) of women in Romania, headed by the matriarch and symbolic Great Mother, Valeria. *A Theft* brings together the archetypal figures of maiden, matron, and crone in the figures of Lucy, Gina, and Clara, as Clara moves from a fragmented concept of self and love to a stronger sense of wholeness (Friedrich). In *Ravelstein* Rosamund is certainly the most independent and sympathetic of Bellow's women. In *More Die of Heartbreak* the central point of reference is Allan Bloom's prop-osition in *The Closing of the American Mind* that the human longing for completeness in love is allied to the longing for education. Bel-low's hero, Benn Crader, undergoes erotic testing at the hands of several mythologized women, renegotiating his relation to erotic desire. In the novel Bellow attempts to reconnect Eros and education by insisting on love as the conduit to higher ideals, rather than as a product of the unconscious. The narrative design of the book, structured on conversations between uncle and nephew, represents a carefully constructed project to put the sublime back into sublimation and Psyche, the Soul, back into psychology. Love thus features as *pharmakon*, both the poison and its remedy.

Throughout his work Bellow is particularly alert to the dangers of converting the individual into a representative or symbolic figure ("Deep Readers"). When Henderson becomes a fertility symbol, he narrowly escapes death. Augie March spends most of the novel evading others' attempts to convert him to their version of the world. Mr. Sammler refuses to allow others to see him as a symbol of the Holocaust survivor and witnesses a climactic fight between the wielders of different symbols—a black pickpocket (previously seen exposing the phallus, the basis of Freudian symbolic order) and Eisen, in whose hands crudely patriotic symbolic medallions become vicious weapons. For Bellow literature must do more than represent and must offer more than a war between different representations—or representations of difference. Robustly independent of temporary critical and cultural fashions, Bellow remains a deeply thought-provoking novelist for whom there are never any easy answers.

Works Cited

Bellow, Saul. *The Adventures of Augie March*. New York: Viking Press, 1953.
_____. *The Bellarosa Connection*. New York: Penguin, 1989.
_____. "The Civilized Barbarian Reader." *New York Times Book Review* 8 Mar. 1987: 1, 38.
_____. *Dangling Man*. New York: Vanguard Press, 1944.
_____. *The Dean's December*. New York: Harper & Row, 1982.
_____. "Deep Readers of the World Beware!" *New York Times Book Review* 15 Feb. 1959: 1, 34.
_____. *Henderson the Rain King*. New York: Viking Press, 1959.

_____. *Herzog*. New York: Viking Press, 1964.

_____. *Him with His Foot in His Mouth, and Other Stories*. New York: Harper & Row, 1984.

_____. *Humboldt's Gift*. New York: Viking Press, 1975.

_____. *It All Adds Up: From the Dim Past to the Uncertain Future*. New York: Viking Press, 1994.

_____. *The Last Analysis*. New York: Viking Press, 1965.

_____. "The Mexican General." *Partisan Review* 9 (May-June 1942): 178-94.

_____. *More Die of Heartbreak*. New York: William Morrow, 1987.

_____. *Mosby's Memoirs, and Other Stories*. New York: Viking Press, 1968.

_____. *Mr. Sammler's Planet*. New York: Viking Press, 1970.

_____. *Ravelstein*. New York: Viking Press, 2000.

_____. *Seize the Day*. New York: Viking Press, 1956.

_____. "A Sermon by Dr. Pep." *Partisan Review* 14 (May-June 1949): 455-62.

_____. *A Theft*. New York: Penguin Books, 1989.

_____. *To Jerusalem and Back: A Personal Account*. New York: Viking Press, 1976.

_____. "Two Morning Monologues." *Partisan Review* 8 (May-June 1941): 230-36.

_____. *The Victim*. New York: Vanguard Press, 1947.

Bloom, Allan. *The Closing of the American Mind*. New York: Simon & Schuster, 1987.

Borkin, Joseph. *The Crime and Punishment of I.G. Farben: The Birth, Growth, and Corruption of a Giant Corporation*. London: André Deutsch, 1979.

Breit, Harvey. *The Writer Observed*. London: Alvin Redman, 1957.

Caracciolo, Peter L., ed. *The Arabian Nights in English Literature: Studies in the Reception of "The Thousand and One Nights" into British Culture*. London: Macmillan, 1988.

Clayton, John J. *Saul Bellow: In Defense of Man*. 2d ed. Bloomington: Indiana UP, 1979.

Cronin, Gloria L. *A Room of His Own: In Search of the Feminine in the Novels of Saul Bellow*. Syracuse, NY: Syracuse UP, 2001.

Epstein, Helen. *Children of the Holocaust*. New York: G. P. Putnam's Sons, 1979.

Friedrich, Marianne M. *Character and Narration in the Short Fiction of Saul Bellow*. New York: Peter Lang, 1995.

Gray, Rockwell, Harry White, and Gerald Nemanic. "Interview with Saul Bellow." *TriQuarterly* 60 (1984): 12-34.

Hayes, Peter. *Industry and Ideology: I.G. Farben in the Nazi Era*. New York: Cambridge University Press, 1987.

Hyland, Peter. *Saul Bellow*. London: Macmillan, 1992.

Kremer, S. Lillian. "The Holocaust in *The Victim*." *Saul Bellow Journal* 2 (1983): 15-23.

Newman, Judie. *Saul Bellow and History*. London: Macmillan, 1984.

Pifer, Ellen. *Saul Bellow: Against the Grain*. Philadelphia: University of Pennsylvania Press, 1990.

Rank, Otto. *The Double: A Psychoanalytic Study*. Trans. and ed. by Harry Tucker, Jr. Chapel Hill: U of North Carolina P, 1971.

Rodrigues, Eusebio L. "Bellow's Africa." *American Literature* 43.2 (May 1971): 242-56.

Saul Bellow Journal. Special issue on *More Die of Heartbreak* 11.1 (1992).

Steers, Nina A. "'Successor' to Faulkner? An Interview with Saul Bellow." *Show* 4 (Sept. 1964): 36-38.

The Holocaust and History in Bellow and Malamud

Daniel Fuchs

In *Zakhor: Jewish History and Jewish Memory*, Yosef Hayim Yerushalmi points out that the fathers of transcendent meaning in history were the Jews, that "human history revealed God's will and purpose" (8). This set up a pattern of "divine challenge and human response . . . a tense dialectic of obedience and rebellion." Thus there was a profound sense in which traditional Jews considered the destruction of the First and Second Temples a result of their sins. The Holocaust has shaken this mentality to near oblivion. Few contemporary Jews would consider the Holocaust their fault. Yet many consider the Holocaust.

In the tradition, God reveals himself historically. Moses speaks of "God of our fathers" who says, "I have surely remembered you" (Exodus 3:16) and "I am the Lord . . . who brought you out of the Land of Egypt" (Exodus 20:2). Memory, therefore, becomes crucial to faith and its very existence. "Only in Israel and nowhere else is the injunction to remember felt as a religious imperative to an entire people," as Passover remembers the exodus. As the tradition develops into long-lived rabbinic Jewry, a Jewry of exile in its inception, the meaning of history is derived more from the prophets than from the historical narratives of the Bible, "as collective memory is transmitted more actively through ritual than through chronicle" (Yerushalmi 21). Memory is sanctified through mythic time. There was no Jewish historian for fifteen centuries. Maimonides, so attuned to the universalizing of philosophy, considered the reading of history "a waste of time" (33).

Modernity radically changes this, particularly the Enlightenment, where the Haskalah movement, a secularizing vanguard of German Jewry, scientifically, nonapologetically, considers the nature and viability of Judaism. Judaism becomes historicized, no longer a sacred text; it is something defined rather than revealed. "Jewish historiography," Yerushalmi says, is "divorced from Jewish collective memory"

(93). History, he says laconically, "is the faith of fallen Jews" (86). The Holocaust, like the Spanish Inquisition before it, led to historical involvement but in a historicizing time. Yerushalmi feels a part of this modernity, part of this disintegration that brings such great gains in consciousness. He feels the losses as well. And, for him, there is something intrinsic to the nature of history that can never recapture the deeply affective context of the prophetic tradition.

Enter literature. For even though "the Holocaust has engendered more historical research than any single event in Jewish history," Yerushalmi has

> no doubt whatever that its image is being shaped, not at the historian's anvil, but in the novelist's crucible. Much has changed since the sixteenth century; one thing, curiously, remains. Now, as then, it would appear that even where Jews do not reject history out of hand, they are not prepared to confront it directly, but seem to await a new metahistorical myth, for which the novel provides at least a temporary modern surrogate. (98)

Presumably the Jewish fiction writer would have a special access to this subject. Yerushalmi believes that "those who are alienated from the past cannot be drawn to it by explanation alone; they require evocation as well" (100). Saul Bellow and Bernard Malamud are American exemplars. They help to define Yerushalmi's desired affective context. The few works of fiction considered here may seem small in the tremendousness of the event, but there is a literary brilliance to be observed, and the longest journey begins with a few steps. Surely these writers are representative of the contemporary consciousness Yerushalmi describes and exemplifies.

"The Holocaust haunted him always as a writer," according to Malamud's friend Nicholas Delbanco (*Talking Horse* 162). Malamud wrote about it at a remove, never directly but through the refugee experience, in some of his most memorable stories, including a few from his best book of stories, *The Magic Barrel*. In "The Last Mohican,"

Fidelman, a failed painter turned would-be critic, is the central intelligence. His soul is tested by the enigmatic refugee Susskind. Serious though it is, in its sense of accelerated importunity the story is almost an extended Jewish joke, with Susskind a variation on the classic *schnorrer*, or shameless hanger-on. (In one version of the joke, a *schnorrer*, after endless, humiliating pleading, is invited to a party where he does not belong—and brings a guest!) The *schnorrer* is an emblem of an East European Jewry that was often on the borderline between respectability and desperation. At first blush, Susskind fits the typology, an illustration of folk memory. But the joke, as Malamud has it, is on Fidelman, whose unexpected new awareness is the epiphanic center of the tale. The exquisiteness of the story lies in Malamud's making the necessary moral object so nearly impossible to like, let alone save.

In his oxblood shoes and tweed suit, Fidelman is an American type, a relatively well-off innocent (even though a poor student) suddenly confronted with the impressive monuments of experience. He sees the Baths of Diocletian, thinks of Michelangelo's role in converting them to a church and convent, and then of the museum it ultimately became. From the politically autocratic to the religious to the aesthetic—or the course of European consciousness in a nutshell. "Imagine," thinks Fidelman, "imagine all that history. . . . It was an inspiring business, he, Arthur Fidelman, after all, born a Bronx boy" (*Magic Barrel* 156, 162). Fidelman experiences the standard reverence and stupefaction. But there is a complication. For Fidelman, "history was mysterious, the remembrance of things unknown, in a way burdensome, in a way sensuous experience" (162). Like Henry James in the Louvre, Fidelman experiences a confusion that signifies both love and fear. And well he might—for the aspect of history that the story involves him in is one that he seems not strong enough to assimilate.

The Holocaust is European history as well, history with a capital *H* at that. Fidelman feels the burden of history in the form of skinny Susskind, whose lack of weight suggests another Jewish folk figure, the *luftmensch*, or impoverished soul who apparently lives on air. He is the test of Fidelman's humanity, and Fidelman almost fails it. "Am I responsible for you then, Susskind?" says Fidelman. Susskind loudly replies, "Who else? . . . because you are a man. Because you are a Jew" (165). Again Malamud relates to Jewish typology—am I my brother's keeper? But if he almost fails the test it is with good reason. The crowning indignity from Susskind is the theft of his manuscript. Poor Fidelman, a "tightly organized" (162) anal-retentive obsessive-compulsive, who records his research expenditures in a notebook and who is disoriented without a work schedule, runs head-on into this whirlwind of need, unexpectedness, and slovenly disproportion named Susskind. Comedy is indeed about the juxtaposition of opposites, and there is a Kafkaesque comedy in this crisis in the life of a well-ordered existence.

Looking for the elusive Susskind in a cemetery, Fidelman comes across a gravestone that screams, "My beloved father/ Betrayed by the damn Fascists/ Murdered at Auschwitz by the barbarous Nazis/ *O Crime Orrible*" (176). Some resistance in Fidelman breaks. That night he dreams he is in a cemetery, with Virgilio Susskind rising up out of an empty grave, asking, "Have you read Tolstoy?" and "Why is art?" Tolstoy's *What Is Art?* makes a strong, an excessive, argument for morality in art. But it is nonetheless the right direction for Malamud. The switch from "what" to "why" presents art as a moral imperative. Art must be moral, says this Virgil to his willing Dante. Fidelman is then in a synagogue apparently converted from a church with a Giotto fresco that shows St. Francis "handing an old knight in a thin robe his gold cloak" (181). This is a perfect venue for the ecumenical Malamud. The dream galvanizes Fidelman's moral sense. Susskind will get his suit, which he offers to him with the particularly Yiddish wish, "Wear it in good health." This is Fidelman's only Yiddish expression in the story. But when he discovers that Susskind has burnt his chapter, using it apparently for candle lighting page by page, he wants only to complete what the Holocaust failed to do—annihilate Susskind. The refugee says, "The words were there but the spirit was missing" (182). Fidelman is violently struck by the rightness of this judgment and forgives everything. How Susskind is suddenly set up as a critic of a critic of Giotto, the story does not explain. But Malamud is impelled by two logics: the proud logic of narrative, which takes the story to its fantastic end whether it is believable or not, and the logic of morality, which insists that the spirit is higher than the letter. Two of Malamud's obsessions, writing stories and "giving," come to a glaring conversion, and we are left to wonder whether Malamud's self-described moral aesthetic is too didactically stylized.

"Giving" is so intense in "Take Pity" that it transcends the bounds of realism into fantasy. Malamud is creating a fable, the old Jewish habit of transforming history into myth. Giving is not only a primary obligation in the tradition but also a heightened obligation in cases of suffering engendered by the Holocaust. So it is to Rosen. This is a story about a man who offers everything, including, finally, his life (he commits suicide so that a widow can collect his insurance). Rosen is trying to preserve her from a second "graveyard" as well, a Malamudian grocery store. Despite the somberness, the story once again has the elements of a Jewish joke, with Eva and Rosen as accelerators in terms of her ever-mounting refusals of anything from the more and more giving Rosen. In a line that could have come only from Malamud, Rosen notes, "Here . . . is a very strange thing . . . a person that you can never give her anything.—*But I will give*" (94). The reader is not quite sure whether to laugh or cry. He makes out his will and takes gas: "Let her say now no" (94), he says in Malamud's impeccable immigrant Yinglish syntax. But Eva has come to his perch in limbo, beseeching him now, but too late.

What Malamud's fiction often shows is the power of fantasy even to the extent of going all the way to symbolism, as in "The Jewbird," itself perhaps an example of Holocaust fiction in its chilling final image of the decimated bird. In holding fantasy so high, Malamud gives us a secular version of an essentially religious sensibility. "One effect of fantasy," he says, "is to give a feeling of timelessness, another of universality" (*Talking Horse* 51). In his discussion of "Take Pity" Malamud cites the classic Yiddish writers in their folk fantasy showing "ordinary people in time of stress" being saved by "unreal or supernatural beings" (59). As if expanding on Yerushalmi's distinction between myth and history, Malamud says that the classic Yiddish texts "show how God tries the Jews and are clearly derived from certain books of the Bible," adding that his works deal "not so much with the miraculous element but the trials and sufferings of poor people." Malamud tells us that "Rosen is being judged for his suicide, perhaps even paying for" it (58), in his super-realistic purgatory, complete with an anaesthetized angel who has seen it all and then some. "Perhaps he is being punished for his pride, for giving when it isn't wanted," Malamud says. As for Eva, "perhaps because of an embittered quality, stubbornness, pride or simple incapacity, through lack of generosity," she cannot accept his generosity and compassion (61). However intricate the plot, Malamud wants to suspend it in the realm of moral fable. "Fantastic, symbolic, mythic, timeless, universal, poetic, or anything else that fantasy may be, the truth it tells is true" (61).

Malamud's Holocaust stories are not all in the fabulist mold. "The Lady of the Lake" is realistic and Jamesian, juxtaposing New World and Old in a tale of intrigue and duplicity, all in an exotic European setting. Though even here plot hangs so heavily in the air that we are only a few steps from fable. Malamud has said that in writing a book, "generally I have the ending in mind, usually the last paragraph almost verbatim. . . . The destination is already defined" (Stern 64). If this is true of his novels it is that much more true of his stories. So of "The Magic Barrel" he has said, "the story was almost all thought out before it was written, usual with me" (*Talking Horse* 85). "The Lady of the Lake" is so preconceived that, effective though it is as dramatic irony, the characters are basically a function of plot. The story of Henry R. Freeman, né Henry Levin, is one of Jewish deidentification. As he emotes over the romantic Italian lake district he thinks, "who ever got emotional over Welfare Island [he means Ellis Island]?" (106). The answer is millions, most of them the children of immigrants, like himself. He wants to radically transform his "unlived life" (109). This Jamesian desire is in itself commendable, and the name Freeman indicates an American expansiveness, but his embarrassment about his own history, in contrast to his fascination with "thees 'eestorical palatz" of the family del Dongo and the attraction of the Lady's "dark, sharp Italian face [that] had the quality of beauty which holds the mark of history" (113), is something Malamud does not forgive. Freeman's present is saturated in her imagined past: "Her past he could see boiling in her all the way back to the knights of old and then some, his own history was something else again" (115). His own Jewish past had brought him nothing but "headaches, inferiorities, unhappy memories" (126). Well, perhaps, but it is a pity that it has brought him nothing else. His Lady is not Isabella del Dongo and she is Jewish and a Holocaust survivor (the only one in Malamud's fiction to have actually been in a concentration camp), who must reject his proposal of marriage because, as she says, "My past is meaningful to me. I treasure what I suffered for."

In Malamud's Holocaust fiction not all pasts have meaning in her sense, and not all suffering is a treasure. Far from it. In "The German Refugee" Oskar Gassner is an assimilated German Jew whose main connection with Judaism is the hatred it inspired in his native countrymen. A well-known Berlin critic and journalist, he is lucky enough to have gotten out of there before and, again, after Kristallnacht, leaving his wife and appallingly anti-Semitic mother-in-law behind. He is quite different from his East European fellow Jews in that he must leave a country he was very much a part of. He feels lost in the United States. Depressed, he cannot learn English, though any possibility of employment makes it necessary to do so. His speech has none of the nervous, witty, ironic vigor of Yiddish, the language of East European Jewish immigrants, but is rather a forlorn patchwork that falls between the stools of German and English, usually with a loud plop. The history he lives is the history we all know from the newspapers. His private life mirrors public life, his past is the present. The only fantasy element of his life is the world of fact. His story is in the realistic, heartbreak manner of Anton Chekhov and early James Joyce, a subtle psychological narrative culminating in a personal insight, an illumination of a missed connection. Malamud takes the story from his own experience as a tutor of German refugees at just this historical and biographical moment. But because Gassner is so deeply depressed—he had attempted suicide during his first week in America—Malamud converts his own depression of the period into the balanced sunniness of his narrator, whom we trust to give an objective account of this extremely painful case.

Malamud gives us fine images of Gassner as a fish out of water—his dressing in full regalia (coat, tie) even in the oppressive New York heat, his sitting in the New York Public Library unable to read. The narrator thinks of him "always suspended between two floors," neither here nor there. His Kristallnacht of the soul keeps him from writing. It is, he says, "as though someone has thrown a stone at a window and the whole house—the whole idea, zmashes" (*Idiots First* 206). He cannot get over his feeling that his wife too is an anti-Semite, she too is complicit. Gassner becomes unblocked, though, and gives a lecture on German poets in German, when the tutor points to their connection with Walt Whitman, particularly his feeling of *Brudermensch*. This breakthrough occurs as the Nazis invade Poland in 1939. The reader is all too aware that "'all men ever born are also my brothers/ and the women my sisters and lovers,/ And that the kelson of creation is love'" is but another window waiting to be smashed. Gassner's wife, he discovers, was shot by the Nazis after she had converted to Judaism and left in an open ditch "with the naked Jewish men, their wives and children, some Polish soldiers, and a handful of gypsies" (212), a tableau that is a ghastly inversion of Whitmanesque brotherhood.

"People say I write so much about misery, but you write about what you know best," said Malamud to an interviewer. He elaborated significantly: "As you are grooved, so you are grieved. . . . the grieving is that no matter how much happiness or success you collect, you cannot obliterate your early experience" (Kakutani 93). Malamud makes a key link between the grocery story and the tomb. His best books—*The Assistant, The Magic Barrel*—relate to this link. Malamud's work is a product of the two Great Depressions, economic and psychological. Janna Malamud Smith, his daughter, sheds light on his psychological makeup in her absorbing memoir, *My Father Is a Book.* As a psychiatric social worker she is particularly sensitive to the sorrows stemming from youth. "I was gypped," said Malamud of his nonexistent youth (6). She says that in Oregon, on good days, he would say, "Some day I'm going to win" (20). Well, he did, through the transformation of suffering. His boyhood friend Ben Loeb notes that in 1939, the time the narrator of "The German Refugee" met his tutor, "He is badly depressed. He once allowed to me that he'd felt enough despair at some moments during these years to at least glance at suicide" (Smith 51). The winter of 1939 into 1940 was "the lowest, loneliest ebb" (Smith 52). And his daughter says that a favorite poem of his was Keats's "When I have fears that I may cease to be." It did not help that his psychotic mother attempted suicide. She died when he was fifteen.

Depression links to his work in another way. His brother was very seriously depressed. Smith tells us that when Malamud left New York for Oregon his father felt abandoned, and brother Eugene, "who after many years of struggle had ventured out into the world and was working, fell apart when Dad moved away" (95). In a wrenching letter of January 7, 1952, Malamud's father writes to him, "He told me that he received writing paper and a Pen from you. But he through [*sic*] everything out the window. . . . Maybe you will find the Pen" (101). As Smith writes, "The Pen carries connotations of Dad's writing, Max's illiteracy, Eugene's inevitable recognition that his older brother had escaped and he had not" (102). She adds, thunderously, "I have always believed that Dad had to leave Brooklyn and his family before he could write freely. What I didn't understand until I read these letters was the price he paid. Neither his father nor his brother really survived his departure" (103).

The Magic Barrel is dedicated to Eugene, and the story "Idiots

First," which, as Robert Solotaroff puts it, involves "a heightened commitment to otherness—for Malamud the glue that holds together the moral world" (69), might also have been dedicated to his brother. Eugene lived twenty years beyond father Max's death, dying at age fifty-five. Despairing, he "sometimes wished to end his life. My father knew this, and it haunted him" (104). Malamud felt a certain guilt about his freedom, felt that in some sense he was not "giving" enough, that a major suffering was due to him. This is one of the reasons—the Jewish ethical tradition is the other—that he writes deeply about Holocaust survivors and the necessity to "give." They are the very image of need. One must give the coat (or suit) off one's back, as Fidelman does to Susskind. Yet giving may be a compulsion amounting to a kind of life-destroying sickness, as it is to the fatally masochistic Rosen of "Take Pity." Gassner of "The German Refugee" could not give his love, his trust, and that too proves fatal. And Freeman of "The Lady of the Lake" is a personification of a respectability so constipated that he will not recognize his own historical vulnerabilities. For Malamud, the Holocaust proves to be an opportunity to redeem the nongiving self. Some take it and some do not. Either possibility comes with difficulties, but Malamud's preference is obvious.

"The German Refugee" is a rarity in Malamud for being a narrative concurrent with contemporary public events. What in Malamud is the exception in Bellow is the rule. Bellow's oeuvre is, by and large, *in history*, tales of private lives synchronous with public events. Bellow writes centrifugally, Malamud centripetally. In *The Bellarosa Connection*, Bellow employs his typical procedure of starting with a real character or two in mind. Unlike Malamud, Bellow generally does not know how his story will end; he is not nearly as dependent on plot. There is a gain in energy that may be offset by a loss in unity. He is involved in a process of discovery—in this case, self-discovery. Malamud is involved in a process of invention. (The categories overlap somewhat in any writer but remain valid.) Bellow's method is expansive, Malamud's selective. In an exchange between them about *The*

Adventures of Augie March, Malamud said that the freedom of the book made him realize how much he himself had "been so entirely conditioned by the constructivist approach" (Salzberg 8). Bellow's response was that his novel "declared against what you call the constructivist approach. A novel, like a letter, should be loose, cover much ground, run swiftly, take the risk of mortality and decay" (9). He might as well have been speaking about his Holocaust novella. That Malamud's short stories are his highest achievement is an indication of how deeply connected to the constructivist approach Malamud is. Malamud once said of Bellow, "I can never write as he does. His books are idea-centered, mine are people centered" (Masilamoni 70), a weak judgment on so prominent a novelist of character. Bellow told an interviewer, "The main reason for rewriting . . . is to discover the inner truth of your characters" (Enck 157). That his narrators may be capable of deep reflection does not diminish their stature as human beings. In *The Bellarosa Connection*, Bellow discovers the inner truth of his surrogate. This truth uncovers his true connection to Jewish history.

The Bellarosa Connection presents the reader with a double narrative, that of Harry Fonstein, who flees Nazi Lemberg (L'vov), and that of the "I" narrator, who wrestles with the meaning of the event. Fonstein's father, a jeweler, did not survive the confiscation of his valuable property in the Vienna of 1938. Most of Fonstein's family were killed by the Germans. He himself is an American success story. After the war, he arrives in the United States from Cuba via Milan, where he did kitchen work, and Turin, where he was a hall porter and shined shoes. He eventually makes good in the heating business in New Jersey—all this despite his being hampered by an orthopedic boot. He lives, he thrives. In his refusal of victimization, in his resurrection as a forceful character, Fonstein reminds us of a crippled Einhorn and Grandma Lausch of *Augie March*, characters notable for their self-overcoming.

Bellow's rendering of event is saturated in history. The narrator contemplates Fonstein's fate:

In Auschwitz he would have been gassed immediately, because of the orthopedic boot. Some Dr. Mengele would have pointed his swagger stick to the left, and Fonstein's boot might by now have been on view in the camps exhibition hall—they have a hill of cripple boots there, and a hill of crutches and of back-braces and of human hair and one of eyeglasses. (4)

The conflation of the particular and the historic is almost breathless in this case for Bellow, a writer not used to backing up his coordinating conjunctions as if he were an incredulous child. The Roman Jews, the narrator reports, "were being trucked to caves outside the city and shot" (9) in the Adreatine Caves, the same mentioned in "The Last Mohican," an allusion not picked up by Fidelman in his ignorance.

Historical particularity consistently animates the prose. The narrator's parental retirement home in Lakewood is "near Lakehurst, where in the thirties the Graf Zeppelin had gone up in flames" (5). In Poland, the "Nazi paratroopers dressed as nuns spilling from planes" (6). Bellow reaches his apogee in the description of Billy Rose, the showbiz entrepreneur who is Fonstein's skittish savior. The narrator can hardly believe it: "Billy Rose? You mean Damon Runyon's pal, the guy who married Fanny Brice?" (9). Yes, Billy was running an Italian underground operation in Rome to free Jews.

The late Billy, the business partner of Prohibition hoodlums, the sidekick of Arnold Rothstein; multimillionaire Billy, the protégé of Bernard Baruch, the young shorthand prodigy whom Woodrow Wilson, mad for shorthand, invited to the White House for a discussion of Pitman and Gregg; Billy the producer, the consort of Eleanor Holm, the mermaid queen of New York's World's Fair; Billy the collector of Matisse, Seurat, and so forth . . . nationally syndicated Billy, the gossip columnist. A Village pal of mine was a member of his ghostwriting team. (12)

Bellow is the master of the portrait that is at the same time an epitome of social history. When the narrator adds, "I assume that Mafia people from Brooklyn had put together Billy's Italian operation. After the war, Sicilian gangsters were decorated by the British for their work in the Resistance," we have the typical Bellovian juxtaposition of respectability and crime. This too is part of social history. We see, then, that where Malamud tends toward fable, Bellow tends toward realism in the nineteenth-century sense; the novelist presents society as its own historian.

Billy Rose is a beautifully rendered character partly because he is given in full ambiguity. He saves Fonstein but does not want to acknowledge him or any saved refugee personally. He wants no emotional scenes, "perhaps fearing" as Janis Bellow, Bellow's last wife, puts it, "that they will lean on him or mouch from him indefinitely" (vii). The narrator seems to make a balanced judgment of him. Sorella, Fonstein's wife, is Billy's nemesis and accuser.

The narrator points out that Billy's benign and successful scheme "was Billy acting alone on a spurt of feeling for his fellow Jews and squaring himself to outwit Hitler and Himmler and cheat them of their victims." He recognizes that "on another day he'd set his heart on a baked potato, a hotdog, a cruise around Manhattan on the Circle Line." He insists, though, that "there were, however, spots of deep feeling in flimsy Billy. The God of his fathers still mattered" (13). Proof of this is that despite his "buglike tropism for publicity . . . his rescue operation in Europe remained secret." So his turning away from Fonstein at Sardi's in New York and, a few years later, at the King David Hotel in Jerusalem is something that he feels needs no defense. Billy tells the pressuring, well-dressed Sorella, "I did what I could. . . . Now what do you want from me—that I didn't receive your husband! What's the matter? I see you did all right. Now you have to have special recognition?" (54). Billy holds firm: "What I did, I did. I have to keep down the number of relationships and contacts" (56). The narrator, who is neutral, tells Sorella, "I can understand that."

Adding to Billy's stature as a giving Jew, it seems, is his desire to donate a sculpture garden designed by Noguchi, consisting of many masterpieces he owns, to the city of Jerusalem. Again, the narrator describes his motives favorably: "His calculation in Jerusalem was to make a major gesture, to enter Jewish history, attaining a level far above show business" (60). He tells Sorella, "You were asking too much. You could not have gotten very far with him" (61).

Billy certainly has his personal weaknesses. He apparently underpays and intimidates his workers. He has a shady and depressing sex life. Yet even here Billy has a disillusioned clairvoyance. When Sorella wants to tell him more about Fonstein's story, he says that he does not care for stories, adding, "I don't care for my own story" (58-59). Luckily, Bellow does. Not admirable but remarkable, Billy's character is probed in the narrator's attempt to calm Sorella. First, the narrator attempts to reduce it to showbiz, but even Sorella rejects this as inadequate. Next comes a deeper explanation: "Maybe the most interesting thing about Billy is that he wouldn't meet with Harry. . . . He wasn't able to be the counterexample in a case like Harry's. Couldn't begin to measure up" (65).

Sorella is a competent, intelligent woman whose practical watchfulness is instrumental in Fonstein's business success. She is also a high school teacher of French who understands the Nazi Ubuist style. She too overcomes obstacles, principally her own weight problem, and, after a lifelong drought, marries the club-footed Fonstein. She is insistent on Billy's personal recognition of Fonstein, but, seeing that he will not do it, gives it up. The moral of the story for her: "The Jews could survive everything that Europe threw at them. I mean the lucky remnant. But now comes the next test—America. Can they hold their ground, or will the U.S.A. be too much for them?" (65). The implication is that Billy's moral failure, as she sees it, derives in part from an American inability to comprehend the deepest suffering. It is this idea that has a lasting impact on the narrator.

So who is right, Billy or Sorella? The narrator is the deciding presence. He is a totally assimilated Jew, complete with Main Line Philadelphia wife named Deirdre, an antebellum house with twenty-foot ceilings, eighteenth-century furniture selected by Deirdre, a closed garden, and an 1817 staircase photographed in *American Heritage*. How goodly are thy tents, O Jacob! Will success spoil Rock Hunter? "I force myself to remember," he says, "that I was not born in a Philadelphia house with twenty-foot ceilings but began life as the child of Russian Jews from New Jersey. A walking memory file like me can't trash his beginnings or distort his early history" (3). Still, he has to force himself. Like Billy, like almost all Americans, he has two identities. And the American identity is not, he says, "inclined to discuss Jewish history," but "damn it," after Nazi Germany "you had to listen" (27-28). Yet the narrator's total assimilation leaves him squeamish from time to time about things Jewish. So he thinks of having the long-lost Fonsteins "for Thanksgiving, for Xmas" rather than Passover because Passover "never comes to pass" (67)—a monumentally false judgment but in character. The conversation about Fonstein's impoverished relative with the rabbi in Jerusalem is described as "a Jewish conversation" (67). And when the rabbi mentions the word *mitzvah* (moral obligation), his silent reaction is "Christ, spare me the mitzvahs" (69). Vaguely optimistic, scientifically oriented contemporary American that he is, he says, "I didn't want to think of the history and psychology of these abominations, death chambers and furnaces. Stars are nuclear furnaces too" (29). He is nonetheless absorbed in Fonstein's case and thinks that the Holocaust refugee "saw me, probably, as an immature unstable Jewish American, humanly ignorant and loosely kind: in the history of civilization something new in the way of human types, perhaps not so bad as it looked at first" (7).

The novella is divided into two parts: the first is full of wonderful character description and dramatic complication that culminates in the Billy/Sorella shootout; the second revolves around the narrator's nightmare. The narrator finds himself in a pit at night. He tries to get out but cannot. His legs are tangled in "ropes or roots," implying the context of part 1. "What made the dream terrible," he tells us, "was my complete conviction of error. . . . I had made a mistake, a lifelong mistake: something wrong, false now fully manifest" (87). His American innocence—"in the New World . . . you could not be put to death, as Jews there had been"—has been deeply shaken by darkest experience. "It wasn't death that scared me, it was disclosure," he thinks. "I wasn't what I thought I was. I really didn't understand merciless brutality" (88). It seems that the price one pays for being this benign entity, an American, is an inability to deal with radical evil. He has apparently read Whitman but not Melville. That the lamp in the room then suggests Abraham, Isaac, and the ram brings him to a moment when Jewish belief was so intense that one would sacrifice everything for it. He relates for the first time to one of a number of "illuminated particles of Jewish history" (89). Having gone definitively from innocence to experience by virtue of his momentous dream, he can conclude, "I had discovered for how long I had shielded myself from unbearable imaginations—no, not imaginations, but recognitions—of murder, of relish in torture, of the ground bass of brutality, without which no human music ever is performed" (90). This may be more than he has actually discovered, since he seems to be confusing Nazi barbarism with the tragic sense of life.

The second part of the story, which includes the pivotal dream, takes place thirty years after the first part. The narrator makes the connection: Sorella's Douglas Fairbanks remarks were "meant for me. . . . There was no way, therefore, in which I could grasp the real facts in the case of Fonstein. I hadn't understood *Fonstein v. Rose*, and I badly wanted to say this to Sorella. You pay a price for being a child of the New World" (89). But it seems to me that the two parts of the story remain somewhat disjunctive. After all, the narrator's modulated judgments of Billy are not wrong in that the first part was about a question of behavior, of style. Billy's heart is, in its idiosyncratic, even distorted, way, in the right place. Not even Sorella wants a change of heart from Billy. He may not have a profound relationship to Jewish history and to Holocaust history in particular—or to anything else—but he does have a relationship. His actions are not mere vanity, but even if they are they have a positive outcome. Billy's lack of personal sympathy does not preclude an *active* cultural sympathy, however spectacular, with his fellow Jews. It is different from the narrator's frozen-over *passivity*, a form of self-denying and meretricious respectability and exclusivity characteristic of the overassimilated Jew. True, Billy might well have shaken hands with Fonstein, spoken to Fonstein, even adored Fonstein, but how much does this have to do with the metaphysics of evil the narrator considers in part 2?

It is possible to consider *The Bellarosa Connection* as an act of self-exorcism, with the narrator an extension of Bellow. "I came late to the Holocaust," he told his son Gregory (another psychiatric social worker) (Talk n.p.), adding that it was only after 1970 that he no longer objected to being called a Jewish writer. In any case, it was the Trotskyite and rather Jewish *Partisan Review*, with its view of World War II as an imperialist standoff, that delayed Bellow from seeing Hitler "for what he was. . . . I was horrified by the positions they—we—had taken" (*Bostonia* 273). But it was not only *Partisan Review*. He says that prior to writing *The Adventures of Augie March*, "things got away from me. The Holocaust for one. I was really very incompletely informed. I may even have been partly sealed off from it because I had certainly met lots of people in Paris who had been through it. I understood what had happened. Somehow I couldn't tear myself away from American life" (*Bostonia* 276). (Could it be, in part at least, because America was key in decimating the Nazi colossus?) He later (in 1991) sees that in writing *Augie March* he

> was still focused on the American portion of my life. Jewish criticism has been harsh on this score. People charged me with being an assimilationist in that book. They say I was still showing how the Jews might make it and that I saved my best colors to paint America. As if I were arguing that what happened in Europe happened because Europe was corrupt and faulty. Thus clearing the U.S.A. of all blame.

The interviewer says, "For a Jew to say that is like saying to be a Jew is to be condemned." Bellow answers: "That's right. That's as much as to say the West has nothing to offer Jews" (*Bostonia* 276).

Of course, Bellow knows that America and the West generally have much to offer—the freedom to write, for example. As for the Holocaust, it was not until Bellow

> went to Auschwitz in 1959 that the Holocaust landed its full weight on me. I never considered it a duty to write about the fate of the Jews. I didn't need to make that my obligation. I felt no obligation except to write—what I was really moved to write. It is nevertheless quite extraordinary that I was so absorbed by my American life that I couldn't turn away from it. I wasn't ready to think about Jewish history. . . . Not until *The Bellarosa Connection.* (*Bostonia* 276-77)

(Bellow is not forgetting *Mr. Sammler's Planet,* which precedes the novella by two decades. Sammler is Bellow's only character to have escaped from a mass grave during the Holocaust, the only one to have killed a Nazi. The novel, though, is mainly about a survivor's view of late 1960s America.)

This work, then, is charged with great personal significance. The gap in Bellow's consciousness accounts for the thirty-year hiatus in the story, the guilt of omission for the narrator's nightmare. It is also the reason the two parts of the story are somewhat discontinuous. Bellow's story reveals a literary love of Billy that works against a simple judgment of him. Bellow is harder on his narrator-surrogate. Truth comes in blows, says Bellow's Henderson, and the blow here takes the form of the nightmare, a welling up from the unconscious, like Fidelman's dream. The commercial specialist in memory neglected to remember one of the profound things. The novelist too, or Bellow in particular, as he has said in a number of places, is a specialist in memory. *The Bellarosa Connection* transcends the commercial and scientific application to present memory (as it is in *Zakhor*) as the essence of Jewish being. This is why the narrator's generally successful Mnemosyne Institute fails in Tel Aviv. The narrator recalls the Jewish Yizkor service, where God is asked to remember a particular soul who is gone. This may give a religious dimension to what happens to the secular narrator of *The Bellarosa Connection*.

With the advent of postmodernism, the reputation of American Jewish writers generally has diminished. Their humanism is seen to be inadequate in the face of the absurdity that is us. Many, not buying into postmodern assumptions, still read them with intensity. Bellow's reputation among this part of the reading audience remains high among novelists and critics and the broad reading public. There has been some recent discussion, however, as to why Malamud has "faded." Perhaps this essay can shed some light. Three of the four Malamud stories here are among his best. The Bellow selection is very fine Bellow. Malamud's characters are so intense that they transcend the charges of narrowness or parochialism brought against them. Their alienation is more real than the conformity that was a salient part of the 1950s, in which they were written. Yet the tone of depression and loss misses something. Malamud is writing about failure in a time when America is moving toward "success." (Of course, success brings failures of its own, and failure may be a form of redemption.) Bellow's great virtue as a writer lies in his ability to construct fictions to view this new fat America, while Malamud remains devoted to pursuing his skinny Susskinds as avidly as Fidelman does. It is as if Malamud missed the boat, missed the great American Jewish turn to affluence for better or worse that Bellow's vibrant prose records so brilliantly. Too often Malamud sings in the *veynedich* (tearful) cantorial style. It is moving but somewhat outdated. Bellow moves on to the wider energetics of contemporary American harmonics, thriving in the dialectical air between assonance and dissonance, writing with what Janis Bellow calls "Stendhalian brio . . . lightness of touch" (x). The *Bellarosa Connection* is a case in point. She informs us that "Saul was writing this powerful, even horrible book with intense heat and joy, dipping into his brightest colors" (x). For Malamud the Holocaust evokes the tearful past. Bellow brings the Holocaust into the pleasure-and-money-ridden present.

Works Cited

Bellow, Gregory. Informal talk on Saul Bellow, American Literature Association Conference on Jewish American and Holocaust Literature. Salt Lake City, Utah, Sept. 2008.

Bellow, Janis. Preface. *Collected Stories*. By Saul Bellow. New York: Viking Press, 2001. v-xii.

Bellow, Saul. *The Bellarosa Connection*. Harmondsworth: Penguin, 1989.

Bostonia. "A Half Life: An Autobiography in Ideas." *Conversations with Saul Bellow*. Ed. Gloria L. Cronin and Ben Siegel. Jackson: UP of Mississippi, 1994. 258-77.

Enck, John J. "Saul Bellow: An Interview." *Contemporary Literature* 6.2 (1965): 156-60.

Kakutani, Michiko. "Malamud Still Seeks Balance and Solitude." *Conversations with Bernard Malamud*. Ed. Lawrence Lasher. Jackson: UP of Mississippi, 1991. 92-95.

Malamud, Bernard. *Idiots First*. New York: Farrar, Straus, 1963.

_____. *The Magic Barrel*. New York: Farrar, Straus and Cudahy, 1958.

_____. *Talking Horse*. Ed. Alan Cheuse and Nicholas Delbanco. New York: Columbia UP, 1996.

Masilamoni, E. H. Leelavathi. "Bernard Malamud: An Interview." *Conversations with Bernard Malamud*. Ed. Lawrence Lasher. Jackson: UP of Mississippi, 1991. 69-73.

Salzberg, Joel. "Malamud on Bellow, Bellow on Malamud: A Correspondence and Friendship." *Saul Bellow Journal* 14.2 (1996): 3-16.

Smith, Janna Malamud. *My Father Is a Book*. Boston: Houghton Mifflin, 2006.

Solotaroff, Robert. *Bernard Malamud: A Study of the Short Fiction*. Boston: Twayne, 1989.

Stern, David. "The Art of Fiction: Bernard Malamud." *Conversations with Bernard Malamud*. Ed. Lawrence Lasher. Jackson: UP of Mississippi, 1991. 54-68.

Yerushalmi, Yosef Hayim. *Zakhor: Jewish History and Jewish Memory*. Seattle: U of Washington P, 1982.

Saul Bellow:
The Critical Reception _____

Gloria L. Cronin

Saul Bellow dominated American literature from the late 1950s to the early 1980s. He came of age in the wake of the legendary Ernest Hemingway, whose existential despair and celebrations of hard-boiled masculinity the small, nonathletic Jewish intellectual urbanite scorned. Instead of celebrations of warrior masculinity, bullfights, wars, big-game hunting, and deep-sea fishing, Bellow wrote of twentieth-century Chicago, its colorful street life, teeming immigrant populations, and newly minted American voices as carefully as Charles Dickens and James Joyce had mapped London and Dublin. And then he wrote about the entire gamut of twentieth-century philosophical and social ideas. But more of that later.

Bellow grew up in Montreal and Chicago hearing his parents' stories of Russian pogroms, revolutions, anti-Semitism, World War I, the great influenza epidemic of 1918-19, and the Great Depression. Not surprisingly, Bellow entered his high school and college years as a devoted utopian socialist. In the 1940s, when he was about to be recruited into the Navy and the atrocities of the Holocaust were just becoming known, Bellow's greatest fear was that Civilization, which almost split apart several times during the twentieth century, might finally be rendered too fragile to endure. Accordingly, Bellow wrote in defense of the reality of the human soul, spiritual ways of knowing, and Western humanism. More specifically, his writing was a lifelong sustained attack against philosophical nihilism, rationalism, skepticism, capitalism, and European modernist philosophical angst.

From his very earliest 1940s novels on, Bellow was received as the writer most likely to fill the space previously occupied by the legendary Hemingway. Unfortunately for Bellow, not even with the Nobel Prize in hand would he or any other writer after Hemingway ever command such celebrity status, or such a legendary persona, far less attract such a broad readership. That era was over. Nevertheless, his first two books, *Dangling Man* (1944) and *The Victim* (1947), impressed the critics as tightly wrought fictions written to a polished Flaubertian standard and influenced by his early reading of Dostoevsky, Tolstoy, Diderot, the French existentialists, and biblical notions of social contract. They also noted imagery suggestive of the fiery afterburn of the Holocaust and a compelling account of the pervasive ennui of the young generation of Americans entering the postwar era. Some noted Bellow's nostalgic yearning for the age of Emersonian Transcendentalism, his austere assessments of post-World War II inquiry into human freedom, and how unlikely it was that anyone could escape history, anti-Semitism, and manufactured ideas.

Most agreed, however, that Bellow had captured the dilemma of Joseph and Asa Levanthal's generation, dangling as they were between 1930s idealism and 1940s pragmatism, post-World War II and an undisclosed future, the anti-Semitic WASP (white Anglo-Saxon Protestant) world that was America, the Jewish future in the new promised land. They also saw that Bellow had thrown down the gauntlet to Hemingway, and that perhaps the future of the American novel would be Robert Cohn's, not Jake Barnes's. Though many disliked *Dangling Man*'s journal form and complained about the lack of plot in both books, Bellow was marked for success. He was among that cadre of American-born descendants of Jewish immigrants to enter the WASP literary mainstream of American literature during the 1940s and 1950s, now called by literary historians the Jewish decades. However, Bellow vigorously refused to be categorized as a "Jewish-American" writer, especially since he was already disaffiliated from the painful Jewish family history of his childhood. His ambition was to be a world-class writer, not an American hyphenated subcategory. Not until the final decade of his life would he accept the designation Jewish American with pride, and by then he had spent many decades recuperating his Jewish religious heritage, albeit on his own terms.

The Adventures of Augie March (1953) completely broke from the philosophical darkness and tight European formulas of *Dangling Man* and *The Victim*. It was begun in the *grisaille* of 1949 postwar Paris, while Bellow was suffering a deep depression. Breaking free from it all, Bellow threw his current manuscript, "The Crab and the Butterfly," down a Paris rooming house garbage chute. Freed from its hold over him, he then embraced his American heritage and voice to produce the picaresque romp through the Chicago of his childhood that *The Adventures of Augie March* represents. He described the experience of writing the book as joyous and freeing. Critics greeted it as his breakthrough novel, quickly identified its picaresque form, European antecedent forms, debt to Goethe, reliance on the Sentimental Novel, and salute to *The Adventures of Huckleberry Finn*. They commented on its powerful reclaiming of American optimism, its insistence that a man's character is his fate, and its complete reinvention of American literary language and voice. Literary historians now see it as the first significant Anglo-American literary break with the mesmerizing power of the high mannerism of the modernist novel. Later Bellow confessed to his anxiety about confronting a WASP worldview, abandoning his former Flaubertian standard, and making a case for the Russian American immigrant experience and its language habits as a literary subject.

Meantime, critics pointed out its Cervantesque chivalric allusions, mock-heroic comparisons of ancient and modern-day heroes, wacky humor, personal family history, classical lore, Dreiserian naturalism, Whitmanesque catalogs, Dickensian caricature, and Hogarthian character portraits, and its rich vernacular language of street, bar, and poolroom juxtaposed with eccentric inset philosophical essays. It was packed with Bellovian homily and Yiddish wit. Most concurred that Bellow had found the middle ground between romantic idealism and existentialist nihilism. They quickly identified the novel's Heraclitan belief that fate is to be determined by character, not by biology or environment, and its flat denial of modern historicism—the idea that twentieth-century men and women were living at the diminishing end of times. As a sort of carnival in the Bahktinian sense, *The Adventures of Augie March* represents a fantastic journey, a lively tale of the road through 1920s-1950s big-city America. It offers a sophisticated treatment of that potent American nexus of ethnicity, power, money, love, urban milieu, young manhood, and an uncertain future.

More recently critics and readers on both sides of the Atlantic have also recognized the groundbreaking accomplishment of its uniquely racy Yiddish-inflected street language—that simultaneously erudite and humorous compound of Bellow's polyglot linguistic heritage of Hebrew, Yiddish, French, Russian, and the American urban language newly emerging among Chicago's North Side immigrant populations. Only very recently have critics seen beneath the optimism of the book and pointed out that come the end of the novel Augie has not clearly embraced a future, that the afterglow of the gas ovens flickers just beneath its surface, and that Augie is only too aware he is literally driving over the war dead of Europe. Critics then and now agree that *The Adventures of Augie March* is not quite a great novel.

Embarrassed by the sheer exuberance and stylistic excesses of *The Adventures of Augie March*, Bellow vowed to return to more tightly restrained forms. Hence *Seize the Day* (1956), with its tight form and philosophical seriousness, seems to have more in common with *Dangling Man* and *The Victim* than with *The Adventures of Augie March*. Critics have wondered if it actually belongs to the earlier period of Bellow's fiction, and Bellow himself refused to quite remember whether this was so or not. The novel was initially seen as an exploration of the "divided self" of Laingian and Jungian psychology, a reprise of the playwright Arthur Miller's themes, a Freudian critique of the fathers and sons of the immigrant generation, Bellow's updating of the Dostoevskian antihero, a treatment of Freudian narcissism and infantile regression, a critique of Wilhelm Reich's character-armoring theories, and an exploration of Wordsworthian notions of immortality. Critics were quick to note Bellow's introduction of the stock comic figure the Yiddish schlemiel to American belle lettres and saw the book as a remarkable image of midcentury America replete with an updated Eliotic wasteland set in a geriatric boardinghouse in New York. It was also received as a book on the dialectics of consciousness and, more recently, a work deeply woven of dense patterns of Jewish religious allusion to Yom Kippur, or the Jewish Day of Atonement. Gender critics also wondered if it was Bellow's diagnosis of fractured American male identity appearing in the vacuum left by the hypermasculine Hemingway hero. Most, however, recognized its treatment of suffering, humanist triumph, and redemption—the price of reclaiming the human soul. Because it is the most anthologized of Bellow's novels, it is also the work most readers are familiar with.

The period of Bellow's great middle novels began with the appearance of *Henderson the Rain King* (1959). Eugene Henderson, one of Bellow's few WASP protagonists, is a burlesque of the absurd, violent, artist-hero of the James Joyce Stephen Dedalus variety. Violinist and pig farmer, he is a menopausal social outcast, a quintessential gentile, and a parody of the hypermasculine Hemingway stoic or narcissist. Henderson is metaphysically earnest, introspective, solipsistic, bumbling, violent, egocentric, and naive. He believes with the mythic fisher kings that there is a curse on the land and that he must restore fertility to himself and those around him. He is Bellow's answer to a generation of modern writers who reacted with exaggerated disappointment to the failed promises of Rousseauistic romanticism. With his initials E. H., his drinking, his .357 magnum rifle, his private firing range, his fascination with African safaris, and his participation in a foreign war, he is Bellow's response to the literary giant, Hemingway, whose reputation and literary formulas continued to dominate the literary world. After alienating his wife, children, and friends, and after shouting his housekeeper to death, Henderson knows he is cursed. His solution is to flee to Africa on a spiritual pilgrimage to remove the curse. It is a fantastic mental journey to the heart of contemporary American spiritual darkness, and its realistic furnishings are reminiscent of the long colonial tradition of African travel literature as it calls up the myth of a savage and childlike primeval Africa uncontaminated by modernity.

Critics have identified the novel as Bellow demythologizing his protagonist's nineteenth-century Transcendental inheritance, romantic disappointment in the contemporary moment, and personal preoccupation with death. Through Henderson's mystical impasses, many point out, we can read Bellow's comment on the utter failure of nihilism and existentialism to teach us anything humanizing about the meaning of death. Hemingwayesque stoicism also seems to have failed in this book, since it does not produce for Henderson any worthwhile social ethics. Through hilarious therapeutic romping sessions with Atti, the lioness, Bellow provides his ultimate comment on the castrating effects of the modernist preoccupation with death as he lopes around the arena, his genitals shriveled in fright, with Atti sniffing his behind.

Critics have also noted in *Henderson the Rain King* Bellow's comic use of *shtetl* humor, intertextual engagement with Joseph Conrad's *Heart of Darkness*, Blakean spiritual quest, an inner fantastic safari, vanquishing of anthropological romanticism, and staging of a crazy modern-day grail quest. His parodic use of Joseph Campbell's archetypal hero journey fascinated structuralist critics, while those familiar with the violent therapeutic methods of Wilhelm Reich were quick to note the hilarious existentialist and Reichian roaring and howling that went with it. Many intertextual parallels were found between *Henderson the Rain King* and Cooper, Cervantes, Whitman, Emerson, Sartre, Melville, Conrad, Eliot, Hemingway, the Bible, cultural anthropology, Jesse L. Weston's *From Ritual to Romance*, Lawrence, Freud, and even Graham Greene. Most recently, post-1980s critics revisited the novel and accused Bellow of racism for his comic, demeaning, or demonizing depictions of Africans. However, most concurred that this novel was Bellow's first mature masterwork, and his most radical break thus far with literary modernism. Many consider it his finest comic writing.

Herzog (1964), thought to be Bellow's great masterwork, was immediately hailed as a modern European confessional novel, the great urban fiction of the day, a devastating critique of university intellectuals, a portrait of contemporary moral decay, a study of the intellectual Jew embattled in Western history, and a massive critique of Anglo-American modernist philosophy. Critical attention has focused on its reinvention of the eighteenth-century epistolary novel and the actual structure of the letters. Critics have noted Bellow's return to mystical religious values, and some have also likened Herzog to those earlier hapless lovers, Prufrock and Bloom. Quite recently, some have treated Herzog as an updated version of the nineteenth- and twentieth-century flaneur or urban street wanderer, and as a contemporary Job.

However, most critical attention still focuses on *Herzog*'s massive rejection of modern philosophical thinkers and social theorists, most of whom are named one by one in Herzog's impassioned, comic, and even snide letters addressed directly to them. Critics have noted Bellow's use of the alienated, marginalized Jew as representative of modern man, his depiction of the modernist historical neurosis, deep investment in biblical references, and use of Oriental patterns of meditative thought. Others have commented on how in this novel Bellow denies forever the possibility of that grand romantic synthesis of knowledge beloved of structuralism and reclaims a biblical God back into the spiritual void created by nihilistic existentialism. When the novel appeared, most critics were impressed with its stylistic virtuosity, the sheer authority of its vision, and its brazen intellectualism. Some few, however, called the book unwieldy, unreadable, overly intellectual, and even turgid. Given the grandeur of its reach, *Herzog* was clearly Bellow's answer to James Joyce's *Ulysses*.

Not surprisingly, *Mr. Sammler's Planet* (1970) came as something of a literary letdown to critics and readers alike. Many critics rejected it as a gloomy, misogynistic work and complained of Bellow's deepening political conservatism and his repudiation of an entire generation of post-1960s youth. They noted his refusal to concede the point of the women's movement or the civil rights movement, or the betrayal of a generation of young Americans over the atrocities of the Vietnam War. Now the book is designated as a somewhat secondary work compared to *Henderson the Rain King, Herzog*, and, in retrospect, *Humboldt's Gift* (1975). A new generation of critics attuned to racial stereotyping noted with increasing anger Bellow's depiction of the superstud black pickpocket who frightens the fixated, voyeuristic old Holocaust survivor, Sammler, by drawing him into a doorway and exposing himself to him. Others saw the book as Bellow's new historicist analysis of European Jewish male misogyny and sexual neuroses, and possibly as Bellow's veiled self-portrait and mea culpa. Regardless, it was Bellow's rejection of the 1960s generation, and younger readers did not appreciate it. Bellow had waited longer than he felt he should in writing a Holocaust novel and was disappointed that the responses to it were so very mixed. By this time he had developed a profound distrust, if not lively hatred, of the whole critical establishment.

   Humboldt's Gift pays homage to Bellow's departed friends and fellow writers Delmore Schwartz and Isaac Rosenfeld. Here Bellow remembers his dead and details the devastation America wreaks upon its artists. He asks whether the artist still has the strength to imagine God or the transcendent after immersion in contemporary America. However, what has enduringly fascinated critics about this book is Bellow's rehearsal and critique of the anthroposophical ideas of quack philosophers Rudolf Steiner and Owen Barfield. In contrast to their responses to *Mr. Sammler's Planet*, critics found *Humboldt's Gift* to be comic, ebullient, inventive, and optimistic. It seemed a serious treatment of the last thirty years of catastrophic and paradigm shifting in American cultural history, and many treated it as one more attempt by Bellow to purge American life of the banalities of modernism and revisit the Emersonian Transcendentalism of his youth. In other words, it was yet another attempt to reconcile the mystical with the rough ground of American experience. By now some critics had clearly lost interest in Bellow and saw *Humboldt's Gift* as the sign of Bellow's decline. Some decried what they saw as a digressive style, and others saw it as evidence of Bellow's careful anatomy of several Western and Eastern meditative strains of thought and practice. Nevertheless, it remains one of his great middle-period novels.

To Jerusalem and Back: A Personal Account (1976) was written in 1975, the year in which Bellow accompanied his then wife to Israel. During this three-month visit he interviewed numerous political and military leaders for his journalistic assignments; hence the book is a collection of interview material, journalistic anecdotes, reported conversations, fictional material, travelogue, bits of essays, snippets of public addresses, and firsthand reporting on the Six-Day War. It was Bellow's attempt to take the measure of the Israeli experiment. The critical response was instantaneous rejection. Critics complained he had not interviewed enough people in the arts, that his political history was sketchy at best, that he misunderstood Zionism, Israel, Islam, and world politics. They complained that the book was shallow, negative, and lacking in any coherent plan or vision, and that Bellow, like most Westerners, could not come to any sense of wakefulness about Israel. It was in the midst of this critical firestorm that Bellow went to Stockholm to receive his Nobel Prize in Literature, the final acknowledgment that he had indeed secured an international audience. This book is rarely visited now.

The Dean's December (1982), which followed, was received by readers and critics as a somewhat wintry piece lacking any balancing comedy. Critics noted that it was a Dickensian tale of two cities, a somber prophetic work that details the morally rotten life of contemporary Budapest and contemporary Chicago both, with their police states and doomed inner-city populations. Some described the book as a clanky kind of mechanism, a top-heavy work without much delight. Others read it as an exquisite work done in a minor key. However, most critical ink was spent on Bellow's depiction of Chicago's and Budapest's urban wastelands, false experience, failed language, media noise, crime rackets, cultures of murder, prison populations, and inner-city degradation. After all, its central metaphor is the lead poisoning of the planet.

Perhaps it was Bellow's last-ditch effort to discover once and for all whether creatures made of variously evolved materials might still apprehend higher orders of existence. Most noted how roundly *The Dean's December* condemns the media, city planners, academicians, scientific minds, and prison culture. Some were shocked that Bellow's picture of the degradation of both cities is cast in the racial metaphor of the regressively savage primeval African jungle. This has been an increasing matter of concern to critics focused on postcolonial and race studies. Yet others saw it as Bellow's statement on the breakdown of language and its final failure to convey either the transcendent or human feeling. However, as a retrospective meditation, some noted, it does provide two of Bellow's most balanced and admirable characters, Dean Corde and Valeria Raresh, both of whom are confronted with broken history and broken critics. On balance however, critics noted the book seemed tired, lacking in the usual linguistic high jinks and intellectual fireworks of the earlier novels, a generally lackluster transitional novel in which Bellow conducts a dialogue between East and West, democracy and totalitarianism, life and death, loss and discovery, male and female. Too few noted that it does contain Bellow's most moral and complex female character—Valeria Raresh. *The Dean's December* is really a distillation of all Bellow's themes, strengths, and weaknesses, replete with strong evidence of his mastery of tonal shifts, variations in sentence structure, clarity of perception, and mastery of eccentric verbal styles. The less enthusiastic described it unkindly as a bleak, lumpy carryall, indicating perhaps that Bellow had lost interest in making fiction. However, its use of a dread-filled Africanity as a metaphor for the collapse of Western Culture remains troubling to many.

It is clear that critical attention had shifted away from Bellow come the mid-1980s, and that his literary reputation had significantly waned. Bellow and his critics had truly lost patience with each other. *More Die of Heartbreak* (1987), though it recaptures much of the old Bellovian comic energy, is generally thought to fall short of the intellectual scope of *Herzog* and *Humboldt's Gift*. It illuminates the tragicomic manner in which modern heterosexual relationships have failed and functions as a Prufrockian lament about failed men, missing mermaids, misogynous nutty love-lore, and botched loves. Without precedent in the Bellow canon, it is based on the old Gogolian farce of the flight of the bridegroom and features two entirely endearing wacky characters: the misogynous Kenneth Trachtenberg and his beloved uncle, Benn Crader. After numerous failed attempts at love by these two bumblers, the book comically offers only celibacy and bachelorhood as solutions. Critics received this as a witty commentary on Eros, the influence of Balzac on American letters, a critique on materialism, and an experiment in farce. Critics also commented on the novel's wit and the energetic buzz of its language, the droll Dickensian characters, and the crackling intelligence. They saw its meditative depth and mercilessly comic examination of the tradition of romantic love. Even though some minor characters fail to come fully alive, they are mostly successful comic delineations. As an anatomy of romantic love in the postmodern age, *More Die of Heartbreak* is brilliant, entertaining, and full of long flights of ideas and comic scenes that redeem it from many other faults.

A Theft (1989) is Bellow's first attempt at reviving the short form of the novella. It stages another Bellovian romp on the comic dynamics of the heterosexual pair. Critics applauded its depiction of the fatal allure of the male intellect for the female lover, the classic evasions of the male lover, the Hawthornian theft of the human heart, the social chaos of "gogmagogsville," the seeming impossibility of higher synthesis, the failure of psychiatry, the agony of contemporary boredom, power politics, the chaotic proliferation of ethnic others, and the increasing absence of "civilized" city spaces. It too received disapprobation from race critics. Even though Bellow declared his fondness for his first female protagonist, Clara Velde, gender critics thought Clara to be stereotypical, fogged over, and generally unimpressive. Some complained that the book lacked mythic power and metaphorical oomph, and that it had insufficient Bellovian wit and comedy. Others praised the book for its faith in heterosexual romance and for its distinctive language, neatness, and control. However, the majority complained of its lack of any genuine large-scale significance, failing to note that Bellow's experiment in novella form precluded any such large-scale novelistic treatments. It was Bellow in cameo.

The Bellarosa Connection (1989), another experiment in the novella form, features an unnamed narrator who is a memory freak, an elderly person trying desperately through memory to reclaim his lost relationship with the remarkable Sorella Fonstein. He has left it far too late, however. She and her Holocaust survivor husband are now dead, and the narrator must face his own identity as an assimilated American Jew who has not valued them soon enough. Critics weighed in anxiously about the work's treatment of the Holocaust in comic mode. It appeared to be a philosophical fable on issues of memory, the Holocaust, human valuing, and Jewish identity. Some noted its elegant shaping and narrative strength, while others complained it was somewhat artificial, too little engaged with the telling, and overly schematic. Some took umbrage at the ethical issue of Bellow's rewriting the historical Billy Rose inside an obviously unflattering fictional narrative. Jewish critics took to heart Bellow's commentary on the moral fate of Jews assimilated into the American experience. Some critics praised Sorella as a marvelous female invention, while others wondered about Bellow's caricaturist's delight in her fatness, failing to understand its finer religious resonances within Jewish cultural history. Altogether most agreed it was a lean and resonant book and a remarkable summary on the subject of memory and the Holocaust. Both of these novellas made publishing history, having been first published as paperbacks.

The Actual (1997) appeared first in hardcover, unlike *The Bellarosa Connection* and *A Theft*. It is the familiar Bellow story of an old adolescent love that is finally admitted to and resumed. The worldly and clever Harry Trellman, a grand noticer of things and ambassador of the arts, is invited to "notice" on behalf of another grand old noticer, Sigmund Adletsky, who soon discerns the nature of Harry's great unrequited adolescent love, Amy Wustrin, and finally brings the two back together. Critics noted its familiar Bellovian theme—the human failure to recognize one's Platonic "actual," or the other half of one's own soul. As a love story about two elderly people, *The Actual*, critics noted, is told with all the familiar descriptive realism of other Bellow works and invokes Bellow's fond belief in the embodied nature of the soul. Reviews were mixed, and in truth a new Bellow publication was no longer the hot item it had once been. Critics complained that Harry Trellman actually notices a whole lot less than Sigmund Adletsky and that this book, despite its upbeat ending, proves to be thin gruel, with its featureless characters and tin-ear dialogue. Others suggested that were it not for Bellow's stature, he might not have gotten away with this piece. Some critics noted a few flashes of vintage Bellow here, but thought the author had lost his sure touch. Worse, some critics thought many passages seemed like bad pastiches of abstracts from other books, particularly *Humboldt's Gift*, and that only a brief description or two of Chicago had the old Bellow power. Most concluded that age had taken its toll on Saul Bellow's genius. A few admirers still held that the book displayed just as much soul as Bellow's earlier work, that Bellow had reached the "prophet stage" typical of old American Jewish radicals, that the book was written in fine scale, and that it qualified Bellow for a place among the great existential writers, such as Dostoevsky and Sartre, Dreiser and Melville. *The Actual* is more a Jamesian work of sensibility, a distillation and an elegy. Though muted in energy, it contains many sparkling sentences, remarkable passages of physical description of aged people, women's bodies, and the Chicago landscape.

Ravelstein (2000), Bellow's last published work, excited far more critical interest than the previous three books. As a career endgame it is an ethnographic fiction about the lives of the children of the Russian Jews, as well as Bellow's ostensible tribute to his great friend, the late

Allan Bloom of the University of Chicago. It is also a paean to the miracle of Jewish survival, a celebration of male friendship, and a prayer for the dead. Critics variously called it death-haunted, masterful, short on plot, an overvaluation of Bloom's ideas, a meditation on Eros, and evanescent with the beauty and mystery of human existence. Some were aghast that Bellow had outed his homosexual friend, to which Bellow responded that he thought everyone knew, and reluctantly removed a few passages.

Some saw Ravelstein as a huge ugly imago of tragicomic proportions, a Jewish Falstaff exaggerated to comic proportions out of love, and noted with pleasure that the novel is streetwise, lyrical, and full of verbal escapades, brotherly love, revelations, and explorations. Others, however, saw it as cantankerous, disloyal, homophobic, cobbled together with poor transitions, and a clear sign of authorial tiredness. Then there were those who insisted it was powerful, familiar, fresh, cerebral, young in spirit, and full of new light on the human spirit. A great sense of loss permeates the pages of this Bellovian end-of-times sermon. It is an old man's book written in gold-standard prose, and many of the contradictory critical responses owe much to the fact that an older generation of critics familiar with Bellow's work weighed in alongside a younger generation with fewer tolerances and a well-developed taste for a very different kind of fiction.

The occasion of Bellow's death on April 5, 2005, was preempted in the media by the deaths of Terri Schiavo (March 31) and Pope John Paul II (April 2). However, during 2005 more than four hundred critical eulogies of Bellow appeared in print. Taken together they provide an interim summing up of Bellow's literary achievement. The word "great" appeared frequently in these pages, and most agreed that Bellow's status in the post-World War II period of American literature is comparable only to that of Mark Twain, Henry James, Ernest Hemingway, Eugene O'Neill, Robert Penn Warren, or William Faulkner. An impressive cast of international literary scholars, writers, and reviewers variously described Bellow as the greatest chronicler since Walt

Whitman, a wise soul, and a spiritual genius. All agreed that his greatest contributions were his spiritual and ethical contributions to his age, his linguistic innovations in the history of the Anglo-American novel genre, and his status as a major twentieth-century writer alongside other such architects of twentieth-century American literature as Faulkner, Warren, and Hemingway. The large representation of British, Australian, Israeli, Italian, French, German, Japanese, Korean, Chinese, and Eastern European critics who wrote suggest his growing international readership and literary reputation. Most acknowledged Bellow's brilliant moral mapping of the exigencies of the twentieth-century soul, his blend of high and low styles, and his wisecracks, mandarin moments, and monologistic style. They noted that though Bellow was not a conventionally religious individual, he was a satirist in search of God whose particular combination of intellectuality and vitality was category-shattering. For many of the contemporary writers Bellow's principal legacy was his polyglot linguistic heritage, which allowed him to reinvent prose literature in the twentieth-century Anglo-American tradition.

By way of eulogy, American critic and scholar James Wood opened up a whole new critical conversation by providing the most extensive accounting of Bellow's lifelong study of the Hebrew Bible and the Christian New Testament. In his article "The Jewish King James Version: Saul Bellow—Not Exactly English But Biblically English," he identifies literally hundreds of biblical references throughout the works, causing him to describe Bellow's prose certainly as Dickensian, Tolstoyan, Lawrentian, Conradian, but ultimately "biblically English." He points out its run-on sentences, loose melodic compounds, repetitions, semantic parallelisms, obtrusive overflowing lyricism, vaguely antique ring, and amassing of adjectives, overflowing quality all faithfully carried over from Hebrew into the King James version and down into Bellow's Yiddish-inflected American works. He says that forever after he has "measured all prose by Saul Bellow's high and low registers, Melvillean cadences, jivey Yiddish rhythms spoken by his crooks, frauds, and intellectuals, Dickensian amplitude full of music and high lyricism lacking in the contemporary English novel" (12).

However, the most colorful eulogist of Bellow's linguistic legacy, David Kipen, enthusiastically called Bellow's heroes "word-sozzled, life-hungry . . . semiautobiographical antiheroes" who "chiseled and loved," "humped and swore," all "in a vernacular that owed a leg-breaking debt to Yiddish, and borrowed from Greek and Latin to pay it back" (A1). He further noted that despite the fact that in the past twenty years Bellow had "slowly fallen off the radar" on the U.S. side of the Atlantic, he was widely influential in the previous three decades because of this trademark prose style of weblike, wild, elaborately looping sentences that baffled readers and impressed critics with their "high mix of erudition" and "jazzy colloquialism" (A1). However, a more moderate note was struck by American scholar Jay Parini, who acknowledged that while for two decades or so Bellow had been a guiding light to younger British novelists such as Ian McEwan and Martin Amis, that for him Bellow had become a representative figure who sadly lived past his 1976 moment of fame. Parini notwithstanding, it was leading American novelist Philip Roth who wrote most authoritatively that Bellow now belongs to the unofficial international and national halls of fame in American literature, currently presided over by the great nineteenth-century British and European writers, as well as Melville, Twain, and Faulkner. Roth insisted that the backbone of twentieth-century American literature was provided by two novelists: William Faulkner and Saul Bellow.

The broad international response to Bellow's death is not a particularly surprising phenomenon. Since the late 1980s, Bellow's readership has been growing steadily on the international scene, aided by the aggressive production of translations undertaken by Bellow's publishers. Bellow began his writing career selling book reviews for ten dollars each. He ended it as a literary great and internationally acclaimed Nobel laureate.

Works Cited

Kipen, David. "Saul Bellow: 1915-2005; Nobel-Winning Novelist Shook Up Literary World." *San Fransicso Chronicle* 6 Apr. 2005: A1.

Parini, Jay. "'When I Sit at the Typewriter, I Open My Heart': Saul Bellow: 1915-2005." *Chronicle of Higher Education* 22 Apr. 2005: B5.

Roth, Philip. "Author Saul Bellow Dies." Associated Press. 5 May 2005. Web. 25 May 2010.

Wood, James. "The Jewish King James Version: Saul Bellow—Not Exactly English But Biblically English." *Times Literary Supplement* 5 Aug. 2005: 12-13.

CRITICAL
READINGS

Exhausting Ennui:
Bellow, Dostoevsky, and the Literature of Boredom _____

Jean-François Leroux

> Now since boredom . . . is the root of all evil, what can be more natural than the effort to overcome it? . . . My method does not consist in a change of field, but resembles the true rotation method in changing the crop and the mode of cultivation. Here we have at once the principle of limitation, the only saving principle in the world. The more you limit yourself, the more fertile you become in invention. A prisoner in solitary confinement for life becomes very inventive, and a spider may furnish him with much entertainment.
>
> —Søren Kierkegaard, *Either/Or*, 1843

Sifting through his "notes" for an unfinished "essay on boredom," the "slothful" narrator-protagonist of Saul Bellow's *Humboldt's Gift* (1975), Charlie "Melancholy" Citrine, stakes his claim to originality as follows: "I saw that I had stayed away from problems of definition. . . . I didn't want to get mixed up with theological questions about *accidia* and *tedium vitae*. I found it necessary to say only that from the beginning mankind experienced states of boredom but that no one had ever approached the matter front and center as a subject in its own right" (1996b, 308, 311, 199). The statement is striking, if not downright paradoxical, flying in the face as it does of a long and considerable literary history. Indeed, though he points here disparagingly to the tradition of medieval scholasticism and goes on to single out "Modern French literature" (to wit, Stendhal, Flaubert, Baudelaire) as "especially preoccupied with the theme of boredom" (200), Citrine fails to acknowledge boredom's considerable literary-intellectual pedigree in the intervening period. Given the importance of much of the literature and culture so elided to Bellow's repeated efforts to awaken humankind to its slumbering powers not only in *Humboldt's Gift* but in his other novels as well, that omission invites a reconsideration of boredom as a central subject in his own work and of the relationship of that work to the actually vast literature of ennui. Abridged but no less tacit in Citrine's "boredom notes" and in much of Bellow's later fiction, this relationship is writ large in his first novel, *Dangling Man* (1944). For this reason, the novel in question repays closer scrutiny.

Though the parallels between various "classics" of Existentialism and Bellow's *Dangling Man* and subsequent novels have been widely discussed, the debate provoked by such analyses and their findings has tended only to confirm Walter Kaufmann's conclusion regarding the so-called Existentialists themselves, namely that "one essential feature shared by all these men is their perfervid individualism" (1956, 11).[1] There is, however, something else which these latter share besides "the refusal to belong to any school of thought, the repudiation of the adequacy of any body of beliefs whatever . . . especially of systems, and a marked dissatisfaction with traditional philosophy as superficial, academic, and remote from life" (Kaufmann 1956, 12)—and that is the intellectual genealogy of boredom. Unlike Citrine's "boredom notes" (Bellow 1996b, 199), Sartre's *Nausée* (1938), with which *Dangling Man* has often been juxtaposed,[2] contained a nod to that genealogy in its original title *Melancholia*, after Dürer's rendering of the ambiguous Renaissance disease/pleasure. And more overtly, in his study of Baudelaire, Sartre acknowledges the emotional-intellectual kinship between Existential "nausée" and Romantic "ennui" (1947, 36). The (proto)Existentialist author who seems most aware of and is most explicit about boredom's complex genealogy, however, is the author with whom Bellow is most often compared.[3] By way of justifying his "violent spleen," the Underground Man of Dostoevsky's *Notes from Underground* asserts that "excessive consciousness is a disease" and that its "direct, inevitable product is inertia" and "boredom" (1981, 2, 5, 18). He explains:

> naturally, to enter upon any course of action, one must be completely reassured in advance, and free of any trace of doubt. And how am I, for in-

stance, to put my mind at ease? Where are the primary causes I can lean on, where are my basic premises? Where am I to find them? I exercise myself in thought, and hence, within my mind, every primary cause immediately drags after itself another, still more primary, and so on to infinity. Such is the very essence of all consciousness and thought. We're back, then, to the laws of nature. And what is the ultimate result? Why, the same thing again. (Dostoevsky 1981, 18)

Here, in keeping with the literary-intellectual roots of his "illness" in Renaissance and Enlightenment thought (Dostoevsky 1981, 1), the Underground Man presents the typical outcome of philosophical doubt as found in the "essayistic" tradition extending from Montaigne to Sartre (Kwaterko 1994, 166).[4] Unlike Montaigne and Sartre, however, the Underground Man sees fit to recall a proverbial, moral wisdom inconsistent with his own: "pernicious idleness . . . as everybody knows, is the mother of all vices," he quips, self-mockingly as it were (Dostoevsky 1981, 37). Thus though he earlier describes his "inertia" as "voluptuous" (14), it obviously does not sit quite as well with him (or his creator for that matter) as it does with the former.[5] The reason is plain. In *Herzog* (1964), Bellow himself reflects, "The question of ordinary human experience is the principal question of these modern centuries, as Montaigne and Pascal, otherwise in disagreement, both clearly saw.—The strength of a man's virtue or spiritual capacity measured by his ordinary life" (2003, 117). That is, although they share a similar starting-point in life's bewildering perplexities, Montaigne and Pascal represent opposite moral ideals, the one conducive to the classical virtues of indisturbance and indolence, the other to moral conversion and ethical action. The same goes, of course, for Montaigne and Dostoevsky. Though committed like Montaigne to exploring the self-in-flux, "the doctrinaire prophet" (so Camille La Bossière concludes in his analysis of Dostoevsky, Gide, and Montaigne) "remains at odds with the indifferent artist" on the "question of the end(s) proper to art" (178, 186, 175).

Mirroring as it does in reverse the dramatic situation of Dostoev-sky's *Winter Notes on Summer Impressions* (1863) even as it frames Bellow's critical introduction to that work, Bellow's narrative of a "cold winter" spent in a Paris prostrated "under a perpetual fog" sug-gests his "agreement" with the "prejudices" of the "great radical" on this score if not on others (1994, 41, 39). In his *Winter Notes*, it will be remembered, Dostoevsky begins by tracing the origins of Russian "idleness" and "boredom" back to "the ways in which Europe has been reflected in us at various times and has imposed its civilization upon us" (1988, 10, 15). He then goes on specifically to indict the modern, French counterpart of that civilization for its boredom-inducing indi-vidualism and materialism. "Depressed and sunk in spirit," Bellow too finds Paris, with the "pervasiveness of [its] literary culture" (Balzac, Stendhal, Zola, Strindberg, Camus, and Sartre are all mentioned in support), unusually given to "melancholy and bad temper" (1994, 43). In fact, so demoralized by his milieu is Bellow that, in true Dostoev-skian fashion, he is willing to defy the law in the name of the spirit by purchasing the coal his feverish son needs for warmth on the black market. For Bellow as for Dostoevsky, it seems, there is no such thing as "innocent sloth" (Bellow 2003, 75). Rather, as much criticism has urged, Bellow shares Dostoevsky's moral commitment to overcoming "the self-imprisonments of the 'wastelanders'" (Braham 1982, 17).[6] "The central impetus in both writers" avers Daniel Fuchs in his "Saul Bellow and the Example of Dostoevsky," "is the quest for what is mor-ally real" (1984, 29). More specifically, Fuchs educes in favor of his case for "Russian influence" Bellow's advocacy of "[t]he idea of a writer as teacher rather than martyr, citizen rather than artist, journal-ist rather than aesthetician; the idea of . . . a literature that refuses to adopt the pose of objectivity, detachment, and disenchantment with life" (29).

A look at Bellow's reprise of Dostoevsky's pivotal novel of 1864 of-fers plenty of circumstantial evidence in support of Fuchs's premises and conclusions. A "moral casualty of the war" in that he is driven into idleness and solitude while waiting to be called up, Bellow's *Dangling Man* echoes Dostoevsky's *Underground Man*. "*Radix malorum est* weariness of life," he notes in his third journal entry, borrowing from Goethe's description, in his literary autobiography *Dichtung und Wahrheit*, of "the sorest evil, the heaviest disease" (1996b, 18). Like the Underground Man, Bellow's hero is a man without qualities drawn to anonymity and (ostensibly) averse to Romantic sentimentality. Thus Joseph immediately confesses himself "deeply disappointed" by Goethe's claim that "Nothing occasions this weariness more than the recurrence of the passion of love," preferring his anecdote about "an Englishman" who "is said" to have "hanged himself that he might no longer have to dress and undress himself every day" (18-19). Indeed, as if to make patent his "compulsion to the centre of indifference" (Fuchs 1984, 42), Bellow's narrator-diarist even provides a literary analogue to Goethe's Englishman in the person of Shakespeare's "murderer Barnadine in *Measure for Measure*[,] whose contempt for life equaled his contempt for death, so that he would not come out of his cell to be executed" (1996b, 18-19).

The allusion to Shakespeare's morally ambiguous play of love stifled if not stymied calls attention to the true source of Joseph's "state" of emotional and spiritual malaise (Bellow 1996b, 37). Like Goethe, who "leave[s]" the "moral causes" of ennui "to the investigation . . . of the moralist" (1900, 2.159), Bellow does not specify this cause, but it is sufficiently tacit throughout *Dangling Man*. Joseph's "narcotic dullness" (1996, 18), after all, has its literal counterpart in the drunkenness of his loveless "Dostoyevskian double" Vanaker (Clayton 1979, 118), as well as in the behavior of his friends at the Servatius party. These, in an episode which seems inspired by Eliot's *The Waste Land*, resort to booze and even hypnosis "to free the charge of feeling in the pent heart" and so make themselves insensible to "pain" (Bellow 1996b, 46, 52). Likewise, well before that party, Joseph admits to using a form of self-hypnosis akin to that by which Abt makes Minna "feel cold" (52). Sensing he is "grow[ing] rooted to [his] chair," he remarks, "I have always been subject to such hallucinations. In the middle of winter, isolating a wall with sunlight on it, I have been able to persuade myself, despite the surrounding ice, that the month was July, not February. Similarly, I have reversed the summer and made myself shiver in the heat" (13). Later, stuck "[i]n bed with a cold," a feverish Joseph persuades himself that January is July: "The icicles and frost patterns on the window turned brilliant . . . and the bold, icy color of sky and snow and clouds burned strongly" (118). Moments after, however, he recalls a dream of a "few nights ago" in which he guiltily because passively witnesses the ravages of war in "an atmosphere of terror such as [his] father many years ago could conjure for [him], describing Gehenna and the damned" (120, 121).

In short, like Dostoevsky's Underground Man, who concludes after his "forty years underground" that "the best thing is to do nothing" (1981, 31, 42), Joseph suffers from sloth or accidie as defined by Chaucer's Parson, who likens the condition to "the peyne of helle [traditionally a place of contradiction, of fire and ice] . . . for they that been dampned been so bounde that they ne may neither wel do ne wel thynke" (X.I.685). Indeed, Joseph exhibits all the classic symptoms of accidie (lit. "carelessness") found in the "early ascetics" he studied "[b]efore he interested himself in the Enlightenment" (Bellow 1996, 128). Thus, although he longs to go out, he "can't even bring [himself] to go to the store for tobacco" (13); at "noon," the traditional hour of the *daemonium meridianum*, he grows "restless, imagining that [he is] hungry again," but finds that he is "not hungry at all" once he arrives at the restaurant (15); he feels discontent with his society, longing for "a 'colony of the spirit,' or a group whose covenants forbade spite, bloodiness, and cruelty" (39), but at the same time is "for refusing" "invitations to Christmas dinner" (31); and finally, as underlined by numerous laconic entries—"Slept until eleven o'clock; sat around all afternoon and thought of nothing in particular" (57); "Slept until one o'clock. Out at four for a walk, I lasted ten minutes and then retreated" (78); "Fairly quiet day" (112)—he is typically idle.[7] And so, with time, even he comes to suspect that he is "practicing some terrible vice" (148).

Not surprisingly, then, Joseph's entry for January 13 contains an allusion to Part Two of Dostoevsky's *Notes*, "On the Occasion of Wet Snow," which points to a parity of moral insight between Bellow and Dostoevsky. Having "walk[ed] through large melting flakes" of snow, Joseph "wander[s] through a ten-cent store, examining comic valentines," but buys "a bag of chocolate creams" instead; he also goes "into a Christian Science reading room and pick[s] up the *Monitor*," but does not read it, ostensibly because he is busy "trying to think of the name of the company whose gas stoves used to be advertised on the front page of the *Manchester Guardian*" (Bellow 1996, 107). Meanwhile, as Valentine's Day approaches, he finds himself "intensely hungry" and eats ravenously, showing a predilection in particular for sweets (oranges, caramels, mints, and especially chocolates) (117). But Bellow's diarist remains unsated. Given the reference to Part Two of Dostoevsky's *Notes*, in which the Underground Man similarly makes his way through "the still falling wet and seemingly warm snow" (1981, 96), the explanation seems obvious. As numerous commentators have observed, by means of its two-part structure Dostoevsky's *Notes* implicitly underscores the logical disjunction between the life of studied indifference and the one of self-realization through sacrifice and moral choice spelled out, for example, in Kierkegaard's *Either/Or* (1843).[8] Simply put, both Dostoevsky's Underground Man and Bellow's Dangling Man suffer because they are "unable to love" (Clayton 1979, 113). Both begin with the self and so end, coincidentally, by complaining of a "loss of contact with anything alive" (Dostoevsky 1981, 152)—a state of hellish indifference or accidie.

Indeed, like the "half-cleaned chicken" he finds "on the kitchen sink . . . its yellow claws rigid, its head bent as though to examine its entrails which raveled over the sopping draining board and splattered the enamel with blood," Joseph is intent on the "troubled density" of his "interior life" even as he looks without for sustenance (Bellow 1996,

24, 26, 24). "Mists faded and spread and faded on the pane as I breathed," he writes and then compares the "ruins before [his] eyes" to the "color of the fateful paper that [he] read[s] daily" (25, 26). No wonder then that he admires his aptly named cleaning woman Marie at "work" as she "washe[s] the windows": "cleaning has its importance as a notion of center, of balance, of order," he explains, somewhat unnecessarily as it were. "A woman learns it in the kitchens of her childhood, and it branches out from sinks, windows, table tops, to the faces and hands of children, and then it may become, as it does for some women, part of the nature of God" (112, 113). By contrast, Joseph, with his "fever of vacillations" (Dostoevsky 1981, 12), might be likened to the darkly comical figure he sees hanging "above the restaurant" where he eats, a pasteboard "hamburger with arms and legs balanced on a fiery wire, lean[ing] toward a jar of mustard" (Bellow 1996b, 107). That is, whatever alleviation his hunger finds in food will ultimately be bitter, not sweet, since it feeds only on itself. John Jacob Clayton concurs, adopting Dostoevsky's moral compass in describing "Joseph's selfhood" as "destructive": "it is his selfhood which keeps him isolated, which makes him hurt those around him" (1979, 83).

There is a certain ironic justness, then, to Joseph's insistence that "[i]t isn't love that gives us weariness of life" (Bellow 1996b, 168). In fact, had he continued to read from Goethe's literary autobiography, he would have seen that what Goethe stresses in the sequel as before is not so much the "passion of love" itself as the "melancholy" that its "return" can occasion by leading the youth (the context is a discussion of *The Sorrows of Young Werther*) to "a contemplation of the transient nature and worthlessness of all earthly things." "[M]oral epochs change as well as the seasons of the year," writes Goethe. "The graciousness of the great, the attachment of the multitude, the love of individuals,—all this changes up and down. . . ." Not even virtue and vice escape change and revolution: "how late do we learn to see, that, while we cultivate our virtues, we rear our faults at the same time! The former depends upon the latter as upon their root . . ." (1900, 2.160-61). Such musings find their echo in the Humanist Joseph. And with reason. In sympathy with Bellow's Dangling Man, who prefers the philosophical indifference of Shakespeare's Barnadine and Goethe's Englishman to the passion of love, Goethe goes on to single out English literature, in particular that of the neoclassical period, the early Milton and Shakespeare, for its profound melancholy (2.161-63). However, though "all diseases are apt to be of foreign origin" (Bellow 1994, 39), the origins of ennui are of course historical, not national. As such, it hardly seems a coincidence that like the Underground Man, who cites Schiller and Kant on the "lofty and the beautiful" and Rousseau on man in the opening pages of his *Notes* (Dostoevsky 1981, 6, 10) and like Sartre's Roquentin, who is held up by epistemological doubts in the midst of a study of a paradoxical eighteenth-century figure, Joseph, too, begins "to dangle" as he is at work on a series of essays on Diderot and other eighteenth-century philosophers. Indeed, the phrasing he uses is tantalizingly apposite in its ambiguity: "it was vaguely understood, when I began to dangle, that I was to continue with them" (Bellow 1996b, 11-12).

Appropriately, in view of the above, Fuchs has shown that Joseph's "Spirit of Alternatives," or "'*But on the Other Hand*,' or '*Tu As Raison Aussi*'" as he alternately dubs him (Bellow 1996b, 135), is modelled not on Goethe's but on Dostoevsky's Mephistopheles—that is, on "the incarnation of world boredom" distilled in the leading (post)Enlightenment ideas (Mochulsky qtd. Fuchs 1984, 41). Joseph himself invites this parallel when he relates an anecdote from his childhood in which he is referred to as "Mephisto" (Bellow 1996b, 77). And yet, though he follows Ivan Karamazov's and Luther's example in repulsing the "two-faced," "equivocal" spirit of non-being (141), Joseph, in Fuchs' view, ends by capitulating to him. Indeed, judging *Dangling Man*'s conclusion from a Dostoevskian perspective, Fuchs finds "little of the ambiguity sometimes attributed to it": "Joseph joins the army in the same way one joins the Grand Inquisitor's church," he concludes (1984, 43). By contrast, Clayton, assessing the book's ending from a Humanist perspective, sees little else than ambiguity: "The ending of the novel is not happy; it is complex and ambiguous, partially hopeful. . . . Joseph is joining not only the army but the human race" (1979, 119).

A closer look at Bellow's critical introduction to Dostoevsky's *Winter Notes on Summer Impressions* provides an explanation for this strong difference of views and perspectives on *Dangling Man*. Noting the anti-Western and anti-Semitic attitudes posted in plain view in Dostoevsky's *Winter Notes* and in "the huge, crazy, foaming, vengeful, fulminating book called *A Writer's Diary*," Bellow concludes that "his personal opinions were not rational" (1994, 45). But Bellow immediately adds a coda. "As an artist," he writes, "[Dostoyevsky] was both rational and wise" (45). Whereas Dostoevsky the "journalist" is "fanatical" in his "principles," explains Bellow, Dostoevsky the artist is, like the author of *The Marriage of Heaven and Hell*, a psychologist of unitary reality well acquainted with the coexistence of "love and hate" (44). As evidence of Dostoevsky's artistic impartiality Bellow cites his correspondence about the composition of *The Brothers Karamazov*:

> Dostoyevsky had just concluded the section of The Brothers in which Ivan had declared that he doubted the existence of God—had offered to return his "ticket" to the Creator. Having made a powerful case for atheism, Dostoyevsky now prepared the answer of faith. For this he turned to Father Zosima. He hoped, he told Pobedonostyev, to avoid polemics. These he considered "inartistic." To answer artistically is to do full justice, to respect propositions and harmonies with which journalists and polemicists do not have to bother their heads. . . . The writer's convictions, perhaps fanatically held, must be tamed by truth. (Bellow 1994, 45)

Bellow concludes, "The degree to which you challenge your own beliefs and expose them to destruction is a test of your worth as a novelist" (45).

Needless to say, it is this Dostoevsky, the visionary artist with the "amphibian soul" (Wilson 1996, 34), the "child of light who saw best in darkness" (Fuchs 1984, 38), with whom Bellow finds himself in closest accord. "His [Bellow's] novels render clearly the barriers that can be erected against [the process of transcending]," writes E. Jeanne Braham, adding that "[i]n this effort, Bellow is closer to the marrow of Dostoevsky than similarities of plot or the uses of doubles can ever document" (1982, 14). Contrary to what Fuchs argues, then, the disjunction implied in "[t]he idea of a writer as teacher rather than martyr, citizen rather than artist, journalist rather than aesthetician" (1984, 29) is in fact weak in Bellow's case. No mere "journalist and publicist" such as Marx, Rousseau, Marat, Saint-Just, or even H. G. Wells (Bellow 2004, 175), Bellow might rather be described, like Dostoevsky in Soloviev's assessment, as an "artist . . . in the publicist business" (1916, 213).[9] In fact, in his fiction Bellow consistently reads Dostoevsky's art, and by extension his own, as a synthesis of these opposed activities or impulses. Thus surveying "the classics of [the] condition" of "spiritual loneliness" to which his protagonists are similarly given in his *The Dean's December* (1982), a late novel which persistently sets up the East as foil to the West (and by analogy, Dostoevsky as double to Bellow), Bellow lists "Dostoevsky's apathy-with-intensity, the rage for goodness so near to vileness and murderousness, Nietzsche and the Existentialists, and all the rest of that" (1998, 161).

The aim of Bellow's implicit rapprochement between his art and Dostoevsky's, it seems clear, is to read the one as a natural outgrowth of the other and so, by extension, to reconcile his own dual vocation as artist and polemicist. Thus, like Hermann Hesse, who opposes the "Asiatic Ideal" of "amoral impartiality" evinced in Dostoevsky's late work to "a European . . . a hard and fast moral, ethical, dogmatic standpoint" (1922, 607-08), Bellow finds in the "equivocal consciousness" of the author of *The Possessed* a counterpart to his own Western skepticism (1998, 130); in the words of *Siddhartha*, Hesse's novel of Eastern Enlightenment modelled on Schopenhauer's *The World as Will and Representation*, "in every truth the opposite is equally true. . . . Everything that is thought and expressed in words is one-sided" (Hesse

1951, 115). Accordingly, the Dostoevskian artist-polemicist who would remain true to the riddling syntax of existence, "a murky glass" in which we see only "guessingly" (Knapp 1998, 192), is vowed to silence or enigma on matters of ultimate significance.[10]

Bellow's doubling of Dostoevsky thus speaks a truth no less eloquent for being understated, for passing under silence what unites (and divides) them. Mirrors, however, invert as well as reflect. In reality, the harmony that Bellow and his critics see as existing between Dostoevsky and himself is far from complete. Indeed, as Fuchs's about-face on *Dangling Man* suggests, Bellow's tacit likening of himself to Dostoevsky has much in it that is jarring to a reader of Dostoevsky. As Bellow himself more amply explains in an updated version of his essay on Dostoevsky, "[the novel of ideas] becomes art when the views most opposite to the author's own are allowed to exist in full strength. . . . The opposites must be free to range themselves against each other, and they must be passionately expressed on both sides" (qtd. Braham 1982, 15). However, speaking of *Dangling Man*, Clayton detects a "conflict" or "schism" between "Joseph the spokesman and Joseph the character" (1979, 64, 68). A devotee of the neoclassical harmonies found in Haydn and Brahms, Bellow's Dangling Man shares more in common with Kierkegaard's Mozart-worshiping Aestheticist than with his strait-laced Ethicist. He, too, "satiate[s] the hunger of doubt at the expense of existence" (1959, 100). Indeed, as an allusion to his "warm[ing] [him]self" "at a salamander" on an already warm day and in the midst of "[s]cenes of love and horror" suggests (Bellow 1996b, 107), hellish contradiction and indifference are Joseph's natural element.[11] And yet, like Bellow's other heroes, Joseph is made to seek that "highest 'ideal construction'" which "unlocks the imprisoning self" (153).

It is here that Bellow and Dostoevsky part ways, for if Bellow's Mephistopheles is Dostoevsky's, his Faust is Goethe's. Hence Joseph recurs to Goethe as to an *âme sœur* later in *Dangling Man*, tacitly conceding that he is descended from the "Werthers and Don Juans" and moreover giving Goethe's work a decidedly Existentialist ring: "The sense in which Goethe was right: Continued life means expectation. Death is the abolition of choice. The more choice is limited, the closer we are to death," he writes (1996, 89, 148). Bellow's defection from Dostoevsky's camp may be traced back to his redefining of acedia here in *Dangling Man* and afterwards. Charlie Citrine, who like Bellow is fond of quoting Blake, Whitman, and Goethe on the "imaginative soul" and who even plans to retire to the Goetheanum at the conclusion of *Humboldt's Gift*, explains: "Some think that sloth, one of the capital sins, means ordinary laziness. . . . But sloth has to cover a great deal of despair. Sloth is really a busy condition, hyperactive. This activity drives off the wonderful rest or balance without which there can be no poetry or art or thought—none of the highest human functions" (306). Leonard Forster has pointed to Goethe's similar redefining of sloth as "a slackening of idealism" in his *Faust:*

> Earlier theologians had defined the sin of sloth as 'aversion to spiritual and divine things'; in the secularized language of the eighteenth century it becomes equivalent to an absence of the desire to strive for something higher, or the loss of that desire. It may result on the one hand in pointless activity, on the other in sheer idleness, disinclination for physical or mental effort of any kind, and thus finally in apathy. (Forster 1971, 55)

Concurrently, Goethe's *Faust*, unlike Marlow's, "is not about the final destruction of a lost soul, but about the ultimate redemption of an earnestly striving, though necessarily erring, human being" (Forster 1971, 54). Similarly, for Bellow's heroes, the "Faustian spirit of discontent and universal reform" is antidote to "a life of innocent sloth," to quote more amply from Herzog's first letter to himself (2003, 75).[12] That is, like Goethe's *Werther,* Bellow's novels fuse the modes of "soliloquy" and "dialogue" by "summon[ing] . . . contradicting spirits" to engage in "a mental dialogue" (Goethe 1900, 158). What strife there is in Bellow, accordingly, is the artist's not the moralist's strife.[13]

Bellow's relative agreement with himself, however, necessarily comes at the price of his disharmony with his predecessor, since as evidenced by his choosing to follow his "artist's instinct" and not to reinsert in Part One of *Notes from Underground* the censored passages where "[he] had" (in his own words) "deduced the need for faith and Christ" (Fanger 1981, xxv), Dostoevsky presents the spectacle of an artist "at war with himself" (Magarshak 1975, 3).[14] In contrast, by conflating the roles of artist and polemicist which he would keep distinct in his polemic with Dostoevsky, Bellow effectively sins against not only the moralist's but the artist's creed he finds at work in Dostoevsky as well, thus at best duplicating a conflict found in the original and overcome, by most critical accounts, only in *The Brothers Karamazov.*[15] In other words, and as might be expected, given their important differences, Bellow and Dostoevsky's relationship in the history of words and ideas does not so much correspond to a dialogue in the traditional sense as to "a vicious circle" (to borrow Bakhtin's figure for boredom's confinement in *Notes from Underground*) in the form of an "internal polemic with another and with [one]self." From this "endless dialogue" of the mind with itself (1984, 230), Dostoevsky escapes in the direction of religious asceticism, Bellow in that of gnosis and silence. Here and in this sense only do the two meet, Western skepticism answering to Eastern mysticism, doubt unto faith, as deep unto deep.

From *College Literature* 35.1 (Winter 2008): 1-15. Copyright © 2008 by *College Literature.* Reprinted with permission of *College Literature.*

Notes

1. For a survey of the "contradictory views among the critics concerning Bellow's existentialist tendency" (Aharoni 1983, 44), see the first three pages of Ada Aharoni's "Bellow and Existentialism." Aharoni quotes Helen Weinberg to the effect that "Bellow would repudiate any systematized finding," including those of existentialism (1983, 43).

2. Clayton (1979, 57-59) and Aharoni (1983, 42).

3. Although he "can see no reason for calling Dostoevsky an existentialist," Kaufmann believes that "Part One of *Notes from Underground* is the best overture for existentialism ever written," anticipating as it does all "the major themes" of that liter-

ature (1956, 14). Comparisons between Bellow and Dostoevsky are not hard to find, in particular in the early reception of Bellow's novels. Less explicit, but no less telling, are the allusions to such Bakhtinian notions as "heteroglossia," "dialogic," "double-voicing" and "interillumination" which have become *de rigueur* in current Bellow criticism. For some recent examples, see the essays by Kuzma (1990, 1993), Kemnitz (1982), and Nevius (1972).

4. Whether we proceed inductively or deductively, Montaigne argues in the *Essais*, X must be investigated by way of –X, –X by way of another, unknown term, and so on "à l'infini": "nous voilà au rouet," he says of such vicious circling (1962, 2.12). All reflexive thought, Sartre concurs, is inconclusive and so characterized by the "languissante dégustation" or slow delectation of the self by the self: "Il s'ennuie, et cet Ennui . . . c'est le goût que l'homme a nécessairement pour lui-même, la saveur de l'existence" (Sartre 1947, 33). Though the statement is applied here to the nineteenth-century *flâneur* Baudelaire, it is the figure of an indolent Montaigne which comes to Sartre's mind in *Nausée* when he seeks to paint the contrast between the inward-looking contemplative and the duty-bound man of action (1979, 119). Not surprisingly, given his aversion to such men of action and to all forms of positivism, Dostoevsky's protagonist in *Notes from Underground*—"neither bad nor good, neither a scoundrel nor an honest man, neither a hero nor an insect" but *un homme moyen sensuel* in his middle age (1981, 3)—is also reminiscent of Montaigne.

5. Montaigne's indolence is legendary. More complex is the case of Sartre, but although Existential ennui may be worrying, Sartre explicitly describes this feeling as a metaphysical not a moral phenomenon (1947, 33).

6. On the connection between Eliot's *The Waste Land* and the sin of sloth or "acedia," see Winters, who takes Eliot to task for confusing "principles which fall . . . into two contradictory groups, the romantic . . . and . . . the classical and Christian" and so "mak[ing] a virtue of what appears to be private spiritual laziness" (1943, 116).

7. For a similar list of the symptoms of acedia, see Forster (1971), who cites the fifth-century writer John Cassian. These symptoms include, for example, "dislike of the place, disgust with the cell, and . . . disdain and contempt of the brethren who dwell with him. . . . It also makes the man . . . lazy and sluggish about all manner of work which has to be done. . . . It does not suffer him to stay in his cell, or to take any pains about reading, and he often groans because . . . he can do no good while he stays there, and complains and sighs because . . . he can bear no spiritual fruit so long as he is joined to that society . . ." (Cassian qtd. Forster 1971, 56).

8. Chiefly Weisburg (1984, 28-41), Frank (1986, 342-47), and Todorov (1990, 89-92).

9. Indeed, just as Soloviev's phrase covers all the stops in Dostoevsky criticism, so, too, "an intensive sort of personal public-relations project" (Bellow 1996, 65) summarizes Bellow's undertaking for most of his critics.

10. On the negative way of the "coincidentia oppositorum" found in the Eastern Church and on Dostoevsky's substituting of that synthetic logic for the Western principle of non-contradiction, see Lossky (1944, 116-17) and Berdyaev (1934, 15) respectively.

11. Concurrently, the Bellovian hero's confrontation with the hellish element is

typically far from harrowing in comparison with the experience of Dostoevsky's protagonists. Though seemingly an exception, Dean Corde's stay in an Eastern underground alternating between the decidedly uncomfortable and uncomforting "extremes of heat and cold," "frost and flames," only emphasizes the rule, for obvious reasons, especially as it is juxtaposed with a Western underground of more moderate "heat and chill" in which kidney patients are "cleansed" of their spleen and treated with an "amorphous pity, a powerful but somehow indiscriminate love" (Bellow 1998, 214, 213, 166, 167).

12. Defending Bellow, and in particular his conclusions, against his many "detractors" on the grounds that his is "another way of transcending," Braham concurs: "Bellow's protagonists fear the cessation of striving, initially at least, because they confuse it with somnabulence. Peace, serenity, harmony seem dangerous opiates to Joseph, Asa Leventhal [in *The Victim*], Tommy Wilhelm [in *Seize the Day*] who, with Henderson [in *Henderson the Rain King*], cry out to 'burst the spirit's sleep.' The sign of their spiritual health is striving" (Braham 1982, 14, 16). Concurrently, in *Dangling Man* the Dostoevskian view of transcendence is represented by a "sickly" pauper peddling Christian Science literature. To the already fever-prone Joseph—a mere ordinary "poor, human devil" after all, who plays at "fir[ing]" guns but is himself harmless— "she suggest[s] the figure of a minor political leader in exile, unwelcome, shabby, burning with a double fever" (Bellow 1996, 77, 107, 162). Indeed, though he says that "[w]e are all drawn toward the same craters of the spirit—to know what we are and what we are for, to know our purpose, to seek grace," Joseph makes it clear that he will not owe this "grace" to "any divinity": "Out of my own strength it was necessary for me to return the verdict for reason, in its partial inadequacy, and against the advantages of its surrender" (154, 68).

13. Viewed "aesthetically," Kierkegaardian despair becomes, according to Sanford Pinsker, "the peculiar Muse who makes . . . [Citrine/Bellow's] Art possible" (1980, 125). For his part, André Gide allies Montaigne's philosophy with Goethe's "sagesse païenne" or Pagan wisdom in order to divorce Montaigne more forcefully from Christianity (1962, 20).

14. Like Ivan, who succumbs to madness when skeptical reason fails him, the Underground Man is supposedly self-defeated, but his inertia remains a vexing problem. On this score, even Dostoevsky apologist Joseph Frank concedes the *Notes'* "total lack of effectiveness as a polemic" (1986, 347).

15. See for example Girard (1963) and Berdyaev (1923/1934).

Works Cited

Aharoni, Ada. 1983. "Bellow and Existentialism." *Saul Bellow Journal* 2.2 (Spring): 42-54.

Bakhtin, Mikhail. 1984. *Problems of Dostoevsky's Poetics*. Trans. Caryl Emerson. 1929. Reprint. Minneapolis: University of Minnesota Press.

Bellow, Saul. 1955. "The French as Dostoyevsky Saw Them." Foreword. *Winter Notes on Summer Impressions*, by Fyodor Dostoyevsky. New York: Criterion.

_____. 1994. *It All Adds Up: From the Dim Past to the Uncertain Future: A Nonfiction Collection*. New York: Viking.

_____. 1996a. *Dangling Man*. 1944. Reprint. New York: Penguin.

_____. 1996b. *Humboldt's Gift*. 1975. Reprint. New York: Penguin.

_____. 1998. *The Dean's December*. 1982. Reprint. New York: Penguin.

_____. 2003. *Herzog*. 1964. Reprint. New York: Penguin.

_____. 2004. *Mr. Sammler's Planet*. 1970. Reprint. New York: Penguin.

Berdyaev, Nikolai. 1934. *Dostoievsky*. Trans. Donald Attwater. 1923. Reprint. London: Sheed and Ward.

Braham, E. Jeanne. 1982. "The Struggle at the Center: Dostoevsky and Bellow." *Saul Bellow Journal* 2.1 (Fall): 13-18.

Clayton, John Jacob. 1971. *Saul Bellow in Defense of Man*. 1979. Reprint. Bloomington: Indiana University Press.

Dostoevsky, Fyodor. 1981. *Notes from Underground*. Trans. Mirra Ginsburg. 1864. Reprint. New York: Bantam.

_____. 1988. *Winter Notes on Summer Impressions*. Trans. David Patterson. 1863. Reprint. Evanston, IL: Northwestern University Press.

Fanger, Donald. 1981. Introduction. Dostoevsky. *Notes from Underground*. Trans. Mirra Ginsburg. 1864. Reprint. New York: Bantam.

Forster, Leonard. 1971. "Faust and the Sin of Sloth; Mephistopheles and the Sin of Pride." In *The Discontinuous Tradition: Studies in German Literature in Honour of Ernest Ludwig Stahl*. Oxford: Oxford University Press.

Frank, Joseph. 1986. *Dostoevsky: The Stir of Liberation, 1860-1865*. Princeton: Princeton University Press.

Fuchs, Daniel. 1984. "Saul Bellow and the Example of Dostoevsky." In *Saul Bellow: Vision and Revision*. Chapter 2. Durham, NC: Duke University Press.

Gide, André. 1962. Preface. *Essais de Michel de Montaigne*. Vol. 1. Paris: Gallimard.

Girard, René. 1963. *Dostoïevski, du double à l'unité*. Paris: Plon.

Goethe, Johann Wolfgang. 1900. *Truth and Fiction*. Trans. John Oxenford. 1810-1833. Reprint. Boston: Dana Estes.

Hesse, Hermann. 1922. "*The Brothers Karamazov* or The Downfall of Europe." Trans. Stephen Hudson (Sydney Schiff). *The Dial* 72.6 (June): 607-18.

_____. 1951. *Siddhartha*. Trans. Hilda Rosner. 1922. Reprint. New York: New Directions.

Kaufmann, Walter Arnold, ed. 1956. *Existentialism from Dostoevsky to Sartre*. New York: World Publishing.

Kemnitz, Charles. 1982. "Narration and Consciousness in *Herzog*." *Saul Bellow Journal* 1.2: 1-6.

Kierkegaard, Søren. 1959. *Either/Or*. Trans. David F. Swenson, Lillian Marvin Swenson, and Walter Lowrie. In *A Kierkegaard Anthology*, ed. Robert Bretall. New York: The Modern Library.

Knapp, Lisa. 1998. "Myshkin Through a Murky Glass, Guessingly." In *Dostoevsky's* The Idiot*: A Critical Companion*, ed. Lisa Knapp. Evanston, Illinois: Northwestern University Press.

Kuzma, Faye. 1990. "Mental Travel in *Henderson the Rain King*." *Saul Bellow Journal* 9.2: 54-67.

_____. 1993. "'We Flew On': Flights of Imagination in *Humboldt's Gift*." *Michigan Academician* 25.2: 159-77.

Kwaterko, Józef. 1994. "Ducharme essayiste ou 'Sartre maghané.'" In *Paysages de Réjean Ducharme*, ed. Pierre-Louis Vaillancourt. Quebec: Fides.

La Bossière, Camille. 2003. "Of Montaigne, Dostoevsky and Gide: A *Sotie*." *Back to Sources: Essais Métis from the Outaouais*. Ottawa: Tecumseh Press. 174-89.

Leroux, Jean-François. 2000. "Henri-Frédéric Amiel." In *Nineteenth-Century French Poets. The Dictionary of Literary Biography*, Vol. 217, ed. Robert Beum. Detroit: Gale.

Lossky, Vladimir. 1944. *Théologie mystique de l'Eglise d'Orient*. Paris: Editions Montaigne.

Magarshak, David. 1963. *Dostoevsky*. 1975. Reprint. Westport: Greenwood.

Montaigne, Michel de. 1962. *Essais*. Ed. Pierre Michel. 3 vols. Paris: Gallimard.

Nevius, Blake. 1972. "Saul Bellow and the Theater of the Soul." *Neuphilologische Mitteilungen* 73: 248-60.

Pinsker, Sanford. 1980. "Saul Bellow, Søren Kierkegaard and the Question of Boredom." *Centennial Review* 24: 118-25.

Sartre, Jean-Paul. 1947. *Baudelaire*. 1938. Reprint. Paris: Gallimard.

_____. 1979. *Nausée*. 1938. Reprint. Paris: Editions du Club de l'honnête homme.

Soloviev, Evgeny. 1916. *Dostoïevsky: His Life and Literary Activity*. Trans. C.J. Hogarth. London: George Allen and Unwin.

Todorov, Tzvetan. 1990. *Genres in Discourse*. Transl. Catherine Porter. 1978. Reprint. Cambridge: Cambridge University Press.

Weisburg, Richard H. 1984. *The Failure of the Word*. New Haven: Yale University Press.

Wilson, Raymond J., III. 1996. "Saul Bellow's *Herzog* and Dostoevsky's *The Brothers Karamazov*." *Saul Bellow Journal* 14.1 (Winter): 27-39.

Winters, Yvor. 1943. *The Anatomy of Nonsense*. Norfolk: New Directions.

The Double Vision:
The Victim by Saul Bellow _____

Jonathan Baumbach

> For no one can judge a criminal until he recognizes that he is just such a
> criminal as the man standing before him and that he, perhaps, is more than
> all men, to blame for that crime.
>
> —*The Brothers Karamazov*

1

Saul Bellow is a rarity among American novelists. He is not a child
prodigy. I say *is* not because most of our "marvelous boys" have, in the
face of time, stalwartly refused to age, have instead become elder states-
men-child prodigies, senile innocents, imaginary boys in real bull rings.
Bellow was twenty-nine when his first novel, *Dangling Man* (1944),
was published. At twenty-nine so many of our talented writers had already indicated that their most significant work was behind them that
they had neither other voices nor other rooms, only new dust jackets for
the nostalgic recreations of their earlier works. What is so remarkable
about Bellow's career is that, while continuing to grow as a writer, he
has risked transaction, each time out, with a different unchartered territory of the novel. In *The Victim* (1947) he has written the best of our
nightmare novels. *The Adventures of Augie March* (1953), for all the dif-
fusion of its picaresque variety of incident, is as rich and dense in experience as any novel written in our time. And *Henderson the Rain King*
(1959), set in that undiscovered Africa of the spirit, is something else
again—a serious comic fantasy with the pitch of insight of a major
novel. It seems clear, as of 1964, that Bellow is our most valuable living
novelist, an adventurous talent of extraordinary resources of vision.

Bellow's longer fiction readily divides itself into two main groups:
the novels of depth, of claustrophobic internal exploration, influenced
by Dostoevsky (*Dangling Man*, *The Victim*, and *Seize the Day*), and

the novels of breadth, of sensation and experience, of physical and spiritual quest (*The Adventures of Augie March* and *Henderson the Rain King*). Inevitably, since Bellow is not two men, the preoccupations of each group reside to some extent in the other. It is somewhat unfortunate that Bellow's reputation, for good and ill, rests so heavily on *The Adventures of Augie March*, a remarkable if over extended picaresque novel with all the vices of its ambition. At its best, *Augie March* has real beauty, particularly the scenes of Augie's childhood and the portrait of Grandma Lausch; but too much of the second half of the book, in striving for a kind of grandiosity (what the New York *Times* book page calls "greatness"), seems willfully eccentric and inflated. I have chosen to deal with *The Victim* not only because it seems to me one of the important novels of our time, but because it is exemplary of the complex concerns of all of Bellow's novels. Since *Dangling Man* anticipates it, treats in less dramatic and more explicit fashion the same victim-victimizer paradox, it may be useful to move into *The Victim* by way of a brief analysis of Bellow's first novel.

The dangling man, Joseph, might be characterized as a sensitive and intelligent Robert Cohn who did not go to Princeton. This is not as patently facetious as it sounds. Bellow is so much at odds with the Hemingway code that the two form a significant polarity. In his first journal entry—the novel is written in the formal guise of a journal (notes from the nether world of uncommitment)—Joseph writes:

> Today, the code of the athlete, of the tough boy . . . is stronger than ever. Do you have feelings? There are correct and incorrect ways of indicating them. Do you have an inner life? It's nobody's business but your own. Do you have emotions? Strangle them. To a degree, everyone obeys this code. And it does admit of a limited kind of candor, a close-mouthed straightforwardness. But on the truest, it has an inhibitory effect. Most serious matters are closed to the hardboiled. They are unpracticed in introspection, and therefore badly equipped to deal with opponents they cannot shoot like big game or outdo in daring.[1]

Joseph's main "opponent" is himself and though ostensibly well equipped to deal with him—Joseph is *practiced* in intellection—he comes off second best; he is ultimately self-defeated.

Joseph dangles because he is denied context; he is 1-A, unemployed and unemployable, waiting to be drafted into the Second World War, in effect waiting to die. The novel chronicles Joseph's deteriorating state of soul. As his life passes in review like the Movietone March of Time, Joseph reflects on its meaning, searching in vain for an existential moral code to which he can anchor his commitment. Since Joseph has nothing to do, is a kind of nonparticipant in the "real world," he can function (he thinks), if function is the word for it, as a detached observer. Detachment, however, is not easily come by. Joseph is a sufferer (like all Bellow's heroes), and detachment while others are being killed in war can only occasion feelings of guilt and impotence. Like Proust's narrator, Joseph has no real present and so must recapture the past if only to assert his existence, to justify himself to himself. The present, he tells himself hopefully, offers him a one-shot freedom, a time to come to terms with ultimates.

But his freedom, like his detachment, is illusory, another of the degrading ironies life plays on him. He discovers that there is no freedom without choice, and no choice without commitment, that while he is an isolate, his spiritual quest is a fraud: "And goodness is achieved not in a vacuum, but in the company of other men, attended by love. I, in this room, separate, alienated, distrustful, find in my purpose not an open world but a closed, hopeless jail" (p. 92). Joseph's symposiums with his imaginary alter ego, the Spirit of Alternatives (which anticipate the Leventhal-Allbee confrontations in *The Victim*), indicate the futility of the inner life divorced from the possibility of outward participation; finally, they become a kind of intellectual onanism, a further manifestation of Joseph's spiritual deterioration.

Though a man of rigorous principle, Joseph is continually betrayed by unrestrainable impulses. A partisan of nonviolence (Joseph is violently antiviolence), victimized perhaps by the ethos of war, he commits one act of violence after another. The outer world represented by the war and its degenerative ramifications—Joseph's profiteering brother Amos, his feeble-minded exhibitionist neighbor Vanaker, his cold-blooded intellectual friend Abt—has become sterile and brutal, brutalizing Joseph in its image. Joseph's aimless rages, though directed at particular objects, are really, Bellow indicates, aimed at himself. When his identity is denied, he asserts it by striking out in rage at the man who has ignored him. When a Communist who knew Joseph when he was in the party refuses to recognize him in a restaurant, Joseph confronts the man and makes a public scene. When his landlord turns off his heat and electricity, the affronted Joseph beats him up. Joseph is saying in effect, "I beat you, therefore you know I am, therefore I am."

The most "symbolic" of Joseph's acts of violence is his unauthorized spanking of his barbaric teen-aged niece Etta. In a finely rendered scene, Etta, who like her successful parents, identifies poverty with unimportance, treats Joseph rudely, refusing to let him listen to Haydn on *her* phonograph because *she* wants to hear Cugat. That she strongly resembles Joseph suggests that, in spanking her, Joseph is beating what he finds detestable in himself, or rather (like Leventhal with Allbee), is beating the objectification of himself. Etta succeeds in further victimizing Joseph by letting her parents infer that Joseph's attack was sexual (because of their physical resemblance, a kind of transferred onanism). Joseph, victimized further by his own free-floating sense of guilt, is unable to deny it.

Joseph's sense of guilt, indeterminate and obsessive, haunts him like an idiot ghost, forcing him to assume responsibility for sins not his own. Jeff Forman, a classmate of Joseph's whose plane was shot down in combat, provides Joseph with an objective occasion to accommodate his guilt. By not participating, by not risking his life, Joseph had let others die for him. Forman is the personal symbol—his falling plane looms through the novel shadowing Joseph's fall—of Joseph's culpability. A self-conscious Dostoevskian, Joseph wants to enter the war, not to kill but to be killed, to be purged of his guilt. Unable to bear the terrible responsibility of his nominal freedom, he gives himself up to the army, seeking redemption perhaps through death, seeking escape from the consciousness of his guilt through mindless action. Joseph writes: "Long live regimentation!" On this high-pitched irony, the novel ends.

By using the form of a journal in *Dangling Man*, Bellow avoids, one would think, the purely technical problem of structure. Though the organization of *Dangling Man* seems arbitrary—there is no apparent link between one incident and another and, consequently, no dramatic progression—it is a rigidly disciplined work. Nothing takes place in the novel that is not directly relevant to the central concern. If anything, *Dangling Man* is too tightly constructed, too sparse of novelistic flesh. Joseph, isolated from his brethren like his Biblical counterpart, has no world. Similarly, the novel exists in no real world, only a peripheral one, limited by Joseph's abortive contacts outside himself.

2

The Victim, Bellow's second novel, is traditionally plotted, well-made in the Jamesian sense. Yet even with its tightness of structure, *The Victim* has a real—a suffocatingly real—sense of life. The novel opens:

> On some nights New York is as hot as Bangkok. The whole continent seems to have moved from its place and slid nearer the equator, the bitter gray Atlantic to have become green and tropical, and the people thronging the streets, barbaric fellahin among the stupendous monuments of their mystery, the lights of which, a dazing profusion, climb upward endlessly into the heat of the sky.[2]

This passage is impressive as description, evoking the oppressive humidity of a hot New York summer night, but it serves also to set an emotional atmosphere in which the victims, Leventhal and Allbee, will be seen sweltering throughout the novel, and it suggests Leventhal's spiritual malaise. Bellow follows with, "On such a night, Asa Leventhal alighted from a Third Avenue train," and we are gradually led into the anteroom of Leventhal's hothouse consciousness. By introducing Leventhal in conjunction with the suffocating heat, Bellow makes the atmosphere a reflector of Leventhal's interior suffocation.

In his way, Leventhal is also a dangling man (as Joseph is also a victim). Waiting for his wife to return from a stay with her widowed mother, he lives (like Joseph) in a state of impermanence and unreality. A dangling isolate, Leventhal is at his most vulnerable when Allbee appears, a human ruin from the darkness of Leventhal's past, to accuse him of having destroyed his life. Allbee's case is this: he had recommended Leventhal, then out of work, to his employer Rudiger; Leventhal, out of intentional malice (Allbee had once made anti-Semitic remarks in his presence), had insulted Rudiger; infuriated at Leventhal, Rudiger had fired Allbee; unable to get another job, broken by the desertion and death of his wife, Allbee had gradually degenerated to his present derelict state, for which Leventhal is mostly responsible. Allbee, whose name suggests that Bellow intends him as a kind of objective correlative for existence, or at least Leventhal's existence, assails Leventhal's self-image, and intensifies his thinly repressed sense of inadequacy. Rationally Leventhal knows that Allbee's charges are untrue, but his own comparative prosperity (for which he feels guilty) and his excruciating sensitivity to anti-Semitism make him vulnerable to Allbee's claim on him. In a sense, Allbee makes him believe what he has always believed though never admitted, that he is inadequate, that his success, small as it is, could have been achieved only by some kind of accident—some universal imbalance.

Though he vehemently denies Allbee's accusations, Leventhal feels strangely responsible for Allbee's deterioration. At one point, after he has already committed himself to Allbee, Leventhal has a flash of self-deceived insight. He wonders: "Had he unknowingly, that is unconsciously, wanted to get back at Allbee?" He then, unable to face even this possibility, denies that he had, consciously refuses all responsibility for Allbee's fall. Despite the assurance of his denial, Leventhal continues to behave toward Allbee as if he had in some interior confessional already admitted his culpability. Leventhal is not so much Allbee's victim as his own. A kind of materialized ghost from Leventhal's haunted psyche, Allbee is not the cause but the occasion of Leventhal's victimization—the objectification of his free-floating guilt.

Allbee is Leventhal's reflection, as seen in one of those freakishly distorting Coney Island mirrors: "He was taller than Leventhal but not nearly so burly; large framed but not robust," a kind of stretched-out version of Leventhal. In implication, Leventhal's meeting with Allbee, like Joseph's with his imaginary alter ego, is an existential I-thou confrontation. Allbee, as victim and accuser, not only releases Leventhal's worst and most hidden fears about himself but also embodies them. Bellow defines the nature of their relationship in their first strange meeting in the park.

On a suffocatingly muggy night, Leventhal wanders into the park, seeking refuge from the heat. When he starts to leave he is accosted by a man who seems vaguely familiar, a deformed shadow from some dark corridor of his past. The man, Kirby Allbee, claims that he has sent Leventhal a letter, in which he makes an appointment to meet him in the park. Though he has not received Allbee's note, Leventhal has, out of a kind of psychic insight, come to the assigned spot at the assigned time, unwittingly answering Allbee's request. It is an insane confrontation. In self-righteous heat, each accuses the other of lying, yet ironically both have, from their limited knowledge, been telling the truth. Allbee insists that Leventhal is pretending not to have received his letter.

"Why should I pretend?" said Leventhal excitedly, "What reason have I got to pretend? I don't know what letter you're talking about. You haven't got anything to write me for. I haven't thought about you in years, frankly, and I don't know why you think I care whether you exist or not. What, are we related?"

"By blood? No, no . . . heavens!" Allbee laughed. [p. 29]

This is a moment, in the classic sense, of recognition. Underlying Leventhal's question, which is in impulse no less unpleasant than Allbee's answer, is the notion that his compassion has familial, or, in a sense tribal, boundaries. The anti-Semitic Allbee wants none of Leventhal's tainted blood, yet both sense—this is implicit in the exchange—that they are in some fundamental way, related. Their relatedness is what the novel is profoundly about. The two are secret sharers, though in a Dostoevskian rather than Conradian sense. Allbee is not to Leventhal, as Leggatt is to the Captain, a primordial alter ego, the personification of his evil possibilities; he is, as Smerdyakov is to Ivan (Svidrigailov to Raskolnikov), the grotesque exaggeration of his counterpart. He represents Leventhal's failings carried to their logical insanity. While we learn a great deal about Leventhal's background, we have only a nodding acquaintance with Allbee's life before he became inextricably connected with Leventhal. Allbee is somewhat of a mystery to us in the sense that human personality is never wholly explicable, in the sense that Leventhal, prior to Allbee's confrontation, has been a stranger to himself.

Though Allbee performs a symbolic role in the novel, Bellow has rendered him as real, decaying flesh and blood. As we begin to find Allbee unreclaimably depraved—a bigot and a fraud—we discover that he has, in part, been telling the truth, that the Willistons, honorable people, thought him once a fine man. Our responses are jarred; perhaps we had been wrong about him; perhaps Leventhal *is* somewhat at fault. And in the sense that a man, regardless of his intentions, is responsible for the consequences of his acts, Leventhal is partly to blame for Allbee's degeneration. In any event, we are not permitted to be *wholly* certain about anything. The truth of *The Victim* is complex, and Bellow refuses to be conclusive merely for the sake of neatness; there is always another possibility, a further ambiguity. Rather than cancel one another out as they might, Bellow's complex of awarenesses—each scene has manifold possibilities—enlarges the experience, intensifies and deepens its meaning. Allbee is Leventhal's devil, but he is also, like Leventhal, his own victim. Suffering a vague sense of responsibility for his wife's death, Allbee as a penance uses the money she has left him to destroy himself. Out of a kind of masochistic principle, yet a principle nevertheless, he refuses to profit in any way as a consequence of her death. He is then like Leventhal in that he seeks an occasion to punish himself in order to redeem his guilt. Leventhal is his occasion, as he is Leventhal's. In victimizing Leventhal, Allbee consciously degrades himself. But victimizing Leventhal is not enough; he feels compelled, since Leventhal as Jew is the enemy (his natural victim and unmerciful judge), to love him and finally to identify with him. Allbee manifests the very qualities he claims to hate in Leventhal: his self-pity, his aggressiveness, his defensiveness, his self-righteousness, his, in Allbee's anti-Semitic notion, Jewishness.

When Allbee moves into Leventhal's apartment, their identification is further intensified. Coming home after a two-day absence, Leventhal finds himself (like Golyadkin in Dostoevsky's *The Double*) locked out of his own apartment by his pretender-self. When he breaks down the door and discovers Allbee and a strange (though familiar) woman in different states of undress, he is not so much embarrassed as outraged. ("Leventhal flushed thickly, 'In my bed!'") This is a powerful and complex scene. In finding Allbee in his bed with a woman who resembles the landlady Mrs. Nunez, whom Leventhal has covertly desired, Leventhal is momentarily horrified, as if Allbee has in some way cuckolded him. Leventhal is particularly vulnerable to this humiliation. Before his marriage, when his wife had confessed to him that she was still involved in an affair with a married man, he had reacted violently, breaking off the engagement. In discovering himself locked out of his apartment, Leventhal experiences a sense of dispossession, almost as if Allbee has usurped his identity or even his very existence. Moreover, Leventhal's identification with "his double" has become so complete that as a consequence of Allbee's act, Leventhal feels guilty, as if he himself had been unfaithful to his wife. Finally, Leventhal senses that Allbee has betrayed him, that he has corrupted his bed as he has dirtied his life.

As Allbee attempts to identify with Leventhal, Leventhal, fulfilling the implied pattern of the relationship, unconsciously imitates Allbee. Though he finds drinking, in particular Allbee's chronic drunkenness, repugnant, Leventhal drinks himself into a stupor at his friend Harkavy's house. Getting drunk for Leventhal is the ultimate degradation, a way of sharing Allbee's private Hell. He becomes so committed to his victimizer-self that when Harkavy, with misguided good intention, asks the suffering Leventhal for his confidence, Leventhal is unable to betray Allbee to him. As Leventhal has learned from his previous unsuccessful attempts at communicating his problem, he is, for the time being, condemned to isolation; he must bear the burden of Allbee alone. Ironically, his victimizer, Allbee, becomes the only one with whom he can communicate.

The nature of their communication becomes, out of the similarity of their wounds, increasingly intimate. Their mutual repulsion, an objectified self-repulsion, evolves, or rather inverts, through their sense of likeness, into a grotesque attraction:

> Allbee bent forward and laid his hand on the arm of Leventhal's chair, and for a short space the two men looked at each other and Leventhal felt himself singularly drawn with a kind of affection. It oppressed him, it was repellent. He did not know what to make of it. Still, he welcomed it, too. He was remotely disturbed to see himself so changeable. However, it did not seem just then to be a serious fault. [p. 224]

This is the moment of closest connection between the two. Through the catalyst of their desperation, their hate is transformed into compassion, into something like love. Allbee, vaguely homosexual, then insists on fingering Leventhal's hair. Fascinated by his touch, Leventhal is for a time incapable of resisting, until, horrified by the implications of his reaction, he roughly pushes Allbee away. Leventhal's is less a homosexual response, though it is that too, than a deeply compassionate one; he is capable of loving even his most vicious antagonist. It is also a moment of obscene identification between the two. In experiencing attraction to his worst self, which is, in implication, the evil of the world (Hell), Leventhal is yielding to his self-degrading instincts, resolving his guilt by falling deeper into corruption. Bellow is suggesting here that ultimately the best and worst instincts of man are not always distinguishable. Heaven, which is redemption, can only and finally be reached through Hell.

At its most malicious, Allbee's persecution of Leventhal is compelled by a need to self-dramatize before an audience, to have someone, preferably his natural enemy, recognize him, understand him, and, finally, love him. In the process, Allbee succeeds in identifying with Leventhal to the extent that when Leventhal's brother Max appears, Allbee, who is an only child, finds it difficult to believe that Leventhal could have had a brother, that Leventhal's background might have been different from his. "I don't know what made me think you were an only child, like me." In a rare moment of guilelessness, Allbee impulsively confesses his loneliness: "I often used to wish there were two of us." This is a significant revelation. Having attached himself to Leventhal, Allbee has, in a sense, fulfilled his childhood wish; he has found, for a time, another of himself.

In an act of ultimate identification, Allbee attempts to kill himself, and, or more likely in his stead, Leventhal. Though Allbee only vaguely realizes this at the time, he wants to commit a kind of suicide—a transferred suicide—in which his other self, Leventhal, will die for him. When they come together several years later, Allbee tries to explain his intention to Leventhal:

"I want you to know one thing," said Allbee. "That night . . . I wanted to put an end to myself. I wasn't thinking of hurting you. I suppose you would have been . . . but I wasn't thinking of you. You weren't even in my mind."

Leventhal laughed outright at this.

"You could have jumped in the river. That's a funny lie. Why tell it? Did you have to use my kitchen?"

Allbee glanced around restlessly. The bays that rose into his loose blond hair became crimson. "No," he said miserably. "Well, anyhow, I don't remember how it was. I must have been demented. When you turn against yourself, nobody else means anything to you either." [p. 293]

Allbee, in any event, believes that he is telling the truth. He has, as we've seen, identified with Leventhal as the source and image of his degradation, and so by killing Leventhal—we are led to suspect that Allbee has no real intention of dying himself—he would be destroying the objectification of his debased self, killing himself symbolically. Before they part, Allbee acknowledges his indebtedness to Leventhal ("'I know I owe you something'"). However, Allbee is unable to articulate just what that "something" is. It is the final consequence of their shared identity; in saving his own life, Leventhal saves Allbee's.

As Leventhal makes possible Allbee's physical rehabilitation, Allbee makes possible Leventhal's redemption. At the start of the novel, Leventhal, isolated from himself, can have no real connection with others. By victimizing him, Allbee breaks down Leventhal's self-limiting defenses, destroys him in effect into wholeness. His confrontation with Allbee, which has all the aspects of a nightmare, operates for Leventhal as a spiritual shock treatment. Spiritually ill, Leventhal can achieve salvation only after he has come to terms with the lower depths of his being—his Allbee. His spiritual descent is an illustration of the Heraclitean paradox, that the way up and the way down are one and the same. Leventhal is on the verge of being physically destroyed—the correlative of his moral degeneration—when he is wakened from a fitful, despondent sleep by the gas perfumes (Leventhal associates it with the scent of Allbee's woman) Allbee has jetted from an unlighted stove. Leventhal instinctively acts to save his life, and in almost ritual progression, he chases Allbee out of his house (exorcising his devil), shuts off the gas, and opens the windows: the cold air revives him. Purged of his guilt and his hate, Leventhal (like the hero of Salinger's "For Esmé—with Love and Squalor") is able at last to sleep undisturbed in the grace of his redemption.

The last chapter, which serves as an epilogue and gloss to the experience of the novel is somewhat unsatisfying. What is wrong is not that it is inconclusive—no finally serious novel can be conclusive—but that it seems, for the most part, unnecessary. Several years after the main action has taken place, Leventhal and Allbee accidentally meet again in the lobby of a Broadway theatre. As if in justification of Allbee's thesis that a man has infinite possibilities for changing his life ("'It makes sense to me that a man can be born again'"), both Leventhal and Allbee have ameliorated, if not their lives, at least their situations. Though only moderately prosperous, Leventhal has a better job, has relocated to a better neighborhood, and, as Bellow insists on telling us, no longer feels that "he had got away with it." Though they had been married for some time before his wife Mary's prolonged visit to her mother, Leventhal is about to become a father for the first time. (His potency, Bellow suggests, is a consequence of his redemption.) For the most part, Leventhal's change, though genuine, is hardly noticeable, while Allbee's transformation is ostentatious, yet, as we discover on closer inspection, illusory. The inversion is ironic though somewhat easy. Leventhal, as real man, has through his redemption undergone a real change, while Allbee, the patina of a man, has achieved a factitious rebirth, a rebirth made possible by some kind of interior death.

The subplot, if it may properly be called that, which deals with Leventhal's brother Max's family, is contrapuntal to the main situation. Leventhal's reactions to his brother's family parallel and illuminate his behavior toward Allbee; the two separate and distinct contexts enable us to cross-check the validity of Leventhal's perceptions in each. With Max prospecting in Texas for a job and a place to settle, Leventhal feels responsible for his brother's wife and children, who live in depressed conditions in that oddly isolated section of New York City, Staten Island, and somewhat guilty for what seems to him Max's desertion of them. At the outset of the novel, Leventhal learns that his youngest nephew, Mickey, is sick and he leaves work during a rush period, initiating one guilt to propitiate another, to help his sister-in-law Elena. The ferry ride to Staten Island, which carries with it echoes of the mythic voyage across the river Styx into hell, operates in the novel as one of the physical manifestations of Leventhal's spiritual descent:

> There was a slow heave about the painted and rusted hulls in the harbor. The rain had gone out to the horizon, a dark band far overreaching the faint marks of the shore. On the water the air was cooler, but on the Staten Island side the green tarnished sheds were sweltering, the acres of cement widely spattered with sunlight. The disembarking crowd spread through them, going toward the line of busses that waited at the curb with threshing motors, in a shimmer of fumes. [p. 6]

The physical properties of Leventhal's outer world are always, in some form, manifestations of his inner disturbances—a paranoid's dream world.

At first Leventhal is unable to cope with Elena's old-world superstitions, but he finally persuades her to send Mickey, who has been running a high temperature, to a hospital so that he can be given the care he obviously needs. When Mickey dies in the hospital—it happens just when Leventhal feels himself inextricably trapped by Allbee's accusations—he suffers pangs of guilt as if by insisting on the hospital he has murdered the child. He senses in his confusion that Allbee's accusations are somehow justified in Mickey's death. The objects of his guilt proliferate. His guilt feelings toward Allbee are transferred to Elena who, he is willing to believe, holds him responsible for the death of his nephew. His sense of guilt for his brother's apparent failure as a father and his own failure to save Mickey is transferred in part to Allbee, one implementing and intensifying the other until Leventhal's guilt becomes objectless, all inclusive, unbearable. He drinks himself into oblivion immediately after he hears of Mickey's death, an act for him of moral suicide, an emulation (as penance) of Allbee's self-destructive pattern. Since Elena is not Jewish, Leventhal is particularly vulnerable to her opinions of him. Somewhere in the ether of his consciousness he disapproves of his brother's union, vaguely attributing a mixed marriage to a failure of principle on both sides. Yet, aware of his own inadequacy, and seeing it mirrored in his brother's apparent escape from family responsibilities, he senses that the failure is essentially on his side—his. Consequently, he resents what he imagines is Elena's (and more intensely her old-world mother's) right to disapprove of him. As in his relationship with Allbee, Leventhal feels persecuted because he believes he should be persecuted.

Haunted by the recollections of his mother's madness and the specter of his own potential, Leventhal thinks he sees his mother's tendencies manifested in Elena. Part of Leventhal's terrible sense of loss at Mickey's death comes from his covert identification with him; they are both victims, in a sense, of their mothers' insanity. Insanity, for Leventhal, is the nature of the destroyer, *is* the destroyer. When Allbee first confronts him with his accusations, Leventhal suspects him, though not without cause, of being demented. Out of his own chaos, Leventhal espies madness at every turn—Allbee, Rudiger, Elena, her mother—obsessively attributing to others his darkest fears about himself. However, Leventhal's world is, even from an objective point of view, somewhat insane. Therefore, within his distorted vision, a projecting into others his own deceived sense of himself, his perceptions are in part accurate. At the start of the novel he is somewhat aware of his tendency to misconceive in terms of his own preoccupations. For example, in his first view of Elena,

He observed that her eyes were anxious, altogether too bright and too liquid; there was a superfluous energy in her movements, a suggestion of distraction or even of madness not very securely held in check. But he was too
susceptible to such suggestions. He was aware of that, and he warned himself not to be hasty. [p. 7]

Though he overstates Elena's disturbance, which is temporary hyste-
ria, not insanity, Leventhal has enough control at this point to be aware
of the limited reliability of his view. Yet for all Leventhal's awareness
of his "susceptibility," under the combined pressures of Allbee's persecution and Mickey's illness and death, his rational monitor breaks
down; his vision becomes distorted. Unable to distinguish the external
world from his obsessive internal one, he loses almost all sense of reality and his perceptions become in effect insane.

Much of the impact of *The Victim* resides in Bellow's ability to keep
the reader's point of view limited to Leventhal's, making the reader a
sympathetic participant in his nightmare experience. At Mickey's funeral, Leventhal is horrified at what he is sure must be Elena's reaction
to him:

He gazed at Max's burly back and his sunburnt neck, and, as his glance
moved across the polished rows of benches, he saw Elena sitting between
Villani and a priest. The look she gave him was one of bitter anger. Though
the light was poor, there was no mistaking it. Her face was white and strain-
ing. "What've I done?" he thought; his panic was as great as if he had never
foreseen this. He was afraid to let her catch his eye and did not return her
look. . . . What would he do if then and there—imagining the worst—she
began to scream at him, accusing him? Once more she turned her face to
him over her shoulder; it seemed to be blazing in its whiteness. She must be
mad. [p. 182]

This is at once a powerful, realistic scene and an hallucinatory vision
not unworthy of Kafka. Nevertheless, that Elena hates Leventhal at this

time seems, given the picture we have had of Elena through Leventhal's eyes, more than possible. Nor can we easily dismiss Leventhal's suspicion of her madness—that too seems possible, even probable. We allow for a certain amount of exaggeration in Leventhal's perceptions, but they are, after all, the only ones we have to rely on. However, when we discover through Max's testimony that Leventhal has completely misread Elena's look, that if anything she is grateful to him rather than antipathetic, that she is not by any reasonable standard insane, we are jarred into re-evaluating the import of Leventhal's entire experience. Yet the possibility remains, though it is a slight one, that Max also may be mistaken. Bellow makes the problem of distinguishing appearance from reality, of affixing moral responsibility for particular and universal wrongs, seem all but prohibitively complex. Each discovery that Bellow permits us to make takes us farther away from a pure and simple answer, yet nearer to the final discovery that there is no discoverable final truth, only a profound and ambiguous approximation of it.

Caught up in a cycle of guilt and persecution, as Leventhal becomes more obsessed with being persecuted he becomes correspondingly more guilt-ridden. Leventhal's behavior toward his former employer and friend Williston curiously parallels Allbee's toward Leventhal. Believing out of a sense of persecution that the uncommitted Williston is sympathetic to Allbee, Leventhal goes to his home and irrationally accuses his friend of having done him an injury. Leventhal's accusations, like Allbee's of him, are vague insinuations, implying a conspiratorial awareness on the part of his hallucinated betrayer. Provoked by Leventhal's badgering, Williston satisfies Leventhal's ambivalent quest for absolution and punishment, and admits that he considers Leventhal in part responsible for Allbee's loss of his job. In response, Leventhal asserts, imitating Allbee's manner of defensive attack, that Williston's position is only a more genteel version of Allbee's, that Williston, underneath his platitudinous liberalism, is also anti-Semitic. Defensive, Williston insists that he does not think that Leventhal actually *intended* to hurt Allbee, though it is an admissible possibility, but whatever his intentions the effect was the same; Rudiger fired Allbee because of Leventhal (which is another of their double correspondences). Though the explanations Leventhal wrests from Williston are painful to him, he compulsively provokes them, a fascinated spectator at his own execution. "'So . . .' Leventhal said blankly, 'In a way it really seems to be my fault, doesn't it?' He paused and gazed abstractly at Williston, his hands still motionless at his knees" (p. 117). Though Leventhal has a moment before accused Williston of prejudice, he readily accepts Williston's verdict. This is Leventhal's first explicit admission of blame for Allbee's comedown, though he had implicitly accepted it all along. However, his *conscious* acceptance of responsibility is a moral act that makes possible his ultimate redemption.

This leads us to the central moral dilemma of the novel: How far can a man be held responsible for the unintentional consequences of his acts? Bellow never wholly resolves the question, but he suggests that the intention and the act are not ethically separable, that morality relies on each man's existential responsibility for his acts. Yet Bellow is aware that absolute responsibility is an impossible ideal, a saint's ideal, and that, in a practical, moral sense, an intentional evil is more egregious than an unconscious one. Though Leventhal assures himself that he had not insulted Rudiger to get back at Allbee, he is nevertheless disturbed because he suspects that Williston has not believed him; his persecution, as always, extends beyond his culpability.

What Allbee and Leventhal share most is the feeling that the dark forces that control civilization are for one reason or another persecuting them. A New Englander with aristocratic pretensions, Allbee equates New Yorkers with the "children of Caliban" (Jews of a kind), who have persecuted him by driving out the light as "Moses punished the Egyptians with darkness." Ironically, Allbee is in a sense more Jewish than Leventhal. His anti-Semitic obsessions have made him more profoundly involved with Jewish tradition and more knowledgeable about Judaism itself than his Jewish enemy. If Allbee's is the guilt of the persecutor, then in some essential way the persecutor and persecuted are one. The Jew and Jew-hater, as close as opposing magnetic poles, become, in their mutual isolation and self-hate, interchangeable—indistinguishable.

Leventhal, a victim of real and imaginary persecution, feels guilty because he believes that his suffering, like all suffering, is deserved, yet he cannot recognize his own mortal sin. At the same time he suspects that civilization, alien to the Jew, is a manifestation of a universal conspiracy, malevolent and unseen, determined on persecuting the outsider—Leventhal. Throughout the novel, Leventhal, as if rolling the stone of Sisyphus, seeks to find out if there is a black list in his profession, some vague conspiracy that performs in microcosm the Great Work of Universal Injustice. At various times it seems to him that he has uncovered the conspiracy in action, with its hand in the till, so to speak, though he is never able to confirm his suspicions.

At their final meeting, the "successful" Allbee tells Leventhal that he has "made his peace with whoever runs things." In other words, Allbee has sacrificed his vestigial sense of self to survive in a world he had, though unknowingly, made. The irony is that he has "made his peace" not with the real world but with his own paranoiac version of it. As Allbee leaves, Leventhal, unrestrainedly curious, calls after him: "'Wait a minute, what's your idea who runs things?'" Allbee has already gone; Leventhal never gets an answer. "Who runs things" is the final insoluble mystery.

If Allbee is Leventhal's antagonist, and double, he is also Leventhal's savior, the unwitting means to his redemption. A similar ritual process takes place for Tommy Wilhelm in *Seize the Day* and Henderson in *Henderson the Rain King*. Allbee, like Tamkin, like Dahfu, is a kind of fraud-saint, a redeemer in spite of himself. All of Bellow's novels, with the possible exception of *The Adventures of Augie March*, deal with the sufferer, the seismographic recorder of world guilt who, confronted by a guilt-distorted correlative of himself, seeks within the bounds of his own hell the means to his heaven. Leventhal is redeemed through succumbing to the temptations of his devil; he crosses the threshold of hell, descends to its deepest parts and, heroically, for Leventhal is finally a hero, comes back again, better if not greatly wiser.

3

The best of our novelists seem to achieve one transcendent performance, followed by self-imitation, or loss of energy, or the substitution of will for creation. Wright Morris is an exception; Saul Bellow is another. Though less prolific than Morris, Bellow has a greater range of concerns and is, on the whole, a more profound if less uncompromisingly difficult a novelist. In an essay in *Esquire*, characteristically entitled "No! in Thunder," Leslie Fiedler, one of Bellow's earliest admirers, admonishes Bellow for resolving *Henderson the Rain King* affirmatively, because (and I am somewhat oversimplifying Fiedler's position) the only honest response to the contemporary world is denial. Though Fiedler's construction is not wholly unreasonable, he argues it too literally (as Stevens tells us, "After the final no there comes a yes") and applies it speciously as if it were an aesthetic principle. Moreover, in making his point, Fiedler misreads, or rather narrowly reads, the ending of Bellow's novel. What is being affirmed in Henderson's ecstatic run across the Newfoundland ice? Contemporary civilization? The universe? Hardly. The regeneration of the self, the endurance of the spirit? In part. It is Henderson, however, not Bellow, who is euphoric; it is Henderson who is celebrating his survival, who is affirming the regeneration of his life. It is rather late in the day to be confusing a first-person protagonist with his author, but that, in effect, is what Fiedler has done. In other parts of the novel, Henderson experiences a similar euphoria (he is chronically manic), an hallucinatory sense of well-being, only to discover afterward that he has beguiled himself. The ending is at least in part ironic; otherwise why have Henderson's affirmation of life take place on a lifeless wasteland? One might answer, of course, because it happens in Newfoundland. But isn't that just the point of Bellow's irony? The new-found land is desolate; Henderson's new-found self is also somewhat illusory. Here, as throughout the novel, Henderson is quixotic. Bellow is not, however, wholly undercutting his hero. The scene is not *just* ironic as it is not just affirmative. Henderson's survival of his adventures in that treacherous dream Africa of the spirit, with all his extraordinary powers of strength and energy undiminished by the bruises of time, is in itself remarkable. As always, Henderson reasons with his feelings, not his brain, and it is his energy—the source of his life—not his self-knowledge, that he is celebrating. Henderson's ecstatic self-affirmation, "running—leaping, leaping, pounding, and tingling over the pure white lining of the gray arctic silence," is possible only where there is no real world about to deny it—where there is nothing crucial at stake to expose his well-meaning ineptitude. That Henderson, in spite of all evidence to the contrary, retains his blind illusions is his absurdity as well as his redeeming grace.

Where Bellow's first two novels are somewhat indebted to Dosto-evsky and Kafka, *Henderson the Rain King* is a unique and adventurous work. It is also a conspicuously American book in the great tradition of the romance novel from Hawthorne and Melville through Faulkner. After Faulkner, Bellow is our major novelist, and his achievement (with Faulkner's) has provided seed for what appears to be one of the strongest crops of fiction in our history. The confrontation of Leventhal with Allbee, of man with his own distorted image, his fallen self, and the consequent recognition of an apparently boundless guilt, for which he suffers and for which he achieves through suffering the possibility, or illusion, of redemption, has become in various disguises one of the abiding concerns of the contemporary American novel and one of the profound moral myths of these anguished, bomb-haunted times.

From *The Landscape of Nightmare: Studies in the Contemporary Novel* (1965) by Jonathan Baumbach. Copyright © 1965 by New York University Press. Reprinted with permission of New York University Press.

Notes

1. Saul Bellow, *Dangling Man* (New York: Vanguard Press, 1944), p. 9. All quotations are from this edition.
2. Saul Bellow, *The Victim* (New York: Viking Press, Compass Books, 1956), p. 3. All quotations are from this edition.

Saul Bellow:
The Adventures of Augie March_____
Donald Pizer

Saul Bellow's third novel, published in 1953 when he was thirty-eight, differs sharply from his first two works of fiction, *Dangling Man* (1944) and *The Victim* (1947). These are novels of conscious compression and chill intellectuality in which the theme of man as victim and sufferer predominates.[1] In *The Adventures of Augie March*, however, Bellow sought a new manner and a new theme, as is suggested by his choice of a picaresque title. Informality, looseness, and a corresponding expansiveness of subject matter characterize this new work. The book "came easily," Bellow later recalled. "I kicked over the traces, wrote catch-as-catch-can, picaresque. I took my chance."[2] This "chance" included Bellow's endowing Augie with one of the most richly evocative prose styles in modern American fiction, a style dense with colloquial diction and rhythms (often Yiddish in origin), with classical, literary, and historical allusions, and with frequent echoes of Thoreau, Whitman, and Mark Twain. They also include his creation of Augie as an urban Jewish transcendental hero—a figure Chicago-born but seeking his identity and thus his fate with confidence that at the center of his nature (the "axial lines" of self) there lie as well the great moral absolutes of life: truth, love, peace, and harmony.

Augie March has therefore often been viewed as Bellow's most engaging novel but as both simpler and more positive than either his earlier or later fiction. The appeal of the work, it is felt, lies largely in its "gritty social texture"[3] (particularly the depiction of Augie's Chicago youth) and in the witty freedom of Augie's narrative style. Augie's quest for a "better fate" is an appropriately self-apparent theme within this obviousness and looseness of form and style. In fact, however, *The Adventures of Augie March* is neither ingenuous nor obvious. Rather it explores with considerable complexity and depth the naturalistic absorption in the precarious balance between the conditioning forces of life and man's desire and need to discover centers of value and affirmation despite the presence of these forces.[4]

Perhaps the best way to introduce this theme is not through such often cited passages as the breezy opening or the "axial lines" section or the Columbus metaphor of the final lines but rather in the incident of Augie and the maid Jacqueline in the last chapter of the novel. Augie is dropping off the old, fat, and ugly Jacqueline at her Normandy home for Christmas when their car breaks down and they have to trudge the last few miles through the mud. Jacqueline tells him, as they sing to keep warm, of her dream of going to Mexico some day, a dream which Augie later recalls as he continues his journey to Bruges on a cold and dark December afternoon, amid the ruins of war.

> But, thinking of Jacqueline and Mexico, I got to grinning again. That's the *animal ridens* in me, the laughing creature, forever rising up. What's so laughable, that a Jacqueline, for instance, as hard used as that by rough forces, will still refuse to lead a disappointed life? Or is the laugh at nature—including eternity—that it thinks it can win over us and the power of hope? Nah, nah! I think. It never will. But that probably is the joke, on one or the other, and laughing is an enigma that includes both.[5]

Augie March is about the "rough forces" of experience, about all that compels and conditions and shapes man, particularly the shaping power of other human wills. It is also about the darkness in nature, the nature of decay and death rather than of eternal renewal. And it is also about the human effort to maintain hope despite these realities, the hope which musters as much grace and wit as is possible in the face of the permanent and insoluble enigma of man's condition. *Augie March*, in short, for all its comic vibrancy, picaresque swiftness of movement, and larky prose is also a naturalistic novel of ideas. Events and people represent specific phases of Augie's effort to understand both the "rough forces" of life and the nature of hope. They represent as well specific contributions to his ultimate discovery that in comic awareness there is a means toward accommodation, if not resolution, of the fundamental conflict between experience and expectation.

* * *

Bellow has often commented in his interviews and essays that "we live among ideas"[6] and that "it is a great defect of American novelists that they shun thinking."[7] But Bellow the ideologue—the honor graduate in anthropology and the *Encyclopedia Britannica* editor—is also Bellow the admirer of "hard facts"[8] in fiction who was first drawn to the possibilities of the novel by his interest in the midwest realists.[9] These two qualities of Bellow the novelist merge in *The Adventures of Augie March* to produce a picaresque novel in which Augie's adventures are not only among ideas but themselves represent a number of large-scale ideas. Augie is both a Chicago-bred youth of the 1920s and 30s and the universal seeker of the permanent values of life. He is a grail quester in the guise of a young man from the city, and the grail he seeks is his own identity.

One of Augie's major characteristics as a seeker is his pretense of dullness or ignorance—somewhat like Henry James' Maisie or Mark Twain's Huck Finn—in order to avoid capture by the armed marauders of the world. He is also—and more significantly—like Dreiser's Carrie in that his seemingly aimless drifting, which includes a willingness to be convinced and directed, is in fact a capacity to drift in directions which he himself desires. Augie for the most part is an absorber and receiver, "a listener by upbringing," who gives "soft answers" to affronts (72, 81). Part of his survival capacity derives from his ability to absorb the hard knocks of experience without "special grief, . . . being by and large too larky and boisterous" to take them "to heart" (12). To survive while continuing to search, without doing harm to others, is his operative ethic; all other moral questions are a matter of context. He steals on several occasions but not on others, despite the opportunity, and he sleeps with some girls but not with one who appears reluctant, since "you never know what forms self-respect will take" (243). As the archetypal seeker, he is above all, despite occasional dry thoughts in dry seasons, a man of hope. After the disappointments and calamities of his Mexican adventure, he is "aged by hard going and experience" (431) and "more larky formerly than now" (447), but the close of the novel still finds him a believer in "the power of hope" (536).

Augie's world also has an unchanging character despite his twenty years of adventure in Chicago, Mexico, New York, and Europe. Because Augie is everywhere a seeker of his own identity, he finds everywhere those anxious for various suspect reasons to offer themselves as guides. Only the superficial character of life changes—man as Machiavelli, as manipulator of others for his own ends, is omnipresent.[10] Bellow expresses this theme of the repetitive nature of experience in a number of ways. One is the device usually foreign to the picaresque novel of the reappearing and unchanging minor character. Augie back in Chicago after his Mexican venture soon encounters almost all the figures, in their accustomed "humour" roles, who made up his Chicago experience before his journey, and several of these characters later reappear in New York and Paris. It is perhaps above all Sylvester, a drifter like Augie whom Augie meets some half-dozen or more times in wildly unlikely places, who symbolizes the notion that Augie's world is the same wherever he goes. It is no wonder that at the close of the novel, even while living in Paris, Augie can claim that "it's all the same to me where I live" (531). Another way in which Bellow enforces the theme of the unity of experience is by enclosing Augie's adventures within a repetitive mesh of personal relationships, in which someone always knows someone else—not only in Chicago, where the device is almost a running joke—but elsewhere as well. So, for example, in an incident which epitomizes this aspect of the novel, Augie in a lifeboat in the North Atlantic finds that he and the only other occupant of the boat are from the same Chicago neighborhood and have acquaintances in common.

Perhaps the most striking evidence of Bellow's insistence on the underlying similarity of all experience is his attitude toward the past. Of course, he suggests in *Augie March* that the distant past and the present are different in many superficial ways, and that they are significantly different in that the values derived from a pastoral world have little meaning in a modern urban civilization. But at the heart of Augie's adventures is the assumption that the figures he encounters—figures who constitute his experience of the present—are universal types with evocative historical prototypes. As a reader of the Harvard Classics, among other such works, Augie is aware of these parallels and thus often creates a rich layer of allusion to suggest the similarities between past and present. This is a strategy we are most familiar with in modern literature in the "epic" poetry of Eliot and Pound. Augie adopts this technique, however, not to suggest the decay of value in the present, which is Eliot and Pound's intent, but rather, as in his comparison of Einhorn to Caesar, Ulysses, and Louis xiv (or as in Bellow's own "Roman texture" in the novel as a whole, with such character names as Augustus, Thea, Stella, and Caligula) to suggest the permanence and continuity of the heroic temperament, even in a crippled Chicago small-time operator. When Einhorn also indulges in such comparisons, Augie comments, "If you want to pick your own ideal creature in the mirror coastal air and sharp leaves of ancient perfections and be at home where a great mankind was at home, I've never seen any reason why not" (76).

Yet the theme of the unchanging in time and place—and therefore of the archetypal in Augie's quest—is but one of two major threads in *Augie March*. For within the broad configuration of the statically universal in Augie's experience is also a theme of variation and change. Augie encounters different kinds of pressure to accept some qualification of his quest, and he gradually clarifies the nature of his search. The naturalism of *Augie March* lies in the collision at various points in the novel of experience and vision.

"Experience"—for Augie, his "adventures"—is principally social, and "vision" also arises from an understanding of oneself in relation to others. Augie rejects the two traditional alternative sources of wisdom—the plumbing of nature and the isolation of the self. The modern world, he soon discovers, contains "no shepherd-Sicily, no free-hand nature-painting" where he can find his Edenic self, but only "deep city vexations" where "you are forced early into deep city aims" (84). Complete withdrawal into the self is also dismissed by Augie. His friend, the "melancholy and brilliant" Kayo Obermark, "thought the greatest purity was outside human relations, that those only begot lies and cabbage-familiarity" (259). But though Augie admires the intellectual idealism of Kayo's view, he also resists it. "I had the idea," he thinks, "that you don't take so wide a stand that it makes a human life impossible, nor try to bring together irreconcilables that destroy you, but try out what of human you can live with first." "Imperfection," Augie concludes, "is always the condition as found; all great beauty too, my scratched eyeballs will always see scratched" (260).

So when Augie early in the novel offers the Whitmanesque formula that "all the influences were lined up waiting for me. I was born, and there they were to form me, which is why I tell you more of them than of myself" (43), he means people, just as at the end of the novel he means people when he remarks that he will continue his quest among "those near-at-hand" (536). The people in Augie's life have a general sameness, as I noted earlier and as Tony Tanner states even more strongly in his comment that they "tend to add up to a sort of general presence of the not-Augie as opposed to the Augie."[11] The "not-Augie" figures in Augie's life do indeed share a number of qualities. Many of them are like the owner of a dog grooming service for whom Augie works briefly. The owner's relations with the animals, Augie recalls, "was a struggle. He was trying to wrest something from them. I don't know what. Perhaps that their conception of a dog should be what his was" (185). Figures of this kind wish to help Augie, to groom him for life (in fact, many do reclothe him), but they also wish him to share their conception of what he is. "Sharing" is thus a loaded term in *Augie March:* it implies the use of someone for one's own emotional or psychological purposes disguised as a wish to help. As Augie says of a particularly troublesome friend in Mexico, "He saw to it that his lot was shared, like everybody else, and did something with you to compel you to feel what he felt" (368). Augie's relations with such figures are similar to that of Huck Finn with the Duke and Dauphin. Augie resists them as best he can, but he is saved largely by the inherent weakness of the figures—Grandma Lausch's pride, Thea's inhumanity, Basteshaw's "brain fever"—which causes their fall from power. Yet Augie, like Huck, often finds himself pitying and looking after those who sought to control him and mold his fate.

Not all of the "not-Augie" characters in *Augie March* are Machiavellian controllers. The influences which are lined up in wait for Augie include several different kinds of relationship, from the crudest users of raw power in order to control to those who shape and mold through the giving of themselves in love. The reappearance of basically similar types in Augie's life suggests that the form of *Augie March* is only superficially the linear one of most picaresque fiction, in which different kinds of adventures follow each other in no apparent order. *Augie March* is really a series of circles, of repetitive patterns without end as Augie encounters again and again characters whose involvement with him represents a reappearance of one of the basic ways in which one person affects another. *Augie March* is therefore much like *U.S.A.* in that the superficially disparate—the twelve narratives of *U.S.A.*, the many adventures of Augie—in fact constitute a deeply interwoven and thematically unified structure.

The earliest cluster of figures whom Augie encounters is that of a number of "adopters"—those who in the act of helping Augie as a fatherless and almost destitute youth also require that he play specific roles within their families. Grandma Lausch is the first such figure in Augie's life. Deprived of a base in her own family because her daughters-in-law refuse to countenance her domineering ways, she "adopts" all the Marches in order to fulfill her need "to direct a house, to command, to govern, to manage, scheme, devise, and intrigue" (5). Her shrewdness and strength of will contribute to the survival of the Marches, but she asks in return obedience and fear. Her hold is broken when she as well as Augie and his brother Simon grow older, and Augie next comes under the influence of the Coblins, an earthy and generous family for whom he works. Since the Coblins have a son who has run away to the marines and a daughter who stutters, they welcome Augie as a candidate for both son and son-in-law. But though Augie is attracted by the larger-than-life warmth and vitality of the Coblins, he resists these roles and moves on to the Renlings. The Renlings are well-to-do—they clothe Augie in princely fashion from their store— and thus offer him a major social advance. But Mrs. Renling is child-less and wishes to enclose Augie in the silken threads of her mater-nal longing. When she mentions adoption, Augie flees her "tender weights" (152). The last and most powerful of the families which want to adopt Augie are the Magnuses. Large, gross, vulgar, and extremely rich, they have already absorbed and almost devoured Simon, provid-ing him with both a wife and a business. They offer to Augie the luxury and power of great wealth, of an opulence which intimates that he is to be adopted not so much by the family as by "things themselves" (238).

From Grandma Lausch to the Magnuses, the "adopters" derive their strength from Augie's material needs. As Augie matures, however, he comes under the equally powerful influence of "true believers" who seek to enlist him in the pursuit of their vision of life. These are the "theoreticians" whom Augie berates toward the close of the novel— the "big personalities, destiny molders, and heavy-water brains, Machiavellis and wizard evildoers, big-wheels and imposers-upon, ab-solutists" (524). The appeal of these figures is analogous to that of the adopters. The first offer the security of material comfort, the second of unquestioning belief. The first provide within the closed structure of the family a refuge against the world, the second within the equally closed structures of such intellectual systems as primitivism and sci-entism an equally snug refuge against intrusive ideas. Yet both in fact are prisons of body, mind, and spirit.

Thea is Augie's first major theoretician. Augie is drawn to her initially by her extraordinary will and "strong nerve" (145) and then is bound by his love. He accompanies her to Mexico because "I went where and as she said and did whatever she wanted because I was threaded to her as if through the skin" (315). Her goal in Mexico is ostensibly to train an eagle in falconry, but in reality it is to uncover in animal life the courage and strength of will which she believes lacking in man and, more specifically, in Augie. If Caligula the eagle can be trained to display these qualities, perhaps Augie can; perhaps man, in short, can rise to the purity of animal power. But in a wonderfully comic parody of the primitivism of Lawrence's *The Plumed Serpent* and Hemingway's *Death in the Afternoon* and *The Green Hills of Africa*, Caligula turns out to be not a "cruel machine" of nature but cautious and even cowardly (355).[12] His fear of the sharp-clawed lizards which he is asked to hunt confirms not the potential inhumanity of man but the potential humanity of animals. As Augie wryly comments after one of Caligula's failures, "Well, it was hard to take this from wild nature, that there should be humanity mixed with it" (355). Man, with his "faulty humanity" (379), cannot absorb from nature codes of life which in fact do not exist either in man or in nature. Thea the theoretician cannot accept this, and she responds to Caligula's failure by discarding both him and Augie and by moving on to snakes. "'You're not special,'" she tells Augie. "'You're like everybody else'" (396).

The other major theoretician whom Augie encounters is Basteshaw, the biologist and ship's carpenter with whom he shares a lifeboat after their freighter is torpedoed during the war. If Thea wishes to confirm an idea about nature, Basteshaw wishes in his experiments to manipulate nature itself. Neither has respect for nature or man, only for the imperatives of his own belief. Basteshaw wants to discover the secret of the origin of life, and when Augie resists enlistment in this effort ("Damn you guys," he cries, "you don't care how you fiddle with nature" [506]), he finds himself batted over the head with an oar and made part of it willy-nilly. So the mad scientists of the world, Bellow's miniature allegory goes, have made us all captives of their "fiddling" with nature.[13]

The adopters and theoreticians in Augie's life wish to control him. But Augie also encounters two other important groups of figures in his adventures who, though they occasionally use him, function principally to reveal to him the nature and dangers of the pursuit of an independent fate. The first such group consists of characters who appear to be seeking their own destinies but who in fact are fulfilling themselves only superficially or incompletely. Sylvester is an obvious example of a figure of this kind. Trying this and that—movie manager, engineer, subway guard, revolutionary—in all parts of the world, he appears to mirror Augie's own life. But unlike Augie, his "adventures" are without a center; he is merely physically footloose and intellectually unanchored and he thus reveals that to move is not necessarily to seek.[14]

Augie's brother Simon is a far more significant foil to Augie's quest. Of Augie's two brothers, Georgie is mentally defective and therefore "simple" while Simon is shrewd and worldly. He appears to be pursuing his fate with insight and strength as with "singleness of purpose" (29) he seeks to reach particular goals at particular moments of his life—to be top boy in high school, to be a gentleman, and to have attractive women and great wealth. He is a kind of latter-day Frank Cowperwood (who also flourished in the tough competitive world of Chicago) in that he too makes "I satisfy myself" the guiding principle of his life. "'You don't care what happens to anybody else as long as you get yours'" (196), he tells Augie. He gets his by becoming a Magnus and thus acquiring Cadillacs and mistresses. But if Augie is in part Simon in his fondness for opulence, Simon is in part Augie in that he cannot be happy in an identity which is not entirely his own. "'We're the same and want the same'" (199), he tells Augie, meaning that they both desire the power of wealth. But their more important similarity is that neither is comfortable playing roles. Simon therefore desperately hopes that Augie will also marry into the Magnus family and thus confirm the role of loud vulgarian which is now Simon's as a Magnus. The violent rage with which Simon confronts all life by the end of the novel is really a rage against himself. If Sylvester's mobility is directionless, Simon's success is empty. In the end, he is simple Simon.

Whereas the fates of Sylvester and Simon suggest to Augie that in the pursuit of one's identity the means can be confused with the end, Einhorn and Mintouchian express values which help Augie in the crystallization of the nature of his quest. They are, in short, less foils than mentors, albeit themselves flawed examples of the values they endorse.

Einhorn, whom Augie meets while still in early adolescence, remains for him throughout the novel a source of admiration for his "philosophical capacity" (60) and his freedom from custom and cant. Augie particularly values Einhorn's desire to be free from the ideological bonds which tie most men. "'There's law, and then there's Nature,'" he tells Augie. "'There's opinion and then there's Nature. Somebody has to get outside of law and opinion and speak for Nature'" (67). So Einhorn is "absolutely outspoken about vital things" (74). As Augie remarks, "Much that was nameless to many people through disgust or shame he didn't mind naming to himself or to a full confidant (or pretty nearly so) like me, and caught, used, and worked all feelings freely" (68). The deep irony of Einhorn's life is that he himself is severely crippled and is thus seemingly a victim of the nature he speaks for. But the same spirit which refuses to accept convention will not accept that desire can be confined and limited by a wheelchair. As far as sex is concerned, "He wouldn't stay a cripple, Einhorn; he couldn't hold his soul in it" (78).

Augie comes to esteem Einhorn greatly—particularly for "the fight he had made on his sickness" (100)—and to recognize the complexity and richness of his character beneath the layer of petty shystering. Einhorn is thus something of a naturalistic hero—a figure of depth and pathos despite his shabby ways. In one of the more striking scenes of the novel, we encounter him taking Augie to a whorehouse as a high school graduation present and riding on Augie's back from the car to the house composed and dignified, with aplomb and in control. He is also something of a father to Augie and is well positioned to effect an "adoption," since he offers both an understanding of Augie's character ("'You've got *opposition* in you'" [117]) and an illustration of the ideal of freedom. Yet Augie holds back because he senses an important limitation in Einhorn's character—that he does not understand the nature of love. For out of his needs and out of his philosophical materialism, Einhorn conceives of relations between the sexes as entirely physical and of relations among men as destructively competitive. He cannot understand, for example, Augie's unwillingness to revenge himself on Simon (who has wronged Augie and deserves vengeance) because Augie loves Simon, since he holds that "in the naked form of the human jelly, one should choose or seize with force" (183). So Augie drifts away from Einhorn, despite what he has learned from him. He senses that his fate is neither the role nor the burden of the youth who bore Einhorn to the whorehouse.

Late in the novel, Augie meets Mintouchian, a figure who closely resembles Einhorn, as Augie himself remarks. An operator on an international scale, as Einhorn was in the Chicago neighborhoods, Mintouchian, like Einhorn, recognizes few restraints to his personal freedom while expressing an appealing philosophical position. "A great man," Augie comments, "he was another of those persons who persistently arise before me with life counsels and illuminations" (478). Appropriately as an internationalist of the 1940s, Mintouchian's principal "illumination" is an existential emphasis on man's need for self-definition through experience. He tells Augie, who requires endorsement of this idea at this point, "'You must take your chance on what you are. And you can't sit still. . . . It is better to die what you are than to live a stranger forever'" (485). But again like Einhorn, Mintouchian is flawed in his distrust of love. Since he believes that all life, including love, is change, he is unable to accept that love can exist without the deception and deceit which change brings. For Augie, who is about to marry Stella, this view is as unacceptable as was Einhorn's advice about Simon.

* * *

Augie's journey through life in search of his identity involves not only encounters with those who are able to influence his sense of him-self—the adopters, theoreticians, and counselors of the world—but also experience of the permanent and irremediable conditions of life which threaten selfhood itself. The most important of these conditions is that of the inevitability of material dissolution and thus the certainty that death and oblivion are the only ends we can know. Augie's quest contains the fundamental irony that the process of finding oneself in time is also that of losing oneself. No wonder that he responds feel-ingly to Einhorn's fear of death, "who maybe was the only real god he had" (83), and that he remarks that "it takes some of us a long time to find out what the price is of being in nature, and what the facts are about your tenure" (362). In Mexico, where graves and corpses are ne-glected, Augie observes "how openly death is received everywhere, in the beauty of the place, and how it is acknowledged that anyone may be roughly handled—the proudest—pinched, slapped, and set down, thrown down; for death throws even worse in men's faces and makes it horrible and absurd that one never touched should be roughly dumped under, dumped upon" (338). And the meaning of this unavoidable real-ity, Augie comes to recognize fully at the close of the novel in a Europe crowded with ancient and fresh dead, is that "Death is going to take the boundaries away from us, that we should no more be persons. That's what death is about" (519).

Death in its "rough handling" of human individuality has an equiva-lent in life itself—the "darkness" of man at his most indiscriminately bestial and thus least distinctive and individual. In a West Side police station, in a strikingly Dreiserian passage, Augie notes that it was very dark. It was spoiled, diseased, sore and running. And as the mis-minted and wrong-struck figures and faces stooped, shambled, strode, gazed, dreaded, surrendered, didn't care—unfailing, the surplus and super-abundance of human material—you wondered that all was stuff that was born human and shaped human, and over the indiscriminateness and lack of choice. (229)

Yet despite the "rough handling" of death and the "darkness" of animal man (images which are to peak in Augie's final reflections about Jac-queline), man, Augie decides, still must live and hope. After his crimi-nal friend Joe Gorman—a figure out of *Studs Lonigan*—is captured and beaten by the police, a depressed Augie makes his way back to Chicago:

However, as I felt on entering Erie, Pennsylvania, there is a darkness. It is for everyone. . . . Only some Greeks and admirers of theirs, in their liquid noon, where the friendship of beauty to human things was perfect, thought they were clearly divided from this darkness. And these Greeks too were in it. But still they are the admiration of the rest of the mud-sprung, famine-knifed, street pounding, war-rattled, painstaking, kicked in the belly, grief and cartilage mankind. (175)

We accept that darkness is for everybody, but we admire those who believe in the light, and we model our lives on this paradox. So Augie decides to write up his "adventures" not because this act will help him to escape oblivion but as an act of "being what he is" and thus of living in the spirit of Greek (and existential) idealism. He writes, he tells us, "not in order to be so highly significant but probably because human beings have the power to say and ought to employ it at the proper time. When finally you're done speaking you're dumb forever after, and when you're through stirring you go still, but this is no reason to de-cline to speak and stir or to be what you are" (519).

Bellow wrote in a characteristic statement in 1960 that "this society with its titanic products conditions but cannot absolutely denature us. It forces certain elements of the genius of our species to go into hiding."[15] Augie's adventures occur within these limits, since they are experiences which identify the conditioning forces of modern life while revealing the difficulty of discovering one's humanity and selfhood. Because Augie's identity is "in hiding," he can express it only in opposition (his "great desire to offer resistance and to say No!" [117]) or in vagueness ("a good enough fate" [28]). "What did I . . . want for myself?" he asks at one point. "I couldn't have told you. . . . I knew I longed very much, but I didn't understand for what" (84). So Augie "tries various things on" (206) throughout his career—from the intellectual life to union organizing, from the coal business to the international black market—and at the close of the novel is still doing so, is still engaged in "this pilgrimage of mine" (424). He does so not in pride—"who was I, not to make up my mind and be so obstinate" (424)—but in fear. As he tells Mintouchian, though "'I have always tried to become what I am . . . , what if what I am by nature isn't good enough?'" (485). Augie's aimlessness thus has strength and courage at its core. To be "in opposition" requires these attributes when the forces seeking control are everywhere and when the outcome of the quest is so much in doubt.

Throughout his indefinable search for a better fate, Augie encounters the view that most men have their fates determined for them. Einhorn supports a belief in the conditioned nature of experience when he notes that the slums will produce each year a large number of criminals and syphilitics. "'It's practically determined,'" he says. But Einhorn goes on to qualify his deterministic ideas when he tells Augie, "'And if you're going to let it be determined for you too, you're a sucker'" (117). Knowledge of a conditioning force, Einhorn implies, offers potential evasion of that force. Later, Augie discusses with the tough and cynical Mimi a more significant and for Augie a more relevant kind of determinism—that our characters are our fates in the negative sense of the effect of our unchangeable weaknesses upon our lives. Mimi notes that most people suffer greatly in life: "They suffer from what they are, such as they are. . . . They'll never change, one beautiful morning. They can't change. So maybe you're lucky. But others are stuck; they have what they have; and if that's their truth, where are we?" (254-55) But, Augie responds, "Me, I couldn't think all was so poured in concrete and that there weren't occasions for happiness that weren't illusions of people still permitted to be forgetful of permanent disappointment, more or less permanent pain . . . ; and maybe most intolerable the hardening of detestable character, like bone" (255). Augie himself lives out these qualifications of a conditioned life. He escapes a slum fate in part because of his knowledge of that fate, and he and Mimi find that all is not poured in concrete, that happiness can be real despite the deep disappointments of life caused by permanent flaws of character. Mimi becomes pregnant by the aloof and self-centered political science student Hooker Frazer and requires an abortion. But unlike Roberta in *An American Tragedy*, whose pregnancy is an example of the misery of human powerlessness, she and Augie discover, in the very effort to resolve her dilemma, "occasional happiness"—the happiness of their pride and strength of will and mutual commitment as they work together, in the face of the indifference and cruelty of their Chicago boarding house world, to liberate her from her condition.

In Mexico, Augie feels himself especially powerless, caught as he is in his love for Thea. Nevertheless, in a moment of insight he arrives at a deep understanding of the compensations for powerlessness within the human condition. On a porch he notices some poinsettias and also a small caged animal, and comments: "It said a lot to me that these flowers should have no power over their place of appearance, nor over the time, and yet be such a success of beauty and plaster the insignificant wall. I saw also the little kinkajou who roved over his square of cage in every dimension, upside down, backwards. In the depth of accident, you be supple—never sleepy but at sleeping time" (366).[16] The rebellious and resistant No, a self-preserving knowledge, occasional happiness, beauty and suppleness—so we not only endure but often flourish within our conditioned existence, in our cages of whatever kind. And these compensations, Augie claims, exist not merely in our imaginations and hopes (the conventional source of compensation) but in the "real world," as Augie himself has found during his adventures: "Everyone tries to create a world he can live in, and what he can't use he often can't see. But the real world is already created, and if your fabrication doesn't correspond, then even if you feel noble and insist on there being something better than what people call reality, that better something needn't try to exceed what, in its actuality, since we know it so little, may be very surprising" (378).

Augie's "axial lines of life" declaration is thus not an isolated triumphant discovery of man's distinctive potential (as it is often viewed) but rather one of a number of compensations for man's conditioned state which Augie has found. Augie, as he tells his friend Clem, "'was lying on the couch here before and they [the axial lines] went quivering right straight through me. Truth, love, peace, bounty, usefulness, harmony!'" (454). This experience of truth, Augie realizes, is available to all men, to "'man himself, finite and taped as he is. . . . Even his pains will be joy if they are true, even his helplessness will not take away his power. . . . The embrace of other true people will take away his dread of fast change and short life'" (455). Man's helplessness, his condition of finiteness as a "taped" creature within "fast change"—all the rough forces and darkness of life—are not denied in this passage. Rather, they exist in conjunction with various compensating counter forces, in this instance that of the joy and power and community contained in the recognition of the great truths of human aspiration.

It is in the human capacity to love deeply that Bellow in *Augie March* offers his most moving example of the naturalistic paradox which runs throughout the novel—that in imprisonment we still find value and meaning. Augie is first introduced to the idea that love can be a destructive controlling force by Grandma Lausch, who tells him that "'The more you love people the more they'll mix you up'" (9) and by Jimmy Klein, who explains to him that the desire for sex leads inevitably to the prison of the family. But Augie's first major encounter with the full ambivalence of love is in the example of Mimi, whom he meets before he himself falls deeply in love with Thea. Mimi is a hard, tough, spirited girl who is very much like Augie himself in her larkiness and opposition. But she is also a slave to love; all meaning in life for her "rested on the gentleness in privacy of man and woman" (270). Mimi in love is therefore a striking example of the human tendency to engage others in one's own fate—"that everyone sees to it his fate is shared. Or tries to see to it" (211). Mimi's fate is her need to love, and she seeks to enlist others in the fulfillment of this need, with her "recruiting place" her "actual body" and her weapons of persuasion "her clinching will, her hard reason, and her obstinate voice" (211). And although Mimi's need locks her into a deeply troublesome relationship with the distant and neglectful Hooker Frazer, it also brings her a "tough happiness" (253), a sense of fulfillment within pain and enclosure.

So when Augie falls in love with Thea, he knows that he is surrendering a large part of himself—in particular his freedom to pursue his own fate—for love. He realizes that he is "abandoning some mighty old protections which now stood empty. . . . Oh, you chump and weak fool, you are one of a humanity that can't be numbered and not more than the dust of metals scattered in a magnetic field and clinging to the lines of force, determined by laws, eating, sleeping, employed, conveyed, obedient, and subject. So why hunt for still more ways to lose liberty?" (316). Yet Augie, when deeply in love, also believes that love is not only an adequate substitute for an independent fate but that fate itself. He tries to tell Thea that "I had looked all my life for the right thing to do, for a fate good enough, that I had opposed people in what they wanted to make of me, but now that I was in love with her I understood much better what I myself wanted" (318). For Thea, however, as Augie discovers, love is not a value or goal in itself but is rather a means of making Augie into what she wants him to be. No wonder, then, that Augie can later sum up his love experiences as an insoluble paradox: "I didn't want to be what they made of me but wanted to please them. Kindly explain! An independent fate, and love too—what confusion" (401).

Yet Augie ultimately grasps and endorses this paradox despite its contradictions and confusions. Love, he comes to feel, is both a hindrance to an independent fate and a vehicle for the achievement of this goal. Back in Chicago after his Mexican adventure, Augie in a "dry" season expresses to Kayo Obermark his belief that man is shaped by "the technical achievements which try to make you exist in their way" (450). Kayo responds, "What you are talking about is *moha*—a Navajo word, and also Sanskrit, meaning opposition of the finite. It is the Bronx cheer of the conditioning forces. Love is the only answer to *moha*, being infinite. I mean all forms of love, eros, agape, libido, philia, and ecstasy. They are always the same but sometimes one quality dominates and sometimes another" (450).

Augie later believes that his love for Stella confirms Kayo's explanation of the role of love. Not only does Augie feel that he and Stella are united in opposition since they are "the kind of people other people are always trying to fit into their schemes" (384), but that his love for Stella will permit him to escape the determining forces of life. Or, to use his own imagery, through love he will avoid being a volitionless metal filing sited on a magnetic line but will rather locate himself freely on his own axial lines of meaning. As he explains when he is about to marry Stella, other people "were subject to all the laws in the book, like the mountain peaks leaning toward their respective magnetic poles, or like crabs in the weeds or crystals in the caves. Whereas I, with the help of love, had gotten in on a much better thing and was giving this account of myself that reality comes from and was not just at the mercy" (488).

But of course both Kayo and Augie are in part wrong. Despite the "answer" of love to *moha*, Augie's activities as a black market dealer at the close of the novel contribute to the control of man by his technology. And his relations with Stella return him to the subjugation of love. "I understood," he comments, "that I would mostly do as she wanted because it was I who loved her most" (515). Yet despite Augie's discovery that life has not changed very much since his boyhood in Chicago—that adopters and controllers are still everywhere, and that the rough forces and darkness still flourish—he has himself become a theoretician, a "fanatic" (522), of love, and is willing to take his stand within its ambivalences. For love, he now realizes, in its fusion of the determined and the free, the destructive and the life-enhancing, the other and the self, epitomizes the experience within which man must live and die. Augie at the conclusion of the novel has therefore not ended his adventures. He refuses to lead the disappointed life, despite his disappointments, and will continue to search for his better fate within love of "those near-at-hand" (536)—Stella, a home and children, teaching the young ("It wasn't so much education as love. That was the idea" [514-15]). His quest for meaning and value in that which controls him is not fatuous. It is rather a deeply felt response to the human condition as that condition is perceived within the naturalistic tradition.

From *Twentieth-Century American Literary Naturalism: An Interpretation* (1982) by Donald Pizer. Copyright © 1982 by Southern Illinois University Press. Reprinted with permission of Southern Illinois University Press.

Notes

1. See Bellow's own comment on *The Victim* in his 1965 *Paris Review* interview in *Writers at Work: The "Paris Review" Interviews, Third Series*, ed. George Plimpton (New York: Penguin, 1977 [1967]), p. 187.

2. Harvey Breit, "Saul Bellow," *The Writer Observed* (Cleveland: World, 1956), p. 273. The interview occurred in 1953.

3. The phrase is James H. Justus's in his review of Bellow criticism for 1976 in *American Literary Scholarship: An Annual/1976*, ed. J. Albert Robbins (Durham, N.C.: Duke Univ. Pr., 1978), p. 297.

4. Some other discussions of *Augie* as a naturalistic novel are: Kingsley Widmer,

"Poetic Naturalism in the Contemporary Novel," *Partisan Review* 26 (Summer 1959): 467-72; Richard Chase, "The Adventures of Saul Bellow," *Commentary* 27 (April 1959), 223-30, reprinted in *Saul Bellow and the Critics*, ed. Irving Malin (New York: New York Univ. Pr., 1967), pp. 25-38; Malcolm Bradbury, "Saul Bellow and the Naturalist Tradition," *Review of English Literature* 4 (Oct. 1963): 80-92; and Earl Rovit, "Saul Bellow and Norman Mailer: The Secret Sharers," in *Saul Bellow: A Collection of Critical Essays*, ed. Earl Rovit (Englewood Cliffs, N.J.: Prentice-Hall, 1975), pp. 161-70. Among other essays on *Augie*, I have profited in particular from Albert J. Guerard's "Saul Bellow and the Activists," *Southern Review* 3 (Summer 1967): 582-96.

5. *The Adventures of Augie March* (New York: Viking, 1953), p. 536. Citations will hereafter appear in the text.

6. Sanford Pinsker, "Saul Bellow in the Classroom," *College English* 34 (Apr. 1973): 976.

7. John Enck, "Saul Bellow: An Interview," *Wisconsin Studies in Contemporary Literature* 6 (Summer 1965): 156-57.

8. The phrase occurs in Bellow's "The Writer as Moralist," *Atlantic Monthly* 211 (Mar. 1963): 60, where Bellow writes, "If a novelist is going to affirm anything, he must be prepared to prove his case in close detail, reconcile it with hard facts."

9. See Bellow's "Starting Out in Chicago," *American Scholar* 44 (Winter 1974/75): 73.

10. As has been frequently noted, Bellow's working title for *Augie March* was "Life Among the Machiavellians."

11. *City of Words: American Fiction, 1950-1970* (New York: Harper & Row, 1971), p. 71.

12. Bellow on several occasions has expressed his contempt for the Lawrence of *The Plumed Serpent*. See his "Where Do We Go from Here: The Future of Fiction" (1962), in *Saul Bellow and the Critics*, ed. Malin. p. 212, and his *Paris Review* interview (1965), p. 182.

13. Augie also encounters a number of other "theoreticians"—Manny Padilla, Clem Tambow, and Robey—who are scientists manqué and who seek to enlist him in their visions of truth. But since he is neither in love with these figures nor confined in a boat with them, he is more readily able to dismiss their threat to his freedom.

14. Sylvester (along with Mimi's lover Frazer) also plays a role in the satire of 1930s radical politics which runs through *Augie March*. Both are expelled from the Communist Party for "Infantile Leftism and Trotskyist Deviationism" (p. 212) and Frazer ultimately becomes a major in U.S. Army Intelligence.

15. "The Sealed Treasure," *Times Literary Supplement*, July 1, 1960, p. 414. See also Bellow's 1965 statement that "'I seem to have asked in my books, How can one resist the controls of this vast society *without* turning into a nihilist, avoiding the absurdity of empty rebellion?" (*Paris Review* interview, p. 196).

16. On his return from Mexico City, Augie discovers human parallels to the flower and kinkajou in his brother George and his mother. George is mentally defective and his mother blind. Besides being imprisoned by their defects, both are also encaged in "homes." Yet both accept their fate with dignity, Augie decides, and thus embellish it (see pp. 419-21).

"The Hollywood Thread" and the First Draft of Saul Bellow's *Seize the Day*

Allan Chavkin

The collection of manuscripts for *Seize the Day* (1956) at the Humanities Research Center of the University of Texas at Austin is substantial. The numerous manuscripts, arranged chronologically by the Center's staff, are divided into thirteen sections. The first section contains the earliest surviving version of the novel, a holograph entitled "One of Those Days," written in two bound notebooks.[1] With the exception of several small holograph fragments, the later manuscript materials in sections II-XII are typescripts; many of these typescripts are replete with holograph revisions. Section XIII consists of sixteen miscellaneous typescript and holograph leaves not identifiable with a particular draft. Although some of the drafts of *Seize the Day* are no longer extant, there is a wealth of material for investigation; in fact, a systematic examination of the numerous manuscripts would reveal much about the development of the novel and Bellow's artistic genius. Such an examination would require a book-length study, however, and is therefore beyond the scope of this article. My purpose must be more modest. By examining the earliest surviving draft of the novel, I intend to show Bellow's primary concerns in this difficult work.

Although "One of Those Days" closely resembles *Seize the Day*, there are some notable differences between the two works. Wilhelm's recollection of his meeting with Maurice Venice (the second half of chapter 1 of the novel) is not in the first draft, and there are other omissions, too. Tamkin's admonition not to "marry suffering,"[2] Wilhelm's feeling in the subway of love for humanity and a number of less well-known passages do not appear in "One of Those Days." The minor characters, such as Rubin, Perls, Rappaport, and Wilhelm's sister Catherine, are not developed, and Olive, Wilhelm's Catholic mistress, is absent from the first draft. Tamkin's storytelling and preaching are not so extensive in the first draft as they are in the published version.

For example, his Egyptian escapade which he exuberantly recounts in *Seize the Day* is only briefly summarized by Wilhelm in "One of Those Days," and his didactic analysis of his poem "Mechanism vs. Functionalism" is not in the first draft. Similarly, Wilhelm's meditations are not very elaborate in the first draft.

As with *Herzog* and *Mr. Sammler's Planet*,[3] Bellow painstakingly worked upon his novel until it exactly conveyed his sense of the human condition. Although some of this revision included pruning, the process of composing *Seize the Day* was mainly one of adding on. Bellow enriched his work until it grew to almost three times its original length and became much more complex than the first draft. "One of Those Days" provides a rare look, then, at Bellow's central purpose in *Seize the Day* because this first draft presents the core of the novel before it evolved into the complicated work of art that critics have grappled with for the last several decades. Specifically, there are five major sources of ambiguity: (1) the water imagery and Wilhelm's metaphoric drowning; (2) the final scene; (3) the complex point of view with its pervasive irony; (4) the allusions to the works of Milton, Keats, Shelley, and others; and most important, (5) the complicated characters who are, to use Wilhelm's language, "like the faces on a playing card, upside down either way" (*S*, p. 63). In "One of Those Days" the water imagery, the allusions, and the irony are of minor importance, and the final scene of the novel is briefer and less subtle than that in *Seize the Day*. In short, these four sources of ambiguity are absent in the first draft of the novel. Moreover, in the earliest version of the novel there are passages, later omitted or substantially altered, which reveal much about the motivation of Wilhelm, Adler, Margaret, and Tamkin, and I shall focus upon these passages in my discussion to help elucidate the most perplexing source of ambiguity in the novel—the characters.

One should state at this point that the published version of the novel is much superior to the first draft and that Bellow was not trying to be cryptic by making *Seize the Day* much more complex than "One of Those Days." The published novel is complex because Bellow sees the world as extraordinarily complicated. Wilhelm, like so many Bellovian protagonists, searches for some kind of truth that will provide order in this chaotic universe, or "multiverse" as it is referred to in *The Adventures of Augie March* (1953).[4] He envisions the modern city as a Babel where even the simplest communication between its self-centered residents is nearly impossible. One of the underlying attitudes that prompts Tamkin's stories is the feeling that this topsy-turvy world is full of people who are both sane and insane at the same time and that underneath deceptive surface appearance exists a disturbing reality. After listening to Rappaport relate a bizarre anecdote of his experience in the Spanish-American war, the appalled Wilhelm reflects: "Oh, things are too strange" ("O," p. 91). To help convey this sense of the world's strangeness and complexity, Bellow uses a sophisticated point of view, full of irony, and the garrulous psychologist, Tamkin.

A detached ironic narrator and a confused, self-mocking protagonist tell the story, and within the overall story Tamkin relates his own fictions, inextricable mixtures of fantasies and sensational facts. During most of the novel we are looking at the world through Wilhelm's eyes. Tormented and desperate, Wilhelm constantly changes his mind. To complicate matters, the omniscient narrator himself changes his attitude toward the characters; he is alternately sympathetic and scornful toward Wilhelm, for example. The fast-talking Tamkin is hardly more consistent, causing Wilhelm and the critics to ponder how much to believe of the fraudulent psychologist, whose speeches make up a significant portion of the novel. Certainly some of what he says can serve as useful explanation. The problem is to distinguish the wisdom from the nonsense. When one considers this problem and the other major sources of ambiguity in the novel, it is not surprising that some critics have interpreted the novel as optimistic, others as pessimistic.[5]

While the critics are not in agreement on the meaning of the novel, there does seem to be a critical consensus that it is Bellow's "finest piece of fiction."[6] The critics believe that *Seize the Day* comes the closest of his works to achieving perfect form; it is a masterpiece with the compression, intensity, and unity of a lyrical poem. Bellow has interwoven theme, structure, plot, imagery, allusions, and point of view into a rich fabric. By examining "One of Those Days" before it evolves into the rich fabric of *Seize the Day*, I hope to reveal the important beginning thread of the novel.

* * *

On the back cover of the second notebook of "One of Those Days," Bellow jotted down some notes to himself for subsequent revision of his novel. Most of these notes indicate minor changes to be made in the plot, but one phrase is particularly revealing—"Hollywood thread throughout." Bellow's reference to Hollywood here is not merely a note to himself to develop the story of Wilhelm's pathetic attempt to become a Hollywood star, which is only alluded to in the first draft. The Hollywood thread is a catchall phrase under which the main themes of the novel can be subsumed, themes often associated with Hollywood: dreaming, narcissism, self-deception, role-playing, hedonism, greedy materialism, cynicism, and the futile pursuit of eternal youth and beauty. The world of *Seize the Day* is one in which all the avaricious characters, self-absorbed in their own fantasies, evade reality; and Hollywood, sometimes referred to as the "dream factory," is an appropriate symbol for such a world. This self-absorption in a dream world can most clearly be seen in Wilhelm's insipid attempts to become a "success," but Adler, Tamkin, and the other characters show this propensity to escape reality, too; they refuse to recognize suffering and death that are part of the human condition. To use Tamkin's metaphor, they have "pretender souls" which parasitically dominate their hosts, the "real souls." According to Tamkin, the real soul, which seeks truth, not social goals, desires to kill the false pretender soul, and thus mankind becomes murderous. Because of their egotism and their lack of love, pity, and sympathy for humanity, the characters of this Hollywood society create a hell on earth.

Tamkin's speech on the internecine warfare between man's two souls, essentially the same in both the first draft and the published version of the novel, expresses one of the key ideas at the foundation of *Seize the Day*. Another key idea, which complements Tamkin's concept of the two souls, is his carpe diem belief. One must not only be true to one's real soul and learn to love but must reject the orientation of a money-obsessed, exploitative society and instead seize the "Here-and-Now." Tamkin foists this philosophy on Wilhelm by showing him his poem "Mechanism vs. Functionalism" ("O," p. 61; *S*, p. 75). Admittedly, the didactic poem is crudely written, but it cogently expresses Tamkin's carpe diem philosophy which, he believes, Wilhelm must embrace if he is to escape his self-destructive existence. All of the titles Bellow successively chose for his work, "One of Those Days," "Here and Now—Here and Now," "At the Foot of Mt. Serenity,"[7] and "Seize the Day," point to Wilhelm's self-destructive view of time. Wilhelm does not live in the present but is remorsefully absorbed in the past or anxiously immersed in the future. Contrary to Horace's injunction to "seize the day, put no trust in the morrow," Wilhelm reveals his basic inclination to ignore the present and put his faith in an illusory future when he tells Margaret at the end of "One of Those Days" that he plans to start anew. "I've run into a little bad luck. As a matter of fact, I don't know where I am. It's one of those days and I can't think & better not even try. Tomorrow I'll go see [some] a guy I know who's a sales manager" ("O," p. 101). Margaret points out to Wilhelm that he's "thinking like a youngster" and deceiving himself again ("O," p. 101).

Despite what Wilhelm claims, this is hardly just another ordinary day, and the title of the first draft is ironic, of course. Similarly, the three subsequent titles of the novel, "Here and Now—Here and Now," "At the Foot of Mt. Serenity," and "Seize the Day," are also ironic. While Bellow does believe that one must "seize the day," as Tamkin exhorts, he would modify Tamkin's carefree carpe diem philosophy to better account for man's suffering. Bellow believes that one can only "seize the day" when he recognizes suffering as an inextricable part of the human condition. "Do you not see how necessary a World of Pains and troubles is to school an Intelligence and make it a soul?" Keats rhetorically asks.[8] Bellow's version of the carpe diem philosophy is very similar to that of the English romantic poet. Life itself with all its joys and sorrows is the highest value, and the immersion in dreams in order to ignore the inexorable process of aging and decay, an escapist tendency pervasive in the Hollywood world of *Seize the Day*, prevents one from living intensely and fully in the present.

Apparently at the forefront of Bellow's mind when he began the novel, the Hotel Ansonia best symbolizes the dreary neighborhood of Upper Broadway with its dreamy inhabitants. In the first draft he described the hotel in the opening paragraph: "On a sunny day you can't find a place on the benches in Verdi Square, opposite Stanford White's Ansonia Hotel, the neighborhood's chief landmark. It looks like a palace from Munich or Prague, only a hundred times more huge, swollen with towers bays and domes and black antennae feeling into the sky. The whole neighborhood is a little like that" ("O," p. 1). The description of the Ansonia becomes subtler in the published novel, where it has been moved to the middle of the fourth paragraph and the explicit connection between the hotel and "the whole neighborhood" is not mentioned, but it still evokes the gaudiness, pretentiousness, and unreality of Upper Broadway. In the published novel Rubin and Wilhelm gaze dreamily at the monstrous hotel, as if mesmerized by it.

In short, this is a society whose escapist inhabitants are so self-absorbed that they have no sympathy or love for anyone but themselves. Contrary to conventional expectations, Bellow has selected the character often considered heroic—the hard-boiled, successful doctor—to embody this self-centeredness and inability to sympathize. Dr. Adler has worked his way from the bottom of the economic ladder to the top, and in his eighties he wants to spend his remaining days in peace. Much to his annoyance the polite, rational doctor finds himself continually challenged by his only son, whose life has been a failure. While Bellow cogently depicts how repulsive the disheveled, emotional Wilhelm is to his proper father, Bellow's real sympathy is with Wilhelm, for he believes fathers and sons have a moral responsibility to one another that transcends any differences. In his refusal to become involved in the suffering of his son, Adler reveals his cold-heartedness and lack of moral worth. He is completely self-absorbed, striving to ignore his obsessive anxiety over his inevitable death. He has "made himself into the idol of the hotel" and like a Hollywood starlet enjoys the residents' worship: "They pampered him and flattered him, and he was exactly like a pretty girl" ("O," p. 7). Sometimes it fills Wilhelm "with boiling indignation to consider how madly his father loved himself" ("O," p. 7).

Several passages in the first draft, which were later cancelled, reveal the depth of hostility between Adler and Wilhelm and make evident some unspoken feelings between father and son in *Seize the Day*. The unfinished conversation below that never found its way into the text proper probably represents Bellow thinking on paper: it seems to have been jotted down quickly, and I've indicated the apparent speakers, whom Bellow omitted in his haste.

[Wilhelm] You hate me

[Adler] Yes, perhaps I do But I have to go to my grave soon [and] while you . . . and I am much more of an individual than you

[Wilhelm] If I had money, by God, you wouldn't Father

[Adler] Yes, I admit it would make a difference

[Wilhelm] It's because you can't brag about me

[Wilhelm] "You haven't accomplished so much yourself," he spoke to himself. ("O," p. 20; Bellow's ellipsis)

Much that is only implied in the published version of the novel is made explicit here—Adler's hatred of his son because of his youth, his lack of "rugged individualism," and his failure to make money and be a "success." As the last sentence of the above passage implies, Wilhelm feels that despite his father's material accomplishment he has not achieved much spiritually. Another passage, which also never found its way into the text, indicates this idea more clearly: "You fuckn hearing, he swore mentally, haven't you got any characteristics? What are you anyway" ("O," p. 14). Wilhelm, who at another point confuses "morale" with "moral" and is corrected by his father ("O," p. 19), means "character," not "characteristics," here. Despite the incorrect word choice, he poignantly expresses Bellow's criticism of Adler—he is a cold-hearted, compassionless man, whose failure as a father makes a mockery of his material success.

Perhaps hoping that Wilhelm soon may have his father's inheritance to invest if father and son do not become completely estranged, the conspiring Tamkin defends Adler to his son. "Of course, old people's [hearts and] sympathies and emotions [die] are faded out long ago. Your dad can't care about you any more. It's not his fault. Nature does it. He has to envy you" ("O," pp. 87-88). There is some truth to Tamkin's explanation. Adler is envious of Wilhelm's youth, and he does feel that at his advanced age he should not have to deal with his son's problems. But the crux of the matter is that Adler does not have any real affection for his son. He feels Wilhelm is capable of anything. His "suspicion of him was boundless. There was nothing he wouldn't think" ("O," p. 33).

Like Adler, Margaret is self-centered and has no love for Wilhelm. A passage in the first draft, later cancelled, reveals much about the motivation of Wilhelm's wife. In the passage Tamkin suggests that she is a middle-class woman, jealous of her husband's putative freedom, who sees him as an investment that she cannot afford to lose. Tamkin associates her with the masquerading, predatory women ubiquitous in the Broadway area who worry that their aging will prevent them from obtaining a husband. There is more trust in Tamkin's analysis of Margaret than in Wilhelm's view of her as merely a vindictive woman bent on punishing him. Tamkin lectures Wilhelm on Margaret as the two men sit in a restaurant full of the middle-class women on the Broadway area:

"She thinks, 'He's free. He has women. While what is my life like?'" He glanced about at the idle, elderly, discontented ladies who were conversing, and preening and calling and eating. Clearly [his] the expression of his eyes said "Before long she'll be like this too. "A woman makes her investment. . . . I was married." ("O," p. 88; Bellow's ellipsis)

Tamkin's view of marriage as an investment is perceptive. In a money-obsessed society where a father can have no respect for a son who cannot earn a substantial salary, even love and marriage are defined as a business proposition.

Despite his astute analysis of society, the self-absorbed Tamkin is very much a product of it. He, too, is obsessed with making a "killing" on the market, and he is desperate. Tamkin, a shadowy figure who has provoked more diverse interpretations than any other character in Bellow's canon,[9] bears some resemblance to the desperate Wilhelm, a fact often overlooked. His self-aggrandizing stories remind one of Wilhelm's self-glorifying lies about his Hollywood "career." Furthermore, his fantasies of success, his pill-taking, and his messy room suggest a parallel with Wilhelm—he is another insecure failure frantic to save himself.

Nevertheless, Tamkin differs considerably from Wilhelm, for there is a basic fraudulence underneath his flamboyance. He is clearly a fast-talking charlatan, who manipulates Wilhelm by his "hypnotic" power—a power that is "something studied and put forth" ("O," p. 43). Referring no doubt to Tamkin's flamboyant personality and his persuasive language, Adler succinctly comments: "He's one of those Hungarians with the mesmeric gift" ("O," p. 23). But while Tamkin, who has spent time in Hollywood, is a better actor and salesman than the man whom he dupes out of his last seven hundred dollars, he should not be seen as a malevolent figure; after all, he does indirectly help Wilhelm attain his salvation even though he is motivated by self-interest. Not only does Tamkin show Wilhelm that he has allowed his social soul to strangle his real soul, but under Tamkin's influence Wilhelm begins to recall and take to heart his past reading of the great English poets. He resembles the other fast-talking gurus and eccentrics in Bellow's fiction, such as Mintouchian, Dahfu, and Dr. Scheldt, who speak both foolishness and wisdom to a Bellovian protagonist eager for some kind of redeeming truth. Both attracted to and skeptical of these eccentrics, Bellow suggests that while not all of what they say is true, they do help the protagonist to reach an important understanding of his situation or experience a change of consciousness, even if it is by a circuitous path.

Like Tamkin, the self-absorbed Wilhelm is very much a product of society. He defines himself in the social terms of "success" and "failure," and he is clearly a failure according to this definition. At times he is a kind of Dostoyevskian buffoon[10] and a Reichian masochist.[11] His past humiliation and defeat have badly damaged his pride and made him resentful and self-denigrating. A person of deep feeling and much energy but with little scope for them, he is racked by contradictory emotions. His mood can change quickly from insouciance to self-abasement. Overweight, gross in his personal hygiene, and self-pitying, he is the least attractive of Bellow's protagonists. The remarkable achievement of the novel is Bellow's ability to make us sympathize with a character who is so often unattractive and unpleasant. Before his father, Wilhelm acts the buffoon, and his absurd role-playing tendency is especially evident in the first draft. "He put on his great, his supercilious, his civilized and worldly air. He was genteel, he was mannered, he thinned his lips, he dropped the ends of words" ("O," p. 13). But while he is repugnant at times, he does have a number of redeeming qualities that the other characters in the novel do not have: an ability to love, sensitive emotions that enable him to experience things intensely, and an idealism which allows him to reject the pervasive cynicism of the successful and instead search for a higher truth beyond the omnipresent materialism of contemporary society. Like Bellow's other protagonists, he "is a visionary sort of animal. Who has to believe that he can know why he exists" (S, p. 39).

One moment puerile and hostile, the next mature and compassionate, Wilhelm is, in short, a contradictory character. "One of Those Days" helps explain his complex motivation and the anxieties at the root of his character. The negative side of Wilhelm—his sloppiness, his poor judgment, his continual failure—can be seen as a kind of instinctive protest against the limitations imposed upon him, directly or indirectly, by his father, his wife, and his society. One of Bellow's notes aptly states: "His ineptness a form of defiance."[12] To assert his freedom against those who would limit it, Wilhelm feels he must act, but, unsurprisingly, his actions are usually rash and ill-conceived. His assertion of his independence and autonomy reveals only his impotence; his rebellion seems childish, not ennobling. A conversation between Wilhelm and his father suggests as much.

> "I have to have some action. I can't let them do everything to me. I have
> to do something too."
> "Isn't it late for you to [act] be like a boy." ("O," p. 24)

Wilhelm's father and wife monopolize his life; he is unable to act without thinking of how they will consider his actions. He has left his wife and acts contrary to his father's wishes, but he is not free from them despite his rebellious behavior. Tamkin bluntly points out Wilhelm's enslavement in the first draft:

> "You worry what your father & your wife will say. Isn't that the truth?"
> "Not the whole truth," said Wilhelm rather weakly.
> "They still control you." ("O," p. 87)

Wilhelm lacks self-knowledge and therefore does not understand the reasons for his actions. As his name-changing implies, he lacks a firm identity; unable to find a proper course of action, he plays a variety of roles. When confronted by his father, he violates the norms of propriety, engages in histrionic behavior, and rejects reason. Though he does not understand its source, he is full of rage against himself and his father. "He was ridiculous in his own [sight] eyes when he was so stiff, so proud, when he said 'you don't know me yet father!' No, how could he know him? He didn't know himself. . . . But he was horribly angry at the old man too" ("O," p. 37).

The source of Wilhelm's periodic rage and self-hatred is his lack of love. With Wilhelm in mind, Tamkin expresses the universal need for love in his speech on the two souls: "'If thou canst not love what art thou?' Nothing" ("O," p. 51). Apparently, the death of Wilhelm's mother with the consequent loss of maternal love was a personal catastrophe from which he has never recovered. This idea was in the forefront of Bellow's mind when he began writing the novel, for he refers to Wilhelm's obsessive recollection of his mother in the opening of "One of Those Days." "The [color] gray of his shirt suddenly reminded Wilhelm of the color of his mother's shroud. She had died seventeen years ago, but he still remembered" ("O," p. 3). This recollection is omitted after the first draft, but Bellow does add a number of other references in the published novel to suggest Wilhelm's deep commitment to his mother, a commitment made stronger because of his poor relationship with his father.

Undoubtedly, an even more important crisis for Wilhelm than this loss of maternal love is his separation from his wife, a point that is not obvious in the published version of the novel. Uncertain of his mental stability, Wilhelm confesses to Tamkin in "One of Those Days": "Woe, I know I am not one-hundred-percent. Sometimes I feel I have lived and died and lived and died again. [I] Maybe it's age. Several separate lives have like passed by. Do you think I am normal? or am I distorted? The most painful experience of all was when I broke up with my wife. I thought it was all up with me—my life was finished" ("O," p. 57). The separation from his wife further intensifies Wilhelm's desperate need for love. Not only has the love between him and his wife vanished, but he fears the loss of his children's love. This anxiety is added to his guilt over his feelings of partial responsibility for the breakdown of the marriage and to his fear that aging will prevent him from remarriage and love with someone else. In a very revealing passage in the first draft, one gains much insight into the psychological pressures plaguing Wilhelm.

> Then he started to think whether his two boys believed that he cared for them. The doubt hurt him greatly. Margaret would have turned them against him. They were old enough to reflect on sex and they would talk about all the women in his life. This part of his father's accusation was dangerously near the truth. In almost every town he had someone to go out with. How could he stand this life otherwise. There was nothing worse than to have to spend the night alone. This was the main thing. And he was growing older and now could not afford to remarry even if Margaret were to let him off the hook at last. Furthermore, he was losing his looks. His neck was growing short and his shoulders squaring upward and his nostrils flared too high, and a dozen other signs were apparent. A woman would have to love him enough to [pardon] overlook his [shortcomings] years and his shortcomings and pity him. If she knew everything about him and saw him clearly and still had charity. And he himself would have charity. They both could cease from struggle and pain. ("O," p. 73, p. 75)

The preceding passage also clarifies a passage describing Wilhelm when he is arguing with his father at the beginning of "One of Those Days": "He too was old [and] an old sinner and a liar. He was tired of himself & his lies" ("O," p. 8). Even in the earliest version of the novel, Bellow conceived of Wilhelm as a character who was at least partially responsible for his situation, not merely an innocent victim of a situation not of his making. Wilhelm's extramarital affairs link him with Herzog and remind one of the profound dissatisfaction that prompts both of them to leave their orderly domestic lives, forsake their professional careers, and seek amid much "struggle and pain" for some kind of redeeming truth. It is important to note that in contrast to "One of Those Days," in *Seize the Day* Wilhelm does find Olive, a woman who can overlook his shortcomings and love him for himself. With her he could have ceased from "struggle and pain," but it is clear that he has lost this opportunity. Wilhelm is unable to obtain a divorce from Margaret, and therefore his relationship with Olive is doomed. The failure of Wilhelm's relationship with Olive emphasizes how desperate his situation is—she was his last hope. His loss of Olive in *Seize the Day* evokes his fear, so poignantly expressed in "One of Those Days," of being doomed to live his remaining years deprived of love.

At the brink of total despair, Wilhelm experiences an emotional catharsis and is transformed in the final scene of the novel. Absorbed in self-pity, Wilhelm accidentally stumbles into the funeral of a stranger. When he looks at the corpse, he breaks down and cries not merely out of self-pity, but for all humanity. For the first time Wilhelm transcends his self-absorption and recognizes his solidarity with the brotherhood of man, whose undeniable common bond is that they all must suffer and die. Wilhelm's acceptance of his humanity in the final scene suggests that he will be able to forsake his pretender soul for his real one. One sentence in the first draft is particularly revealing: "He tried to stop, but it was as if the source of all tears had suddenly sprung open within him, black and fathomless, and they were pouring out and convulsed his body, bending his stubborn head *at last*, bowing his shoulders, twisting his features, crippling the very hands with which he tried vainly to wipe away the endless flowing tears" ("O," pp. 106-7: italics added). There is a similar sentence in the final text, but Bellow has subtly omitted the phrase italicized here—"at last." While Bellow's novels typically end affirmatively, they also conclude with deliberate ambiguity to suggest that existence, so often irresolute and mysterious, cannot be reduced to a single meaning. Bellow omitted the phrase "at last" in the published version of the novel because he did not want to assume the role of omniscient narrator making a categorical statement about the final meaning of the novel. The cancelled phrase "at last" does reveal, however, what he had in mind when he was first composing his modern fable of an ordinary man's secular redemption, and it provides evidence for what most critics have argued Bellow was suggesting by the novel's conclusion. Wilhelm is not merely enjoying another bout of self-pity or indulging in masochistic glorification of suffering; in a moment of heightened awareness he transforms himself, "bending his stubborn head at last."

In the past Wilhelm's stubbornness prevented him from recognizing that his pains and troubles were part of humanity's suffering. When he confronts the corpse and recognizes that death and suffering are part of the human condition, he finally humbles himself and breaks out of the self-imprisonment of excessive self-consciousness and dreaming. Forced for the first time to admit to himself the ineluctable reality of his mortality, he recognizes that life itself is the highest good. In the beginning of the novel Wilhelm suddenly recalls at one point the final line of Shakespeare's "Sonnet 73," "To love that well which thou must leave ere long" ("O," p. 7; *S*, p. 12), and in the final scene he understands not only intellectually but emotionally the need for a love of life in the face of death. In its dramatic presentation of the spiritual rebirth of a desperate man on the verge of complete ruin, the novel ends with a profound affirmation and suggests a powerful alternative to the negation of the Hollywood society.

From *Studies in the Novel* 14.1 (Spring 1982): 82-94. Copyright © 1982 by the University of North Texas. Reprinted with permission of the University of North Texas.

Notes

1. With these notebooks spread open before him, Bellow typically wrote on the right-hand page, leaving the left-hand page for revisions. For the last twenty pages of the 107-page manuscript, however, he wrote on both the right-hand and left-hand pages. Since he did not number the pages, I have done so, numbering them consecutively through the two notebooks. All quotations from "One of Those Days" will follow the holograph exactly (with cancellations in brackets), and page references will be given parenthetically in the text, with the designation "O."

2. Saul Bellow, *Seize the Day* (New York: Viking Press, 1956), p. 98. Subsequent references will be given parenthetically in the text, with the designation *S*. Originally, the entire novel appeared m a slightly different form in the *Partisan Review*, 23

(Summer 1956), 295-319, 376-424, 426-28, 431-32. When I refer to the published novel in this article, I shall be referring to the Viking Press edition, which is a revision of the *Partisan Review* text and therefore should be considered Bellow's final version.

3. See the manuscript studies by Daniel Fuchs, "*Herzog:* The Making of a Novel," in *Critical Essays on Saul Bellow*, ed. Stanley Trachtenberg (Boston: G. K. Hall, 1979), pp. 101-21, and Keith Cushman, "Mr. Bellow's *Sammler:* The Evolution of a Contemporary Text," *Studies in the Novel*, 7 (1975), 425-44, rpt. in Trachtenberg.

4. Saul Bellow, *The Adventures of Augie March* (New York: Viking Press, 1953), p. 95.

5. Keith Michael Opdahl, *The Novels of Saul Bellow: An Introduction* (University Park: Pennsylvania State Univ. Press. 1967), p. 116, can be considered as representative of the majority view, which sees the novel as one of affirmation because Wilhelm finally attains spiritual "redemption," while Andrew Jefchak, "Family Struggles in *Seize the Day*," *Studies in Short Fiction*, 11 (1974), 301-2, can be considered as representative of the minority view, which sees the novel as one of "incipient despair" because Wilhelm in the final scene "perceives that his unshared life looms permanent."

6. William H. Pritchard, "Saul Bellow," in *The Norton Anthology of American Literature*, ed. Ronald Gottesman et al. (New York: W. W. Norton, 1979), II, 1952. See also John J. Clayton, *Saul Bellow:* in *Defense of Man*, 2nd ed. (Bloomington: Indiana Univ. Press, 1979), p. 302; M. Gilbert Porter, *Whence the Power? The Artistry and Humanity of Saul Bellow* (Columbia: Univ. of Missouri Press, 1974), p. 102; Ralph Ciancio, "The Achievement of Saul Bellow's *Seize the Day*," in *Literature and Theology*, ed. Thomas F. Staley and Lester F. Zimmerman (Norman: Univ. of Oklahoma Press, 1969), p. 49; and J. R. Raper, "Running Contrary Ways: Saul Bellow's *Seize the Day*," *Southern Humanities Review*, 10 (1976), 158.

7. "At the Foot of Mt. Serenity," a line from Tamkin's poem, was used only once as a title. On the front page of the second draft, a typescript with holograph corrections, one finds the typewritten title "One of Those Days" and the holograph title "At the Foot of Mt. Serenity." Both are deleted and replaced with the holograph title "Here and Now—Here and Now."

8. Keats's 21 Apr. 1819 letter to the George Keatses, *The Letters of John Keats*, ed. Hyder E. Rollins (Cambridge, Mass.: Harvard Univ. Press, 1958), II, 102. For a discussion of the influence of the romantic view of suffering on the novel, see my article "Suffering and Wilhelm Reich's Theory of Character-Armoring in Saul Bellow's *Seize the Day*," forthcoming in *Essays in Literature*.

9. Critics have interpreted the enigmatic Tamkin as a dispenser of Reichian wisdom (Eusebio Rodrigues, "Reichianism in *Seize the Day*," in Trachtenberg): as a *schnorrer* (Sarah Blacher Cohen, *Saul Bellow's Enigmatic Laughter* [Urbana: Univ. of Illinois Press, 1974], pp. 103-4); as a shaman (Lee J. Richmond, "The Maladroit, the Medico, and the Magician: Saul Bellow's *Seize the Day*," *Twentieth Century Literature*, 19 [1961], 21-24); as a kind of literary artist who sacrifices factual accuracy in order to express essential truths (Gilead Morahg, "The Art of Dr. Tamkin: Matter and Manner in *Seize the Day*," *Modern Fiction Studies*, 25 [1979], 113); and as a "psycho-

analyst as a figure of fun whom even the patient can think of as being part faker" (Daniel Weiss, "Caliban on Prospero: A Psychoanalytic Study on the Novel *Seize the Day* by Saul Bellow," *American Imago*, 19 [1962], 304).

10. Irving Howe, ed., "Introduction to *Seize the Day*," in *Classics of Modern Fiction* (New York: Harcourt Brace and World, 1968), p. 461.

11. Rodrigues provides the most detailed discussion of Bellow's use of Reich's theory of character-armoring to depict Wilhelm's masochism.

12. From section XIII of the *Seize the Day* manuscripts.

The Fifties Novels:
The Adventures of Augie March, Seize the Day, and Henderson the Rain King[1]

Malcolm Bradbury

I looked in at an octopus, and the creature seemed also to look at me and press its soft head to the glass, flat, the flesh becoming pale and granular— blanched, speckled. The eyes spoke to me coldly. But even more speaking, even more cold, was the soft head with its speckles, a cosmic coldness in which I felt I was dying. The tentacles throbbed and motioned through the glass, the bubbles sped upward, and I thought, "This is my last day. Death is giving me notice."

—*Henderson the Rain King*

Bellow has often spoken of a change of style and perception that came into his work after his first two novels; it is an unmistakable feature of his fiction of the 1950s. Starting with *The Adventures of Augie March* (1953), he began to write a new kind of novel, one that broke out of the tight, Europeanized, soul-searching and *Angst*-ridden form of his first books and opened into an exuberant and positive comedy. Bellow has remarked that 'modern comedy has something to do with the disintegrating outline of the worthy and humane Self, the bourgeois hero of an earlier age'; he has also seen that there is a modern comedy that ridicules the conditions of this misery, releasing pain as laughter.[2] He has remarked too on the power of the comic in the Yiddish tradition: 'Laughter and trembling are so curiously mingled that it is not easy to determine the relations of the two',[3] and this evidently has much to do with his own developing direction in comedy—one that sought to reach from the sad humour of human suffering to comic aspiration toward human grandeur, from the historical and diurnal world to the world of the transcendent and eternal. Bellow's heroes began to change; they became less victimized sufferers of insight and discovery, more positive, questing seekers after it. In the process, Bellow seemed to become a more affirmative writer, though in looking to that affirmation we must always observe the struggles and human pains out of which it grew.

As these new preoccupations shaped into matters of style and form, Bellow's novels changed. The old naturalist and existential containments did not by any means disappear, but they became a material to be contended with; his new books were texts of expansion and flow, novels of character-formation in which the heroes, especially Augie March and Henderson, became large mental travellers in quest through large social, psychic and neomythic landscapes to find the measure of their being, the nature of their human tenure. This released in Bellow a potential for mythic, fantastic and comic writing he had earlier contained, and along with it a Bellovian metaphysical vernacular, one of his larger offerings to the contemporary novel. In *The Victim* Bellow's style had already shown more suppleness, a freer motion between the hard social world and the world of thought and feeling. Now, by bringing a vital new energy and ebullience to his central characters, a new texture to his prose, Bellow was able to convert that social world into a landscape adequate to the enquiring spirit. Bellow's writing of the 1950s is thus a great opening out; in it he creates both a new form and a new kind and condition of hero. The form was that of picaresque metaphysical comedy; the heroes were self-creators, men who command large dimensions of their own fate, and move through expansive open landscapes and comic self-venturing into a growth of the spirit. The structural form expands toward contingency, toward vastly enlarged social content in *The Adventures of Augie March* (1953), toward mythic and psychological metaphor in *Henderson the Rain King* (1959), and the dominant rhetoric takes on vastly greater splendour, wit and comic self-awareness.

Bellow has since reflected that this release, coming in *The Adventures of Augie March*, was at first 'too effusive and uncritical'. 'I think I took off too many [restraints], and went too far, but I was feeling the excitement of discovery', he said in an interview. 'I had just increased my freedom, and like any emancipated plebeian I abused it at once.'[4] One form of release was to admit the voice of the extravagant self-narrator; the first-person mode of *The Adventures of Augie March* immediately opens out to display him as the first of Bellow's heroes who are larger than the world in which they live. Augie may have grown up in classic Chicago, that city of naturalism, 'just plain brutal and not mitigated', and come off its mean streets. But it is clear to him that the *Studs Lonigan* containments that have limited his predecessors in fiction are not meant for him, as his expansive opening utterance makes clear:

> I am an American, Chicago born—Chicago, that sombre city—and go at things as I have taught myself, free-style, and will make the record in my own way: first to knock, first admitted; sometimes an innocent knock, sometimes a not so innocent. But a man's character is his fate, says Heraclitus, and in the end there isn't any way to disguise the nature of the knocks by acoustical work on the door or gloving the knuckles. (*AM*, p. 7)

Augie is extravagant morally, intellectually and emotionally, and in a sense he has a character by becoming a character, fictionally dense and detailed, moving in a vastly more various and established world—unlike Joseph who retires into his room and has 'in a word, no character'. As Augie feels he has all human history behind him, and wishes to embrace the quality and texture of life, to become a Columbus of the near at hand, so Bellow, with a Dickensian abundance, provides him with it. The book is Bellow's most specified and episodic, a rich, character-filled, sprawling account of 'adventures' where, in scenes of very broad texture and significance, Augie passes beyond the Machiavellians and instructors of his childhood who seek to enlist him under laws of control and limitation, and moves out into a wider kingdom of abundance where he learns not just from other men and women but from all to hand: animals, nature, books.

But, appropriately enough for a novel dealing in part with a massive, energetic, material and indeed 'sombre' Chicago during the Depression years, the battle of determinism and independence is an essential structure to the book. 'All the influences were lined up waiting for me', Augie notes. 'I was born, and there they were to form me' (p. 52). Indeed all things seem to intersect in him: the flow of history, the interaction of races and classes, intellectual theories and their 'terrible appearances' within the world. Historicism and romantic independence struggle: at one point he nearly becomes secretary to the exiled Trotsky in Mexico, the man of history and historicism who shares with Augie's other heroes the wish to navigate by the great stars. But the great stars are not quite enough for him, because there is also the matter of nature. Augie sees around him a great massed weight of human ideas, with as much bulk as the massing, in a world of endless random energy, of material and men, an exciting but excessive abundance of thought turned into life:

> There's too much of everything of this kind, *that's* come home to me, too much history and culture to keep track of, too many details, too much news, too much example, too much influence, too many guys to tell you to be as they are, and all this hugeness, abundance, turbulence, Niagara Falls torrent. Which who is supposed to interpret? Me? (p. 525)

It is this swamping, exciting mass of 'it' that becomes the point of anxiety for all of Bellow's later heroes, raising in new form the problem of trying to discover the human mean.

Augie's quest therefore takes him beyond the social and historical world and into nature, seeking to find the basis of his tenure there: 'It takes some of us a long time to find out what the price is of our being in nature, and what the facts are about your tenure', he reflects. 'How long it takes depends on how swiftly the social sugars dissolve' (p. 421). He tries to acquaint himself with biological and bodily laws, often in comic form (like the eagle-training session in Mexico), and with an openness far beyond that accessible to Joseph and Leventhal, both of whom are characterized by their suppression of emotional aspects of their lives. Augie struggles in sexual relationships and friendships, at the same time hoping to find a stillness somewhere that will afford access to life's 'axial lines', those angles of guidance and revelation where 'life can come together again and man be regenerated' (p. 524). But he is a comic hero, forced, like all Bellow's heroes, to mediate between the world of action and that of thought, to make some sense of the life constituted for him in the book. He ends, as he must, in contingency, knowing that no one is special, that mortality threatens, that there is no possession of anyone or anything, that man is both good and evil, that the historical amassing of the world and the anxiety it generates is real and cannot be refused. He acquires a chastened sense of history's powers, but also a 'mysterious adoration of what occurs'.

He has learned, in short, the passion for self-constitution that permits him to constitute the narrative, lets him write as a chastened comedian of possibility, celebrating 'the *animal ridens* in me, the laughing creature, forever rising up'. The laughter is against human hope, but also is that hope:

> . . . is the laugh at nature—including eternity—that it thinks it can win over us and the power of hope? Nah, nah! I think. It never will. But that possibly is the joke, on one or the other, and laughing is an enigma that includes both. (p. 617)

And this is exactly the enigma the book distils, as it looks both into the dark weighty claims of modern historical experience and the passions that might be expended against it.

* * *

But the claims of the material world do not leave Bellow's fiction, as *Seize the Day* (1956) went on to show. Indeed, after the contingent open style and comic abundance of *The Adventures of Augie March*, this

---

could well be read as a step backward toward his earlier manner of writing. It is a tight novella set in New York over a very short time-span, a period of twenty-four hours, one seized day; and, like a short story, it moves toward one single dense instance of illumination. (Suitably it appeared in the American edition along with three of Bellow's best short stories, 'A Father to Be' (1955), 'Looking for Mr Green' (1951), 'The Gongaza Manuscripts' (1954), and his one-act play *The Wrecker.*) In *Seize the Day* an exact economy prevails, the story's world being created only as it impinges on its hero, in a sequence of instants. Likewise the title asserts this notion of instantaneousness, so opposite, in a sense, to Augie March's abundant inclusiveness. But this book, too, is a comedy, exploring the relationship between an absurd human being and an act of affirmation; indeed it has been rightly seen as a classic story of the Jewish *Schlemiel* (the type of whom Jewish lore has it, 'If he went into the hat business, babies would be born without heads'), the clown of failure who also contains a virtuous suffering compassion.

Tommy is certainly a superfluous man, an ex-actor who has appropriately worked for seven years as an 'extra', in films, a clown-victim for whom nothing ever goes quite right, who is tugged together out of chaos. His Hollywood ambitions, career in salesmanship and marriage are all on the rocks; he is at the mercy of an accusing father and an exploiting wife. There is a wild absurdity about his body and clothes ('He liked to wear good clothes, but once he had put it on each article appeared to go its own way' (*SD*, p. 9)). On this one day, just before Yom Kippur, he is drowning in his stock of experience—a middle-aged semi-failure in a seedy hotel who still just hopes, like the pigeon he sees beyond the hotel window, to fly. Yet he knows himself to be a clumsy animal, needing help, a man of sorrows from whom everything goes and to whom nothing comes back, but who dreams beyond his own imperfection of a larger body and a larger soul. Already a man of ten false decisions, he is about to make another, by entrusting his money to the commercial manipulations of Dr Tamkin, a superb figure of the charlatan, a psychic adviser and classic confidence man who is able to see into the uncertainties and contentions of Tommy's burdened soul, offers to lead him through the money-markets to spiritual release, and gives him the advice he wishes to hear: 'The past is no good to us. The future is full of anxiety. Only the present is real—the here-and-now. Seize the day' (p. 72). A man of love must have help in a world like this, if he is to transform soul into social power, to take, as Tamkin puts it, a 'specimen risk'.

For all its tight economy, *Seize the Day* is very much in Bellow's new manner, a story of man as a suffering joker divided between the practical material world and a larger world of being. It is one of his most poised pieces of writing, tonally very exact and developing according to elaborate metaphorical codes, careful analogies and parallelisms, a matching of experience in objects and nature. The secondary characters are all aspects of Tommy's quest—the stifling father, the exploiting wife, the various false guides of his life, like his corrupt agent Maurice Venice. Its comedy is metaphysical and complex, especially as it is distilled in the figure of Tamkin, the sage-like reality-instructor, the man who hints he has been one of the Detroit Purple Gang, headed a mental clinic, invented an unsinkable ship, and 'understands what gives'. A reader of everything, author of the self-help poem 'Mechanism vs Functionalism: Ism vs Hism', he promotes 'spontaneous emotions, open receptors and free impulses'. Tommy is the trapped comic victim, the clown of desire imprisoned in the biological facts of his existence, burdened with his 'inescapable self':

> The spirit, the peculiar burden of his existence, lay on him like an accretion, a load, a lump. In any moment of quiet, when sheer fatigue prevented him from struggling, he was apt to feel this mysterious weight, this growth or collection of nameless things which it was the business of his life to carry about. That must be what a man is for. (p. 44)

But that self is the treasure, if it can be not a 'pretender soul', trapped in the social mechanism and so existing only in a state of suffering, but a true soul, a larger body, that can go with joy. And it is this that Tamkin offers to release, by using money to go beyond money, to pass beyond a stock-market 'killing' to a curing, a more than material state. Tamkin displays Bellow's gift for superb character invention, and is the forerunner of many such figures; between them, Tommy and Tamkin and their metaphysical chatter make the book a moral farce.

But it is a serious farce, as we follow the essential metaphor— Tommy's motion from 'drowning', constriction, congestion to its final release in an opening of the heart. It comes through a strange path: Tamkin leads Tommy through the massed, overwhelming city to a brokerage office, where he is to make his 'killing' on the lard market, and restore his battered fortunes. Of course the money is lost; so is Tamkin, who promptly disappears. Materially destroyed, Tommy seems defeated. But Tamkin is guru as well as charlatan; he has always suggested that his promises are more than material, that through counterfeit meanings we might come to a humane truth. So it is appropriately the glimpsed figure of Tamkin, or someone like him, who leads Tommy to his final step. Chasing the trickster, he jostles through the crowds to find himself in a funeral parlour, where an unknown corpse lies in its bodily mystery, the ultimate double. Tommy, drowning in his unreleased tears and the watery grave of his circumstances, weeps at last over the stranger-corpse, tears that take him, we are told, 'deeper than sorrow, through torn sobs and cries toward the consummation of his heart's ultimate need' (p. 126). Such is the precise economy of the story that this is both its metaphorical and its humanistic outcome— Tommy's weeping is the final concentrating image of the chokings and drownings that have been threatening him, and a sacral resolution of the chaos of his so far unseized day.

His final release may thus be supposed to be his restoration, his atonement, his discovery of his own mortality but also of its potential. Tommy weeps for the body of another, and his own insufficient and debased body; he weeps, too, to find that that 'killing' to which he has devoted his day has a meaning; being part of the compromised struggle that life makes with lifelessness. He weeps also to find himself a part of the city's moving crowd, a crowd to which he has been helplessly trying to reach; and he weeps to discover the mortality that makes the living and the dead into one community, making life senseless but making living activity into a value, because it is simply all there is. At the same time the scene trembles, characteristically and comically, on the brink; Tommy is the comic mourner at the wrong funeral, mistakenly assumed by the crowd to be a close relative of the dead man ('The man's brother, maybe?') even though they are not alike. Tommy remains absurd to the last, yet it is the condition of absurdity that now comes to recognition; it is what we share, for there *is* a meaning in our lumbering body, our mortal existence, our clownlike status in the material world. The luminous moment on which the story ends both affirms and questions that daily absurdity. Thus, rather like Augie, Tommy, though absurd, is potential, and moves comically through an insufficient world to a humane outcome. And it is indeed this possibility of comic humanism that, with these novels of the 1950s, comes to seem the prime matter of enquiry in Bellow's work.

* * *

With *The Adventures of Augie March* and *Seize the Day*, Bellow seemed to have undertaken a new enterprise in comic perception. The first book uses autobiographical, picaresque, adventurous contingency to explore both the inescapability of history and the possibility of its dissolution in redemptive laughter; the second uses a method of poetic metaphysical distillation to dissolve the contingent material world into absurd tears. With his next book, *Henderson the Rain King* (1959), Bellow went on to draw the two enterprises together, mixing spacious picaresque construction and metaphorical concentration in a novel that seeks—just like its first-person narrator, Eugene Henderson—for 'grandeur', but seeks it in a mythic intensity and a symbolistic method.

Henderson the Rain King is indeed a book of enormous rhetorical and narrative extravagance; like *The Adventures of Augie March*, it is structured on a capacious self-narrating and a free and open pattern of 'adventures'. But, where Augie passes through a world of loosely enlarging social experience with metaphoric potential, Henderson explores *his* vitalistic desires in a landscape that is quickly transformed from one of social and historical specificity, from the amassed stuff of contemporary America or Europe, into legendary time and mythic space, so that the laws of ordering function differently. The bulk of the novel is placed in the landscape of an imaginary Africa (a continent Bellow had not visited) which is deliberately made prehistoric rather than historic, a world beyond human footprints, a place where 'all travel is mental'. And where Bellow's earlier books amend but respect the laws of realism and naturalism, *Henderson the Rain King* moves in another direction that also has deep roots in the history of American fiction, into the form of 'romance'.

'Romance' was the classic American Transcendentalist form, the mode of a fiction preoccupied neither by laws of realism deriving from social specificity nor by the prevailing rules of the normal. It was, said Nathaniel Hawthorne, the place where the actual and the imaginary might meet, each imbued with the properties of the other, and where a displayed fictional invention, a taste for the fantastic *and* the self-reflexive, might contend with and qualify the claim of empirical fact, the life of social and historical existence. It was a structure for enunciating American romantic idealism, but in modern fiction it has undergone a significant revival as a result of modern scepticism about realism. Robert Scholes has noted that one of the reasons for the solvency of realism in contemporary writing, and the movement of the novel toward what he calls 'fabulation'—to modes of romance, fantasy, myth, grotesquerie and self-conscious fictionality—has been the need to depict the power and dominance of the inner life.[5]

The comment applies well to *Henderson the Rain King*, a book that steps out of the social and historical world and at the same time evokes many of the romances of the past (it has appropriately been compared with Melville's *Moby Dick* (1851), where Ishmael likewise leaves the dull, land-based life of debasement and irritability to begin his quest into nature; and with Mark Twain's *A Connecticut Yankee in King Arthur's Court* (1889), where that romantic quest soon turns toward destruction). *Henderson the Rain King* likewise leaves realism behind in order to quest for 'reality'—Henderson describes himself as a man who, learning that T. S. Eliot's nightingale tells us that humankind cannot stand very much reality, asks how much *un*reality it can stand ('I fired that question right back of the nightingale. So what if reality may be terrible? It's better than what we've got' (p. 100)). The difference between classic American romance and Henderson's quest is that his is certainly comic and to a considerable degree parodic, and so needs reading very differently.

Bellow's achievement in the book is that, without ponderousness or over-assertion, he can provide the elaborate constituents of a modern journey into spirit, nature and culture, and so create a texture of contemporary mythography; at the same time he can ironize such a romantic and self-vaunting enterprise. Henderson is thus conceived—by Bellow and by himself, as first-person narrator—in the grand manner. He suffers none of the outward victimizations of Bellow's earlier heroes, being his first non-Jewish central figure, a millionaire of Anglo-Saxon Protestant stock who is recipient to a large heritage of wealth, historical responsibility and social service, a massive access to the history of American and western culture. His utterance is a vaunt, and extravagance is the functional state of his being. He has an excess of body, with a height of 6 ft 4 ins, a weight of 230 lbs; his face is, as he says, like Grand Central Station, or an unfinished church; he has 'the bulk of a football player and the colour of a gypsy'; he clothes himself in the clothes of farce. His inward life matches; he is, he says, to suffering what Gary is to smoke. He is a man of excess over-stated in nature:

The sun is like a great roller and flattens the grass. Beneath this grass the earth may be filled with carcasses, yet that distracts nothing from a day like this, for they have become human and the grass is thriving. When the air moves the brilliant flowers move too in the dark green beneath the trees. They burst against my open spirit because I am in the midst of this in the red violet dressing gown from the Rue de Rivoli bought on the day when Frances spoke the word divorce. I am there and am looking for trouble. (p. 31)

Disconcertingly positioned in relation to others, to society, objects and the natural world, rough, violent, physical, powerful, disoriented and soul-searching, Henderson is a metaphysical comedian, a supernatural bumbler with aspirations for his soul, a psycho-braggart speaking the great romantic vaunt of the Self.

So his wealth and scale, his violence and his frantic and grandiose marrying, loving and soul-searching, his heavy hand holding the delicate violin he wishes to play, all translate into a discourse that moves freely from vernacular confession to biblical incantation, and is the most marvellous quality of the book. His soul as readily to hand as his clothes, Henderson's language becomes a remarkable device for mediating an action that is equally extravagant and giving it intellectual and mythic possibilities and pretensions. His character is deliberately intended to call forth an analogous world of absurdity in experience: as he says, 'a damned fool going out into the world is bound and fated to encounter damned fool phenomena' (p. 59). And so, in Africa, he does, for Bellow invents a continent bereft of its more familiar contents and replaced by two contrasting states of history, culture, and psychic relation to nature, and these likewise function both mythically and comically.

Henderson is indeed, as Bellow once said, 'an absurd seeker after high qualities'; his adventures both evoke basic myths or archetypes and present themselves as the stuff of eclectic anthropological and cosmic farce. Like all first-person narrators, Henderson is hard to measure, and the book has been very variously read. But Henderson's egocentric story of spiritual hunger, his endless *I want, I want,* his drive to burst his spirit's sleep, is clearly a central part of Bellow's own mythic world. It is a world that starts in society, departs it, and returns to it; where *Henderson the Rain King* most differs from the other novels is in the scale granted to the hero and the degree to which the novel is created as an outward map of his inward psychic terrain.

Above all Henderson is a comic imperial hero appropriate to his time, that of the Eisenhower regnum, the season of material superpowerdom. He recognizes that it is the destiny of his generation of Americans to get out into the world to try to find life's wisdoms, and this means a step from his present material condition, which is that of a 'trophy':

A man like me may become something like a trophy. Washed, clean, and dressed in expensive garments. Under the roof is insulation; on the windows thermopane; on the floors carpeting; and on the carpets furniture, and on the furniture covers, and on the cloth covers plastic covers; and wallpaper and drapes! All is swept and garnished. And who is in the midst of this? Who is sitting there? Man! That's who it is, man! (p. 26)

He belongs to a world stuffed to excess with materials and goods, but feels detached from his antecedents and culture, heir to a meaningless inheritance, 'a displaced person'. 'Nobody truly occupies a station in life any more', he reflects. 'There are mostly people who feel they occupy the place that belongs to another by rights' (p. 35).

Society is again a lunatic contemporary prison, a place of chaotic rush and inhuman madness, creating a dislocated or debased image of the self: so, as an act of deliberate cultural sacrilege, he farms pigs, making great profits while feeling himself as debased as his animals. He is energetic but aimless, powerful but dissipating power, moving toward entropy. Like previous Bellow heroes, if on a characteristically larger scale, he finds that social existence generates depression and rage. His marriage is a disaster, and whenever he goes among people there is, he says, 'the devil to pay'. He accepts that he lives in an age of madness, and that 'to expect to be untouched by madness is a form of madness. But the pursuit of sanity can be a form of madness, too' (p. 27). And it is his rage that brings about his break with society; losing his temper with his family one morning at breakfast, he rages so loudly that it frightens and kills the old lady who comes in to cook his meals. He reads this as the final lesson in his debasement, evidence of the way he disturbs and is disturbed by the surrounding environment, is unfit to live among men. So, threatened too with pointless death, he leaves a note on the corpse (*Do not disturb*), and sets out, a man who has ruined 'the original piece of goods issued to me and was travelling to find a remedy' (p. 74), from the social to the pre-social world.

The Africa he travels to is of course classic mythic ground for the western mind; his journey calls up the history of safari, exploration and buried treasure; Livingstone, Hemingway, Tarzan and 'She', the heart of darkness, the waste land of barbarism secreted in civilization, 'Mr Kurtz—he dead'. But a damned fool indeed encounters damned fool phenomena, and Bellow's is a mock-Africa, anthropologically dense and allusive but populated with African absurdists and Dr Tamkins, black gurus in pursuit themselves of much the same natural, anthropological and determinist lore that preoccupies Henderson's own abundant mind. Africa promptly looks to Henderson like 'the ancient bed of mankind'; the land is all 'simplified and splendid, and I felt I was entering the past—the real past, no history or junk like that' (p. 46). In fact history is not so easily escaped; the two tribes he presently encounters represent two fundamental versions of the relationship between man and nature, myth and history. He travels through the desert with a Christian African guide, Romilayu, who takes him first to the Arnewi, a peaceable tribe of cattle-raisers who appear to live in a prehistoric Golden Age. Their language contains no oppositions, and they live by an unambitious goodness, removed from Henderson's desire to burst his spirit's sleep. Even so, Henderson has little trouble making his metaphysical hungers understood, and most of those he meets are in some fashion conspirators in his soul-searching; even the animals conspire with his psychic needs and ambitions. So, too, does the weather; he arrives in a time of drought, when the cattle are dying from the pollution of their water tank by frogs; the Arnewi's religion of acceptance forbids them to intervene.

As with Mark Twain's Hank Morgan (in *A Connecticut Yankee in King Arthur's Court*) Henderson's innocent American desire for service is aroused: 'I thought, this will be one of those mutual aid deals; where the Arnewi are irrational I'll help them; and where I'm irrational they'll help me' (p. 83). Custom first demands he wrestle with the chief, whom he defeats with his strength, and meet the queen, Willatale, blind in one eye, as Bellow's Sammler (*Mr Sammler's Planet*) will be, and similarly a repository of transhistorical wisdom. She accepts Henderson and tells him that he possesses *grun-tu-molani*, 'man wants to live', the life-force. Feeling he is on the right track, he decides to use Yankee technology and blow the frogs out of the tank with homemade explosives; he blows up both frogs and tank. The drought has already been recognized as internal ('As we turned away I felt as though that cistern of problem water with its algae and its frogs had entered me, occupying a square space in my interior, and sloshing around as I moved' (p. 60)) and the disaster is Henderson's too. Unable to acquiesce in the given, able to counter stagnation only with excess vitality and technique, he has to leave in disgrace and humiliation, 'having demolished both the water and my hopes. From now I'd never learn more about the *grun-tu-molani*' (p. 106).

But his unwilling Vergil, Romilayu, leads him to a second tribe, the Wariri ('chillun darkness', says Romilayu), who were once linked to the Arnewi but now live in a different historical and psychological stage, belonging to the fallen timebound world, an age of violence, action and change. Where the Arnewi manifest a 'female' peacefulness and acceptance, the Wariri manifest a 'male' energy and force. The Arnewi are associated with cattle; the Wariri beast is the lion, and culture and nature are in endless psychic struggle.[6]

This is more appropriate territory for Henderson, and the place of his chief adventures. The Wariri—who have a more complex social system, carry guns, and have a kind of police and immigration service—capture and interrogate him and place him in a room with a corpse, confronting him with his deepest anxiety, that of death; he copes by disposing of the body in a ravine. This is a test of strength; the Wariri have a use for Henderson's excessive, undirected energy. Instead of accepting the drought, they have a rain-making ritual to break it—to 'prime the pumps of the firmament', as their king, Dahfu, puts it. Part of the ritual involves lifting a heavy wooden goddess, Mummah, from one spot to another; after the tribal strongman fails, Henderson, feeling use for his strength at last, asks permission to undertake the task and, in what is effectively a moment of sexual mastery over the idol, he succeeds and feels renewed:

> I was so gladdened by what I had done that my whole body was filled with soft heat, with soft and sacred light. . . . My spirit was awake and welcomed life anew. Damn the whole thing! Life anew! I was still alive and kicking and I had the old *grun-tu-molani*. (p. 181)

Spirit and world seem to meet in a function; part of Henderson's quest is over. But there is the question of social service: Henderson now becomes Sungo, the tribal rain king, being stripped, thrown into a water tank and made part of a shrieking dance as the rain obligingly falls. Above all he must become concerned with the political position of King Dahfu, educated in Syria, and 'a genius of my own mental type'. Dahfu is one of Bellow's richest versions of the wise if sometimes dangerous instructor, who often appears to Bellovian heroes, a man of thought, learning and extreme applications; and, like other heroes of legend, Henderson now has tasks to perform.

Dahfu has evolutionist psychological theories, a compound of Lamarck and Wilhelm Reich, believing that the body originates in the brain, so that man may create his physiology, or change it:

what he was engrossed by was a belief in the transformation of human materials, that you could work either way, either from the rind to the core or
from the core to the rind; the flesh influencing the mind, the mind influencing the flesh, back again to the mind, back once more to the flesh. . . . For
him it was not enough that there might be disorders of the body that originated in the brain. *Everything* originated there. 'Although I do not wish to
reduce the stature of our discussion', he said, 'yet for the sake of example
the pimple on a lady's nose may be her own idea, accomplished by a conversion at the solemn command of her psyche; even more fundamentally
the nose itself, though part hereditary, is part also her own idea.' (pp. 220-1)

And he urges Henderson to adapt the 'exceptional amalgam of violent
forces' in him by introducing him to a lioness he keeps in the palace, a
figurative equivalent of 'the noble' which will have its turn in the
world. He explains that Henderson, in isolating himself, becoming
self-conscious, has grown contracted, whereas the lioness 'does not
take issue with the inherent. Is one hundred per cent within the given'
(p. 245). Henderson's experience of instruction with the lioness, the
killing beast totally unified and in itself, generates scenes of wonderful
invention within a remarkably inventive book; a book which metaphorically turns on the legendary equivalence between animal life and
human states of being. But before the lessons are complete, accident
dissolves the apparently profitable instruction; Dahfu is killed by a
wild lion on a ritual lion hunt, and reveals finally that Henderson is his
successor—and that when he loses the power to carry Mummah and
satisfy the harem of wives he will be sacrificed, and hence that sav-
agery is not capable of being mastered but involves lasting violence.
Henderson's situation returns to extremity; he sees that Dahfu too has
not resolved the problem of relating energy to communal task.

Henderson escapes from the Wariri, taking with him the lion cub
thought to be Dahfu's soul, and a concept of human nobility drawn
from him, which he utters to Romilayu:

We're supposed to think nobility is unreal. But that's just it. The illusion is on the other foot. They make us think we crave more and more illusions. Why, I don't crave illusions at all. They say, Think big. Well, that's baloney of course, another business slogan. But greatness! That's another thing altogether. Oh, greatness! Oh, God! Romilayu, I don't mean inflated, swollen, false greatness. . . . But the universe itself being put into us, it calls out for scope. The eternal is bonded onto us. It calls out for its share. (p. 297)

And, in what is to be a characteristic ending, the path of instruction has itself to be amended: the lessons taken have been to a degree mock lessons. Flying home across the Atlantic, accompanied by the lion cub, reminder of nobility sacrificed to society, and an orphan boy he has met on the flight, his final twin, he realizes that he must settle for his own nature, closer to the fairground bear, that sad humorist, than the lion.

Thus, as before, the novel ends on a contained and measured possibility; Henderson is now no longer matched to the pigs with which he began, nor to the cattle or the lion, but to his own comic shambling largeness. Warrior and female principle, violence and gentleness reconcile; the world contains lasting traces that are more than single occasions. Henderson has found a print in nature to attach himself to:

if corporeal things are an image of the spiritual and visible objects are renderings of invisible ones, then Smolak [the fairground bear he had once worked with] and I were outcasts together, two humorists before the crowd, but brothers in our souls—I embeared by him, and he probably humanized by me . . . something deep was already inscribed on me. (p. 316)

Landing in Newfoundland, Henderson, knowing his imprint, runs with bear and child round the plane, 'leaping, leaping, pounding and tingling over the pure white lining of the grey Arctic silence' (p. 318). It closes on a sense of freedom, a celebration of stark created nature; but also a sense of the conditioned and the bonded. Like Augie before him and Herzog after, Henderson enters the kingdom of knowledge which contains both process and biology and those eternal traces—the limits and the possibilities of self-creation.

Henderson in fact concludes the book as Bellow's most affirmative hero, to the end the abundant comedian of his own self-assertion. Bellow once spoke of Henderson's quest as 'a remedy for his anxiety over death . . . the indeterminate and indefinite anxiety, which most of us accept as the condition of life which he is foolhardy enough to resist.' His struggle has been against 'cosmic coldness'; yet, in the Newfoundland cold, he finds a state of joy in which he can run freely.[7]

It is an ending that Leslie Fiedler has called one of 'unearned euphoria', and it promotes certain doubts. What, though, sustains the lyric note to the end is Bellow's own note of comic metaphysics, which conducts Henderson—with his sense that one must live a thing before one knows it, and that visible objects are the renderings of invisible ones—into a new and promising state of living to know. It is this engaged space between the lyric and the comic, manifesting itself both as metaphysics and wit, that gives Bellow the tones of a major novelist. Henderson's progress through the kingdom of nature, through a world where animals measure out the stuff of human potential, where single instances leave lasting traces, where a commanding biology can be transliterated into an endless becoming, is an extraordinary conceit. The mythic intent makes it very much a book of the fifties: a decade obsessed with the hope that the imagination might generate at last the saving fable, the tale of the waste land redeemed, the desert of civilization watered by some humanist or metaphysical discovery. But the myth both asserts and mocks itself, takes on a neoparodic form; and it is the method of comic fabulation, of expansive and pyrotechnic farce, of absurdity finding a path to human measurement, that makes *Henderson the Rain King* so strangely notable a novel.

Notes

1. *The Adventures of Augie March* (New York: Viking Press, 1953); *Seize the Day* (New York: Viking Press 1956); *Henderson the Rain King* (New York: Viking Press, 1959).

2. Saul Bellow, 'Some Notes on Recent American Fiction', *Encounter*, 21 (November 1963), pp. 22-9; reprinted in Malcolm Bradbury (ed.), *The Novel Today: Writers on Modern Fiction* (Manchester and London: Manchester University Press and Fontana, 1977), pp. 54-70. Also, Saul Bellow, 'Literature', in Mortimer Adler and Robert M. Hutchins (eds), *The Great Ideas Today* (Chicago, Ill.: Encyclopaedia Britannica, 1963), pp. 163-4. For Bellow's views of comedy and a reading of his comic methods see Sarah Blacher Cohen, *Saul Bellow's Enigmatic Laughter* (Urbana and Chicago, Ill., and London: University of Illinois Press, 1974).

3. 'Introduction', in Saul Bellow (ed.), *Great Jewish Short Stories* (New York: Dell, 1963).

4. Quoted in Harper, op. cit.

5. Robert Scholes, *The Fabulators* (New York: Oxford University Press, 1967).

6. Judie Newman, in an unpublished lecture, has taken these points further, observing that Bellow always takes seriously Ortega y Gasset's dictum, quoted in *The Adventures of Augie March*, that 'Man has not a nature but a history', and that Henderson encounters fundamental models of history in Africa: the Arnewi live in a Golden Age timeless pastoral, the Wariri in a fallen cyclical history, and Henderson has the American prophetic-progressive view; hence the 'supposedly "mythic" or "romance" setting is merely a pretext to an exploration of the very bases of the historical sense.'

7. In the valuable study *The Novels of Saul Bellow: An Introduction* (University Park, Pa, and London: Pennsylvania State University Press, 1967), K. M. Opdahl usefully emphasizes that when Henderson feels at last at home in the cold he has come to terms with the 'cosmic coldness' of death and inanimation which has haunted him through the book.

"Weirdly Tranquil" Vision:
The Point of View of Moses Herzog_____

M. Gilbert Porter

The consensus among Bellovian scholars and critics is that, all things considered, *Herzog* remains Bellow's best novel. Here artistic vision finds its appropriate concretions; meaning is achieved through form. Point of view is complicated and directly reflective of the emotional and intellectual condition of the protagonist. The end of the novel grows organically out of the exposition and resolves the initial conflict without making larger claims than the condition of the central intelligence can support. The theme is significant and presented with intensity. Views opposite to those of Herzog are given more than ample play in the characterizations of a large cast of antagonists and in the fundamental ambivalence in Herzog himself. The conflict in Herzog between his intellect and his sensibilities provides the integrating principle in the novel, setting up the complex point of view, inviting the "lessons" of the reality instructors, intensifying Herzog's anguish, and leading him, finally, to his transcendental affirmation, in which he frees himself from the compulsion of intellectual systematizing and relaxes in the freedom of an emotional/intuitional synthesis. *"The intellectual has been a Separatist,"* says Herzog as he approaches clarity. *"And what kind of synthesis is a Separatist likely to come up with?"* (322).

What passes for plot in the novel is a narrative strategy that moves Herzog from a state of agitation to a state of rest, from a frantic search for direction to a discovery of that direction. The events that attend Herzog's transformation, though, are presented mainly through Herzog's own perceptions as the central intelligence in a sophisticated and often convoluted narration. Thus, point of view is central to the assessment of Bellow's achievement in *Herzog*, yet most critics have settled for summary statements rather than detailed examinations of narrative technique. Earl Rovit, for example, observes that Bellow "reshuffles time sequences expertly, shifts Herzog's point of view from first- to third-person, employs the device of the fragmentary 'mental' letters as a masterly bridge between solipsism and communication, and casts an ambience of irony over his entire construction" (24). According to Peter Bischoff,

> *Der Roman ist zum wesentlichen Teil im Bewußtsein der Hauptfigur abgesiedelt. In einer technisch sehr ausgefeilten Verschachtelung von beschreibenden und szenischen Rückblenden sowie im Geiste konzipierten, mitunter aufgezeichneten, jedoch nie abgesandten Briefen spielt sich das "Psychodrama" Herzogs ab. Durch den Kunstgriff der wechselnden Perspektivierung verleiht Bellow der solipsistischen Selbstanalyse seines Protagonisten eine psychische Dynamik, die die beschreibenden und szenischen Erzählelemente in einer Mischung verschiedener Zeitebenen verbindet. Die Erzählperspektive wechselt zwischen figürlicher, figürlich-auktorialer, und auktorialer Erzählweise, wobei die figürliche Perspektive des Protagonisten ständig zwischen "I," "you," und "he" variiert. Ein solcher Wechsel innerhalb der Figurenperspektive wird dadurch ermöglicht, daß sich Herzog seines Bewßtseins stets bewußt ist. Indem Herzog sich nicht nut als Subjekt, sondern auch als Objekt betrachtet, entfremdet er sich von sich selbst. (96)*[1]

In a similar vein, Eusebio L. Rodrigues writes that "the narrative angle jumps around shifting wildly from one mode to another without warning and often within the same paragraph, creating an illusion of constant rapid nervous motion and a continuity of tempo that offsets the tortoise pace of the action and the cramping time schedule" (162). And Malcolm Bradbury comments that "this is a book set primarily *within* consciousness, and there is a parallel formlessness or oblique design in the novel's structure—until, finally, both Herzog and the book transfigure the plurality of words and explanations into significant silence" (138).

These remarks are all thoughtful and perceptive but remain, as far as point of view is concerned, within the realm of general observation. What follows here is an attempt to explore in some detail, but without becoming tedious, the actual functioning of narrative technique in the novel as it contributes to the development of Herzog's character.

The opening section of the novel presents Herzog as seriously distracted. The adulterous Gersbach and Madeleine are saying he is insane, and others have agreed with them. Herzog reports the rumor accurately without being disturbed or intimidated by it, behaving oddly but feeling "cheerful, clairvoyant, and strong" (1). In a Wordsworthian exercise, Herzog is recalling emotion in tranquility—and he approaches total recall—in the interest of justifying, putting into perspective, and clarifying the events that have led him to distraction.[2] Although the opening section precedes the ending section by only a few days of the week of the narrative time covered by the novel, the bulk of the book between beginning and end focuses on the domestic strife of the past year and includes memories and reflections extending as far back as Herzog's childhood.[3] Most of the events of the novel, then, are images recreated and relived—in pain, trembling, and humor—by a suffering mind, but the recollection leads ultimately to peace, though the journey is circuitous indeed.

The end of the introductory section shows Herzog viewing himself in the windowpane of the old house in Ludeyville that is as imposing and disordered as Herzog himself:

> He was taking a turn around the empty house and saw the shadow of his face in a gray, webby window. He looked weirdly tranquil. A radiant line went from mid-forehead over his straight nose and full, silent lips. (2)

The reflection of the self—"weirdly tranquil"—in the murky pane and the line bisecting the head are emblematic of both a divided consciousness and a narrative technique. Herzog is at once involved in and detached from his experience—pained, amused, bewildered, evaluative. The shifts in narrative from past to present, from private to public, from abstract to concrete, and from third to first person are reflective of Herzog's ambivalence. His intellectual fervor and emotional pain heighten his perceptions, making his observations in all areas vivid, intense, and—at least in terms of his own character—reliable.

Like Mr. Sammler in *Mr. Sammler's Planet*, Herzog looks both inward and outward. He is in his experience as participant; he is detached from it as spectator, witness, and judge. The shifting point of view keeps the reader aware of a protagonist who is consciously experiencing his experience. "Awareness was his work; extended consciousness was his line, his business. Vigilance" (278). That Herzog is a self examining himself is fundamentally revealed by a series of reflections in glass, water, and various mirrors, beginning with the image of the divided self in the murky windowpane. When Herzog recalls the scene in which Madeleine announced her intention to obtain a divorce, he looks back from his New York apartment on himself in Chicago putting up storm windows on the house Madeleine had ordered him out of:

> . . . lying with no more style than a chimpanzee, his eyes with greater than normal radiance watched his own work in the garden with detachment, as if he were looking through the front end of a telescope at a tiny clear image.
> *That suffering joker.* (11)

The present self sees the past self here through the perspective provided by elapsed time, but the subject and object are still one; the suffering joker in the garden is now the suffering joker on the couch. Shopping for clothes on Ramona's suggestion, Herzog examines himself in the store's "triple, lighted mirror": "His body seemed unaffected by his troubles, survived all blasts. It was his face that was devastated, especially about the eyes, so that it made him pale to see himself" (20). This is one of many such assessments of his condition. He is frightened by his condition, but he refuses to be intimidated by it or to take himself and his suffering too seriously: "Alone, he put his tongue out at himself and then withdrew from the triple mirror" (21). Looking back further still, Herzog remembers a moment in a subway after a visit with Marco in Philadelphia:

> The mirror of the gum machine revealed to Herzog how pale he was, un-healthy—wisps from his coat and wool scarf, his hat and brows, twisting and flaming outward in the overfull light and exposing the sphere of his face, the face of a man who was keeping up a front. Herzog smiled at this earlier avatar of his life, at Herzog the victim, Herzog the would-be lover, Herzog the man on whom the world depended for certain intellectual work, to change history, to influence the development of civilization. Several boxes of stale paper under his bed in Philadelphia were going to produce this very significant result. (104-05)

The pattern is constant. Recalling pain in the past produces a smile in the present, mitigating the pain but certainly not negating it. Although his anguish often ambushes him in the form of involuntary tears, Her-zog tells Himmelstein, "I'm going to shake this off, I'm not going to be a victim. I hate the victim bit" (82). Herzog's recurrent smile despite his tears signifies both resilience and resistance, acknowledging the pain but promising to transcend it.

The desire for transcendence sometimes assumes the form of imagi-native reflection. Waiting for the ferry at Woods Hole, Herzog looks into the water "at the net of bright reflections on the bottom. . . . There was no stain in the water, where schools of minnows swam. Herzog sighed and said to himself, 'Praise God—praise God'" (91). Like the Ancient Mariner blessing the water snakes, Herzog is moved to prayer by the clarity and beauty of the water. He yearns to see his essential be-ing at one here with the brilliance of nature. "If his soul could cast a re-flection so brilliant, and so intensely sweet, he might beg God to make such use of him. But that would be too simple. . . . The actual sphere is not clear like this, but turbulent, angry" (91). Despite Herzog's yearn-ing, the albatross of his mortality does not drop from his burdened neck, and he must continue his quest for clarity in the realm of the actual. In the mirror in Ramona's apartment he sees reflected the same struggling self, and in the police station Herzog reads in Madeleine's eyes the vote for his death, his total nonexistence, a reflected wish that frees him from any residual hold Madeleine could have over him. These reflections of the self are symbolic of Herzog's anguished spirit, his heightened consciousness, his compulsion to revisit his pain, to tell all in order to overcome chaos and prevent nervous collapse. The reader—a transfixed Wedding Guest—is thus compelled to attention and to sympathy, and the narrative framework is neatly established for the credible juxtaposition of memories, letters, dramatic scenes, philosophical discourses, *obiter dicta*, social commentary, and assorted musings in a convolution of Herzog's present and past.

Herzog's struggle toward clarity and balance as revealed in various physical reflections is established further through Bellow's use of the shifting point of view in the modified technique of a central intelligence who requires the reader to share his pain, his humor, his humanity, and his process of discovery and transformation. The pattern usually starts with traditional third-person objective point of view (Herzog in the narrative present), shifts to first person (Herzog recalling an antecedent event, reliving it in scenario), shifts to first-person editorial (Herzog analyzing the event in retrospect), and then shifts back to third-person (Herzog from authorial perspective resuming the pace of narrative present). The letters typically provide the stimulus for the interruption of third-person narrative to follow Herzog, in dialogue and dramatic episode, through one of his excursions into his past. One example will suffice to illustrate the technique:

En route on the train to visit Libby Sissler, Herzog, in a New Haven car, is described in the third person from the point of view of an objective author: "He sat in a cramped position, pressing the valise to his chest, his traveling-desk, and writing rapidly in the spiral notebook. *Dear Zelda . . .*" (34). Addressing Zelda in the second-person vocative places Herzog in the first-person role, in which he returns in memory to hockey games with Herman and conversations with Zelda both before and after the divorce—these memories presented dramatically and through narrative summary, but here the third person is Herzog describing himself, and the first person is Herzog in action: "He tried to get a grip on himself. Half buttoned, red-eyed, unshaved, he looked disgraceful. Indecent. He was telling Zelda his side of the case: 'I know she's turned you against me—poisoned your mind, Zelda'" (37). As Herzog dramatically renders the scene from the past with himself as both first and third person, he recreates what he said as well as what he thought, and this scenario is interrupted in its turn by the continuation, in italics, of the letter to Zelda in the narrative present:

"Well, I know you aren't like the other wives out here. . . ."

Your kitchen is different, your Italian lamps, your carpets, your French provincial furniture, your Westinghouse, your mink, your country club, your cerebral palsy canisters are all different.

I am sure you were sincere. Not insincere. True insincerity is hard to find. (38)

With sarcasm, with equivocal attempts at fairness, with bemusement and discomfort, the "he" of the present relives the "I" of the past: "(Recalling, in the still standing train, the thwarted and angry eagerness of these attempted explanations, he had to laugh. Nothing but a wan smile passed over his face). . . . He saw himself in the train window, hearing his own words clearly. 'I think you're on the level'" (40). With this reflection of the self viewing the self, Herzog ends his letter in the narrative present—and this episode into the antecedent past—with an editorial comment in first person evaluating himself and Zelda: "*But I'm no criminal, don't have it in me; frightful to myself, instead. Anyway, Zelda, I see you had tremendous pleasure, double excitement, lying from an overflowing heart*" (41). The self-effacing author now resumes control in the narrative present and advances the movement of Herzog in the third person: "All at once the train left the platform and entered the tunnel. Temporarily in darkness, Herzog held his pen"

(41). Bellow then records his central intelligence making a Freudian-inspired notation suggested by the memories of Madeleine and Zelda as they have conditioned his present state of mind: "Herzog wrote, *Will never understand what women want. What do they want? They eat green salad and drink human blood*" (41-42).

The whole novel, of course, is a reflection, beginning and ending with Herzog practicing the self-examination that Socrates and Thoreau advocated to make life worth living. The section immediately preceding provides a paradigm of the technique that makes the novel work as an extended reflection in which Herzog prepares himself through hyperawareness for a better future. In a typical passage, Herzog describes his own rhetorical stance:

> We must be what we are. That is necessity. And what are we? Well, here he was trying to hold on to Ramona as he ran from her. And thinking that he was binding her, he bound himself, and the culmination of this clever goofiness might be to entrap himself. Self development, self-realization, happiness—these were the titles under which these lunacies occurred. Ah, poor fellow!—and Herzog momentarily joined the objective world in looking down on himself. He too could smile at Herzog and despise him. But there still remained the fact. *I* am Herzog. I have to *be* that man. There is no one else to do it. After smiling, he must return to his own Self and see the thing through. (66-67)

My main point is that Bellow's use of strategic shifts in person and time—the special employment of an intricate central-intelligence point of view—embodies particularly well the condition of the protagonist, torn as he is between the realm of thought and the realm of feeling, between the evidence for despair in the world and the desire for affirmation in himself, between the active man and the reflective consciousness. The intimacy of the first person enlists our sympathy; the objectivity of the third person, whether Herzog's voice or Bellow's, lends credibility to the perceptions. The vacillations in Herzog find engaging and natural expression in the vacillating point of view in a masterful narrative technique that enables Bellow as an artist to display his shiniest wares.

From *Saul Bellow Journal* 8.1 (Winter 1989): 3-11. Copyright © 1989 by *Saul Bellow Journal*. Reprinted with permission of *Saul Bellow Journal*.

Notes

1. "The novel is located essentially in the consciousness of the protagonist. The 'psychodrama' of Herzog is played out in a technically refined labyrinth of descriptive and scenic flashbacks, and of letters which are conceived in the mind, sometimes recorded, but never sent. Through the artifice of the changing perspective, Bellow grants to the solipsistic self-analysis of his protagonist a psychical dynamism which combines the descriptive and scenic narrative elements in a mixture of various time levels. The narrative point of view alternates between character, persona, and omniscient author; thus the point of view of the protagonist varies constantly between 'I,' 'you,' and 'he.' Such a change within the character-perspective is made possible by the fact that Herzog is always conscious of his own consciousness. In observing himself not only as subject but also as object Herzog becomes a stranger to himself" (translation mine).

2. For a discussion of elements of English romanticism in *Herzog* and elsewhere in Bellow's work, see Allan Chavkin.

3. Time is kept strategically vague in the novel, but as Herzog gathers his forces in the Berkshires toward the end of the narrative, he muses, "But was it only a week—five days? Unbelievable!" (326). The narrative goes on, then (327), with Herzog's report of his desultory activities ("For the next two days—or were there three?—Herzog did nothing but send such messages, and write down songs, psalms, and utterances.") before he shaves to meet his brother Will, makes a date with Ramona, and ends the novel with "no messages for anyone" (341).

Works Cited

Bellow, Saul. *Herzog*. New York: Viking, 1964.

Bischoff, Peter. *Saul Bellows Romane*: Entfremdung und Suche. Bonn: Bouvier, 1975.

Bradbury, Malcolm. *The Modern American Novel*. London: Oxford UP, 1983.

Chavkin, Allan. "Bellow and English Romanticism." *Studies in the Literary Imagination* 17.2 (1984): 7-18.

Rodrigues, Eusebio L. *Quest for the Human: An Exploration of Saul Bellow's Fiction*. Lewisburg: Bucknell UP, 1981.

Rovit, Earl. *Saul Bellow*. Minneapolis: U of Minnesota P, 1967.

The Holocaust in *Mr. Sammler's Planet*_____

S. Lillian Kremer

Three years after the Arab nations invoked the rhetoric of liquidation in their anti-Israel propaganda, Saul Bellow returned to and expanded treatment of the Holocaust in his fiction. In his pre-1970 novels the Holocaust was evoked symbolically and allusively and the six million were peripheral phantoms; in *Mr. Sammler's Planet*, they live. Unlike the European Holocaust chroniclers Elie Wiesel and Andre Schwarz-Bart, who set their fiction in the Holocaust era and confront the concentration camp world, the American novelist eschews the dramatization of atrocities and camp life. Instead Bellow evoked the past through haunting recollections of survivors and examination of current behavioral and emotional disorders stemming from wartime brutality. Although this method sacrifices the immediacy of Nazi horror, the lasting effect of the barbarism is powerfully conveyed. Holocaust survivors continue to suffer decades after their initial victimization. Wartime clamor echoes in their minds; tormenting visions reach across chasms of time and space oppressing the victims. For the survivors, contemporary American reality is marred by the European disaster. Bellow's focus is on the consequences of survival: death or distortion of the creative impulse; impairment of the capacity to love; and religious confusion.

The novel's protagonist is Artur Sammler, an aging introspective intellectual who wonders if he has a place among the living and is convinced that he is marked forever by his Holocaust experience. Risen from the dead, the survivor, whose name comes from the Yiddish word *zammlen* (to gather) is a Tiresias figure, a one-eyed observer and judge of the post-Holocaust wasteland. He collects evidence of violence, corruption, and degeneration. As the horror of the Holocaust forced Sammler out of pre-war complacency in 1939, confrontation with a black felon in New York City is the catalyst for propelling him from post-war spiritual withdrawal into contact with the violence and excesses of the Vietnam era. A victim of irrational cruelty, Sammler speaks for reason, order, tradition, and human dignity in the midst of chaos. World War II has been a cataclysmic disruption of Sammler's pleasant, productive life. The son of a wealthy assimilated Polish-Jewish family, Sammler was part of the Bloomsbury group and enjoyed the privileges of the British intelligentsia. After a twenty year career in London as a correspondent for Warsaw journals, he returned to wartime Poland to reclaim the family land. There he was engulfed by his ancestral legacy of persecution: his wife was killed, and he suffered the loss of an eye and damage to his nervous system. These injuries continue to plague Sammler, erupting periodically in the form of migraine headaches which "put him in a post-epileptic condition."[1]

Rather than employ a single extended flashback, Bellow renders Sammler's war memories in segments of spontaneous recollection at crisis periods in the protagonist's post-war life. This approach is evident in the first chapter. Sammler associates his encounter with a New York criminal with his Polish era of terror. Fear of the thief is manifested in a constriction of the nerves, muscles, and blood vessels at the base of the skull which suggest "The breath of wartime Poland passing over the damaged tissues—that nerve spaghetti, as he thought of it" (9). As he tries to escape from the pickpocket, the old man is reminded of his European fugitive status:

he knew something about lying low. He had learned in Poland, in the war, in forests, cellars, passageways, cemeteries. Things he had passed through once which had abolished a certain margin of leeway ordinarily taken for granted. Taking for granted that one will not be shot stepping into the street, nor clubbed to death as one stoops to relieve oneself, nor hunted in an alley like a rat. This civil margin once removed Mr. Sammler would never trust the restoration totally. (47)

Late in the second chapter, we discover that near the war's end, Sammler was hidden in a Polish tomb by a cemetery caretaker who had no particular fondness for him. We then move further back in time to Sammler's recollection of the mass murder of Jews. In this episode, Bellow constructs an horrendous series of images which move the reader to indignation, while at the same time he maintains artistic distance and avoids overt moral judgment:

> he and sixty or seventy others, all stripped and naked and having dug their own grave, were fired upon and fell in. Bodies upon his own body. Crushing. His dead wife nearby somewhere. Struggling out much later from the weight of corpses, crawling out of the loose soil. Scraping on his belly. Hiding in a shed. Finding a rag to wear. Lying in the woods many days. (86-87)

A more complete account of the graveside experience appears at the novel's midpoint. Here, the remembrance of Holocaust times moves beyond physical description to include philosophic speculation and moral judgment. As Sammler examines his obsessive concern with the past, he hypothesizes that some Navajo or Apache must have risen from a near fatal interment in the Grand Canyon and put it out of mind. As a moralist, Bellow juxtaposes this speculation about a hypothetical accident with a calculated government program of genocide. He adds the chilling reference to Adolf Eichmann's discomfort at the fresh swelling of blood around his boots at a similar mass grave. He thus underscores the crucial distinction between accidental violence and the organized brutality European Jewry suffered. As though he anticipates the remonstrance of those weary of hearing of the Holocaust, Sammler asks, "Why speak of it?" Because, as Elie Wiesel reminds us, survivors need to bear witness, to remind the world of its acquiescence, of its silence and its complicity in the annihilation of European Jewry.

In the final chapter, Bellow sketches the mass murder scene in even greater physical detail. Concrete sensory images and specificity of detail and image vividly evoke the landscape of death:

The hole deepened, the sand clay and stones of Poland, their birth-place, opened up. He had just been blinded, he had a stunned face, and he was unaware that blood was coming from him till they stripped and he saw it on his clothes . . . the guns began to blast, and then came a different sound of soil. The thick fall of soil. A sound of shovel-metal gritting. . . . He had clawed his way out. If he had been at the bottom, he would have suffocated. . . . Perhaps others had been buried alive in that ditch. (249)

Whereas earlier passages stressed philosophic meditation and psychological terror of time past, this passage focuses on the torment of anticipation. This emphatic graphic portrayal of physical movement toward death and the first rendering of the mass graveside scene contribute to the novel's structural unity. The Holocaust becomes the reader's preoccupation, as Bellow forces one to consider the experience in its diverse ramifications.

Bellow parallels Sammler's Holocaust experiences with a psychosocial probe of the long-term effect of Nazism on survivor-victims by surrounding Sammler with a community of survivors whose Holocaust induced disorders are variations and reverberations of Sammler's troubles. Sammler's son-in-law, Eisen, a painter, foundry worker, and metal sculptor, manifests his disturbance in violent behavior and the distortion of the creative impulse. A dehumanized creature of iron, Eisen has survived the violence of the war, but is permanently psychologically damaged. Physically mutilated in war, he remains a psychological cripple in peacetime, three decades after his mistreatment. His creative potential aborted, he has become grotesque, a craftsman of the ugly.

Eisen's painting reflects the trauma of his existence. Sammler finds the art appalling, the work of "an insane mind and a frightening soul" (62). All the people in the paintings resemble corpses. Eisen also fashions metal medallions into traditional Jewish symbols, Stars of David, branched candelabra, scrolls, and ram's horns with Hebrew inscriptions. The inscriptions he selects, "*Nahamu*, comfort ye," and God's command to Joshua, "*Hazak*, Strengthen thyself," defy those wishing to destroy him. The victim of homicidal maniacs, Eisen has become a madman himself. While using his sculpture to attack a criminal who is endangering another person, Eisen transforms the creative to the destructive act. Whereas Sammler's ordeal in suffering has added depth to his character, left him with the compassion to weep for a fallen enemy of his people, Eisen responds only to the law of the jungle: kill or be killed.

The histories of both Sammler and Eisen are marred by non-Aryan anti-Semitic persecution. Having escaped Nazi slaughter, both men encounter the hatred of their comrades-in-arms. Polish partisans determine to "reconstruct a Jewless Poland" (129), and begin to massacre the Jewish partisans. Sammler's escape from his anti-Semitic fellow citizens is reiterated in Eisen's deliverance from Russian soldiers. After being wounded at Stalingrad, Eisen was traveling in a troop transport with other casualties and was treacherously thrown from the moving train, "Apparently because he was a Jew" (25). Speaking of the incident years later in Haifa, Eisen remarks ironically, "Good fellows–*tovarishni*, but you know what Russians are when they have a few glasses of vodka" (26). In these accounts of non-German anti-Jewish violence, Bellow adds his voice to those with the courage to condemn the active complicity of Christian and Communist countries in the Nazi effort to rid Europe of its Jewish population. "*J'accuse*" is clearly heard in Bellow's stark references to non-Aryan efforts to apply Germany's Final Solution to the "Jewish Problem."

Sammler's daughter, Shula-Slawa, whose name indicates her identity conflict, suffers prolonged religious and cultural schizophrenia, as a result of four years spent hiding from the Nazis in a Polish convent. Although Sammler is outraged by Shula's present-day antics and will not excuse them, he interprets her post-Holocaust lapses from decency as the direct result of her wartime deprivation. Shula, too, manifests the connection in her regression to her native tongue when she is confronted with criminal charges. Although Sammler recognizes the connection, he resents Shula's effort to exploit her victimization. Shula's portrait reflects the plight of some Jewish survivors who were protected from the Nazi menace by Christian religious orders and subsequently experienced religious confusion stemming from indoctrination by their protectors. Many years after the war, Shula's confusion recurs, most poignantly during the Easter season.

> Things that ought but failed actually to connect. Wigs for instance suggested orthodoxy; Shula in fact had Jewish connections. She seemed to know lots of rabbis in famous temples and synagogues. . . . She went to sermons and . . . lectures. . . . She became well acquainted with the rabbi, the rabbi's wife and family—involved in Dadaist discussions about faith, ritual, Zionism, Masada, the Arabs. But she had Christian periods as well. . . . Almost always at Easter she was a Catholic. Ash Wednesday was observed and it was with a smudge between the eyes that she often came into clear focus for the old gentleman. (24-25)

Thus it is obvious that Shula's interest in Catholicism, focusing as it does on the period when the observant religious ponder physical death and spiritual rebirth, is but another instance of her Holocaust-haunted life. In addition to religious schizophrenia, this passage demonstrates Shula's obsession with survival as illustrated by its allusion to Masada, the site where a band of Jewish zealots resisted the mighty Roman legions for two years before committing suicide. The survivor of the Nazi attempt to annihilate Jewry remembers another fallen empire's attempt to destroy the Jewish people. That she dwells on the matter of Jewish persecution and survival in the context of Masada suggests also the post-war Israeli attitude toward Masada as a symbol of defiance and strength against the enemies of Israel. It is symbolic of both Jewish defeat and victory.

Loss of faith or religious confusion, major themes in European Holocaust literature, appear not only in Shula's Jewish/Christian dichotomy and another survivor's apostasy, but in Sammler's Jobian probings. Although his ancestors were Orthodox Jews, his parents were freethinkers and Sammler had not been observant prior to the war. Nevertheless, in a post-war analysis of his spiritual evolution he claims that the Holocaust was the catalyst for his doubts concerning God's purpose:

> During the war I had no belief, and I had always disliked the ways of the Orthodox. I saw that God was not impressed by death. Hell was his indifference. But inability to explain is no ground for disbelief. Not as long as the sense of God persists. I could wish that it did not persist. The contradictions are so painful. No concern for justice? Nothing of pity? Is God only the gossip of the living? (215)

To question God is within Jewish tradition. What historic period could be more trying to one's faith than the Holocaust? Temporary apostasy and atheism were not uncommon responses. Josephine Knopp finds Sammler's assessment of God strikingly parallel to that in Elie Wiesel's presentation of the catastrophe. "There is the same indictment of God for His failure to uphold the covenant, the same attempt to reject God completely, the same involuntary, unwelcome persistence of belief."[2] From the vantage point of the late 1960s Sammler can rationalize his judgment against God from within the framework of religious doubt. The partisan who rejoiced at his capacity to kill a German soldier was the atheistic, acculturated Bloomsbury litterateur dehumanized by Nazi and Polish anti-Semitism. It is not until his post-war concern with spiritual values that Sammler responds to a similar situation, the death of an Egyptian soldier in the Six-Day War, with compassion.

Sammler's lack of interest in recovering his pre-1939 cultivated Anglophile identity is consistent with the views of Elie Wiesel, inmate of Auschwitz, that the Holocaust "put into question everything that we had believed before."[3] After Auschwitz, civilization could not and should not be the same. As a result of the apocalyptic experience of the Holocaust and its paralytic aftermath, Sammler seeks spiritual understanding.

> He wanted, with God, to be free from bondage of the ordinary and finite. A soul released from Nature, from impressions, and from everyday life. For this to happen God Himself must be waiting, surely. And a man who has been killed and buried should have no other interest. He should be perfectly disinterested. . . . What besides the spirit should a man care for who has come back from the grave? (109)

Bruch, a Buchenwald survivor and an acquaintance of Sammler's, evinces frustration in his determined effort to reject God and Judaism. Anger and spite seem to be Bruch's primary motives for denouncing God and faith. Although Bellow chooses to treat Bruch's "apostasy" ironically, he explores the serious implications of Holocaust-inspired Jewish doubt of God. Bruch's grandstand "rejection" of God and Judaism is, in essence, an expression of his desperate disappointment in God's apparent indifference to the suffering of His people. In the end, Bruch does not abandon God or religion; he merely changes denominations, revolting from orthodox piety and strict adherence to Torah to a less stringent form of Judaism. Unlike Sammler, who actually denies God for a time, Bruch simply rejects one form of worship in order to practice another.

In addition to representing a crisis in religious identity, Bruch's character is also a reflection of the psychic wounding of Holocaust victims. He lives in perpetual suffering as a result of his degrading experiences in Buchenwald. His illness takes the form of re-enactment of death scenes in his private theatre of the absurd. The pathology of the Third Reich continues to claim its victims. The tormented survivor relives his traumatic experiences, repeatedly playing the corpse, to the accompaniment of his own choral funeral chant. Bruch and another German Jewish refugee "used to hold Masses over each other, one lying down in a packing case with dime store beads wound about the wrists, the other doing the service" (56). The theater metaphor is evident also in Bruch's alternate routine in which he holds a pot over his mouth for an echo effect and rants in imitation of Hitler, "interrupting himself to cry 'Sieg Heil'" (56).

In Bruch's story Bellow presents the concentration camp universe. The barbarous is juxtaposed with the ridiculous to suggest the absurdity of Germany's venture in Aryan superiority:

saucepans . . . were offered to the prisoners for sale. Hundreds of thousands, new from the factory. Why? Bruch bought as many pans as he could. What for? Prisoners tried to sell saucepans to one another. And then a man fell into the latrine trench. No one was allowed to help him, and he was drowned there while the other prisoners were squatting helpless on the planks. Yes, he suffocated in the feces! (56)

Repeated use of *pan, saucepan, pot,* and death references tie the Buchenwald recollection and Bruch's contemporary psychological problems. Causal relationship between the Holocaust experience and the current psychological disorder is thereby established. This method also provides structural unity as it corresponds to Bellow's established pattern of identifying the survivor's malady and then demonstrating its genesis in the Holocaust.

Bellow's penchant for symbolic naming and irony is indulged in Bruch's story. He is among those who have suffered the crime of the century. His obsessive funeral masques testify to his on-going suffering. Life, which Jews are taught to value as a blessing, has in Bruch's experience been a curse at worst; and far less than hallowed at best. In naming the character, Bellow deletes the vowel sound from *Baruch* (a popular Hebrew name meaning blessed) to convey the concept of disrupted or incomplete blessing. Similarly appropriate for our consideration is *Bruch* as a transliteration for the Yiddish noun signifying a disaster, a break, in this case aptly connoting the destruction of the Holocaust.

Elements of the absurd and the theatrical associated with Bruch's memory of Buchenwald resurface in Bellow's uproarious Lodz Ghetto labor camp rendition. The novelist introduces this episode with words and phrases such as "deformed," "obsessed," "abnormality," "play acting," "dramatic individuality," "theatricality in people," again juxtaposing concepts of mental illness and theater as he had in the earlier Bruch section. Theatrical posturing, grotesque humor, and emphasis on the unnatural, unreal order of existence characterize Bellow's recreation of Nazi rule. Eight years prior to Leslie Epstein's novel based on the career of Chaim Rumkowski, *King of the Jews*, Bellow treated the macabre in his own rendition of Rumkowski, the mad Jewish king of Lodz Ghetto. Disorientation and the disruption of reason dominate in a scene of chaotic life in the ghetto restructured as labor and death camp. Relying on historic records, the novelist incorporates details from Chaim Rumkowski's reign as *Judenaltester*, Nazi installed dictator of the Jews, whom Bellow dramatizes as an elderly, corrupt, failed business man, "a distasteful fun-figure in the Jewish community" (210). Amid tragic suffering, the bizarre Rumkowski, dressed in ceremonial royal robes, rode through the ghetto in a broken, but ornate nineteenth-century gilded coach. In addition to the pageants and plays he had organized in his own honor, the mad king printed money and issued postage stamps with his picture. This terror of the Jews, whose first name is derived from the Hebrew word *chai*, meaning life, ironically presided "over the death of half a million people" (211).

Bellow uses the Rumkowski section for a rare instance of direct moral commentary in order to criticize the Nazi mentality. In Sammler's voice, Bellow notes the hateful nature of the Nazi mind:

This theatricality of King Rumkowski evidently pleased the Germans. It further degraded the Jews to have a mock king. The Nazis liked that. They had a predilection for such *Ubu Roi* murder farces. . . . Here at any rate one can see peculiarly well . . . the blood-minded hatred, the killers' delight taken in its failure and abasement. (211-212)

Thus, approached from the perspective of order created by authorial intrusion, the outrageous and insane aspects of this scene are heightened. The idea that ordinary people could endure this abuse is difficult to accept. That a country reputed to be one of western civilization's most enlightened nations could have implemented and carried out such obscenity is difficult to comprehend. That the world acquiesced in this barbarism is difficult to justify. The historic Rumkowski data force the reader beyond the normal environment of literature and into the lunatic realm of the Third Reich. Just as the events of the Holocaust radically alter the survivors' conception of reality, the mad king of Lodz scene dislodges the reader from comfortable illusions and forces one to experience a severely disordered universe. Bellow creates the nightmarish quality of this episode through an extended juxtaposition of comic absurd detail and realistic scenes of suffering and death, of parodic ceremony and tyrannical oppression. The reader is shocked into comprehension of the enormity of Nazi crimes via Bellow's insightful association of normal bureaucratic functions of state with barbarism, his refusal to engage in meaningless separation of the banal bureaucratic functionaries and the leaders.

Bellow controls the relatively short Rumkowski section on multiple levels. Paralleling the parodic grotesque is a stark graphic portrait of the ghetto labor camp environment. The reader is not permitted to forget human misery and degradation.

> The ghetto became a labor camp. The children were seized and were deported for extermination. There was famine. The dead were brought down to the sidewalk and lay there to wait for the corpse wagon. (211)

Bellow considers the possibility of ambiguity in Rumkowski's character. On the one hand, he is depicted as a grotesque clown, an exhibitionist. However, this posture is qualified by a serious lapse in the clown facade and with authorial speculation about his motivation for acting the role of mad king. Bellow follows an account of Rumkow-

ski's nonsensical behavior with reference to an occasion when he pro-
tested the arrest, deportation, and anticipated murder of his council.
For this breach of conduct, he was severely beaten. The motives of the
victim-king are open to question. Bellow alludes to the double role of
Jewish leaders who accepted the *Judenaltester* position, attempting to
use it to help their co-religionists in some small way: "Perhaps his secret thought was to save a remnant. Perhaps his mad acting was meant
to amuse or divert the Germans" (211). Rumkowski's ability to continue in his appointed role of dictator, arbiter of life and death for half a
million people in the German spectacle, had its limits: "he voluntarily
stepped into the train for Auschwitz" (212). Although conflicting eval-
uations of Rumkowski's motives and behavior appear in survivor testimony, Bellow's conclusion that the ghetto master volunteered for "re-
settlement" is in agreement with historic accounts which indicate that
he could have stayed behind with the seven hundred people left to
clean up the ghetto but chose instead to join his brother on August 30,
1944 in the last transport for Auschwitz.[4]

Perhaps Bellow relied on images and scenes of the absurd because
he concurred with George Steiner's conviction that "The world of
Auschwitz lies outside speech as it lies outside reason."[5] Perhaps he
abstained from documentary reference to the torture chambers, gas
chambers, and crematoria because he believed that it would be pre-
sumptuous for an American to treat such horrendous events from the
vantage point of safe haven. Although he limits description, Bellow
nevertheless confronts the moral significance of this event as few novelists have.

Moral indignation is voiced through Sammler. The hero-survivor
refuses to absolve the Nazis: he points ironically to the German facility
for bureaucratic slaughter of innocent millions. When urged by his
niece, another survivor, to comment on Hannah Arendt's "banality of
evil" thesis, Sammler rejects Arendt's contention that Nazis of Adolf
Eichmann's ilk were ordinary men, neither monsters nor pathological
anti-Semites, but merely loyal Germans obeying state law. Moreover,

he resents Arendt's conclusion that these Nazis were personalities whose evil deeds emanated not from their own character, but rather from their position in a totalitarian state. Sammler insists on the moral responsibility of the individual. These figures were raised in pre-Nazi, Christian Germany and therefore had no illusions about the nature of the connection between anti-Semitism and murder. Banality is a mask designed to deceive the gullible. Sammler's condemnation of the Nazi mentality, in this instance, is appropriately phrased in Hebraic terms, stressing the Judaic concept of the sacredness of life and denouncing the Third Reich venture as blasphemous. Despite the Holocaust experience, the Jew still values the idea of moral accountability:

> "The idea of making the century's greatest crime look dull is not banal. . . . The banality was only camouflage. What better way to get the curse out of murder than to make it look ordinary, boring or trite? With horrible political insight they found a way to disguise the thing . . . do you think the Nazis didn't know what murder was? Everybody . . . knows what murder is. That is very old human knowledge. The best and purest human beings, from the beginning of time, have understood that life is sacred. To defy that old understanding is not banality. There was a conspiracy against the sacredness of life. Banality is the adopted disguise of a very powerful will to abolish conscience." (20-21)

Thirty years after the Holocaust, Bellow, other American and European writers of note, and respected scholars in various disciplines have awakened interest in a subject which many people had forgotten and others would prefer to ignore. Why return to these horrors in the 1970s and 1980s? Some argue that distance was necessary for philosophic reflection and artistic experimentation to find forms appropriate to such material. Another probable explanation is that Bellow was motivated by the Mid-East crisis. That Bellow has written implicitly and explicitly of the Holocaust in periods when Jewry's physical survival was severely threatened is evident from the publication dates of both *The Vic-*

tim and *Mr. Sammler's Planet*. That the Holocaust is overtly associated in the novelist's and the protagonist's minds with Arab intentions in the Six-Day War is dramatically manifest in the text of *Mr. Sammler's Planet* and in Bellow's own voice in *To Jerusalem and Back*.

Alvin Rosenfeld, who views Artur Sammler as a prototype of the Holocaust writer, a man "possessed of a double knowledge: cursed into knowing how perverse the human being can be to create such barbarism and blessed by knowing how strong he can be to survive it,"[6] argues correctly that the very nature of Sammler's experience has enlarged his sight, that his vocation is "that of a seer, a man of unusual perception whose observations carry the ring of authority."[7] One may say the same of Sammler's creator. Saul Bellow has attained, in the eyes of many contemporary readers, the stature of artist-seer. It is Bellow, after all, who has reminded us, after decades of the tendency of modern literature to be its own source, to be estranged from modern society,[8] that it is now appropriate for the writer to accept the role of moral authority that society imputes to its men of letters.[9] Bellow's career is a testament to this vision of the writer as sage and guide. As a distinguished moral voice in twentieth-century literature, Saul Bellow has confronted the important issues of our times with intelligence and courage.

Notes

1. Saul Bellow, *Mr. Sammler's Planet* (Greenwich, Connecticut: Fawcett Publications, 1971), p. 28. Subsequent citations will be from this edition and appear in the text in parentheses.

2. Josephine Zadovsky Knopp, *The Trial of Judaism in Contemporary Jewish Writing* (Urbana: University of Illinois Press, 1975), pp. 150-151.

3. Elie Wiesel, "The Fiery Shadow: Jewish Existence Out of the Holocaust," *Jewish Existence in an Open Society* (U.S.A.: Jewish Centers Association, 1970), p. 43.

4. Leonard Tushnet, *The Pavement of Hell* (New York: St. Martin's Press, 1972), p. 61.

5. Quoted by Lawrence Langer, *The Holocaust and the Literary Imagination* (New Haven: Yale University Press, 1975), p. 15.

6. Alvin H. Rosenfeld, *A Double Dying: Reflections on Holocaust Literature* (Bloomington: Indiana University Press, 1980), p. 32.

7. *Ibid.*

8. Saul Bellow, "The Thinking Man's Wasteland," *Saturday Review of Literature*, 48 (April 3, 1965).

9. Saul Bellow, "The Writer as Moralist," *Atlantic Monthly*, 211 (March, 1963).

"Farcical Martyrs" and "Deeper Thieves" in Bellow's *Humboldt's Gift*

Allan Chavkin and Nancy Feyl Chavkin

The car walloped the pavement, charging toward the Holland tunnel. Close to the large form of Humboldt, this motoring giant, in the awful upholstered luxury of the front seat, I felt the ideas and illusions that went with him. He was always accompanied by a swarm, a huge volume of notions. He said how changed the Jersey swamps were, even in his lifetime, with roads, dumps, and factories, and what would a Buick like this with power brakes and power steering have meant even fifty years ago. Imagine Henry James as a driver, or Walt Whitman, or Mallarmé.[1]

We turned into La Salle Street where we were held up by taxi cabs and newspaper trucks and the Jaguars and Lincolns and Rolls-Royces of stockbrokers and corporation lawyers—of the deeper thieves and the loftier politicians and the spiritual elite of American business, the eagles in the heights far above the daily, hourly, and momentary destinies of men. (259)

Although *Humboldt's Gift* (1975) has prompted much scholarly writing, critics have neglected to examine the extensive references to cars and drivers in the complex work.[2] This neglect is unfortunate, for the automotive references and driving habits of the major characters clarify the main theme of the book, contribute to its satiric view of modern society, and help reveal not only the status and the social ambitions of the major characters but also their real selves underneath their social masks. At one point the narrator Charlie Citrine states that he has allowed his car "to become an extension of my own self (on the folly and vanity side)," and that statement applies to other major characters in the novel also (36).

In *The Dean's December* Bellow presents a scathing indictment of the totalitarianism of the Communist bloc, where he sees no hope; he also paints a grim picture of the problems confronting modern capitalism which faces a grave moral crisis as the inner cities decay because of the worsening situation of the underclass.[3] Bellow's analysis of the problems of American society in *Humboldt's Gift* is both more subtle and more comical than in the often explicit and somber *Dean's December*. Bellow's focus in *Humboldt's Gift* is upon the absurd situation of the modern writer in a materialistic society full of the cynical "realism" of "deeper thieves"; in such a society, the idealistic writer who hopes to play a great role in the fate of mankind feels as if power has been stolen from him, and he becomes a "farcical martyr," performing the role of failed artist to the satisfaction of ubiquitous cynical "realists." When Von Humboldt Fleisher, who was supposed to be "the great American poet of the century" (340), exults in being "the first poet in America with power brakes" and speculates on what kind of drivers certain famous writers would have been (20, 21), then his artistic collapse and farcical martyrdom are adumbrated.

Humboldt's Gift is actually a long desultory meditation that is prompted by the need of the narrator to understand the cause of the failure, madness, and premature demise of his friend and mentor Von Humboldt Fleisher. Though it often substitutes a comic tone for the solemnity of the romantics, the novel can be considered as an elaborate variation of the discursive meditative ode, the genre initiated by Wordsworth that presents the gradual process of the mind's coming to terms with its anxiety.[4] In an essay published in the same year as *Humboldt's Gift* and appropriately entitled "A World Too Much with Us," Bellow observes that the spiritual crisis which afflicted the English romantics—what "in our modern jargon" we call "alienation"—is our problem today.[5] The form of *Humboldt's Gift* is a crisis meditation in which Charlie finds himself confronted with two radically different "teachers," Ronald Cantabile, a vibrant representative of modern materialistic society, and Humboldt, a spiritual mentor. To illuminate this crisis and its resolution, we will focus upon Charlie, Cantabile, and Humboldt, their automobiles, and their driving habits.

* * *

By conventional standards Charlie is a successful writer, and he takes pride in the symbols of his success, especially his luxury Mercedes 280-SL coupe that his voluptuous young girlfriend Renata coerced him into buying. Charlie has won prizes for his books on historical figures, has written a popular Broadway play based on his friend and mentor Humboldt, and has been commissioned by major magazines to write stories on the Kennedys and other national figures. For these accomplishments he has earned a great deal of money and the French government has made him a Chevalier of the French Legion of Honor. Yet Charlie suffers from writer's block and feels dissatisfied. In an early draft of the novel, it is especially clear that Charlie's belief in "realism" has resulted in his forsaking his potential as a serious artist: "Hamilcar [Humboldt] had always been good natured with him— almost always. Nevertheless, he had not liked being told that the real Orlansky [Citrine] was a strong realist. Not an artist" (*MS* 7.6, pp. 18-19).[6] This passage makes clear the basic opposition between "realism" and art that is at the core not only of this novel but also of Bellow's other work. In its most extreme form, the "realism" that Humboldt refers to here, and which is the dominant modern sensibility, is a brutal cynicism and materialism; it is opposed to the values and outlook of the romantic writer, who believes that there is "the deeper life"[7] or added dimension to existence that cannot be scientifically verified or logically explained.

Although Charlie intended to resist materialism, the fact of the matter is that Charlie abandoned the search for "the deeper life" for easy money and social status. He realizes now that his success is superficial, and his fame temporary. His award by the French government is a trivial one, the equivalent of one given to those who breed pigs or "improve the garbage cans" (187), and even the inept, comical criminal Ronald Cantabile knows the insignificance of the award when he ridicules the writer by reading him part of Mike Schneiderman's column which refers to Charlie the Chevalier as "the Chevrolet of the French Legion" (258).

Although in his youth Charlie had artistic promise that he neglected for the sake of "realism," now the values of his youth are "edging back." Charlie views himself as a Rip Van Winkle who has woken up: "As I was lying stretched out in America, determined to resist its material interests and hoping for redemption by art, I fell into a deep snooze that lasted for years and decades. Evidently I didn't have what it took. What it took was more strength, more courage, more stature. America is an overwhelming phenomenon, of course. But that's no excuse, really. Luckily, I'm still alive and perhaps there's even some time still left" (306).

As though to help Charlie awaken from the deep snooze of middle-class comfort and complacency, a number of disturbing distractions occur. Denise, his ex-wife, her lawyers, hostile judges, and the IRS are consuming his financial assets. Charlie has sunk much money into *The Ark*, a new journal that he intends to publish. Charlie's goal is to revive art and culture in the American cultural wasteland, but his friend Pierre Thaxter is proving to be an unreliable editor; in fact, he is probably embezzling the funds intended for the journal. Moreover, Renata's fidelity is in doubt. She has dallied with a wealthy undertaker named Flonzaley before when she became disenchanted with Charlie, and Charlie worries that he may lose his voluptuous mistress to his rival if he cannot offer her money and marriage.

Charlie is haunted, too, by memories of his close friend Humboldt. As patron, guide, and protector, Humboldt helped Charlie in his early career. He not only helped in material ways, such as getting him a teaching position at Princeton, but also gave him much advice. Humboldt told Charlie to view the "wonderful, abominable rich" "in the shield of art," and that business had the power "to petrify the soul" (14). But neither Charlie nor Humboldt has heeded this advice, and now Charlie feels guilty over both of their failures.

Charlie's biggest distraction, however, emerges in the form of Ronald Cantabile. This "demon" of distraction, whose job it seems is to deflect, misdirect, and manipulate him, smashes up Charlie's prize

Mercedes because Charlie refuses to pay a gambling debt from a poker game in which Cantabile won by cheating.

Charlie is shaken up by the attack on his silver Mercedes because the car has important associations for him. When he first met Renata, Charlie drove a Dodge Dart, but Renata found this ordinary car inappropriate for a man of Charlie's wealth and status: "What kind of car is this for a famous man? There's some kind of mistake." "I tried to explain to her that I was too susceptible to the influence of things and people to drive an eighteen-thousand-dollar automobile. You had to live up to such a grand machine, and consequently you were not yourself at the wheel" (36). But Renata dismisses this argument and criticizes Charlie for being afraid of and for shirking the "potentialities" of his success. She forbids Charlie his Dodge compact, and when Charlie attempts to negotiate with the salesman for a second-hand Mercedes, Renata—"roused, florid, fragrant, large—had put her hand on the silver hood and said, 'This one—the coupe.' The touch of her palm was sensual. Even what she did to the car I felt in my own person" (44). The phallic-shaped car represents for him not only social status but also youth and virility. Renata possesses the power to "turn on" Charlie and the car. "Renata? Why Renata didn't need an ignition key to start a car. One of her kisses on the hood would turn it on. It would roar for her" (260). Denise rightly associates the new Mercedes with Renata and with sexuality. From Denise's point of view, Charlie in his dotage now cools "gypsy Renata's lust" and purchases the expensive Mercedes Benz to satisfy this bimbo's desire for higher social status associated with the luxury car. (Renata drives an old yellow Pontiac that has a hole in the floor covered by a piece of tin.) When Charlie comes to call for his two daughters, Denise tells him to make sure the car is "well aired." "She didn't want it smelling of Renata. Butts stained with her lipstick had to be emptied from the ashtray. She once marched out of the house and did this herself. She said there must be no Kleenexes smeared with God-knows what" (58).

Charlie makes clear that an attack on the car is also an attack on himself (and a low blow at that) because he has allowed the car to become an extension of himself. The car seemed to confer on Charlie an immunity from the mindless violence of the modern city, "the moronic inferno" (35). The elegant Mercedes promoted a sense of security which is destroyed when the automobile is attacked. Charlie's overvaluation of the car which has made him feel not only special but also invulnerable sets him up for a harsh fall. "The attack on this car was hard on me also in a sociological sense, for I always said that I knew my Chicago and I was convinced that hoodlums, too, respected lovely automobiles. Recently a car was sunk in the Washington Park lagoon and a man was found in the trunk who had tried to batter his way out with tire-tools. Evidently he was the victim of robbers who decided to drown him— get rid of the witness. But I recall thinking that his car was only a Chevrolet. They never would have done such a thing to a Mercedes 280-SL. I said to my friend Renata that *I* might be knifed or stomped on an Illinois Central platform but that this car of mine would never be hurt" (35). Apparently there is some truth to this supposition that at least some cold-blooded mobsters have great respect for luxury cars. The distorted values of contemporary society in which worship of materialism results in excessive admiration for an expensive car is suggested when the amoral opportunist Cantabile insists that it was Charlie's fault that Cantabile beat up the elite machine: "You made me. Yes, you. You sure did. You think I don't have feelings? You wouldn't believe how I feel about a car like that" (45).

Stunned by the attack on his car, Charlie describes the damaged Mercedes in graphic detail. His excessive love for his car is revealed by the fact that he unconsciously anthropomorphizes it when he describes the damage to the vehicle. "My loveliest of machines, my silver Mercedes 280, my gem, my love offering, stood mutilated in the street. Two thousand dollars' worth of bodywork would never restore the original smoothness of the metal skin. The headlights were crushed blind . . . (47). The windshield was covered with white fracture-blooms. It had suffered a kind of crystalline internal hemorrhage" (35-36).

* * *

The inept but persistent Ronald Cantabile becomes Charlie's nemesis. Cantabile is a marvelous comic creation—manic, demonstrative, manipulative, and full of outrageous schemes. Ben Siegel observes that "Cantabile also personifies the tightening bonds between an upwardly mobile middle class and a shady world of confidence men and mobsters."[8] In fact, the novel suggests that the worlds of culture and crime are not so far apart any more. It is significant that Cantabile has a wife, Lucy, who is writing her doctoral dissertation on Humboldt, and that the small-time mobster wants Charlie to help her with the project. Charlie refuses to help on Lucy's dissertation and states that such a project is "pure capitalism," suggesting, perhaps, that Lucy hopes merely to exploit the dead poet to advance her career.

Cantabile represents some of the worst aspects of capitalist society in the post-World War II period. While he is flamboyant and elegant, the real Cantabile can best be described as exploitative and avaricious—and his driving habits and his car reveal his true character. Cantabile drives his white Thunderbird in a fiercely aggressive manner, and Charlie describes the red leather upholstery of the mobster's car as "spilt blood" (87) and remarks that it reminds him of "pulmonary blood" (100). Cantabile drives his "showy auto" with its "immense instrument panel" (87) irresponsibly, taking off at top speed from a standstill with tires screeching, "like an adolescent drag-racer" (87). He holds the steering wheel in an aggressive way—"as though it were a pneumatic drill to chop up the macadam" (87). He deliberately runs red lights and tailgates the bumpers of cars ahead of him. He makes other motorists "chicken out" by his reckless driving (88). Entering the expressway, he guns his engine and charges into the merging traffic, and other cars are forced to brake for him.

Cantabile's wild driving is in marked contrast to the masterful driving of his beautiful mistress Polly. In contrast to Denise and other women Charlie has known, her "pleasant cheeks" suggest that "one could be sexually pleasant with Polly." Charlie reflects that she can "gratify" her man and adds: "Why was it that some men knew how to find women who naturally pleased and could be pleased?" (254). In short, Charlie is impressed with Polly and with her "marvelous" driving, which is symbolic of her general competency. Her impressive driving ability is described in the scene in which the domineering Cantabile virtually kidnaps the protesting but largely passive Charlie in order to take him to see a con man named Stronson. This scene in which Cantabile "kidnaps" Charlie is a particularly important one because it not only reveals Cantabile's character, but also suggests the connection between the worship of technology and the decline of wisdom and virtue.

Interested in talking with Pierre Thaxter and avoiding Cantabile, Charlie resists the petty criminal's demand to get into the Thunderbird, but Cantabile aggressively pursues the writer, finally shoving him into the "throbbing" car despite his resistance: "He put his hands on my rear and thrust me in," Charlie states (257). Cantabile's fascination with Charlie is abnormal, and it may be partially the result of an unconscious homosexual attraction. In one bizarre scene, Cantabile shoves Charlie into a lavatory stall and forces the imprisoned writer to witness the mobster's malodorous defecation. At another time he informs Charlie that the writer can "make it" with Polly only "through" Cantabile. "Don't try on your own," he warns the writer (187). Cantabile suggests that the three of them should have sex together and even describes positions in which Polly would satisfy them both simultaneously. The sexual proposition is entirely Cantabile's idea, and Charlie wants no part of Cantabile's sexual circus, which he finds disgusting. In *Herzog* (1964), Bellow had hinted that Valentine Gersbach's intercourse with Madeleine Herzog could be construed as vicarious homosexual intercourse, for Moses Herzog was Gersbach's real object of desire. It is possible that Cantabile unconsciously hopes to "make it" with Charlie "through" Polly.

In any case, Cantabile cannot seem to stay away from Charlie and continually forces himself upon him, as he does when he takes the writer to see Stronson before the fraudulent "businessman" "tears off" in his Aston-Martin (259). With Polly at the wheel, and Cantabile, Thaxter, and Charlie as passengers, the flashy Thunderbird travels through the traffic-filled streets of Chicago, and Charlie, unenthusiastic about becoming involved with Cantabile, meditates. Charlie reflects that John Stuart Mill had said that "if the tasks of *durum genus hominum* were performed by a supernatural agency and there was no demand for wisdom and virtue, O! then there would be little that man could prize in man." Charlie reflects that this is what is happening in America where "the Thunderbird would do as the supernatural agency" (259). Charlie is unable to find any values in this society in which man is dehumanized, merely an inferior machine to the impressive technological marvel of a luxury automobile.

* * *

In an early draft of the novel, Charlie reflects: "Maybe through Humboldt, that goofy apostate poet, I might recover my judgement and shed my need for these misleading types" (*MS* #15.17, pp. 32-33). Charlie is referring to the "wrong types" he has become involved with in the preceding years as he achieved commercial success with his writing at the sacrifice of his talent and promise of possible greatness. Now, obsessed with death, disenchanted with the materialistic ideology of contemporary society which denies the possibility of a "soul," and suffering from writer's block, Charlie is in dire straits. In this crisis Humboldt emerges to rescue him. Amid the distractions of Renata, Denise, Cantabile, Thaxter, lawyers, lawsuits, and children, Humboldt comes out of the world of the dead with his "gift." "But I didn't expect him to come to me as in life, driving ninety miles an hour in his Buick four-holer. First I laughed. Then I shrieked. I was transfixed. He bore down on me. He struck me with blessings. Humboldt's gift wiped out many immediate problems" (110).

It is significant that Humboldt comes from the world of the dead in his charging, "fateful Buick" (33). Throughout the novel Humboldt is associated with luxury cars, especially the big Buick Roadmaster. Even as a child Humboldt was "car crazy" (4). Humboldt's father was wealthy, and the "car crazy" Humboldt would drive with his dad to baseball games in a Pierce-Arrow or a Hispano-Suiza. Later his father lost all of his money in the stock market crash and died of a heart attack. Humboldt never lost his love for fancy cars, however. Although Humboldt did not become as wealthy as his father had before the stock market crash, he did achieve success with *Harlequin Ballads*. Full of car mystique, he purchased a second-hand Buick Roadmaster, of which he was inordinately proud.

One Sunday in September 1952, Humboldt picks up Charlie to take him to his home out in the country. The next day Humboldt will take Charlie to an interview for a position at Princeton. Charlie describes the drive from New York to New Jersey in detail (20-22). Humboldt is a genius and a charming, handsome man, but there is a darker side to him that is suggested by his car and by his driving habits. Charlie vividly recalls the drive on that Sunday in September 1952 in which he visualizes "two odd dolls" in the front seat of "the roaring, grinding four-holer," the muddy Buick Roadmaster looking "like a staff car from Flanders Field." "The wheels were out of line, the big tires pounded eccentrically. Through the thin sunlight of early autumn Humboldt drove fast, taking advantage of the Sunday emptiness of the streets. He was a terrible driver, making left turns from the right side, spurting, then dragging, tailgating. I disapproved. Of course I was much better with a car but comparisons were absurd, because this was Humboldt, not a driver. Steering, he was humped huge over the wheel, he had small-boy tremors of the hands and feet, and he kept the cigarette holder between his teeth. He was agitated, talking away, entertaining, provoking, informing, and snowing me" (21).

Preoccupied with power and hoping to conquer the world of culture with his brilliance and then preside over it, Humboldt is constantly scheming how to outmaneuver his "enemies" and hence the aptness of comparing his Buick to a staff car from Flanders Field. An authoritarian general with "peculiar lusts to consummate" (23), Humboldt assumes that Charlie and his good-natured wife are his loyal lieutenants who will follow his orders and be obedient no matter how demanding and unreasonable he becomes. Humboldt's driving suggests that he can be domineering, reckless, and eccentric.

Eventually Humboldt's eccentricity deteriorates into madness. When his scheme to be awarded a chair at Princeton fails, his paranoia and pathological jealousy increase to an intolerable point. Earlier Kathleen had informed Charlie that Humboldt looked under the hood of his car for "booby traps" (27); he is fearful that as a Jewish man married to a Gentile woman he will be attacked by reactionary groups such as the Ku Klux Klan. The poet is also obsessed with his wife's fidelity. Although Kathleen is an adoring wife, Humboldt believes that she is secretly "wild." In fact, Humboldt, a lover of cities, had escaped to the country largely because of his anxiety over his wife's putative adultery: Humboldt accuses his "wild" wife of allowing her father to sell her as a "white slave" to one of the Rockefellers.[9] In early drafts of the novel, the extent of Humboldt's pathological jealousy and Charlie's attitude toward it are clear. Obsessed with his wife's "purity," Humboldt comments in an early draft: "If she's so innocent, how did she learn what she knows. The way she swings her leg over me—that takes practice. The way she goes down on you. Before I met her she already knew plenty, but now she knows a lot more. And I never taught her. That's what I have to live with. But it's my assignment. I love her" (*MS* #7.25, p. 47). Charlie does not want to become involved in this issue of Kathleen's putative infidelity, but is appalled at Humboldt's obsession. In an early draft, Charlie's repugnance is particularly trenchant: "Madness is supposed to be inventive. But the same nastiness comes out again and again, the same torments and fantasies in the same narrow range. Up the skirts! Out the raunchy cock of the stranger. And they drip their dirty secretions in the corner while the poor husband lies in a helpless trance. I was repelled" (*MS* #20.9, p. 7).

This jealousy becomes life threatening when Humboldt tries with his Buick to run down Kathleen. At a faculty party soon after Humboldt has been informed that the poetry chair scheme has failed, Humboldt witnesses his slightly inebriated wife take some matches out of the pocket of a Negro composer. Kathleen's unfortunate act provokes the poet to sensational jealousy and violence. Earlier, on his way to the party, "the Buick skidding on the gravel and booming through clouds of dust," he had ranted and raved again over Kathleen's imagined infidelity with Rockefeller (144). Now, totally enraged, he runs her into the yard, punches her in the stomach, and pulls her by the hair into the Buick. Unable to back out because of a car parked behind him, he wheels over the lawn and off the sidewalk, "hacking off the muffler on the curb" (145). Driving home from the party, Humboldt keeps punching her, steering with his left hand. At a blinking light, Kathleen escapes from the car, and Humboldt tries to run her down but smashes into a tree. The state police must free him from his car, the doors having jammed shut because of the collision (143).

It is likely that Humboldt's obsession with his wife's alleged infidelity is partially the result of his feelings of sexual inadequacy exacerbated by his anxiety over his role as a poet in a society that values a man with money and power over a man with imagination and culture. To be a poet in a materialistic science-and-technology oriented country is difficult; certainly it is not "macho"—"to be a poet is a school thing, a skirt thing, a church thing" (118). On the way to the party, Humboldt verbally abused his wife with these revealing accusations: "Did Rockefeller's penis thrill her more? Did the billions enter in? Did Rockefeller have to take a woman away from a poet in order to get it up?" (144).

In his posthumous letter to Charlie, Humboldt reveals that he always tried "to keep the upper hand" in the sexual act (338), and Charlie early in the novel speculates that self-centered Humboldt placed the

Critical Insights

compliant Kathleen, and metaphorically Charlie and others too, in a subordinate position that showed no concern for their desires or needs. "Lie there. Hold still. Don't wiggle. My happiness may be peculiar, but once happy I will make you happy, happier than you ever dreamed. When I am satisfied the blessings of fulfillment will flow to all mankind" (23). This reasoning is that of the power-obsessed, deranged tyrant—it is also the reasoning of one who is suffering from feelings of anxiety over his sexuality and from insufficient social status in a society that values money and power over poetry and culture.

When Humboldt finally wrecks his car (53), the accident aptly symbolizes the "smash-up" of his life. Right before they are supposed to leave for Europe, Kathleen escapes from Humboldt, and he degenerates into madness. This downward turn into extreme paranoia leaves no doubt that Humboldt's potential to be the great American poet of the century has been torpedoed. His life quickly deteriorates into ridiculous clowning as he plays with great energy the role of pathetic victim, the sensitive poet crucified by a harsh world full of enemies. Humboldt becomes the star performer in a circus of absurd drama, wild emotions, and scandal, as he involves himself with police, psychiatrists, lawyers, and private detectives. Charlie suggests that he has "a grand time being mad in New York" (53), and there's much truth to that statement, but, of course, Humboldt is not play-acting. In his delusions, he believes that an innocent man named Magnasco is living with Kathleen, and the enraged poet repeatedly threatens him with a gun. When the police come to arrest Humboldt, he fights like an ox. He ends up in Bellevue, and soiled from diarrhea, he is locked away for the night in a filthy state.

When Kathleen dumps Humboldt, the poet's paranoia knows no bounds, and even his "blood brother" Charlie becomes the focus of his rage. Humboldt cannot forgive Charlie for his success, especially since his Broadway play *Von Trenck* "exploited" his character: "But who the hell is Citrine to become so rich?" (2); "And I don't say he actually plagiarized, but he did steal something from me—my personality. He built my personality into his hero [Von Trenck]" (3-4). Humboldt satisfies some of his feelings for revenge by drawing his emergency "blood-brother" check on Charlie's account for $6,763.58. In his posthumously delivered letter to Charlie, Humboldt explains that he bought an Oldsmobile with part of the money but states that he didn't really know what he was going to do with "this big powerful car on Greenwich street." In fact, the expense of keeping the car in a garage was more than the rent in his fifth-floor walk-up apartment. For a while he "drove a hell of a car" and would say to his buddies when he drove past the theater where *Von Trenck* was playing—"There's the hit that paid for this powerful machine" (340).

Ironically, after he received shock treatment, he couldn't remember where he had left the car, the claim check, or the registration and thus lost the Oldsmobile. Humboldt confesses that he "had it in" for Charlie because he expected Humboldt to be the great American poet of the century who would "purge consciousness of its stale dirt" and teach us about "the three-fourths of life that are obviously missing!" (340). Unfortunately, Humboldt explains, he has not been able to read or write poetry in "these last years": "Opening the *Phaedrus* a few months ago, I just couldn't do it. I broke down. My gears are stripped. My lining is shot. It is all shattered. I didn't have the strength to bear Plato's beautiful words, and started to cry. The original, fresh self isn't there any more" (340). It is revealing that Humboldt describes his mental collapse with automotive metaphors; the implication is that Humboldt inordinately identifies with his car and that he is excessively absorbed in materialism with the consequent loss of his poetic powers.

* * *

Humboldt's posthumous gift to Charlie, a film treatment, contains a description of the situation of the contemporary artist as farcical martyr which applies to both Charlie and Humboldt and clarifies Bellow's view of the fundamental situation of the modern artist in a materialistic society unsympathetic to his purpose. "To the high types of Martyr-dom the twentieth century has added the farcical martyr. This, you see, is the artist. By wishing to play a great role in the fate of mankind he becomes a bum and a joke. A double punishment is inflicted on him as the would-be representative of meaning and beauty. When the artist-agonist has learned to be sunk and shipwrecked, to embrace defeat, and assert nothing, to subdue his will and accept his assignment to the hell of modern truth perhaps his Orphic powers will be restored . . ." (345-346). In contrast to the artist as tragic martyr (e.g. Gauguin, Melville), contemporary society has created the artist as self-indulgent buffoon. Having lost all discipline and thoroughly compromised himself, Hum-boldt performs in the farce of his own failed career, becoming an ab-surd caricature of the suffering artist-hero of the past.

Humboldt is only partially responsible for his sad fate, Charlie im-plies. Society must share a large part of the blame, for while it provides the poet with material comfort it renders him socially insignificant and powerless, and he becomes a tragi-comic figure. In the scene in which Cantabile kidnaps Charlie to take him to see Stronson, the Thunderbird is delayed in traffic by those who hold *real* power in this country—by "the deeper thieves" described in the second epigraph. The expression "deeper thieves" refers not only to the fact that the wealthy as a result of their power can steal more money than ordinary thieves but also to their cynical "realism" which has resulted in their "stealing" the re-spect, stature, and power that artists once had. This cynical "realism" is largely accepted by society as a whole and is held by such disparate types as Renata, her mother the Senora, Charlie's brother Ulick, Thaxter, and Cantabile, all of whom might be described with the lan-guage Charlie uses to describe the inept hoodlum—as parts of "the new mental rabble of the wised-up world" (107). This cynical "real-ism" disseminated by the powerful and widely adopted by much of so-ciety results in the artist's values being considered as insignificant or bogus, "children's play" or "fairy tale stuff." According to the literal-minded, the realist can make things happen, while the idealistic artist with his belief in such scientifically unverifiable ideas as the "soul" and "the imagination" cannot do useful work in the real world. Charlie reflects on this cynical point of view held by many: a poem cannot pick you up in Chicago and land you in New York a few hours later; "it had no such powers. And interest was where power was" (155). While in ancient times the poet possessed power in the material world, he no longer does. "The deeper thieves" respect most those who can "make things happen" in the material world; "a poet can't perform a hysterectomy or send a vehicle out of the solar system" (118).

Charlie reflects that the poet's main occupation into be a martyr— that is, to fail and to suffer. In fact, society is proud of its dead poets because their failures validate its cynical "realism." The poet's failure proves that in the U.S.A. only those who are "tough-minded" and devoted to the material world can be triumphant. Poets such as Humboldt are loved only because these martyrs "can't make it here." When a poet such as Humboldt goes mad, the "realist" exults: "If *I* were not such a corrupt, unfeeling bastard, creep, thief, and vulture, I couldn't get through this either. Look at these good and tender and soft men, the *best* of us. They succumbed, poor loonies" (118). It is Humboldt's feeling of social insignificance and powerlessness that results in his doing exactly what society expects and encourages him to do—to become "a hero of wretchedness" and to enact "The Agony of the American Artist" (155, 156). Charlie reflects that Humboldt "consented to the monopoly of power and interest held by money, politics, law, rationality, technology because he couldn't find the next thing, the new thing, the necessary thing for poets to do" (155).

In the film treatment in which Humboldt reveals the role of the modern artist as farcical martyr, he implies that Charlie must transcend this role and find the "next thing" for the poet to do. Like Corcoran, the writer in the treatment, Charlie has lost both his wife and mistress and has compromised his integrity and prostituted the powers of his imagination for commercial gain. Humboldt's gift and accompanying letter contain quotations from and allusions to the English Romantic poets, especially Blake, and suggest the efficacy of the power of the imagination to help the individual achieve spiritual rebirth. At the end of his letter to Charlie, Humboldt reminds his friend that "we are not natural beings but supernatural beings" (347). By the end of the novel, Charlie has struggled through his crisis and concluded that he must seek higher values above the materialism that is aptly symbolized by luxury cars. He can now reject the lucrative offer to write a screenplay despite loss of his wealth, resign himself to Renata's having jilted him for the rich undertaker Flonzaley, and cast off the troublesome Cantabile, who no longer has power over him. In an attempt to win Renata back when she left him for Flonzaley, Charlie had suggested that he would purchase a new Mercedes. Now that idea is forgotten, however, for Charlie intends to "take up a different kind of life" (483), one that will focus on spiritual matters and "The Messiah, that savior faculty the imagination" that can illuminate the commonplace world and redeem it (396).

From *Kansas Quarterly* 21.4 (Fall 1989): 77-88. Copyright © 1989 by *Arkansas Review*. Reprinted with permission of *Arkansas Review*.

Notes
We are grateful for a National Endowment for the Humanities Fellowship and a Southwest Texas State University Organized Research Grant which enabled us to complete the research for this article. We also express thanks to Saul Bellow for allowing us to examine and quote from his unpublished manuscripts.

1. Saul Bellow, *Humboldt's Gift* (New York: Viking, 1975) 21. Subsequent references will be given parenthetically in the text.

2. Barbara L. Estrin, "Recomposing Time: *Humboldt's Gift* and *Ragtime*," *Denver Quarterly* 17 (1982): 16-31, mentions that the destruction of a car "sets into action the most dramatic sequence of both novels," but she does not discuss in any detail the importance of the automotive references in *Humboldt's Gift*.

3. For a discussion of this moral crisis, see Allan Chavkin and Nancy Feyl Chavkin, "Bellow's Dire Prophecy," *The Centennial Review* 33 (1989): 93-107.

4. For a discussion of Bellow's debt to English Romanticism in *Humboldt's Gift*, see Michael G. Yetman, "Who Would Not Sing for Humboldt?" *ELH* 48 (1981): 935-51, and Allan Chavkin, "*Humboldt's Gift* and the Romantic Imagination," *Philological Quarterly* 62 (1983): 1-19, and his "Bellow and English Romanticism," in *Saul*

Bellow in the 1980s: A Collection of Critical Essays, ed. Gloria L. Cronin and L. H. Goldman (East Lansing, MI: Michigan State Univ. Press, 1989): 67-79; originally published in *Studies in the Literary Imagination* 17 (1984): 7-18.

5. Saul Bellow, "A World Too Much with Us," *Critical Inquiry* 21, No. 1 (1975): 1.

6. This quotation is from unpublished drafts of the novel that are part of the Special Collections at the University of Chicago Library, where most of Bellow's manuscript material is held. Occasionally, unpublished passages from the manuscripts confirm what is subtly suggested in the novel. As we do here, when we refer to these manuscripts we shall use the abbreviations MS and the identifying numbers used by the Special Collections staff: 7.9, pp. 18-19, refers to Box #7, Folder #9, pages 18-19. In this article, the quotations from Bellow's early unpublished manuscripts of *Humboldt's Gift* are from "Deposit: 1978 group."

7. Saul Bellow, *The Dean's December* (New York: Harper and Row, 1982) 105.

8. Ben Siegel, "Artists and Opportunists in Saul Bellow's *Humboldt's Gift*," *Contemporary Literature* 19 (1978): 151.

9. Humboldt is modelled on Delmore Schwartz, as James Atlas, *Delmore Schwartz: The Life of an American Poet* (New York: Farrar Straus Giroux, 1977), makes clear. Atlas reveals that Schwartz really believed that his wife was Nelson Rockefeller's lover; seven years after his wife left him he wrote in his private journals that Rockefeller's "great wealth, his status as a married man, and his political ambitions were all very much involved in her effort to conceal the real reasons for her [deceptive] actions" (345).

The Dean's December (1982)[1] _____

Robert F. Kiernan

> There's nothing too rum to be true.
>
> —Albert Corde

Like *Humboldt's Gift, The Dean's December* is a tale of two cities. Its resemblance to the earlier work almost ends with that correspondence, however, and most reviewers pronounced its dynamics moribund in comparison with the whirligig dynamics of *Humboldt's Gift*. *The Dean's December*, it was commonly said, was more heavy-handed than heavyweight. Hugh Kenner observed pointedly that the idiomatic vigor expected of Bellow had been swamped by his protagonist's excessive brooding, and he consigned the novel to "Lower Bellovia."[2] The British reviewer Jonathan Raban argued that *The Dean's December* was "a work of passionate, brooding ratiocination . . . simultaneously magnificent and dull."[3] More intemperately, the popular press tended to ask if America's Nobel laureate was not haranguing his countrymen—if the Nobel Prize had not made him intellectually arrogant. In unusual self-extenuation, Bellow has pointed out that he intended originally to write a nonfiction work about Chicago. Finding the journalistic approach too restricting, he allowed his original concept to evolve into fiction at the price of residual discursiveness.[4] He has also pointed out that the novel suffered the pressure of a book-club deadline.[5]

The protagonist of *The Dean's December* and the perpetrator of its brooding ratiocination is Albert Corde, a newspaperman who has become a professor of journalism and subsequently dean of students in an unnamed Chicago college. As dean, he has embroiled himself in controversy by writing a series of articles indicting Chicago for its racism, its clubhouse politics, and its lack of what he calls "moral initiative." He has also pressed for the conviction of a black man who murdered one of the college's white students, and he has endeared himself thereby neither to the college provost nor to young liberals on the campus—among them, his nephew. In short, the dean is too morally passionate for Chicago. He has jeopardized his professional standing as both journalist and college official by his impulse to take absolute moral readings.

The dean is geographically if not mentally distanced from the Chicago fray when he and his wife Minna spend the month of December in Bucharest visiting her dying mother, the distinguished psychiatrist Valeria Raresh. From the outset of their stay, they find that a Rumanian official obstructs their visits to the dying woman, apparently because of Valeria's history of disdain for the Socialist government. Thirty years earlier she had fallen into disfavor as minister of health; officially exonerated years later, she had declined to rejoin the Party. The government officials respect Minna's international standing as an astrophysicist, but she had defected from Rumania twenty years earlier while studying in the West, and they are not disposed to overlook Valeria's behavior for her sake. Indeed, because she did not formally renounce Rumanian citizenship when she became a citizen of the United States, she is arguably subject to Rumanian authority—a situation that worries Corde. Incautious conversation must never be indulged in her mother's wiretapped apartment, he warns, and he is anxious that they leave as soon as possible after Valeria's death on Christmas Eve.

A childhood friend of Corde named Dewey Spangler happens to be in Bucharest when Valeria dies, and Corde confides in him—imprudently so, because Spangler is an international journalist who fancies himself a Walter Lippmann. Upon the dean's return to America he is embarrassed to find he has given Spangler an interview and is the subject of one of his columns. Insidiously, the column mimics the dean's articles about Chicago in tone and style, and with pseudoanalytical eloquence Spangler concludes that Corde possesses "an earnestness too great for his capacities." So damning is the indictment and so dismissive Spangler's suggestion that Corde went into shock when he glimpsed the world outside academe that Corde feels his professional credibility destroyed, at least in moral matters. He resigns his deanship immediately, intending to write further articles but no longer attracted to controversy. The novel ends with him accompanying Minna to the Mount Palomar observatory and traveling with her in a lift attached to one of the dome's structural arches, following its curve to the apex, and then returning again to the floor. Aware of this obvious analogy to his fall from moral authority, he reflects that it is not the extraordinary cold of the observatory that he minds so much as the coming down again.

Corde is in one sense a familiar Bellovian figure. In his incessant brooding over the biggest human issues, he recalls Joseph in *Dangling Man*, Asa Leventhal in *The Victim*, Moses Herzog in *Herzog*, Artur Sammler in *Mr. Sammler's Planet*, Charlie Citrine in *Humboldt's Gift*. Like those brooders, he is part idealist, part oracle, part disillusioned realist. But more than any of his predecessors, he is concerned with connections between opposites—with cords that bind, as his surname suggests. He recalls an abyss of pettiness in Valeria that offended his compulsive large-mindedness, but he is nevertheless drawn to her affectively, just as he is drawn to others markedly different from himself. The sense of being spied upon by his in-laws would antagonize another man, but it inspires Corde to enlarged vision and he sees himself gratefully with fresh eyes. The horrors of life in Rumania under Soviet domination make him think less of how much better life is in America than of a symbiotic link between the two political powers. "It's the weak democracies that produce dictatorships," he announces to Minna. "You can't help thinking about it," he adds revealingly.

Corde's compulsion to search for a link between opposites manifests itself especially in a dialectical approach to experience. Without quite understanding the impulse, he actively seeks experiences of an alternative kind in the hope of discovering some ultimate synthesis. As a *Tribune* reporter with an international reputation, he abandons a career others would envy and seeks seclusion in academe. Rising to a deanship in a respected college, he then devotes himself to muckraking journalism that embarrasses the college. And after he has established liberal credentials with this journalism, he makes a crusade of bringing a black man to justice, leaving himself open to the charge of racism. "It was beyond him to explain why he became so active in this case," the reader is told. A precise understanding of his career reversals eludes Corde as well. It was the long undergraduate years reading Plato, Thucydides, and Shakespeare in a Dartmouth attic that brought him back to academe, he likes to think, and he speculates variously on his reasons for writing the articles about Chicago. He deduces finally—too vaguely—that "the experience, puzzle, torment of a lifetime demanded interpretation."

Others are less vague than Dean Corde about what ails him. In Provost Alec Witt's estimation, he is simply a fool, an outsider unshaped by the PhD process who has to be led by the nose through his administrative duties. "Muddled high seriousness" is Witt's diagnosis, and the provost comes to the further conclusion that Corde is unteachable—that he has "an emotional block, a problem, a *fatum*." Half smart *alec* and half academic *wit*, Alec Witt seems to enjoy letting Corde know his opinion while assuring him of entire sympathy. Corde is contemptuous of the provost's duplicity but cannot discount his assessment. Indeed, he ultimately agrees with Witt that the articles in *Harper's* were unwise, and he decides at the end of the novel that he would like to rewrite them from a larger perspective. Pressured by Witt to resign his deanship, he confesses to Minna that the provost had been right all along, that academics was never his proper game, that he "wasn't meant to be a dean." The reader is reluctant to credit Witt with insight, but because Corde neither refutes nor resents his judgments, the provost is an important interpreter of his actions.

Dewey Spangler looms as importantly as Witt in his assessment of what ails Dean Corde. He has the advantage of having grown up with Corde in Chicago and being able to maintain that the *Harper's* pieces are "completely characteristic." "Aren't you aware of cutting loose with a lifetime of anger?" he asks the dean. But Spangler is as fatuous as Alec Witt in many ways and an unsatisfactory judge to that same degree. He is surely disingenuous when he says to Corde, "I'm damned if I can explain why you wrote those pieces" inasmuch as he explains quite clearly why Corde wrote them. Indeed, Spangler has multiple theories of Corde's behavior that he propounds with no sense of contradicting himself. Alternately with his theory of "a lifetime of anger," he suggests that Corde is reacting against academe's ivory tower. "You went from active to passive," he says; "Now you're tired of the passive and you've gone hyperactive, and gotten distorted and all tied in knots." Elsewhere he sees Corde as indulging a taste for apocalyptic poetry in the *Harper's* articles. "The dragon coming out of the abyss, the sun turning black like sackcloth; the heavens rolled up like a scroll, Death on his ashen horse. . . . Wow!" Still elsewhere, Spangler hints at stygian perversities and says that Corde "might as well have stirred Bubble Creek with a ten-foot pole and forced the whole town to smell it." Such varying analyses suggest that it is simply inexplicable to Spangler that a man who had established a reputation should turn around and destroy it.

The men in Corde's family are less carefully judicious than Spangler and Witt in their assessments of the dean. Zaehner, his deceased brother-in-law, thought the dean an unworldly fool who invited others to cheat him—his cousin Max Detillion in particular. Knowing the judgment accurate, Corde wonders why he still permits such exploitation. Detillion is a shyster who hides assets and evades court orders, but the dean has given him money to invest and does not really face the fact that Detillion has cheated him of more than two hundred thousand dollars. Detillion compounds that affront by choosing to represent the defense in the murder trial that proves Corde's academic undoing. Yet Detillion's aggressions hardly touch Corde. Merely to see someone like his cousin was to enter symbiotically into his *life*, he suggests, his fascination with connections overriding logic. Zaehner and Detillion may have disagreed in all else, but they would agree on seeing Corde as H. L. Mencken's *Boobus Americanus*, and Corde would not seriously disagree with the judgment.

Zaehner's son Mason, a dropout student of the college, appoints himself the dean's particular critic. Professing to be an intimate friend of Lucas Ebry, the black man who killed the white student, he sees himself a representative of street people and presumes to teach his uncle about Chicago's social realities. His basic point is that establishment intellectuals like his uncle cannot understand a group he fashionably terms the "underclass." But his case against Corde is riddled with a boy's hatred of an uncle too often extolled as a model. He thinks of Corde variously—too ripely—as a "mastermind nemesis," as a racist, and as a voyeur of the macabre, titillating himself with the observation of lives darker than his own. Typically, Corde finds elements of truth in all of Mason's charges. Indeed, he thinks Mason's voice "the true voice of Chicago—the spirit of the age speaking from its lowest register."

To the extent that Mason speaks with the true voice of Chicago, his voice blends with the voices of Zaehner and Detillion, just as his charges reinforce Witt's notion that Corde is a man of "muddled high seriousness" and Spangler's notion that the dean is settling an old score with the city. But the correspondence of these several voices discredits them more than it authenticates them, for there is something ganglike in their tendency to coalesce—something gratuitously offensive in the general determination to underscore inadequacies and faults that Corde acknowledges. The effect is to render Corde a man more sinned against than sinning. The reader does not dispute the specifics of criticism leveled at Corde, but he tends to resent the fulsomeness of its expression. That Corde does not generally rebut his critics' points of view deepens the reader's resentment of his treatment.

This is not to argue that Corde is a milquetoast, so meekly acquiescent as to assent unthinkingly to any reading of his character or plan for his life. An eminent geologist named Beech is impressed by the dean's articles in *Harper's* and invites him to write about his discovery that crime and social disorganization in inner-city populations can be traced to the effects of lead poisoning—to be his "interpreter to the Humanists." Such a role should have the appeal of a connection for Corde. He is in fact flattered by the proposal and finds Beech "a terrific fellow," "a nice man." "And when you considered what a terrific charge he carried, the responsibility for such frightening findings (would the earth survive?), how gallant his mildness was," Corde observes. Yet he resists the role that Beech wants him to play in a conviction that the geologist's interpretation of society's ills is too simple. Just as the dean remains substantially his own man in dealing with his Chicago critics, he is not the dupe of his taste for connective roles in a more pleasant, flattering relationship. Corde makes errors of judgment, assuredly, but his self-determination knows no compromise.

With obvious symmetry, Bellow counters his gang of male Chicagoans with a cluster of East European women. Valeria is the center of a group that includes her daughter, Minna; her sister, Gigi; Beech's Serbian assistant, Vlada; and Valeria's concierge, Ionna. Together with some other women, they make up what Corde perceives as "a love community," "an extended feminine hierarchy." Their community of love is impressive because it survives self-interest and egotism without denying the reality of either compulsion. Ionna reports on the other women to the secret police in order to keep her position as concierge, yet she is utterly devoted to Valeria and Gigi and protects them while she blackmails them. Valeria asserts herself as matriarch of the community, casting Gigi in the role of dithering little sister and Ionna in the role of manumitted housemaid, but her affection for both is real. Impressively, the community of loving women survives physical separation and occupational difference: Vlada in chemistry and Minna in astrophysics share in its emotional symbiosis although they live in Chicago and cannot assist in the usual business of remaking clothes for one another and waiting alternately in queues. Effectively, the community of women is a rebuke to the Chicago gang. Within a repressive political regime that forces each citizen to inform on his associates, the women transcend personal interest and remain committed to human values. Given their head by a more benevolent political system, the Chicago males are locked into their separate egos, each becoming the other's enemy.

As persons more humanly achieved and more sensitive to claims of the human community than their Chicagoan counterparts, women qualify better than men as Corde's judges. Yet the same achievements that qualify them as judges make them less prone than Bellow's men to voice their conclusions—even to *reach* conclusions. They seem, rather, to collect impressions. Their eyes ask Corde, "Could he really, but *really*, be trusted?" but they make no pronouncements on the subject. If Gigi and Valeria make up a parole board in the dean's mind, they debate without resolve the only question that matters to them: "Would he really settle down with their Minna?" Corde does not resent their watch upon his character any more than he resents the Chicagoans judgments, but in tribute to the women's human achievements he allows them a role in his feelings that he does not permit Spangler, Witt, or Mason.

Valeria holds an especially important place in Corde's feelings. Determined to effect a final, human connection with her, he whispers to her on her deathbed that he *loves* her. And after her death she still seems alive to him, still presiding over her community of women like a protective spirit. Her personal humanity came, he speculates, "from the old sources," from "the deeper life," from something atavistic that she tapped like a mother lode of strength. She incarnates for Corde a unity of consciousness lost to modern consciousness. And he has small respect for "advanced modern consciousness":

> Why? Because the advanced modern consciousness was a reduced consciousness inasmuch as it contained only the minimum of furniture that civilization was able to install (practical judgments, bare outlines of morality, sketches, cartoons instead of human beings); and consciousness, because its equipment was humanly so meager, so abstract, was basically murderous.

Appropriately, Valeria's last gift to Corde is an antique pocket watch, an emblem of time running backwards as well as forwards. Her legacy to official Rumania, which has embraced murderous consciousness, is its best hospital. But Valeria's final judgment of Corde is more enigmatic than these symbolic dispositions. When he declares on her deathbed that he loves her, she suffers a galvanic seizure, and it is unclear what causes the seizure, whether delight or dismay. Corde knows that his history as a womanizer has always troubled Valeria. Does she think the declaration an overflow of his love for Minna? Or proof that he is too casual in his loves? Like all the women in *The Dean's December* and unlike the men who surround Corde, she hesitates to reach moral conclusions and expresses herself ambiguously when she seems finally to know her mind. The overlay of her circumspection with Corde's esteem forces the reader to suspect a connection between her moral open-mindedness and Corde's double-minded interest in connections. Like all the women in his world, she is an inspirational model.

But Corde has a philanderer's contempt for women and generally fails to acknowledge that they accomplish the ordinary business of life while he spins theories and devises categories.[6] Although devastated by grief, Gigi steps immediately into Valeria's competent shoes and runs the Bucharest household with an efficiency Corde patronizes as "hysterical." Her sickbed is described with mock admiration as a "command post" from which she directs aged crones to black-market queues formed at 4 A.M. so that Corde might eat grapes, tangerines, and other luxuries. Similarly, he patronizes Vlada's competence as Beech's assistant by reducing her poise to something glandular—"the fully centered assurance of a stout woman." Her intelligence he categorizes as shrewdness. Paradoxically, he also finds her femininity inadequate. Her eyes are not soft enough for his chauvinistic eye. "She did not invite you to take part in dream enterprises," he complains.

Corde patronizes also his sister Elfrida, who has always rejected the protection he likes to offer. He acknowledges that she is inherently skeptical, a "practical woman," "an excellent money manager," yet he thinks of her condescendingly as "a dear girl," one whose letters reveal "a looping, rambling, naive charm, not strictly literate, with feminine flourishes." Corde is fond of women, as he often remarks, but his assumption that they are "not strictly literate" blinds him to the realization that they are more successful than men in dealing with the everyday world.

Corde fails particularly to understand Minna's involvement with the real world. He likes to think of his wife as an otherworldly astronomer and sees his function in their marriage as managing her sublunary affairs. Indeed, it gives him pleasure to instruct her in the business of daily living. More verbal than she, he lectures her incessantly, just as he lectures himself inwardly, and he imagines that she appreciates the tutelage. Only her patience allows their basically strong marriage to survive the ordeal. In an unusual moment of impatience, she says, "I tell you how horrible my mother's death is, and the way you comfort me is to say everything is monstrous. You make me a speech. And it's a speech I've heard more than once." It is nicely parodic that his lectures prove "sometimes instructive even to himself."[7]

Ironies crisscross Corde's statements about Minna, making clear that he misunderstands and misjudges her. "She was not an observer," he maintains, although Minna's profession takes her regularly to space observatories. "She'd have to come down to earth one day," he forewarns on several occasions, not anticipating the final tableau in which he leaves Minna aloft in the Mount Palomar observatory and descends to earth himself. Corde may think that he expedites Minna's dealings with officialdom in Rumania, but Minna ends up making most of the necessary arrangements herself while he sits in their bedroom ruminating upon events in Chicago.

Although Corde especially disapproves of what he thinks to be Minna's fanatical absorption in her work, her humanistic sensitivities are well developed and fully the equal of his. When she observes vaguely, "My mother is a symbol . . . ," Corde demands imperiously, "Of what?" He seems to expect a naive, political answer. But sensing the trap in his question, Minna insists, "It isn't political, it's just the way life has to be lived, it's just people humanly disaffected." When Corde still fails to grasp her point that Valeria was a human symbol rather than a political symbol and asks why officials fear a demonstration at the medical school, Minna speaks with human warmth, not with the scientific remoteness he thinks her wont:

> I told you. It would be sentiment. To approve what Valeria personally stood for. Just on human grounds. . . . Why don't you go and rest for a while, my dear. You're tired. This is hard on you. I can see.

The strength of the Corde marriage is based on minds and sensibilities well matched, then, even if the dean persists in not recognizing the development of Minna's sensibility. Corde's habit of close observation is the intellectual equivalent of her scientific empiricism, and his concern with human awareness finds an echo in her deeply human awarenesses. The crucial difference between them is that Minna does not bring her scientific and humanistic understandings into meaningful conjunction, while Corde tries to make physical perception a vehicle of humanistic understanding. His endeavor can be compared to that of the Sharp-Focus Realists in modern painting, and the comparison points to a limitation in his endeavor. Like the exaggerated clarity in a painting such as Andrew Wyeth's *Christina's World*, Corde's intensity of observation produces a *sense* of signification rather than explicable meanings. From first to last, his acts of passionate attention result not in journalistic "truth" but in intuitive understandings, imagined truths, and clairvoyance, as he vaguely recognizes. Early in the Rumanian sojourn, he meets Mihai Petrescu, a Party watchdog who pretends to be Valeria's friend, and his awareness of Petrescu's physical reality drifts typically into conclusions intuitive and imagined:

> Petrescu was squat, small-eyed; his fedora was unimpeded by hair so that the fuzz of the hat brim mingled with the growth of his ears in all-revealing

daylight. In every conversation about Valeria his sentences had a way of creeping upwards, his pitch climbed as high as his voice could bring it, and then there was a steep drop, a crack of emotion. He was dramatically fervent about Valeria. Studying his face, Corde at the same time *estimated* that something like three-fourths of his creases were the creases of a very tough character, a man you could easily *imagine* slamming the table during an interrogation, capable *perhaps* of pulling a trigger. *It wasn't just in Raymond Chandler novels that you met tough guys.* [emphasis mine]

The drift of Corde's mind is the same at the end of the Rumanian sojourn when he confronts Dewey Spangler. Intensely physical awareness fades once again into a visionary gestalt:

Then for some reason, with no feeling of abruptness, he became curiously absorbed in Dewey: blue eyes, puffy lids, tortoise-shell beard, arms crossed over his fat chest, fingers tucked into armpits, his skin scraped and mottled where the beard was trimmed, the warm air of his breathing, his personal odors, a sort of doughnut fragrance, slightly stale—*the whole human Spangler was delivered to Corde in the glass-warmed winter light with clairvoyant effect.* [emphasis mine]

This drift of Corde's mind into suprasensible apprehension is a symptom of his need to connect mind with sensibility, observation with conclusion, every aspect of experience with every other aspect. Although impressive in itself, that need is vain in the novel's divided world. The differences between Chicago and Bucharest are emblematic of politically irreconcilable differences between East and West. Town and Gown manifest similar dividedness in Chicago. An unbridgeable gulf yawns between the temperaments of men and women, as between Eros and Psyche.[8] Corde involves himself with the terra firma of history and politics; Minna, with boundless space; and each finds the other's pursuit incomprehensible. Liberals and conservatives find no common ground even in pursuit of common ends. Corde and

Beech share an apocalyptic view of the world, but their two apocalypses cannot finally be one—or so Corde concludes.

In demanding coherence of such a world, Corde engages himself in an idealistic enterprise. There is no possibility of synthesis being real without his perceiving it, he asserts. "Reality didn't exist 'out there,'" he says. "It began to be real only when the soul found its underlying truth." Yet Corde is as double-minded about this idealism as about all else. He scorns Witt's and Spangler's allegiance to mind even more than the women's indifference to mind. "The generality-mind, the habit of mind that governed the world, had no force of coherence," he concludes. "It was dissociative. It divided because it was, itself, divided. Hence the schizophrenia, which was moral and aesthetic as well as analytical."

Corde knows himself to be as divided as this double-mindedness suggests, but he rarely faces his internal divisions. He formally acknowledges that he is half Huguenot and half Irish, that he is a scion of both "pullman-car gentility" and "a corrupted branch of humanity." He suggests at times that he is a nihilist, at other times that he is a believer.[9] He is obviously, unreconciledly both academic administrator and journalist. But this dividedness is usually eclipsed for Corde by the larger question of what he represents, and such veiling of the dividedness is symptomatic of his identity crisis. It seems not to occur to him that he might simply *be*, dividedly. Spangler asks him why he has become a professor in Chicago, and Corde alludes to the query as "the really hot question," for he tends to equate his identity and his profession. Yet to all such questions about why he became a professor in Chicago, he offers vague or facile answers. "By the time the latest ideas reach Chicago, they're worn thin and easy to see through," he suggests in answer to a query from Elfrida. Alternately, he says he became a teacher because his modernity was all used up and he wanted to cure his ignorance. Perhaps it was only nostalgia for his undergraduate years, he suggests on another occasion.

If Corde is grateful for clues to who and what he is in the opinions men pronounce upon him, those opinions provide only momentary illumination inasmuch as they seldom agree in particulars. Liberals think the Dean a reactionary on the basis of his articles in *Harper's*; conservatives pronounce him crazy; and Mason thinks him evil. It would seem natural for Corde to relax into dividedness amid such divided opinion and cease to worry the question of what he represents, but he needs to resolve opposite opinion into some ultimate truth. To live with paradox is insupportable, no matter that he lives with it continually. He seems actually to think that the affirmation of paradox is a symptom of mental imbalance, as he indicates when he discovers himself using the language of the Beatitudes:

> So what was the pure-in-spirit bit? For an American who had been around, a man in his mid-fifties, this beatitude language was unreal. To use it betrayed him as a man wildly disturbed, a somehow crazy man. It was foreign, bookish—it was Dostoevsky stuff, that the vices of Sodom coexisted with the adoration of the Holy Sophia.

It is the unexpected denouement of such agonizing that Corde finally reaches an accommodation with dividedness.[10] The self-containment of women like Minna, Valeria, and Vlada has always suggested that accommodation was possible, and in the absence of clearer causality, one has to infer that the women's spirit infects Corde despite his unadmitted contempt for their sex. He is, after all, a susceptible man. "Why was it," he wonders, "that there were people with whom he, Corde, was so tied that his perception of them amounted to a bondage? They were drawn together physically, so tightly that he was virtually absorbed by them. . . . A kind of hypnotic coalescence was what occurred." Corde's double-mindedness has prepared him for the influence of women, of course. Disliking puzzles, he has always criticized his "intermittent consciousness" and "fitfulness of vision," and female composure is enormously attractive to him as an alternative. Bedeviled by puzzles of consciousness, he is generally convinced that he has "read too much, gathered too many associations, idled in too many picture galleries." A gender "not strictly literate" holds interest for him in consequence.

A "hypnotic coalescence" between Corde and his wife seems especially influential upon his final accommodation with dividedness. Because she separates her scientific and her humanistic perceptions, Corde has admired Minna less than he has admired Valeria, and seeing himself as her link with reality, he has never looked to Minna as a model of what he might be. But one suspects that Corde's view of his wife as professionally too-absorbed is the fallout of his own defection from journalism. His final intention to take up journalism again—as a trade rather than as a crusade, and restricting his scope so that he will not find himself agreeing ignorantly with crusaders like Beech— suggests an unconscious imitation of Minna's own behavior. "Don't be smart. Make no speeches," he cautions himself in dealing with Chicagoans once again at the end of the novel, and the admonitions might be Minna's own. "I don't like controversy," he assures his wife as if it were an established fact of his own life, rather than of hers. "I'm not much hurt. . . . I wasn't meant to be a dean," he can murmur after his final interview with Witt, echoing Minna's own sense of the situation.

Corde's "hypnotic coalescence" with Minna and the community of women finds its emblem in the cyclamens that bloom luxuriantly in the chill air of the Bucharest crematorium where Valeria's obsequies take place. Corde recalls someone suggesting to him that the plants produce their leaves and spectacular flowers in a state of sleep—that they represent "perfection devoid of consciousness, design without nerves." An abnormal sleepiness overtakes Corde thereafter, but he does not subsequently—in a word—*sleep*. "He took his cue from them [the cyclamens] and gave up consciousness," the reader is told. Minna falls asleep on the bed beside him at night, but Corde goes into "a state of blankness" that suggests the unsleeping sleep of the cyclamens. He enters, apparently, a state of unconscious life suited to hypnotic coalescence, and he comes to fulfillment in that state as mysteriously and as magnificently as the flowering plants.

The several domes of the novel are also emblematic of this coalescence with Minna and the community of women. Both Valeria and Minna are associated with domes, Valeria with the dome of the crematorium and Minna with the dome of the Mount Palomar observatory, and both domes are inhospitably cold—at least to Corde's conscious sensibility. Entering both, he is brought lower by attendants—to the hot, nether regions of the crematorium, where he identifies Valeria's body, and to the warmer floor of the observatory, away from the freezing heights where he leaves Minna. He thinks on the latter occasion of the "killing cold" that threatens to split open a third dome—the dome of the skull—as if by an ax. "But that dome never opened," he reflects. "You could pass through only as smoke." One wonders if his association is with the crematorial smoke, for to open his own head to the larger worlds of Minna and Valeria is a death experience for Corde, as the sleeping cyclamens, the freezing cold, and the dome-splitting ax conspire to suggest. To open his head is an abandonment of his commitment to ratiocination, his quest for a unified reality, and the warmth he experiences in partisan behavior. It is an abandonment that cannot be effected by an act of the will but only by a "hypnotic coalescence" as evanescent as cyclamens blooming in the cold and as smoke finding its way to an opening.

No passage in the novel describes the moment in which Corde discovers the possibility of relaxing into dividedness, but that silence is a narrative strength, not a weakness, for Corde himself is unaware of the moment and its mysterious evolution. When he decides at the end of the novel that he will collaborate with Beech limitedly, advising him about language only, he has clearly broken his commitment to undivided truth in favor of the unresolved, the problematic, and the contingent. He can connect with Beech simply because he likes him while rejecting the awesome connectiveness of being an "interpreter to the Humanists." He remains and presumably will remain a divided man, but with less compulsion to eclipse his knowledge of that state or to resolve its tensions. His remark in the last paragraph of the novel that he minds the cold of Minna's world at the height of the Mount Palomar observatory but that he also minds coming down to earth again suggests that his doublethink is no longer strained. He has finally relaxed into what a divided world requires him to be.

Does Corde actually suffer a death experience, then? Bellow promotes an alternate understanding of the dean's coming to peace when husband and wife take ten minutes of rest in the cloister of an old California mission en route to the Mount Palomar observatory. If their immediately subsequent visit to the observatory implies that Minna will continue to focus on the largest awarenesses and that chastened Corde will continue to arch high and return to earth again, the monastic interlude suggests that occasional retirement from struggle with the world will also give them rest. Their accommodation to the world of obdurate dividedness is a species of monastic retirement, Bellow seems finally to say—not a death of mind and spirit, but a necessary adjustment of human animals to their world.

Notes

1. Saul Bellow, *The Dean's December* (New York: Harper & Row, 1982).
2. Hugh Kenner, "From Lower Bellovia," *Harper's* (February 1982): 62-65.
3. Jonathan Raban, "The stargazer and his sermon," London *Sunday Times*, 28 March 1982, 41.
4. *See* Michiko Kakutani, "A Talk with Saul Bellow: On His Work and Himself," *New York Times Book Review*, 13 December 1981, 28-30.
5. *See* Al Eisenberg, "Saul Bellow Picks Another Fight," *Rolling Stone* 363 (March 1982): 16.
6. Allan Chavkin has looked more positively than I upon Corde's attitude toward women. *See* "The Feminism of The Dean's December," *Studies in American Jewish*

Literature 3 (1983): 113-27. I disagree with Joseph Cohen's argument that Corde is a completely reformed womanizer, "full of love and admiration for the women around him," but Cohen's observations on the relationship of the novel to Bellow's fourth marriage are illumining. "Saul Bellow's Heroes in an Unheroic Age," *Saul Bellow Journal* 3 (Fall-Winter 1983): 53-58.

7. Allan Chavkin has argued that Bellow's intention in *The Dean's December* was to write "a meditative novel in which the protagonist ponders personal and public problems" and concludes that the dean's discursiveness is unfairly criticized. "Recovering 'The World That Is Buried under the Debris of False Description,'" *Saul Bellow Journal* 1 (Spring-Summer 1982): 45-57.

8. For a discussion of the Eros-Psyche theme in the novel, *see* Judie Newman, "Bellow and Nihilism: *The Dean's December*," *Studies in the Literary Imagination* 17 (Fall 1984): 111-22.

9. In an interview with Melvin Bragg, Bellow attributed to Corde "a sort of nihilistic questioning of the world." "An Interview with Saul Bellow," *London Review of Books* 4 (May 1982): 22. Judie Newman has discussed the novel's interest in nihilism in "Bellow and Nihilism: *The Dean's December*."

10. Matthew C. Roudané comes to a similar conclusion via a different argument. "A Cri de Coeur: The Inner Reality of Saul Bellow's *The Dean's December*," *Studies in the Humanities* 11 (December 1984): 5-17.

On *Him with His Foot in His Mouth and Other Stories*

Daniel Fuchs

Four of the five works in *Him with His Foot in His Mouth and Other Stories* are recent and deal with aging. The fifth, "Zetland: By a Character Witness," is not a story but a fragment of a projected novel about Isaac Rosenfeld; written about a dozen years ago, it does not fit in with the *eheu fugaces* coloration of the rest of the collection. The most ambitious and best fiction is "What Kind of Day Did You Have?"—a novella which reaches a level near that of Bellow's best short fiction. Of the new pieces, Bellow is most deeply involved with this work and with the problematic "Cousins." "A Silver Dish" is a lovely story and the most formally polished, even meeting *New Yorker* standards!—something which even the post-Nobel Bellow is too idiosyncratic a taleteller to always do. The title story is great fun but, once past its original impulse, too reliant on Bellow mannerisms. All in all, this collection is Bellow in fine form. He dramatizes here, with varying degrees of success, a sense of the transcendent value of character. In doing so he is mining his richest vein.

"What Kind of Day Did You Have?" is about a distinguished old man who nearly dies. Given a new lease on life, he pursues familiar eros in the face of thanatos. Though he does this in an imperative way, he even more conspicuously pursues habitual sublimated eros, the life of the mind, against death. For Victor Wulpy is a Marxist intellectual of an imperious stamp whose apparent confidence is matched only by his air of contempt. He is compared to a sultan, a king, a captain, and, more ominously, "a tyrant in thought" (96). The wonder is that he should have an affair with a rather ordinary, upper-middle class, divorced hausfrau. What kind of affair did they have? To answer the question, one must first consider the cast of mind of this particular intellectual, for "What Kind of Day Did You Have?" is one of those dense Bellow works in which idea is made flesh and flesh idea.

Victor Wulpy (modeled on Harold Rosenberg) appears to have im-
bibed Marxism from infancy rather than mother's milk. As a result, everything about the decadence of bourgeois culture seems crystal clear
to him and witheringly cold. Wulpy speaks of the "animal human aver-
age" (122) (like Marx, he is a corrosive wit), the sellout of the intellectuals, and *The Eighteenth Brumaire* which "had America's present
number" (103). He sees social classes prevented from acting politically, with clowns and ham actors filling the void. There is some question as to how to reconcile this partly justified cynicism with proletarian utopianism, but it is never articulated. Focusing on the farcical
parody of revolution in the absence of true proletarian struggle (as in
the late sixties in America), *The Eighteenth Brumaire of Louis Bona-
parte* is a work (as Rosenberg points out in his essay "The Politics of
Illusion" 122), which could be used to refute Marxism in its millenar-
ian aspect. To this indictment Wulpy adds a contemporary twist: fictional personages take over when professional groups con the public
with "standards" that conceal cheating.

Wulpy's icy clairvoyance carries into his personal life. "He could
discuss a daughter," says the narrator, "like any other subject submitted
to his concentrated, radiant consideration—with the same generalizing
detachment" (107). True, his daughter is one of Bellow's wacked-out
younger types, a violinist and rabbi-to-be, who offers her hapless
mother a homosexual sex manual so that the old gal can compete for
Wulpy's affections. Yet with parents like hers, what chance did the kid
have? There was sure to be some outlandish retribution for her
mother's humiliating status as her father's sexual secretary and facto-
tum. The situation is somewhat reminiscent to me, though perhaps not
to the author, of Mady, the philandering Pontritter, and the victimized
Tennie of *Herzog*. But the religiously inclined narrator sees mainly the
idiocy of the child, never thinking that marriage might be a sacrament
(or a social contract) and not a joke. Hence, the more abuse Wulpy's
wife can absorb the more noble we are to judge her to be.

More than this, Wulpy's coldness carries over into his actual love life. With a condescension the narrator does not seem to penetrate, Wulpy thinks of his middle-aged divorcée as a "girl" (74). He values her for the *"caresse qui fait revivre les morts"* (155), yet he cannot help thinking that the affair is "not serious. . . . Such old stuff—*not* serious" (156). Is love, then, a bourgeois illusion, tied up with property rights? Katrina's claim on him is minimal enough. "It wasn't just another adultery," she thinks. "She wasn't one of his casual women" (153). Are we to take this absence of negatives for a presence of positives?

The climax of the story has to do not with the sexual gratification they snatch from the jaws of time but with the meaning of the affair. Wulpy had given Katrina *Journey to the End of Night* to read, Céline's novel in which a central character refuses to tell his lover that he loves her and is shot dead as a result. Rather than with the woman of feeling, however, Céline's modernist sympathy is with the nihilist, a murderer whose honor resides in refusing false ideals. Katrina is not so much shocked by the novel as by Wulpy's commending it, thereby degrading what she wants to value most. While it occurs to her that his aim in doing so was "to desensitize her feelings" (154) so she would feel his loss less, her insight may well err on the side of generosity. Is Wulpy, then, simply a high-powered cynic? Despite his political stance, Wulpy often concedes "that the obscurest and most powerful question, deeper than politics, was that of an understanding between man and woman. . . . Katrina, as a subject for thought, was the least trivial of all" (156). We are so told, but it is not easy to see how Wulpy actually feels such emotion. His affection is very muted, the object of it rather dull, and the whole affair more than a bit tacky. So while we are supposed to concur with Wulpy that "of all that might be omitted in thinking, the worst was to omit your own being" (156), his emotional neutrality all but does just this. Indeed, this relationship has as much to do with the psychodynamics of master/slave as with illumination of thought. Affectionately sadistic to his pathetic wife, Wulpy makes demands on his mistress to which only a masochist would respond. Perhaps it is masochism that compels her when, in the climactic moment of the story, she asks him to say "I love you." (The private plane from Buffalo to Chicago seems to be falling in a winter storm—more love and death.) Surely the icy integrity of Wulpy could not brook such a cliché. "Why," the sympathetic narrator asks, "should Victor declare, 'I love you'? For her sake, he went on the road" (161). False intimacy she can never get from Wulpy. Does she get true intimacy?

Again a personal issue is inextricably bound to the ideational development of the story. Wulpy is pursued by Wrangel, a successful sci-fi Hollywood producer, who had been Wulpy's student thirty years ago. As Wrangel's name indicates, he is persistent in argument. He mounts a critique of a man whose ideas he respects, which, with certain differences noted, we may assume is Bellow's critique of Rosenberg. If sci-fi paranoia and serious intellection seem incompatible, we should recall that his next movie deals with the long reign of quantification, the divine mind overthrown by the technocratic mind—a serious subject in grotesque form. Of course, whether he does the movie or not depends first on financial considerations. In any case, the opulently clothed Wrangel is an unlikely groupie, but he does put Wulpy to the test. Familiar with Wulpy's ideas (including his essay on *The Eighteenth Brumaire*), he rightly sees him as an apostle of the new. The avant-garde is free of "this death grip of tradition." Wulpy admires art which creates "a world of its own, owing nothing to the old humanism" (112), a view with which the humanist Bellow would have to feel uneasy. Also, Wrangel rightly objects to Wulpy's seeing things in terms of class struggle, imposing thereby European conceptions of class on Americans. "'I have a friend,'" (114) says Wrangel, a friend who supplies a viable alternative. The "friend" is Bellow.

Wrangel opts for a Steinerian "created soul," which has been temporarily replaced by "an artificial one." Religious humanism seems more relevant to our moral predicament than does Marxism. Now, Wrangel's friend holds, men live "mainly by *rationales* . . . made-up guidance systems," what Bellow usually calls ideologies. In a typical comic undercutting of his spiritual concerns, Bellow has Wulpy retort,

"'Is this friend of yours a California friend? Is he a guru?'" (114). But Wrangel holds his ground.

Although he has come East to see Wulpy, Wrangel agrees with Sidney Hook that the problem of Wulpy's group is that they are merely talking radicals (a point which activist Marxists also make). Yet Wrangel thinks of Wulpy in a way that preserves him from himself. Wrangel sees past the usual categories to Wulpy's uniqueness: "A subtle mind. Completely independent. Not really a Marxist, either" (132). This is surely Bellow's view of Rosenberg as well. Improbably, the sci-fi producer agrees that "without art we can't judge what life is." Subtly (and this is even more improbable), though, he turns back on himself to say, "but even Victor's real interest is politics" (134), and, one should add, radical politics. Wrangel recalls that during the French student crisis Wulpy "agreed with Sartre that we were on the verge of an inspiring and true revolution" (134-35). This is a crucial mistake, which Wrangel does not or cannot make enough of. All he can say is that "he got carried away" (135). He rightly judges—and again, the judgment is surely Bellow's judgment of Rosenberg—that "in politics Victor is still something of a sentimentalist" (135) about Marx, about revolution. He notes Wulpy's limitations of vision. Yet Wulpy believes that it is precisely his imagination of power that gives him the edge over other intellectuals.

Surprisingly, Wulpy admits that old age has given him the "dispassionate view [he] always preferred" (146). But Wulpy confuses metaphysical and aesthetic passion, on the one hand, with political passion, on the other, under the ambiguous rubric of "a powerful reading of the truth of existence" (146-47). The ideational confusion is personally fruitful, though, in that he is for the first time having "lucid impressions—like dreams, visions—instead of lucid ideas" (147). This is what Bellow meant when, in an interview conducted by D. J. R. Bruckner, he said, "I think Victor was sustained by something he did not know" (62). Wulpy speaks, in Bellovian fashion, of a "shared knowledge that we don't talk about," rising to a positively spiritualist view: "Cryptic persistent suggestions: the dead are not really *dead*. Or, we don't create thoughts. . . . A thought *is* real, already created, and a real thought can pay you a visit" (148). In this context he reluctantly admits that Wrangel supplied "a California parody of things that I had been thinking myself" (147). Wulpy, after all, has had a life in the arts.

Wulpy's reluctant progress, then, under the aspect of mortality, is from tough to tender-minded, cold to lukewarm. But it is an inhibited progress, if it can be considered a progress at all. Sex, apparently, is the last lucidity—a fleeting one. Sexual affection is sexual affection, and love (whatever that is) is love; and he owes it to his self-respect as a mind not to confuse the two. Isn't either motive sufficient? Yes, for Katrina's sake he went on the road. Tenderness will have to do, man-and-womanness. Wulpy, if not Katrina, is sustained by an oblique intimacy. In the haunting climax of the story, the relatively simple, sensuous, middle-class Katrina knows what it is to be intimate with disillusioned truth.

"Cousins" is narrated by a familiar Bellow type—the urban *isolato*—divorced, distinguished, filial. The story is lyrical, our interest being not so much in what happens but in the contemplative consciousness of the central character. Everything depends on Ijah Brodsky's temperament, and an intriguing one it is. This is hardly new, but story as poem in Bellow has rarely been so obvious. The narrative "I" allows for greatest elaboration of intimate detail, retrospection and, above all, sentiment. The protagonist thinks of a series of cousins who are set in something of a dramatic pattern, but it is what Ijah feels about them that counts. Bellow has always been a novelist of "character," and what we essentially get here is a return to his earliest form—pure character sketch. The difference is that where the early sketches were monologues by the characters, here we get a monologue about character—not character as such, but a special version of the *amor fati*, the pull of relation, the mysterious attraction of cousins. I suspect that, generally speaking, Bellow's generation was the last of the earlier immigrant Jewish milieu to feel this kind of intimate involvement—as opposed to the nuclear family involvement, which is still very deep, and which, as his ex-wife points out to him, Ijah does not have—and it is a bit hard to see where sentiment lets off and sentimentality begins. Ijah, an intellectual sort of investment banker (research department), calls his cousins "the elect of my memory" (242), but one may wonder why.

The story begins with a vivid description of Tanky Metzger, a rackets type who could get fifteen years for his activities. The respectable Ijah is asked to write a mitigating letter; he does so because of the special status cousins have for him. Tanky "associates with gangsters, but so do aldermen, city officials, journalists, big builders, fundraisers for charitable institutions—the mob gives generously" (227). While this is not yet the familiar they-all-do-it cynicism, Ijah soon crosses the line. The foundations of political stability, of democracy, are "swindle and fraud," he holds, with the top executives and lawyers "spreaders of the most fatal nets" (244). If so, why not revolution or anarchy or, at least, reform, rather than being part of the establishment? The problem is that in Ijah Brodsky we have another instance of the creeping sentimentality/cynicism that has infringed on Bellow's late work. Ijah sees part of the problem when, thinking of why he wrote a letter for Tanky, he says, "I had no space to work out whether this was a moral or a sentimental decision" (240).

His mind echoing with Hegel and Heidegger, with, in his own description, disintegration and antarctic frigidity, Ijah clings to cousins like an ocean survivor to a life raft. With Tanky, a certain balance between moral and sentimental is achieved. With Tanky's sister, Eunice, whom Ijah doesn't so much contemplate as encounter along the way, American madness takes over. Cynicism finds an objective correlative. Living with a husband who spends what he earns on himself, Eunice pays for her children's tuition with her inheritance. Totally in the money culture, she explains her involvement in a med-school admittance payoff: "You can guess what a medical degree is worth, the income it guarantees" (250). She welches on half the payoff, negating her bond of "integrity." It is hard to judge whether her base or noble motive is worse. Why does she stay with her husband? Because "I'm covered by his Blue Cross-Blue Shield" (252). Marriage has often been a metaphorical insurance policy in bourgeois culture; here it is a literal one. No wonder our investment banker reads anthropological studies of Siberia, where the "powers of darkness surrounded you" and you are confronted by "demanding spirits whose mouths were always gaping. The people cringed and gave ransom, buying protection from these ravaging ghosts" (253). It is the same world as the rackets and the medical schools gone corrupt—and, as Ijah sees it, the world of investment banking, which shores up its Brazils and Irans by the protection of government guarantees, leaving the public to bear the risk. Can feeling be anything but sentimental when reality is so cynical? The "careerists" in his building seem no less bizarre than Siberians. "Human beings, by definition, [are] half the time mad" (254), thinks Ijah, thereby undercutting an earlier Bellow balance. For example, there is Charley Citrine's attack on the Freudian Philip Rieff for suggesting that life is a hospital.

In all this darkness Cousin Motty just does not stand up as representative of what life ought to be, as Bellow's defensive rhetoric all but implies: Motty is "the head of the family, insofar as there is a family, and insofar as it has a head" (258). The tentativeness of the story's movement is partly accounted for by Bellow's admission to Bruckner that "I began to think I was wrong and Nietzsche was right about the disappearance of the gods" (56). This does not literally figure in the story except as resultant mood, the fruits of reading Heidegger on Nietzsche and others. Is the ice broken by such filial-to-the-n[th] displays as observing old Motty's birthday? Maintaining that "the very masses are turning their backs on family," Ijah clings nonetheless to his admittedly "imperfect love" (261) of the old man. He links this affection to the disintegration he sees in the life process and the social order. But even Ijah wonders about the connection: "What do I want with Motty anyway, and why have I made a trip from the Loop to molest him?"

(265). Yet he feels that the old man silently consulting with himself is in touch with the original person, the soul, the perspective of the Blakean divine eye. In the dissolution of mortality and history, "the untenability of existence" releases this original self, which is now "free to look for real being under the debris of modern ideas" (268). The man on the dump, the rose on the dungheap, the crocus in concrete—such minimal images of renewal (the last from *Humboldt's Gift*) occur to me as descriptive of the thinning air of late Bellow. "Getting on top of the collapsed pile" (262) is the way Ijah puts it.

If Tanky, Eunice, and Motty are instances of social and natural disintegration beyond which some form of soul exists, Cousin Scholem represents a putative triumph of spirit over circumstance. But Scholem does not quite come off as a character, being a dubious amalgam of the Isaac Rosenfeld prodigy type and an actual World War II veteran and cabbie whose quest for Soviet-American accord received national media attention. Scholem thinks he has out-Darwined Darwin and has made the first major philosophical breakthrough since the *Critique of Pure Reason*. All this was cut short by the Japanese attack on Pearl Harbor. Volunteering, Scholem comes to the defense of democracy and his theories, culminating in the grand meeting of Americans and Russians at the city of Torgau. His great work postponed, he is presently a taxi driver. The spectacular comedown works for Bellow in a comic context (for example, Wallace Gruner), but it jars in an elegiac one. The elderly Scholem has had cancer surgery, and the doctors say he will soon be dead. He wishes to be buried in Torgau. Bellow is stirred by the positive impulse in the man, which he thinks of as typically Jewish. Amid decadence, Scholem upholds the "moral law," purity of thought, patriotism; he "wanted to affirm that all would be well, to make a distinguished gift [like Humboldt, like the novelist himself], to bless mankind. In all this Scholem fitted the classical norm for Jews of the diaspora" (276). Bellow attributes Scholem's cancer to his effort to be pure in decadent Chicago, adding that driving ten hours a day in traffic also had something to do with it.

A relative with money will get specialists to read Scholem's great work (totally unbelievable at the point), even though he thinks of Scholem as a megalomaniac. Ijah, in typical Bellow fashion, regards such psychological terms as "a menace," thinking that "they should all be shoveled into trucks and taken to the dump" (281). More cultural garbage. In the muted anticlimax of an ending, Ijah barely sees the ailing Scholem in Paris at a convention of taxi drivers, which confirms the basically sentimental quality of the connection. Yet there is a metaphysical perspective. Time wastes us; relation is a kind of immortality or an expression of the *amor fati*. At the story's end, we see Ijah, movingly, in his frailty, like the cousins he observes, an instance of time's depredations.

Bellow anticipates the charge of sentimentality by having Ijah's ex-wife express it. He turned to cousins, she says, because of the lack of real connection with nuclear family. Further, when nuclear families are breaking up, collateral relatives enable him to indulge his "taste for the easier affects." He "lacked the true modern severity" (288). More power to him. Wulpy had that, almost. But one need not embrace the true modern severity to feel uneasy about Ijah's expression of emotion. Nothing here is dramatized. Character sketch does the work of plot. Bellow claims that the story is "metaphysical not sentimental" (Bruckner 56), but it is clear that the two are not mutually exclusive.

There is, I believe, a more deeply felt character sketch in "Zetland: By a Character Witness." Here we get Isaac Rosenfeld without complications, and the prose moves with a greater fluency than in "Cousins." There is much more to the Rosenfeld portrait than is given in this fragment (cf. *Saul Bellow: Vision and Revision* 257-64), including the most brilliant writing Bellow has not published. But he gave up on the projected novel about Rosenfeld because he did not want to portray him as "a kind of Dostoyevskian clown" (Bruckner 60), as a victim, and that is the way the book was turning out.

Though it is less central to Bellow's own patterns of feeling—and was perhaps for this reason easier to mount in terms of dramatic disposition—"A Silver Dish," next to "What Kind of Day Did You Have?" is the best story in the collection. Once again, a central question is "What do you do about death?" (191). Morris Selbst is the sort of man only a daughter could love—or a tender-minded son. A ne'er-do-well and petty con artist, this immigrant "became an American, and America never knew it. He voted without papers, he drove without a license, he paid no taxes, he cut every corner. Horses, cards, billiards, and women were his life interest, in ascending order" (198). This fugitive from a picaresque novel is set in a religious domestic context of Christian proselytizers and Jewish converts so straightlaced as to almost forgive his mendacities. The crisis comes when he steals a silver dish from the kind, paternalistic Mrs. Skogland, to whom, in this Depression story, he had come to borrow money. "Kind has a price tag," says cynical Pop years later to his long-tried son. The story exists in two time frames, that of the embarrassed boy and that of the mellow man in his sixties thinking of the recent death of his ancient father; this contrast is its point. The story is a Sunday morning rumination in which all is retrospective in the son's central intelligence.

Woody Selbst, the son, is his father's opposite. Unbidden, he believes even as a youth that "God's idea was that this world should be a love world, that it should eventually recover and be entirely a world of love." Typically, Bellow must undercut such traditional tender-minded assumptions. "He wouldn't have said this to a soul, for he could see himself how stupid it was—personal and stupid. Nevertheless, there it was at the center of his feelings" (199-200). These feelings serve him well years later in coming to terms with Pop, hospitalized, feeble, rebellious in his deathbed. That's what you do about death; you mitigate its effect by transformations of feeling. Pop dies as Woody holds him, thereby preventing the old man from removing the intravenous needles. "You could never pin down that self-willed man," Woody says admiringly of Pop's perversely resolute spirit (222).

In the hallowed haze of sexagenarian retrospection, the question of sentimentality once again arises. Pop is really a narrow, bastardly sort of guy who, as Woody thinks, "never suffered." Is he so different from Eunice's husband, a contemptible egotist who spends everything on himself? Selfless Woody loves Pop for his selfishness. Sentimentality is much less an issue here than in "Cousins." How can you forget a father—particularly one whose inflexible will helped you escape as a youth the clutches of rather oppressive spiritualism? To this extent Woody shared his desire for freedom.

This desire in Woody sometimes takes the form of travel to exotic places. An image from a recent safari haunts him. A buffalo calf disappears into the White Nile, snatched by a crocodile. But Woody's vision of love persists, a moral, perhaps Jewish world, beyond the victimization of Darwinian nature.

The title story is a bright *jeu d'esprit*, comical in some ways already familiar to the Bellow reader. After the gloom of *The Dean's December*, it is good to see Bellow operating in the boisterous mode. Harry Shawmut is an academic musician whose romantic nature is indicated by the transcendent way he conducts Pergolesi. Music is freedom, but so, alas, is wit; the first, Auden once wrote, is "pure contraption . . . an absolute gift"; the second, like poetry, "fetches/ The images out that hurt and connect" (Auden 125). The story pivots around an insulting remark Shawmut made thirty years back to an innocent spinster librarian, Miss Rose. The crack, presumably unlike the many others which the story gives us, was unprovoked. Shawmut, in true Bellovian fashion, wishes to absolve himself of gratuitous offense. The incident brings to mind the episode of the pink ribbon from Rousseau's *Confessions*. Rousseau was asking to be absolved by his awareness—the purity of honest consciousness. So is Shawmut. But where Rousseau was solemn, Bellow, in contemporary fashion, makes comedy of a neurotic quirk. The story is cast as one long letter of indirect apology to the wronged Miss Rose. Look, cries Shawmut, look how this aggression in me has messed up my life. But what we see becomes so involuted in plot and often moves so far from Shawmut's weakness that we barely remember that the librarian was the cause of this confession, or that she would want to hear all this.

Would she derive gratification, so many years later, from Shawmut's being torpedoed by his shameless brother? And what does this betrayal have to do with Shawmut's famous weakness? Silent people are also betrayed. For her to derive satisfaction from his tribulations, she would not be Miss Rose but Lucretia Borgia.

Shawmut, in his sixties, the quirky, ingratiating "I" of the story, is the only elderly character in this collection not concerned with death. (He does see his ancient mother in a nursing home, but to comic effect—she remembers the terrible brother and has no recollection of Shawmut.) Shawmut is involved in the long perspective, though, as his confession to Miss Rose shows. He is also on the receiving end of abuse, having been written a long, scathing letter on his character by an apparent friend of thirty years—this is the vaguely Gersbachian Walish. But the story is unconvincing here. Walish's rancor is attributed to the success of Shawmut's TV program, to the envious betrayal by friends, and to the plot complications: a felon brother businessman who does him in and a not particularly competent brother-in-law lawyer, who, in order to save Shawmut what money he has left, devises a crafty scheme which leaves Shawmut in exile in Vancouver fearing extradition. We have a familiar scenario: the idealist *putz* ground up in the businessman/lawyer double whammy.

If all this seems mannered, it may be because it is so far from the real-life event on which, in part, it seems to be based. Lionel Trilling informed me in conversation that he wrote such a letter to Bellow (perhaps echoed in Shawmut's fragmentary recollection of Walish's) in response to what he took to be Bellow's misconceived attack on him in a *Harper's* piece the year before. And Bellow wrote the widowed Diana Trilling a letter, which she informed me of, expressing regret that he had caused Trilling any pain. If my assumption is correct, the story is, in part, a larky reworking of a theme that could have been treated very differently—and a remarkable insight into the comic imagination. Of course, Shawmut's trait can produce the comedy we have here and, by Bellow's own account, literally did on two occasions. But the Walish letter seems a bit disconnected in the story. There is a passing allusion to a Trilling work of that period, *Sincerity and Authenticity*, when Shawmut is thinking about the appeal of Allen Ginsberg, who is putting his queer shoulder to the wheel: "this bottom-line materialistic eroticism is most attractive to Americans, proof of sincerity and authenticity" (22). If this means that there are dangers to accepting authenticity as a moral standard, he is reading Trilling rightly; if it means Trilling sets authenticity up as a standard, he is not. I would speculate that an ironic, problematic remark Trilling made in that book (42) to the effect that *Herzog* may be open to "the terrible charge of philistinism" for realigning our attitudes toward modernism vis-à-vis traditional values may have had to do with the flare-up. The incident was unfortunate since, in the cultural wars, both are fighting on essentially the same side—civilization—Bellow as religious humanist, Trilling as Freudian humanist.

Bellow's religious humanism figures in this story as well, again in the comically defensive position. Shawmut is stranded in Vancouver with his landlady, old Miss Gracewell, who reads Swedenborg and the occult, and thinks about poetic justice and the life to come. She is one of the spacey characters the Bellow protagonist feels a secret affinity for. Appearing near the beginning of the story and near the end, she serves to surround the mad events of the normal world in a fragile frame of spirit. Her strangeness—related to Shawmut's passion for religious music—is preferable to the strangeness of the workaday world. "The Divine Spirit, she tells me, has withdrawn in our time from the outer, visible world" (58), notes Shawmut sympathetically. She too posits an "awakened age of the spirit" (59). So we too come full circle in the thematic unity of these works.

From *Saul Bellow Journal* 5.1 (Fall/Winter 1986): 3-15. Copyright © 1986 by *Saul Bellow Journal*. Reprinted with permission of *Saul Bellow Journal*.

Works Cited

Auden, W. H. *Collected Shorter Poems*. London: Faber, 1966.

Bellow, Saul. *Him with His Foot in His Mouth and Other Stories*. New York: Harper and Row, 1984.

Bruckner, D. J. R. Interview with Saul Bellow. "A Candid Talk with Saul Bellow." *New York Times Magazine* 15 April 1984: 56, 60, 62.

Fuchs, Daniel. *Saul Bellow: Vision and Revision*. Durham, NC: Duke UP, 1984.

Rosenberg, Harold. "The Politics of Illusion." *Liberations*. Ed. Ihab Hassan. Middletown, CT: Wesleyan UP, 1969.

Trilling, Diana. A Conversation. Fall 1976.

Trilling, Lionel. A Conversation. Spring 1975.

Trilling, Lionel. *Sincerity and Authenticity*. Cambridge: Harvard UP, 1972.

A Contemporary Fall:
More Die of Heartbreak[1] _____

Ellen Pifer

"Contemplating flowers"—a more serious occupation to Charlie Citrine than the customary business of America—receives even more prominent attention in Bellow's latest novel. In *More Die of Heartbreak* (1987), the protagonist, Benn Crader, is an internationally renowned botanist who, in the words of his nephew, the novel's narrator, is both a research scientist and a "plant clairvoyant" (234, 305). Working "like a contemplative, concentrating without effort," Uncle Benn, a university professor, not only studies plant anatomy but appears to see "behind the appearances" (253). "Studying leaves, bark, roots, heartwood, sapwood, flowers, for their own sake," Uncle Benn, says his nephew, "contemplated them"—that is, "he saw into or looked through plants. He took them as his arcana. An arcanum is more than a mere secret; it's what you have to know in order to be fertile in a creative pursuit, to make discoveries, to prepare for the communication of a spiritual mystery" (27).

This visionary enterprise, "contemplating flowers," delineates only one of the numerous thematic and structural affinities between *Humboldt's Gift* and Bellow's most recent novel. Because *More Die of Heartbreak* takes up, in so many ways, where the earlier novel left off, I have chosen to alter slightly the chronological pattern traced thus far (with the initial exception, of course, of *Mr. Sammler's Planet*) and devote immediate attention to *More Die of Heartbreak*. Thus *The Dean's December* (1982), the novel that appeared directly after *Humboldt's Gift* (1975), will be discussed in the succeeding chapter of this study.

Charlie Citrine, the narrator of *Humboldt's Gift*, reviews the tragic history of his old friend, the poet Von Humboldt Fleisher, as he tells his own story. In *More Die of Heartbreak*, Benn Crader's nephew, Kenneth Trachtenberg, is compelled by a similar bond of love to recount the story of a man he reveres. By reviewing the life of his uncle, whom he regards as his spiritual father, Ken attempts to put that life as well as his own in perspective. Citrine, furthermore, attributes the demise of Humboldt's personal life and artistic vocation to the poet's loss of faith in his visionary imagination. Similarly, Ken Trachtenberg pays tribute to his uncle's gift of seeing, as a "plant clairvoyant," and attributes Benn's recent "fall" to loss of confidence in that visionary power.

The author of many "books and articles," Uncle Benn enjoys a "big reputation" in the field of botany (32). Yet despite Crader's eminence as a scientist, says his nephew, "not even the 'laws' of physics or biology were permitted to inhibit him" (15). "Uncle was sure," Ken later explains, "that nature had an *inside*" (128, Bellow's italics). In his research on plants, Benn Crader has worked "like a contemplative, concentrating without effort, as naturally as he breathes, no oscillations of desire or memory" (253). To his own, characteristically modern "oscillations of consciousness," Ken contrasts his uncle's mode of contemplation—one that, in Ken's description, bears a definite resemblance to Rudolf Steiner's account of "inward" vision: Benn "really *knew* the vegetable kingdom. He practiced the scrutiny of secret things—total absorption in their hidden design." "There were times," Ken also notes, "when you felt [Benn's] power of *looking* turned on you. . . . This is the faculty of seeing; of seeing *itself*; what eyes are actually for" (317, 14, Bellow's italics).[2] In the end, however, Uncle Benn fails to "make the psychic transfer to human relations"; the complexity and deviousness of personal relationships disturb and ultimately foil his powers of insight (106).

Born and raised in Paris, Ken accepts a teaching post at his uncle's midwestern university in order to be near his mentor. It is from Benn that his nephew, a man in his middle thirties, hopes to learn something of the "higher spheres" of existence, knowledge to which Ken's natural father, Rudi Trachtenberg, is wholly indifferent. An American expatriate who remained in Paris after the Second World War, Ken's father is a cosmopolitan whose many accomplishments belong strictly to the sexual and social spheres of life. In "tennis, [his] war record, . . . in sex, in conversation, in looks," Rudi Trachtenberg is, according to Kenneth, an unqualified success. In an era that celebrates physical fitness and erotic invention, Rudi is a paragon—a "Hegelian . . . Master Spirit" (65). "The historical thing which millions of sex-intoxicated men were trying to do and botching, he did with the ease of a natural winner" (37).

The very type or product of those "conditioning forces" against which Augie March seeks to defend the "primordial person," Rudi Trachtenberg is indifferent to the "fundamentals" his son urgently seeks to discover (10-12). Like Herzog, Ken Trachtenberg admits that he "used to be sold on" theories and ideas but "discovered that they were nothing but trouble if you entertained them indiscriminately." There are some "matters"—including the "matter" of Uncle Benn's "fall"—"for which theorizing brings no remedy" (19).[3] Ken's "partial deafness," moreover, directly links him to Artur Sammler, whose partial blindness emblemizes the Bellovian hero's divided consciousness, oscillating between the "superstructures of explanation" and the soul's "natural knowledge" (47). "Modern life, if you take it to heart, wears you out," Ken reflects. "Even my hearing aid was off, and when I fiddled my finger under my long hair and tapped on it, something like a sonic boom went off in my skull" (118). Turning on his hearing aid, Ken tunes into "modern life"; like a "sonic boom" in the "skull," the impact of his re-entry is shattering.

With his uncle, a widower, Ken shares a propensity for ineffectual and "confused relations with women"; he cannot even persuade Treckie, the "childlike" but willful young woman he adores, to marry him. Instead, Treckie has removed herself, along with their little girl, Nancy, thousands of miles away from Ken—to live in Seattle with another man. Aware that he lacks his father's sexual talent, Ken tries "to right the balance" by giving himself "more mental weight." Yet this attempt to compensate mentally for lack of physical or sexual authority only goes to show, in Ken's view, "how far we've fallen below the classical Greek standard. We've split things in two, dividing the physique from the mind" (39-40). Searching for a way to mend this "split," Ken wants to realize his "soul in the making" (37).

Looking to his uncle for guidance, Ken finds, instead, that Benn Crader is also prey to divided consciousness. As Ken says, "I had come to America to complete my education, to absorb certain essential powers from Uncle, and I learned presently that he was looking to *me* for assistance" (92, Bellow's italics). What happens to Benn in the human sphere, Ken discovers, is partly due to his special nature as "a man of feeling"; for Benn, a middle-aged widower, proves acutely susceptible to "*love* longings" and their peculiarly modern distortions (278, Bellow's italics). When, in his mid-fifties, Benn suffers an onslaught of erotic longing—impulses that Rudi Trachtenberg is much more adept at handling—he impulsively sets out to achieve conjugal bliss. Believing himself to have fallen in love with a "perfect" beauty, a woman much younger than he, Benn peremptorily marries Matilda Layamon. Unfortunately, the marriage brings him neither peace nor love. It is a disaster—one that could have been averted if he had paid heed to the warning signals emitted by his "prophetic soul" (326). Distracted by desire, failing to trust in his intuitive powers because they strike him as "irrational," Benn becomes prey to those "oscillations of consciousness" Ken has sought, under his uncle's influence, to quell.

When Ken initially sets out to absorb his uncle's influence, he is not sure whether Benn's gift for "contemplating flowers" may be carried over into the human sphere. Eventually he discovers that Benn's insight into plants does "overlap," to a considerable degree, with the sphere of "human relations" (106). Alarmed, however, by what he sees, Benn decides, like Von Humboldt Fleisher, not to credit his visionary powers. As a poet Humboldt "wanted to drape the world in radiance" but lacked "enough material" (*HG* 107). The "short supply" of "material," which Citrine attributes to the poet's failure to trust in his visionary imagination, similarly plagues Uncle Benn. As his nephew observes, "the whole vegetable kingdom was [Benn's] garment—his robe, his coat. . . . Still, Uncle's garment was incomplete. It didn't quite button" (119). This tragic incompleteness is partly due, of course, to the fact that human beings make far more complex demands on one's powers of insight than members of the "vegetable kingdom." But as Benn and his nephew both come to realize, Benn's failure also derives from his refusal to heed the promptings of his inmost self.

Characterized as a mysterious "daemon" or "inner spirit," Benn's inmost self—which he also calls "that second person of mine"—has guided him at crucial moments in his life. (This "daemon" is the polar opposite of Herzog's "demon" of "modern ideas," whose insistent demand for theories and explanations must be silenced before Herzog can commune with *his* inner spirit.) It was "that second person inside" him that prompted Benn to "become a botanist" in the first place (58, 84). By the same clairvoyant power that allows him to see into plants, he detects something repellent in the "hidden design" beneath Matilda's lovely outward appearance. Not liking what he sees, he attempts to dismiss these "visions" as mere "irrational reactions" (263). Exposed to his uncanny insight, which he cannot explain, certain features of his fiancée, despite her "classic face" and form, appear malign (124). Whether Matilda's "sharp teeth" or wide, mannish shoulders *objectively* reveal her true nature is a moot question (143). For Benn they have disturbing significance, provoking a troubling response that he ought not to ignore. By this time, however, the wedding has been planned, the invitations engraved; thus he chooses to "go against [his] deeper instinct" and marry Matilda (326). Weakly attempting to justify that decision to his nephew, from hindsight, Benn tells Kenneth, "I was warned . . . not to marry. It was a sin to disobey the warning. But a man like me, trained in science, can't go by revelation. You can't be rational and also hold with sin" (298).

By marrying the wrong woman Benn also entangles himself in her family—becoming the pawn of her father's elaborate financial schemes. A rich and prominent physician, Dr. Layamon is far more dedicated to empire-building than to the art of healing. Embroiling his son-in-law in a financial maneuver designed to yield millions of dollars, Dr. Layamon tells Benn, "If you're going to share the bed of this delicious girl of high breeding and wallow in it, you'll have to find the money it takes." By urging Benn to regain several million dollars he has been "screwed out of," Dr. Layamon proposes to help his son-in-law earn the right to "wallow" in Matilda's bed. (Dr. Layamon is obviously heir to the "pigdom" that Henderson summarily abandons.) Years earlier, Benn's Uncle Vilitzer had purchased from Benn and his sister, for a modest sum, a piece of family property that Vilitzer secretly knew would soon be worth millions. Shortly after the purchase, Uncle Vilitzer was able to resell the Craders' family property, for no less than fifteen million dollars, to a multinational corporation as the prospective site of the Electronic Tower, a monstrous skyscraper that presently dominates the skyline of the midwestern metropolis where Benn and the Layamons reside. By threatening to reopen a lawsuit against Uncle Vilitzer at this time, Benn will, according to Dr. Layamon, force his uncle to pay him several million dollars (167-68). In this way, Layamon tells his son-in-law, "you can be made whole" (171).

The ironic effect of Dr. Layamon's pledge is not lost on the reader, who later observes how the purported goal, to make Benn financially sound or "whole," shatters his psychic well being. Instead of making the "psychic transfer" from the plant kingdom to the human sphere, as his nephew had hoped, Benn's vision is severely impaired by his entry into the Layamon family and his descent into the maelstrom of American greed, ambition, desire. His remarkable "marine blue, ultramarine" eyes—eyes that, before his ordeal with the Layamons, seemed to embody "the power of seeing itself, created by the light itself"—are soon beclouded by "sorrow" and guilt, "sin and punishment" (14, 234, 240). The Layamons thus serve "to bring Benn in, that is, to bring him back" into the world of property and power, "down from the sublime regions" of lofty contemplation. They are not, however, entirely to blame. "Benn," says his nephew, "had *wanted* to come down, he had a special wish to enter into prevailing states of mind and even, perhaps, into the peculiar sexuality associated with such states" (165-66, Bellow's italics). By insisting that his fascination with Matilda's alluring beauty *is* love, Benn undergoes his version of the West's current "ordeal of desire"—implicating him in the "fallen state" in which, says Ken, "our species finds itself" (100, 19). Dwelling in "the absence of love" and attempting to compensate for "inner poverty" with "sexual enchantments," contemporary humanity is in dire straits (241, 118, 155). Whether conscious or not of their "human impoverishment," plenty of people are, as Citrine already notes in *Humboldt's Gift*, "oppressed to the point of heartbreak" (*HG* 350).

Even before Benn Crader's disastrous marriage to Matilda Layamon and his subsequent "fall," he has gone on record affirming the universal need for love and the "heartbreak" brought on by its absence. To a journalist who interviews him about the "dangers of radioactivity from Three Mile Island and Chernobyl," Benn makes the unexpected reply that serves as the novel's title and suggests its central theme: "It's terribly serious, of course, but I think more people die of heartbreak than of radiation" (197, 87). Implicit in Benn's unorthodox statement is his perception of two invisible yet deadly forces. While science has made the first one clear to us—warning of the terrible dangers produced by extreme levels of radiation—the lethal condition of "heartbreak" cannot be detected by instruments. As invisible to the naked eye as radiation, the misery of "human impoverishment" is registered, Bellow makes clear, not by scientific instruments but within the human heart.

Nothing less than a new vision of human life—one that breaks through the current "claustrophobia of consciousness" and places love squarely at the center—must be found, Benn's nephew is convinced, if more people are not to "die of heartbreak" (33). Just as Ken traces his uncle's unique visionary powers to an extraordinary "heart" and the love it generates, so he is able, under Benn's influence, to perceive how "an overflow of feeling" transforms the very nature of a person moved by love. When, for example, Ken tells Uncle Vilitzer's son Fishl of the schemes being laid by the Layamons against his father, Fishl's filial piety is profoundly aroused. Right before Ken's eyes, Fishl metamorphoses from a vulgar "entrepreneur and seed-money man" to a dignified and devoted son:

> He didn't even look like the double-chinned suave man who had received me. . . . The eyes, the nose, not a single particular of his appearance remained the same. I thought, You don't even begin to know a person until you've seen the features transformed in an overflow of feeling. A totally different Fishl came before me as soon as he saw that he might be in a position to defend his father, save him from his enemies. (182)

The impact of this transformation becomes even more pronounced when one considers that Fishl has been cut off, financially as well as emotionally, by his father. Heartless and, by all reasonable standards, utterly *un*deserving of affection, Harold Vilitzer continues, up to the moment of his death, to be loved unrequitedly by both his son Fishl and his nephew Benn. Thus Uncle Vilitzer occupies the unusual, and paradoxical, position of denying the reality of love while being its recipient.

Although Ken's revelation of the power of love centers upon Fishl rather than his father, a brief digression on the character of Harold Vilitzer helps to clarify the reality old Vilitzer would deny. Annoyed by Fishl's many bizarre, and failed, business ventures, Harold Vilitzer has refused, for fifteen years, even to see his son. Nor does he appear, in extreme old age, to have any regrets about his behavior—anymore than he regrets having cheated Benn by turning a fifteen-million-dollar profit on the Craders' family property. "Where money is concerned," Uncle Vilitzer declares, "the operational word is *merciless*" (282, Bellow's italics). From Vilitzer's "message" of mercilessness, Ken traces the logic of unalloyed materialism:

> Death is merciless, and therefore the ground rules of conduct have to include an equal and opposite hardness. From this it follows that kinship is

bullshit. You can see how this would reflect on my attachment to Uncle [Benn], on Uncle's attachment to me. Against us there stood Vilitzer's exclusion of his son Fishl. . . . Fishl's emotions towards his father were further evidence [in his father's eyes] of his unfitness, his ignorance of the conditions of existence. (282)

When Benn and his nephew visit Uncle Vilitzer, in order to talk about his swindling of the Craders, the old man gets angry and even tries to "take a sock" at one of them. Catching the octogenarian in his arms, Ken notes that Vilitzer "felt as light as an empty plastic egg carton. . . . He was scarcely even a tenement of clay; he was wickerwork, porous plastic. Only the pacemaker unit under his shirt had any weight" (286-88). Ken's impression is of a man whose heart has been virtually replaced by the tiny machine fitted to his breast. Nearly a corpse, Vilitzer is not so much a skeleton as a hollow shell. A mere semblance of humanity, he honors no human bond that would hamper his grip on his hundred-million-dollar financial kingdom. Nor can this desiccated creature acknowledge the final irony of his existence: that death, to which Vilitzer has opposed his "equal and opposite" code of "mercilessness," will soon arrive to sever his (death)grip on his money. Uncle Vilitzer has built his kingdom not in opposition to death, but under its yoke.

Through Ken's bond with his uncle—the warmth of an "attachment" deemed worthless by Vilitzer—he has become more "receptive" to phenomena and "the power behind" them (299). Gazing at Fishl, who now looks "totally different," Ken recalls Benn's "second person inside"; there may be, he suspects, "such a person also in Fishl" (182-83). Almost immediately, he has the extraordinary "impression" of *seeing* this "second Fishl": "As I watched closely, the singularity of this seemingly comical fatty seemed to detach itself from him and, with a tremor, move away. I give my impression of this just as it came to me. Another Fishl was sitting there in the fully buttoned vest. . . . Intimations, maybe, of a second Fishl." If, at this instant, "the real Kenneth" is perceiving the "real Fishl"—if Ken's "inner spirit" is making contact with Fishl's—then the border between "inner" and "outer" reality has, at least momentarily, been dissolved (186). Under the influence of his uncle, Ken transcends, at least momentarily, the mind-body "split" and penetrates, in Citrine's phrase, "behind the appearances."

The theme of idolatry, although less pronounced in *More Die of Heartbreak* than in *Humboldt's Gift*, permeates the later novel as well. To begin with, Benn's early praise of Matilda's external "perfection"—her "classic face" and "hyacinth hair"—suggests his tendency to idolize her beauty (53, 124). As Ken says, "It wasn't [Matilda's] beauty that I questioned, it was the Edgar Allan Poe stuff [Benn] was giving me about her. . . . Too much of the marble statue in the stained-glass niche" (121). Underscoring the connection, Ken comments on Matilda's silence, "Edgar Allan Poe's Helen standing in her niche had nothing to say. The representative of beauty was dumb, a terrific advantage for a sensitive devotee of classic figures" (139). Like Renata Koffritz's exquisitely preserved beauty, moreover, Matilda Layamon's marble "perfection" is suggestively associated with death. An "extravagant, luxuriant sleeper," Matilda, Benn observes upon marrying her, abandons herself to sleep like "Psyche embracing Eros in a blind darkness" (142). Here, as in the earlier novel, Bellow implies that when Eros is idolized, "the sex embrace was death-flavored" (69).

The gradual "disintegration" of Matilda's image in Benn's eyes—and his attempts, at the same time, to deny his troubling "visions"—ultimately precipitate his "fall" from "whole" vision into "critical consciousness" (265). Benn's "fallen state" is shockingly revealed to the "plant clairvoyant" one night at the Layamons' luxurious duplex. Temporarily staying with his wife at the home of her parents, Benn is awakened by a disturbing telephone call. Too restless, after the call, to return to bed, he wanders about the Layamon residence while the rest of the family are asleep; eventually he enters his mother-in-law's private study, customarily barred to outsiders, in order to "have plant contact" with a beautiful azalea he has admired from afar (299). To his shock and dismay, he finds that this exquisite plant is actually a fake.

Standing in the corner of Mrs. Layamon's study, the red azalea—from whose flowers Benn has, from outside in the hallway, repeatedly drawn inspiration—proves a cunning silk replica wrought by Oriental hands. The "plant clairvoyant" has been duped by a "damn near perfect imitation" that is thoroughly "false." In shock, Benn telephones his nephew in the middle of the night, to report the disastrous news:

> A stooge azalea—a stand-in, a ringer, an impostor, a dummy, a shill! I was drawing support for weeks and weeks from this manufactured product. Every time I needed a fix, a contact, a flow, I turned to it. Me, Kenneth! After all these years of unbroken rapport, to be taken in. . . . The one thing I could always count on. My occupation, my instinct, my connection . . . broken off. (300, latter ellipsis Bellow's)

To Benn this dismal error is much more than a "sign" of professional failure. He blames himself for having severed his "connection" not only to the plant kingdom but to that inner kingdom of his essential self. For betraying his calling—the serious business of "contemplating flowers"—he has, he tells his nephew, been duly "punished": "I've been punished, Kenneth. For all the false things I did, a false object punished me" (300).[4] Gulled by desire, Benn has forfeited "wholeness" for idolatry. Like the "grumpy old man" in Menasha Klinger's story, who takes the mere appearance of a flower for the real thing, Benn has been seduced by "the plastered idols of the Appearances" (*HG* 487).

When Benn reveals to his nephew the humiliating discovery—that he has "lost the privilege of vision, fallen into the opposite and brutal prevailing outlook"—Ken, registering the impact of that "fall," loses heart (328). "What had happened to [Benn] affected me as well," he says. "I could feel the perturbation widening and widening . . . and became aware that I had come to depend upon his spirit. Without its support, the buoyancy went out of me."

That buoyancy gone, Ken feels more convinced than ever of the "inner poverty" of "modern life," which his new country, America, embodies in the extreme: "Your soul had its work cut out for you in this extraordinary country," he laments. "You got spiritual headaches. . . . There seems to be a huge force that advances, propels, and this propellant increases its power by drawing value away from personal life and fitting us for its colossal purpose. It demands the abolition of such things as love and art . . . of gifts like Uncle's" (301, latter ellipsis Bellow's).

Fortunately, just at the moment Ken begins to formulate a general picture of doom, he recovers, if not his former "buoyancy," a more lucid state of mind:

> Of course, we all have these thoughts today instead of prayers. And we think these thoughts are serious and we take pride in our ability to think, to elaborate ideas, so we go round and round in consciousness like this. However, they don't get us anywhere; our speculations are like a stationary bicycle. And this, too, was dawning on me. These proliferating thoughts have more affinity to insomnia than to mental progress. Oscillations of the mental substance is what they are, ever-increasing jitters. (301)

With this revelation Ken breaks off his formulations, pondering his uncle's parting words. It is "time," Benn tells him before hanging up the telephone, "I took hold" (300). "When you've fallen from grace, what do you take hold of?" Ken wonders (301).

Instead of sinking into misery, however, he recollects a story about "Whistler the painter," told to him by his Aunt Lena, Benn's first wife:

> It was Lena who introduced [Ken] to the valuable idea that modes of seeing were matters of destiny, that what is sent forth by the seer affects what is seen. She liked to give the example of Whistler the painter when he was taken to task by a woman who said [of his art], "I never see trees like that." He told her, "No, ma'am, but don't you wish you could?" This could be a variation on "Ye have eyes and see not." (305)

Whistler's retort offers a challenge to those who, like the woman in Aunt Lena's story, worship "the plastered idols of the Appearances."[5] Thus, Ken recalls the biblical passage, "Ye have eyes and see not," the judgment against idolatry that recurs throughout the Old and New Testaments. Entranced by appearances, Whistler's interlocutor "sees not"; the victim as well as the perpetrator of "inner poverty," she deprives herself of a rich and vital picture of the world.

Resolving to "take hold" of his own life, Ken decides to fly out to Seattle to visit Treckie and his daughter. On his way to the city, however, he experiences another setback. In a fit of vengeful fury that recalls Herzog's abortive plan to murder his rival, Gersbach, Ken imagines beating up Treckie's current lover, a ski instructor, and fighting him to the death. Arriving at Treckie's apartment, he finds that the "ski instructor," whom he has mentally stereotyped as thick and brutal, has "gone to Mass." Venting his jealousy and frustration, Ken heads for the bathroom, proceeding to "wreck it" by smashing everything in sight. But then, as in Herzog's case, "actuality" takes over, demonstrating the futility of his actions. Treckie's "settled intimacy" with another man, he notes, is manifested in every concrete detail—confirmed even by the household odors and mundane arrangement of objects (309-10).

His illusions shattered, Ken realizes that he has been guilty of that same "Edgar Allan Poe stuff" he has scoffed at in Benn (311, 121). Even his admiration for another woman, his friend Dita Schwartz, has not released him from this "ordeal of desire."[6] Now, however, face to face with Treckie, the "child-woman," he perceives not a work of "perfection," not a "marble statue" or idol, but a specific human being—a human being, furthermore, who wants no part of him. Although the revelation is "downright shocking" to his ego, Ken faces the fact that, as he puts it, "I failed to turn *her* on" (312, Bellow's italics). For her part, Treckie calmly accepts Ken's "tantrum," regarding his wreck of the bathroom as a "minor inconvenience" and their "mutual quitclaim" (319).

As Ken and Treckie "conclude the matter" of their failed relationship, Uncle Benn is present both in Ken's thoughts and in his conversation with Treckie. "He's a famous man in his field," Treckie says of Benn, "but he does make an awfully flaky impression when he sounds off." His statement, "quoted in the paper," that "more people died of heartbreak than of radiation poisoning," strikes her as "a crazy remark" (315). Meanwhile Treckie, aware that Ken looks down on her interest in trendy "California-type-stuff" like "applied Zen" and "group psychotherapy," defends her "life-style." As their daughter watches television cartoons in the next room, she tells Ken, "We're a pluralistic society, after all. Multiple acculturation is what it's all about." To Ken, in search of "a desperately needed human turning point," Treckie's relativistic chatter is virtually indistinguishable from the "cartoon sound effects" coming from the television set: "the bangs, whistles, buzzings, blams and tooting" (314-16). He sees, nonetheless, that for Treckie he "didn't even exist. That was nothing to get excited about, as it was one of the commoner human experiences—neither to give a damn nor to be given a damn about. In practice it was accepted as a matter of course, though at heart nobody quite came to terms with it" (319).

What human beings know "at heart," this passage reminds us, is quite different from what they *appear* to accept. This is the meaning suggested by the novel's title, which draws attention to the "hidden design" behind the appearances of modern life. To say, as Benn does, that "more people die of heartbreak" is not to diminish the dangers of radiation or the threat of nuclear disaster. It is to say that other, less obvious but still urgent "matters" also threaten us. On the other hand, Benn's statement may have a still more radical implication for contemporary culture. Bellow may be suggesting that the widespread apprehension of material doom is itself symptomatic of a deeper crisis. In any case, Bellow's narrator reaffirms, in words that articulate the novelist's own search for a way out of the current state of "human impoverishment," his commitment to "Project Turning Point" (330). Ken remains convinced "that, really, conscious existence might be justified only if it was devoted to the quest for a revelation, a massive reversal, an inspired universal change, a new direction, a desperately needed human turning point" (315).

After saying goodbye to Treckie and flying back to the Midwest, Ken receives another telephone call from his uncle, one that signals a "turning point" or "new direction" in Benn's life. Taking hold of his fate in radical fashion, Benn has decided to abandon Matilda, her family and Dr. Layamon's schemes. Calling his nephew from a Miami airport, Benn is on his way to the North Pole, where "an international team of scientists" is conducting "special researches. And I signed on," says Benn, "to check out lichens from both poles . . . and work out certain morphological puzzles." Benn's timely escape from Matilda may indicate that he will never overcome his "confused relations with women"; yet his present determination to save himself is a marked departure from his former "evasive action" (233). In contrast to his tortuous attempts to quell his "visions" and to rationalize his alliance with Matilda, Benn's current decision, he tells his nephew, has been "carefully felt through. Rather than thought out. It's a survival measure" (334).

Like Henderson, who went "beyond geography" to save his soul, Benn must take extreme measures for his own "survival." "We're going to be based in northern Scandinavia," he tells Ken, "at the edge of Finland, actually. And beyond." There, at the edge of the world, "night and ice" will provide a "corrective" to internal disarray: "Ice for the rigor. And also because there'll be no plants to see, except the lichens. Because if there's no rapport," says Benn, "if the rapport is dead, I'm better off in plant-free surroundings" (334). Ken does not condemn his uncle's flight from the Layamons; though "mystified," he gives Benn's "expedition [his] blessing." For what his uncle must accomplish, he knows, even "Novaya Zemlya" may not be "remote enough" (335). In so chaotic a time, "when so many supports and stabilities are removing themselves from [the individual]," one must take radical steps to regain a sense of connection. Clearly, Benn must "remove himself" from the distractions of modern life—from the "magnetic attraction of anarchy" (330).

To the North Pole, where "magnetic attraction" does not exert its customary force, Benn Crader sets out to "preserve himself humanly"—and, if possible, to recover his "gift" of vision. Whether or not he will redeem his "fall from grace," Benn's gift for "contemplating flowers" still offers Ken a model for achieving "perfected insight." Minding Benn's apartment and his plants while his uncle is away, Ken will continue, as he says, to "retrieve from my memory bank those wonderful hours when, under [Benn's] influence, not only my lungs were breathing but my mind breathed too. Some of his powers of seeing *had* been transmitted to me. So I saw" (278, Bellow's italics). Having stilled "the oscillations of consciousness," Ken can "breathe" mentally as well as physically—the expansion of the "chest," Lewis's "seat" of feeling, effecting an expansion of the psyche and its powers.

* * *

At the end of *More Die of Heartbreak*, Ken Trachtenberg remains committed to his "Project Turning Point." His author, moreover, appears to be engaged in a similar project: the search for a "turning point," the "quest for a revelation." In the latter stages of this quest, the novels published since *Mr. Sammler's Planet*, Bellow has ventured more and more openly against the grain of contemporary formulations and cultural "orthodoxy." And while he continues to enlist the conventions of the realist novel, the impact or effect of his fiction is to overturn some of realism's time-honored traditions. In most realist fiction from Cervantes to Dreiser to Hemingway, "the conditioning forces" clearly hold sway over the tiny figure of the individual, who is caught in their force-field even as he seeks a "channel" to freedom. Yet the central preoccupation of Bellow's fiction appears to be moving further and further "beyond" that force-field and its "magnetic attraction." In his own rendering of reality the novelist seems headed, like Benn Crader, for "the edge" of the familiarly known world: "And beyond."

True, Bellow still honors the novelist's obligations to the historical moment and the geography of place; and he delights, perhaps more than ever, in rendering the significant details and particular absurdities of the contemporary urban scene. At the same time, however, his handling of these traditional materials tends, like Charlie Citrine's "upside-down" postures, to overturn the realist's ruling premises. What Ken Trachtenberg says of his "Project Turning Point" thus has special relevance for the direction that Bellow's fiction is taking: "The secret of our being still asks to be unfolded. Only now we understand that worrying at it and ragging it is of no use." Instead, the individual "must maneuver [him]self into a position in which metaphysical aid can approach" (330-31). Engaging in his own novelistic "maneuvers," Bellow has been working his way through the local coordinates of history and geography to regions of human experience as remote from Stendahl's "mirror carried along a highway" as "Novaya Zemlya." By effecting this "massive reversal" in the genre's traditional emphases and effects, he may have reached a "turning point" not only in his own career but in the development of the realist novel: a point at which the "primordial person," rather than his alteration by "the conditioning forces," is of crucial interest. In Bellow's own fiction, in any case, it is the "secret" of the human being, his "hidden design," that the novelist's art is increasingly dedicated to unfolding.

Notes

1. Saul Bellow, *More Die of Heartbreak* (New York: William Morrow, 1987).

2. In *Knowledge of the Higher Worlds and Its Attainment*, trans. George Metaxa (Spring Valley, NY: Anthroposophic Press, 1947), Rudolf Steiner instructs a student of his philosophy "to place before himself the small seed of a plant" and to contemplate both its visible and "*invisible*" reality by picturing the "*plant of complex structure*" that will "*later be enticed from the seed by the forces of earth and light*" (60, Steiner's italics). In *An Outline of Occult Science*, Steiner elucidates the relationship between the "force" of "light" and the human capacity to see: "There lies hidden in what is perceived by an organ the force by which that same organ was formed. The eye perceives light; but

without light there would be no eye. Creatures spending their lives in darkness do not develop organs of sight" (86). Echoing Steiner's thought, Ken Trachtenberg says, "The light pries these organs out of us creatures for purposes of its own" (14).

3. While reviewers of *Herzog* tended, to Bellow's dismay, to overlook the novel's "comic portrait of the enfeeblement of the educated man" (Roudané, "An Interview with Saul Bellow," *Contemporary Literature* 25, 3 [Fall 1984]: 268-9), reviewers of *More Die of Heartbreak* were more alert. Even though Terrence Rafferty, "Hearts and Minds," *New Yorker*, 20 July 1987: 89-91, found the novel "phenomenally dull," he noted the "comedy" created when the "characters' high-powered cerebral equipment . . . gets tangled up in the works" of everyday life. More favorably disposed toward the novel, Paul Gray, "Victims of Contemporary Life," *Time*, 15 June 1987: 71, deemed *More Die of Heartbreak* "a consistently funny variation on the theme of intellectual haplessness."

4. Earlier in the novel, Benn is described as perceiving, beneath the plastic dusting on a Christmas tree, that the tree, contrary to all appearances, is *real*. "You couldn't fool Uncle about a tree," Ken confidently asserts (127). Now that statement must be retracted; having "deviated" from his "original, given nature," Benn is duped by a fake. Here too Steiner's influence seems to be operating. In *Knowledge of the Higher Worlds and Its Attainment*, Steiner distinguishes between a real plant seed and its "*artificial imitation*," which does not contain "*secretly enfolded within it*" the "*force of the whole plant. . . . And yet both [the real and the imitation seeds] appear alike to my eyes. The real seed, therefore, contains something invisible which is not present in the imitation*" (60-61, Steiner's italics). It is this "invisible something" or "hidden design" that Benn has lost the power to detect.

5. The incident concerning Whistler is also described by Owen Barfield in his study of idolatry, *Saving the Appearances: A Study in Idolatry* (1957; New York: Harcourt, Brace, 1965): "When a lady complained to Whistler that she did not see the world he painted, he is said to have replied 'No, ma'am, but don't you wish you could?'" Both Whistler and the lady, Barfield points out, are referring to the activity— "which in Whistler's case was intenser than the lady's"—of "figuration": the process by which each individual perceives and represents to himself the phenomenal world. This activity consists, Barfield adds, of "two operations": "First, the sense-organs must be related to the particles [of light, waves, quanta, etc.] in such a way as to give rise to sensations; and secondly, those mere sensations must be combined and constructed by the percipient mind into the recognizable and nameable objects we call *things*" (24, Barfield's italics). Barfield's account of "figuration" articulates in more philosophical terms Ken Trachtenberg's assertion about "modes of seeing": "that what is sent forth by the seer affects what is seen."

6. Though highly attractive in her own right, Dita Schwartz does not produce the illusion of "perfection." She has been marked, and marred, by existence. Her "scarred" face, the result of "an adolescent case of acne," takes on emblematic significance in the novel. In contrast to Treckie's smooth and "pink face," as well as Matilda's "classic face," Dita's blemished skin, though it causes her anguish, bespeaks her honest and straightforward nature (205, 189).

Saul Bellow's *Ravelstein* and the Graying of American Humor _____

Sarah Blacher Cohen

One of Saul Bellow's favorite jokes is "about an American singer who makes his debut at La Scala. He sings his first aria to great applause. And the crowd calls '*Ancora, vita, vita.*' He sings it a second time, and again they call for an encore. Then a third time and a fourth [. . .]. Finally, panting and exhausted, he asks, 'How many times must I sing this aria?' Then someone tells him, 'Until you get it right.' That's how it is with me—I always feel I haven't gotten it quite right, and so I go on singing" (Kakutani 1).

While in his seventies Thomas Mann wrote one of his most comic novels, *The Confession of Felix Krull, Confidence Man.* Similarly Saul Bellow, though in his eighties, goes right on singing by writing one of his most comic novels, *Ravelstein.* The protagonist of Bellow's thirteenth novel is an octogenarian writer, with the incongruously funny child's name of Chick, who is a thinly disguised double of Bellow himself. Throughout the novel, Chick, "stuck in his privacy," employs the humor of wry self-deprecation for his lapses of memory, his schlemiel-like errors of judgment, and his head-in-the-clouds idealism, while tripping over the potholes of life. Like Bellow's other comic bunglers, Tommy Wilhelm, Moses Herzog, and Charles Citrine, Chick marries Vela, the wrong woman who sexually spurns him and financially exploits him. As a renowned Roumanian physicist patterned after Bellow's fourth wife, a renowned Roumanian mathematician, she will not subordinate her professional life to cater to his needs. Like the "blue stocking" (107) Madeline in Bellow's *Herzog,* she views herself as the intellectual superior of her mate and demands inordinate respect from him. Chick is wounded by her hauteur, her corrosive rivalry. He had misconstrued marriage as a deterrent to loneliness in the abyss, yet he, like Bellow's other uxorious heroes, ends up more lonely and harassed in the nuptial state than he would have been unattached and isolated. It would have been preferable for him to heed the Jewish proverb: "It is better to dwell in the wilderness than with a contentious and angry woman" (Ausubel 344). Not content to be the saintly fool, Chick is forced to retaliate with his own sardonic wit in the battle of the sexes against his *belle dame sans merci* wife, assaulting her with a barrage of ironic character assassinations, or as he calls them, "thought murders" (95).

But Chick is not the novel's primary "animal ridens, the laughing creature forever rising up."[1] He is the "first class noticer" (*The Actual* 15) of the present and the tribal memory man of the past, bringing to life the most unforgettable funny man of his university days. In so doing, Bellow sets into motion another of his hybrid comic *roman à clef* novels, whereby the reader is compelled to laugh at the author's caricatured disguises of real-life celebrities and his wryly libelous exposés of their errant behavior. Previously, Bellow had titillated us with his hyperbolic inflations of personality quirks, his mockery of the hypocrisies and affectations of such august figures as the art critic Harold Rosenberg, satirically depicted as Victor Wulpy, the womanizing connoisseur of aesthetic treasures in Bellow's story "What Kind of Day Did You Have?" and the poet Delmore Schwartz, satirically transformed into the Dionysian bard of *Humboldt's Gift*. Now joining Bellow's fictionalized rogues' gallery is his dear, departed friend, Allan Bloom, who becomes the eponymous hero Abe Ravelstein, the larger-than-life Paul Bunyan of Academia, amusing his students with the tall tales of his intellectual pursuits and grandiose theories. His cerebral hijinks as a Professor of Political Philosophy, his injection of "wit and self irony in a democratic society" (2) represent his attempt to provide an indispensable service to humanity, like those public figures before him who chose comedy rather than philosophy for "adversity's sweet milk." But Ravelstein bemoans the fact that the public doesn't often appreciate his or their comic sense:

> Odd that mankind's benefactors should be amusing people. In America at least this is often the case. Anyone who wants to govern the country has to

entertain it. During the Civil War, people complained about Lincoln's funny stories. Perhaps he sensed that strict seriousness was far more dangerous than any joke. But critics said that he was frivolous and his own Secretary of War referred to him as an ape. (1)

Ravelstein joins the company of Lincoln and other such "spoofers and self-spoofers" as H. L. Mencken or W. C. Fields, Charlie Chaplin, Mae West, Huey Long, and Senator Everett Dirksen, who employ self-mockery and "educated insolence" to reform democratic societies. In this capacity, Ravelstein is an eloquent spokesman for Bellow's comedy of ideas, a form of comic which occurs, according to Wylie Sypher, "whenever a society becomes self-conscious about its opinions, codes or etiquette, with the author acting as the intellectual conscience of this self-scrutinizing society. Through sanity and verbal wit, the author is able to magnify comedy of manners to the dimensions of a criticism of life" (211). In the novel, Ravelstein functions as Bellow's manic intellectual and spiritual conscience whose serious preoccupations coexist with his clownishness. Employing comic figurative language to impart both high and low knowledge, Ravelstein, for example, admonishes his class: "Without its longings, your soul was a used inner tube, maybe good for one summer at the beach, nothing more" (25). Or he offers advice about how to avoid being "tapped by idlers": I refuse to be "the pipe at Saratoga Springs, where the Bronx Jews came in summer with cups to drink life-giving waters for free—a remedy for constipation or hardening of the arteries" (44). When teaching his students that "Jerusalem and Athens were the twin sources of Civilization," Ravelstein allows himself to "cut a caper," to be the "Borscht belt comedian":

> "You remind me of Dwight McDonald," he says to Venetzky, one of his friends who is dead broke. "If you're in such a bind, Venetzky, why don't you sell one of your bonds." It never occurs to him that Venetzky has no bonds. The McDonalds have them. The Venetzkys don't. It's like the old depression joke about the hobo who makes a pitch to a rich old lady and

says: "Ma'am, I haven't swallowed a bit of food in three days." "Oh you poor old man. You must force yourself" she says. (21)

Ravelstein, schooled in the classics, often uses the agile insights he derived from them as springboards for his jests: paraphrasing Socrates, he says with tongue in cheek: "Maybe an unexamined life is not worth living. But a man's examined life can make him wish he was dead" (34). To mock trendy practices, Ravelstein, borrowing from the *Phaedrus*, claims that "a tree, so beautiful to look at, never spoke a word and that conversation was possible only in the city, between men." "Plants were not his thing," he said. "He'd eat a salad, but he couldn't see the point of meditating on it" (100).

Ravelstein's sudden rhetorical leaps from the sublime to the ridiculous are like the antic rhetorical strategies of his ancestral Yiddish humorists, wherein, according to Maurice Samuel, "the fusion of the secular and the sacred make possible a charming transition from the jocular to the solemn and back again. Well-worn quotations from sacred texts mingle easily with colloquialisms and dignified passages jostle popular interjections without taking offence" (qtd. in Howe 47). Similarly, Ravelstein mixes his elevated Greek with demotic translations of it and embroiders their higher thoughts with Jewish jokes:

> Ravelstein. With his bald, powerful head, was at ease with large statements, big issues and famous men. [. . .] He was just as familiar with entertainers like Mel Brooks as with the classics and could go from Thucydides' huge tragedy to Moses as played by Mel Brooks. "He comes down from Mount Sinai with the commandments. God had handed down twenty, but ten fall from Mel Brooks's arms when he sees the children of Israel rioting around the Golden Calf." (11)

Ravelstein resembles his Jewish forebears in yet another way. He loves to talk. He instructs, examines, debates, puts down errors. He is a voluminous word-spinner. According to Saul Bellow,

Powerlessness appears to force people to have recourse to words. Hamlet had to unpack his heart with words. He complains. The fact that the Jews of Eastern Europe lived among menacing and powerful neighbors no doubt contributed to the subtlety and richness of the words with which they unpacked. ("Laughter in the Ghetto" 15)

Ravelstein's words are very subtle and very rich. They are principally responsible for the novel's comedy of language. They are created by a Bellow whose mother preferred him to be a fiddler or a rabbi, causing Cynthia Ozick to think of him as a

sentence-and-paragraph fiddler, or a rabbi presiding over an unruly congregation of words. The words are unruly because they refuse to be herded into categories of style: they are high, low, shtick, soft-shoe, pensive, mystical, sermonic, eudemonic—but never catatonic; always on the move, in the swim, bathed in some electricity-conducting effluvium. (27)

Though it may be artificial to make a special distinction for the "comic" in words, since most of the varieties of the comic are produced through the medium of language, there is "a difference between the comic *expressed* and the comic *created* by language" (Bergson 127). The former could, according to Henri Bergson,

be translated from one language into another though at the cost of losing the greater portion of its significance when introduced into a fresh society different in manners, in literature and above all in association of ideas. But it is generally impossible to translate the latter. It owes its entire being to the structure of the sentences or to the choice of words. (128)

Unlike the literature of exhaustion, whose language and characters are drained of vitality, the verbal response of Ravelstein to comparable despairing circumstances—such as his dying from AIDS—is an energetic and feisty one. Or, unlike the literature of the absurd, whose language has been reduced to mechanical phrases, nonsense syllables, incoherent grunts, and even silence in reaction to the banal and the baleful, Ravelstein animates, loosens up, and coins words which increase the novel's mirth rate. He is garrulous, not because he feels powerless like his Yiddish-speaking forebears, but garrulous because he feels the full extent of his powers. Therefore, he can create a risible coexistence of polished English and fractured English, reputable euphemisms and their disreputable four-letter equivalents, ostentatious diction and unassuming diction, philosophical obscurity and gutter clarity. John Leonard likens Ravelstein's comedy of language to the

> prose equivalent of break dancing. Barbed, breezy, disheveled and surreal; salt-savoring and brain-fevered; brilliant twitch patter and Great Book patois; colloquial and mandarin, sentimental and neo-baroque; Talmudic mutter and gangster slang [. . .] the long irony, the low laugh, the short fuse [. . .] such a style miracle-whips. (7)

Thus Ravelstein, with his flood of language, is another of Bellow's "reality instructors," those "heavy water brains" who inundate the Bellow protagonists with their life counsels and illuminations. Though he's younger than Chick, Ravelstein takes the *boychick* in hand and lectures him, much as the specious psychologist Tamkin gives the gullible Tommy his fraudulently comic advice or the brutally candid lawyer, Himmelstein, derides Herzog for his naiveté. But the novel contains more than brotherly advice about how to survive amid the Machiavellians scheming to exploit the credulous protagonist. It is Bellow's comic version of D. H. Lawrence's *Blut Bruderschaft*, the loving bond between brothers, even if Bellow does not have Ravelstein and Chick physically wrestling with all kinds of experiences. Sophomoric at heart, they not only seriously discuss the intricacies of political theories, but they also have fun sharing the intimate details of student confidences and the social gossip about government officials. They love to window shop in Paris's finest boutiques and cook gourmet recipes for one another. They genuinely respect one another, appreciate each other's good fortune, and are inordinately generous to each other. Above all, they are, in the words of Cynthia Ozick, "more entangled—more raveled—than academic colleagues usually are: they were cognitive companions, mutual brain-pickers, and (in Bloom's Platonic lingo) true friends" (27).

Ravelstein, however, wants more than "true friendship" from Chick for the reality instruction he offers him. Dying of AIDS, Ravelstein wants him to be his biographer, to be a reverential Boswell to his flawed Johnson. Controlling in life, he wants to be controlling in death. Instead of being the compliant protagonist of the conventional comedy where *all ends well*, he strives to make everything *appear well* by dictating to Chick the kind of epitaph he wants, thus outwitting the Angel of Death. And Chick, in turn, is committed to giving permanence to his dear friend Ravelstein by providing an intimate portrait of this man "of idiosyncracies and kinks, of gobbling greed for penny candies or illegal Havana cigars, who beneath it all is a Homeric prodigy" (57).

For his biography on Ravelstein, Chick focuses on the most readily discernible kind of external character damage which modern comedy reveals: affectation. According to Bellow, the comedian of the twentieth century has made much of the private shabby person who plays the gentleman. Joyce's Leopold Bloom in *Ulysses* is one such figure— "How grand we are this morning [. . .] the petty individualist of common origins and gentlemanly pretensions" ("Literature," 163-64).

Chick lists many of Ravelstein's acquisitions to reflect his comic vanity: the $4,500 Lanvin sports jacket, the big antique oriental carpets, the French antique sideboards, the $20,000 wrist watch—all to mask his bourgeois Dayton, Ohio, origins and his burly body.

Chick also makes sport of Ravelstein's being tripped up or grounded by the physical. He thus applies Bergson's formula that the comic is produced when the body, "a kind of irksome ballast holds down a soul eager to rise aloft" (Bergson 92). Ravelstein "treated his body like a vehicle, a motorbike that he raced at top speed along the rim of the grand canyon." Yet beneath his attempts to transcend his fallible body, he is still the Dostoevskian buffoon. He

> functions like an amusement park mirror in which you see your face and
> body horribly distorted; yet when you look more closely, you may find that
> the very process of distortion reveals something about you (that leer, that
> grin, that simper, that smirk) which you might not see in an ordinary mirror. In short the buffoon causes us to see a part of ourselves that we do not
> like to acknowledge. (Howe 461)

Like Tommy Wilhelm's father, Dr. Adler, and the inflexible society he represents, we do not like to see part of ourselves in the "large, odd, excited, fleshy, blond, abrupt personality named Wilhelm" (*Seize the Day* 39). We resent having the slightest resemblance to any "weak-willed creature whose life is controlled by pills—first stimulants and then depressants and anodynes followed by analeptics, until the poor organism doesn't know what's happened" (32-33). Above all, we shudder to think we have anything in common with such an uncouth fellow who uses the red tapes of cigarette packages as dental floss and greedily devours the remains of another person's breakfast. Similarly, Bellow makes us want to distance ourselves from the crude Jewish behavior of the buffoonish Ravelstein when dining with a super-important visitor:

> Faculty wives knew that when Ravelstein came to dinner, they would face a
> big cleaning job afterward—the spilling, splashing, crumbling, the nastiness of his napkin after he had used it, the pieces of cooked meat scattered
> under the table, the wine sprayed out after he laughed at a wisecrack;
> courses rejected after one bite and pawed to the floor. An experienced hostess would have spread newspapers under his chair. [. . .] She wasn't going
> to let any kike behave so badly at *her* table. (37-38)

Indeed, Ravelstein does not try to camouflage the "kike" in himself. He does not subject himself to the "ordeal of civility," repressing the

"*Yid*" or "id" in himself. He is secure enough to be the brash, outspoken Jew abroad and at home. Indeed his great comic appeal is that for all his efforts to transform himself into a disciplined Greek Philosopher King, he remains an unbridled Jewish academic sage and street urchin, complete with a peculiar Jewish face, a love of vaudeville Jewish humor and a relentless hatred of the Nazis. "It is impossible to get rid of one's origins," he tells Chick. "It is impossible not to remain a Jew" (179), or as the joke has it, "You can change your noses, but not your Moses." Ravelstein also convinces the assimilationist Chick of the inescapability of his Jewish fate. Unlike Augie March, who proudly asserts, "I am an American—Chicago born" (3), Chick is forced to conclude, "As a Jew you are also an American, but somehow you are also not" (23). Or when a minor Jewish character receives a heart transplant from a non-Jew, Chick has to restrain himself from asking him how "a gentile heart with its shadow energies and its rhythms," could "adapt itself to Jewish needs or peculiarities, pains and ideas?" (148).

Chick is not able to finish his biography during the lifetime of Ravelstein. "It was as if by writing about Ravelstein there would be no barrier between death and me" (163). Furthermore, Chick, like the old furniture appraiser in Arthur Miller's *The Price*, is a great believer in the power of unfinished work to keep oneself alive. Hence the wrong-headed beginnings, the self-censor's deletions, the interminable writer's blocks. Only six years after Ravelstein's death, when Chick himself has faced death from food poisoning on a cruise with his new young wife, is he able to confront the dissolution of the self and complete the biography of his deceased friend. Thus the assignment he had taken on as sport, never believing he would outlive his younger subject, becomes an obligation he must fulfill. The biography he ultimately completes, waylaid by comic ambivalence and procrastination, "is a book, in some sense, about the writing of a book" and a misunderstanding of that book's intention (Gray 71).

Bellow did not intend, as some critics have charged, to violate Bloom's sexual confidences to write a sensationalist best-seller. Nor was

Bellow's motive for writing *Ravelstein* to convey his "unarticulated jealousy of Bloom's sudden fame" (Apple 2). Bellow wrote the novel, not from a desire to attack, but from a desire to pay homage to his friend, who is not only an intellectual *Wunderkind*, but also ultimately one of those comic characters, those "unruly creatures whose life blood pulse richly, whose features are odd and whose (quirky) opinions, gestures, vices and habits control the mechanism of the plot in which they happen to be cast" (Taine, qtd. in Sypher 21). More specifically, Ravelstein is Bellow's comic Jewish man, who is not a "god or a beast, but a savage of somewhat damaged but not extinguished nobility."[2] Like Leventhal in *The Victim*, he becomes a creature who is not "more than human" or "less than human," but "exactly human" (119). Like Bellow himself, he chooses laughter over "complaint as more energetic, wiser and manlier" (Harper 62). From his deathbed Ravelstein asks for stronger doses of vaudevillian Jewish humor to dull the pain:

> "How does the furious husband bit go, again? The heartbroken man who tells his buddy, 'My wife cheats on me.'" "Oh, yes. And the buddy says, 'Make love to her every day [. . .] and in a year that will kill her.'" [. . .] "Then a sign is brought on stage [. . . reading] 'Fifty-one weeks later.' And then the husband is pushed on stage in a wheelchair by the wife. He looks very weak. Muffled by blankets like an invalid. The wife is blooming. [. . .] As she strides off, the feeble husband in a vaudeville stage whisper says confidentially to the audience, 'She don't know it, but she's got only a week to live.'" (117-18)

The Jewish sense of humor, with its mockery of mortality, energizes the dying Ravelstein and the frail Chick. It is also their only dependable life preserver, buoying their sinking spirits. And, ultimately, it is their miraculous boomerang, catapulting them into higher spheres:

> Ravelstein, shutting his eyes [. . .] flung himself bodily backward into laughter. In my own different style, I did the same thing. As I've said be-

fore, it was our sense of what was funny that brought us together, but that would have been a thin, anemic way to put it. A joyful noise—*immenso guibilo*—an outsize joint agreement picked us up together. (118)

What fuels their laughter and keeps it burning to the end is their laughter about death. It enables Ravelstein, the younger, and Chick, the elder, to contemplate their inevitable end with a certain *élan vital*. But the fact that they laughed together doesn't mean that they laughed for the same reasons. The big joke for Ravelstein was that his most serious ideas, previously shunned by the academy, were put into a book which the lay public loved, and, like Bloom's *The Closing of the American Mind*, made him a millionaire. And the rueful joke for Chick, Bellow's *senex*, is that he outlives Ravelstein, his *juvenis*, reversing the comic conventions of youth triumphing over old age.

Beyond the grave, Ravelstein is far from gloomy: "Ravelstein looks at me, laughing with pleasure and astonishment, gesturing because he can't be heard in all this bird noise. You don't easily give up a creature like Ravelstein to death" (233). And we don't easily give up a writer like Bellow to death. He has sung this aria to perfection, and he is still singing strong! Bravissimo!

Notes
1. In *The Adventures of Augie March*, Bellow refers to Augie as an "animal ridens" (536).
2. Presumably written by Saul Bellow, though unsigned, in "Arias," 4-5.

Works Cited
Apple, Sam. "Making Amends." *Jerusalem Report* 7 December 2000: 1-5.
Ausubel, Nathan. "Introduction: Schlemihls and Schlimazls." *A Treasury of Jewish Folklore*. New York: Crown, 1948.

Bellow, Saul. *The Actual*. New York: Viking Press, 1997.
_____. *The Adventures of Augie March*. New York: Viking P, 1953.
_____. "Arias." *The Noble Savage*. 4 (1961): 4-5.
_____. "Laughter in the Ghetto." *Saturday Review of Literature* 36.30 May 1953: 15.
_____. "Literature." *The Great Ideas Today*. Ed. Mortimer Adler and Robert M. Hutchins. Chicago: Encyclopedia Britannica, 1963: 135-79.
_____. *Ravelstein*. New York: Viking, 2000.
_____. *Seize the Day*. New York: Viking, 1956.
_____. *The Victim*. New York: Vanguard, 1947.
Bergson, Henri. "Laughter." *Comedy*. Ed. Wylie Sypher. New York: Doubleday, 1956. 61-190.
Gray, Paul. "Saul Bellow Blooms Again." *Time* 24 April 2000: 70-71.
Harper, Gordon L. "Saul Bellow The Art of Fiction: An Interview" *Paris Review* 37 (Winter 1965): 48-73.
Howe, Irving. "Introduction to *Seize the Day*." *Classics of Modern Fiction*. Ed. Irving Howe. New York: Harcourt Brace and World, 1968. 457-66.
_____. "Introduction." *A Treasury of Yiddish Stories*. Eds. Irving Howe and Eliezer Greenberg. New York: Viking Press, 1953. 1-7.
Kakutani, Michiko. "A Talk with Saul Bellow: On His Work and Himself." *New York Times* 13 December 1981: 1-6.
Leonard, John. "Living the Great American Novel." *The New York Times* 15 October 2000: 1-8.
Ozick, Cynthia. "Throwing Away the Clef." *New Republic*. 22 May 2000: 27-30.
Sypher, Wylie. "Our New Sense of the Comic." *Comedy*. Ed. Wylie Sypher. New York: Doubleday, 1956. 193-214.

Koheleth in Chicago:
The Quest for the Real in "Looking for Mr. Green"

Eusebio L. Rodrigues

Perhaps the most complete and compact short story that Saul Bellow has ever written, a story significant in many ways, is the early "Looking for Mr. Green" (1951). Without striving to be a novel and without violating the unwritten canons of short fiction as his other short stories do, it crystallizes some of the major themes of Bellow's fiction. It also marks the exact moment of transition in Bellow's development as an artist, for it issues from a creative mood poised precariously between the belief that man is somehow a victim of the human condition, and the powerful awareness that man can somehow transcend this condition. "Looking for Mr. Green" is a Bildungsroman that makes use of the basic pattern that underlies Bellow's fiction, that of the quest. It is a minor classic of our time, a story that has the resonance that Joyce's "The Dead" has, releasing ripples upon ripples of concentric meanings that vanish into the mystery of an evocative silence.

It opens with a graphic description of the Negro slums in Depression Chicago: "trampled, frost-hardened lots on one side; on the other, an automobile junk yard and then the infinite work of Elevated frames, weaklooking, gaping with rubbish fires; two sets of leaning brick porches three stories high and a flight of cement stairs to the cellar."[1] Into this desolate wintry urbanscape comes George Grebe, whose job it is to deliver relief checks to people unable to come to the agency to collect them. The story tells of his strange experiences on his first day at the job, the sights he sees, the people he meets, the frustrations he encounters, as he vainly searches for the elusive Mr. Green. A detailed analysis of the story will allow us to watch Bellow use his "lifting power"[2] to transform this simple, Dreiserian piece into a metaphysical parable.

The first few pages establish the vivid reality of the blight-bitten Negro district between College Grove and Ashland with a few, deft impressionistic touches. The persons Grebe meets on his search for Mr. Green are also unmistakably real: the janitor is "very short and stooped. A head awakened from meditation, a strong-haired beard, low, wide shoulders. A staleness of sweat and coal rose from his black shirt and the burlap sack he wore as an apron" (p. 89). It is only after Grebe sees the graffiti on the walls of a devastated building, stark in its ugliness—"the hall toilets ran like springs"—that the narrative shifts to another, a mythohistorical dimension: "He saw WHOODY-DOODY GO TO JESUS, and zigzags, caricatures, sexual scrawls, and curses. So the sealed rooms of pyramids were also decorated, and the caves of human dawn" (p. 90).

The search for Mr. Green, one slowly begins to see, is a quest man has always been pursuing from the very beginning. That Grebe becomes aware a little later of "the earthen, musky human gloom" (p. 92) of the crowded room into which he enters "like a schoolboy," (p. 91) to find people sitting on benches "like a parliament," (ibid.) indicates that the action is moving on to another plane, a shift that is confirmed when Grebe now recalls his morning's interview with his supervisor, Raynor. Instinctively sensing Grebe's confused hunger for knowledge, after poking good-humored fun at both Grebe and himself, Raynor questions the necessity and the worthwhileness of seeking for (to use the Nietzschean phrase) real reality, especially in these tough times: "Were you brought up tenderly, with permission to go and find out what were the last things that everything else stands for while everybody else labored in the fallen world of appearances?" (p. 96). Raynor himself, it is implied, had been powerfully attracted by such an idea in the past. Deliberately twisting the Arnoldian statement, Raynor now proclaims, with ironic hilarity, that he sees life straight and whole, and he bequeaths his "wisdom" to the young George Grebe: "I'll tell you, as a man of culture, that even though nothing looks to be real, and everything stands for something else, and that thing for another thing, and that thing for a still further one—there ain't any comparison between twenty-five and thirty-seven dollars a week, regardless of the last reality" (ibid.).

It becomes clear at this the mid-point of the story that "Looking for Mr. Green" consists of two planes, one concretely actual, the other symbolic, that constantly dissolve, merge and fuse into one another without either plane insisting on its own supremacy. A re-examination of the apparently realistic first half of the story now yields some symbolic meanings missed earlier. The inhabitants of this unreal city do not seem to belong there. Many are newcomers. When Grebe knocks at the door of a room, it is opened by a young Negro girl who does not understand his question about Mr. Green at all: she has a "dream-bound, dream-blind face, very soft and black, shut off" (p. 90); she has taken the room just a week ago. In the street Grebe sees the hurrying, anonymous crowd: "You only saw a man, a Negro, walking in the street, or riding in the car, like everyone else, with his thumb closed on a transfer" (p. 91). The janitor tells Grebe of the utter impossibility of knowing who is who in this chaotic jungle: "I don' know all the tenants, leave alone the tenants' tenants. The rooms turn over so fast, people movin' in and out every day" (p. 89).

The ghetto and its inhabitants become metaphors for man and the dark, incomprehensible world he moves in. Raynor's references to office boys in China and to braves in Tanganyika as attracted by the power of civilization are no longer merely inconsequential and light-hearted, but serve to widen the story's geographical range. The casual details thrown in about Grebe are quite significant: that he is like a hunter inexperienced in the camouflage of his game, that he has an indoors sort of face, that he made no effort to seem what he was not. Raynor's eyes are slightly sardonic, while Grebe has gray eyes that "persisted in some kind of thought and yet seemed to avoid definiteness of conclusion" (p. 86). Grebe is a typical Bellow protagonist (kin to Joseph, to Asa Leventhal, to Moses Herzog), well-meaning, thoughtful, good-natured, forced for the first time (this is his first experience of the Chicago slums) out of his insulated existence and confronted with the bewildering problem of appearance and reality (Henderson will supply an answer to this problem in 1959) and the related question: "How should a good man live; what ought he to do?" (Joseph had asked this question in 1944).[3]

Bellow introduces the Staika incident immediately after the Raynor interview to illustrate one way to meet the challenge of the human situation. Nicknamed Blood Mother of Federal Street because she is a professional donor of blood, Staika drags her six children around with her as she defies the world, giving out with all her might, putting on a noisy show, notifying the press before setting up her ironing board at the agency office to protest their non-payment of her electric bill. Raynor and Grebe both admire Staika's refusal to be trapped in her situation, but Grebe cannot quite accept Raynor's interpretation of Staika as an embodiment of a rampant, destructive force, one that will "submerge everybody in time, and that includes nations and governments" (p. 99). Grebe, he with the gray thoughtful eyes, can see that Staika is the life force and that she expresses "the war of flesh and blood, perhaps turned a little crazy and certainly ugly, on this place and this condition" (ibid.). But he also sees that she expresses her outrage outrageously: "But she behaved like a liar. The look of her small eyes was hidden, and while she raged she also seemed to be spinning and planning" (p. 98).

Grebe continues on his search for Mr. Green, neither disillusioned by Raynor's cynicism nor sustained by the Staikan form of energy. His next encounter is with an Italian grocer who offers him a Dantesque vision of the human hell, loud with crime, thick with abomination, crowded with people bound on the Hindu wheel of *samsāra:* "a swarm amassed by suggestion and invention, a huge, hugging, despairing knot, a human wheel of heads, legs, bellies, arms, rolling through his shop" (p. 100).

He then delivers a check to Winston Field, an old man who knows who he is and, encircled and fortified by his cards and credentials, has protected himself somewhat against the onslaughts of this world. Looking proud and magnificent like Minos, the righteous judge of the underworld, Field has accepted the human plight; and he puts forward two important ways to come to terms with this bewildering world. First, one must accept the fact that money is the sun of mankind, that it lightens the blackness of human existence: "Nothing is black where it shines, and the only place you see black is where it ain't shining" (p. 102). Secondly, Field suggests that a sense of human togetherness and a covenant among people are necessary to achieve a measure of reality.[4]

The second suggestion triggers off a number of thoughts in Grebe as he steps out of Field's bungalow into the surrounding darkness and has an overview of the wastes and ruins of Chicago. He sees it not as Rome, perhaps, the Eternal City, nor as Paris, City of Man, but as a city that speaks of the human condition and forces one to think about appearance and reality. Rebuilt after the Great Fire and in ruins again, Chicago is no continuing city, it is not abidingly real. The ruins of the city do not convey a message of mere desolation. To Grebe they are eloquent of an enormous power that has not been put to proper use; he feels "a faltering of organization that set free a huge energy, an escaped, unattached, unregulated power from the giant raw place" (pp. 103-104). The power let loose in the wastes of Chicago is, for Grebe, that of the human spirit, embodied in its people, one that has been tragically misspent and misdirected.

For the reality behind any city is not its objects and buildings but the agreement and the coming together of its people, the covenants they have formed. The cycles of Chicago speak of the ephemeral agreements that have been made: "It was that they stood for themselves by agreement, and were natural and not unnatural by agreement, and when the things themselves collapsed the agreement became visible" (p. 104). Grebe can now understand Field's principle: that any idea or scheme (like the fantastic El built by Yerkes, the great financier, or even Field's fragile scheme of creating a Negro millionaire every month) depends on the continual co-operation and consent of people to be translated into reality. Grebe can now accept this dimension of reality. But when he asks himself further questions about the problem of evil and suffering—"Why is the consent given to misery? And why so

painfully ugly? Because there is *something* that is dismal and permanently ugly?" (p. 106)—he discovers that he can offer no answers. He
gives up his intellectual quest and continues looking for Mr. Green.

The story ends with a scene that is deceptively simple and apparently inconclusive. The reader attuned to Grebe's metaphysical quest
can however respond to the several vibrations released by Grebe's last
encounter. Bellow deliberately intensifies the realistic plane of this episode: the scenic details are graphic and stark. Grebe rings the bell on
the door with the name Green under the mailbox and finds himself face
to face, not with a dream-bound girl, but with a Negro woman who, furious with drunken rage and completely naked, blunders down the
stairs. Grebe's polite enquiries about Mr. Green are met with curses
and yells. Convinced somehow that Mr. Green is upstairs, he finally
gives her the check.

Grebe's giving of the check should not be interpreted as an act of failure or defeat: it is a symbolic gesture whose significance proceeds from
and is connected with all that he has experienced and learnt that day. The
Negro woman in whose eyes Grebe sees "a dot of blood in their enraged
brilliance" (p. 108) is another manifestation of the spirit of Staika.
Grebe senses this life force all around him after leaving the relief
agency: "He saw her color, in the spotty curb fires, and the fires under
the El, the straight alley of flamy gloom. Later, too, when he went into
a tavern for a shot of rye, the sweat of beer, association with West Side
Polish streets, made him think of her again" (p. 99). Twice in the presence of this naked woman and the powerful energy she radiates, Grebe
has the strange feeling that Mr. Green is somewhere around: he expects
him to appear on the landing above; he feels that he is being observed
by someone on a mountain of used tires next door. Convinced that Mr.
Green is upstairs, Grebe is now certain that "the woman stood for Mr.
Green, whom he was not to see *this time*" (italics mine) (p. 109). He is
overjoyed by intimations of hope and possibility, feeling that Mr.
Green "*could* be found" (ibid.).[5] His face blazes both with self-ridicule
and with a feeling of elation. The self-ridicule hints that Grebe, the sen-

sitive intellectual, might well be mistaken in his belief. But it doesn't undercut the powerful suggestion that a hidden energy burns within Grebe too and that it is this energy that compels him to hand over the check.[6] He does what the epigraph of the story suggests he do: "Whatsoever thy hand findeth to do, do it with thy might. . . ."

The quotation (Ecclesiastes 9:10) provides another dimension to this complex story. One should read "Looking for Mr. Green" as a modern dramatization of Ecclesiastes, which is a congeries of meditations and questions about the impossibility of ever solving the riddle of human life. The writer seeks to make some sense of the bewildering complexity and the vanity of human existence even though he knows that all speculation is futile. He acknowledges the existence of the divine but cannot understand its inscrutable ways. But he does not despair or indulge in a *Miserere*. Ecclesiastes suggests that one must take the world as one finds it, acknowledge the days and ways of darkness, accept life's conditions and direct one's life accordingly. A certain degree of happiness can indeed be attained. *Carpe diem*, one should seize the day: "Go thy way, eat thy bread with joy, and drink thy wine with a merry heart; for God now accepteth thy works. Let thy garments be always white; and let thy head lack no ointment. Live joyfully with the wife whom thou lovest all the days of the life of thy vanity, which he hath given thee under the sun, all the days of thy vanity: for that is thy portion in this life, and in thy labor which thou takest under the sun. Whatsoever thy hand findeth to do, do it with thy might; for there is no work, no device, nor knowledge, nor wisdom, in the grave whither thou goest" (Ecclesiastes 9:7-10). The protection afforded by wisdom and wealth is a help against the terrible onslaughts man has to face. Ecclesiastes also suggests that cooperation with one's fellow-men in a piece of work will result in greater rewards, for unity is strength.

In the *Show* interview, Bellow tells of his reading of the Hebrew Scriptures: "My childhood was in ancient times which was true of all orthodox Jews. Every child was immersed in the Old Testament as soon as he could understand anything, so that you began life by knowing Genesis in Hebrew by heart at the age of four. You never got to distinguish between that and the outer world."[7]

The Old Testament flavor of "Looking for Mr. Green" is unmistakable, and one can sense the pressure of Ecclesiastes on Bellow's creative consciousness in the composition of the story. The word *sun* is repeated throughout; "under the sun" is a recurring phrase in Ecclesiastes for the world and the human condition. Grebe's brushing at the sunbeam that covers his head during the interview with Raynor can now be seen as more than a touch of realistic detail. Winston Field talks about money as the sun of human kind, while Raynor stresses the importance of a comfortable salary and the futility of knowing about the human condition: both, like Ecclesiastes, offer practical suggestions not counsels of despair. Grebe himself is a younger, a modern *Koheleth* (Hebrew for the Greek Ecclesiastes, "the preacher") who hunts for Mr. Green and for the meaning of human existence. His long day in the black ghetto telescopes the cumulative experiences of a lifetime so that Grebe is led to the same conclusions that Ecclesiastes reached after having lived a full life under the sun. No intellectual solutions are offered; no final answers are provided; human existence continues to remain a mystery. As his day draws to a close, Grebe becomes aware of some forms of sustenance that help man in his sojourn on this earth.

"Looking for Mr. Green" needs to be recognized as one of the great short stories of our time, great in its evocation of mystery and in the tremendous reach of its meaning.

From *Studies in Short Fiction* 11.4 (Fall 1974): 387-393. Copyright © 1974 by *Studies in Short Fiction*. Reprinted with permission of *Studies in Short Fiction*.

Notes

1. Saul Bellow, *Mosby's Memoirs and Other Stories* (New York: Viking Press, 1968), p. 88. Page numbers in parentheses refer to the pages in *Mosby's Memoirs*, which includes "Looking for Mr. Green."
2. In "Dreiser and the Triumph of Art." [*Commentary*, 11 (May 1951), 502-503], a

review of F. O. Matthiessen's book on Theodore Dreiser, Bellow refers to the "lifting power" of Dreiser the novelist.

3. Saul Bellow, *Dangling Man* (New York: New American Library, Signet, 1965), p. 27.

4. Bellow's use of names is interesting. Field, for example, suggests order or organization (a magnetic field), or perhaps a controlled stretch of green. Green, on the other hand, is a color, an idea, and abstraction.

5. It is interesting to note that Bellow recast and slightly changed the last paragraph of his story to avoid finality and to achieve a sense of ambiguity and possibility. In the original version of "Looking for Mr. Green," [*Commentary*, 11 (March 1951), 251-261], Grebe considers the giving of the check an act done in a moment of illumination: "However, a moment came, illuminated from the greatest height, when you could not refuse to yield a check. . . ." He offers a reason for the elation he feels and the story ends thus: "'For after all,' he said, 'I *did* get to him.'" The last paragraph of the story, as published in *Mosby's Memoirs* (1968), omits the sentence involving illumination and ends significantly with a mere feeling of elation: "'For after all,' he said, 'he *could* be found.'"

6. David P. Demarest, Jr., offers a different interpretation of Grebe's giving of the check in his insightful essay, "The Theme of Discontinuity in Saul Bellow's Fiction: 'Looking for Mr. Green' and 'A Father-to-be'" [*Studies in Short Fiction*, 6 (Winter 1969), 175-186]. Grebe is seen as a stubborn idealist whose search is a brave, if futile, attempt "to connect logically the worlds of idea & experience."

7. Nina A. Steers, "'Successor' to Faulkner?" *Show*, 4 (September, 1964), p. 36.

Shame and Saul Bellow's "Something to Remember Me By" _____

Andrew Gordon

The comedy in Saul Bellow's fiction is largely the comedy of shame. His heroes are typically vain, proud, and stubborn men who feel they are different, unique, and above the common fate. Events conspire to prove them wrong about themselves: they are not exempt from ordinary reality; they are in fact laughable schlemiels. Characteristically, what happens in Bellow's novels and stories is that the lofty heroes are brought down and taught a lesson by a comic scourging, made to run the full gauntlet of embarrassment, mockery, ridicule, humiliation, mortification, and disgrace. Bellow is not easy on his characters: he gives them the works. Nor are his heroes easy on themselves. There is always a moment in the narrative when the hero thinks to himself, as does Louie in the short story "Something to Remember Me By," "I had no sympathy for myself. I confessed that I had this coming, a high-minded Jewish schoolboy, too high-and-mighty to be Orthodox and with his eye on a special destiny. . . . The facts of life were having their turn. Their first effect was ridicule" ("Something" 213).

I think of such Bellow heroes as Joseph in *Dangling Man*, so ashamed to be unemployed and living off his wife as he awaits being drafted into WW II that he cannot face his friends or relatives and is even afraid to be seen in the streets. I also think of the shame of Tommy Wilhelm in *Seize the Day*, who is bilked of the last of his money by a quack doctor, and who is told by his elderly father when he asks him for help, "'Go away from me now. It's torture for me to look at you, you slob!'" (*Seize* 110). Tommy ends the novel crying at the funeral of a stranger, lamenting, "I'm stripped and kicked out" (*Seize* 117). Then there is Eugene Henderson of *Henderson the Rain King*, who is literally stripped, initiated into an African tribe by having to run naked through the village. Poor Moses Herzog in *Herzog* is a cuckold whose wife had an affair with his best friend, public knowledge to his friends and relatives, but Herzog was the last to find out. Sammler in *Mr. Sammler's Planet* is publicly humiliated by an obscene heckler who disrupts Sammler's speech at Columbia University. Later, a black pickpocket exposes his genitals to Sammler in the lobby of an apartment building. And Charlie Citrine in *Humboldt's Gift* is jilted by his fiancee, who leaves him babysitting her son in Madrid while she is in another city marrying another man. Implicit in all these comedies of shame seems to be the (perhaps masochistic) notion that a dose of humiliation is good for the soul.

For the purposes of this discussion, I want to limit myself to one recent story, "Something to Remember Me By," which encapsulates the ritual degradation of the Bellow hero. The story is cast in the form of a memoir by an old man, told to his son, about a shameful adolescent rite of passage he underwent: tricked by a prostitute who robbed him of his clothes, he had to put on a woman's dress and try to make his way home in the Chicago winter.[1] Louie is another typical Bellow hero, "stripped and kicked out." What interests me in the story is what the psychology of shame might be able to tell us about the Bellow hero's journey, and why the elderly narrator chose to tell this shameful story to his son rather than an incident of which he might be proud.

In recent studies, shame has been discussed primarily in terms of narcissism (Broucek, Morrison, Piers and Singer, Wurmser). But I see the Bellow hero as more of a neurotic character than a narcissist. According to the psychoanalyst Andrew P. Morrison, for narcissists, "shame seems to constitute their central negative affective experience, while for neurotic patients shame shares the spotlight with other painful feelings, principally guilt and anxiety" (Morrison 162). Although shame is a dominant emotion in Bellow's stories, so is guilt and anxiety. Guilt and shame are often associated affects, and both can be evoked by the same act; guilt refers to the sense of having done wrong and shame refers to the diminished self-image from the act (Miller 47). 1 interpret the Bellow hero to be an old-fashioned neurotic, complete with oedipal guilt. This guilt is closely connected with the shame the character feels. In addition, because he is not really a narcissist, and his problems lie primarily in the oedipal rather than exclusively in the preoedipal realm, Bellow's neurotic hero is more capable of true self-object differentiation and object love than the narcissist.

Because the narrator of "Something to Remember Me By" is a typical Bellow protagonist, what I will say about the story could apply as well to many other Bellow stories and novels. I will argue that the Bellow hero, such as Tommy Wilhelm in *Seize the Day*, Moses Herzog in *Herzog*, or Louie in "Something to Remember," usually undergoes a shattering experience of shame which temporarily strips him of his identity and his understanding of his world. Through action, meditation, or the act of narration, he attempts to counter that shame, to rediscover his identity, to reinterpret his world, and, finally, to reassert his capacity to love.

To summarize the plot of "Something to Remember Me By":

Louie, the narrator, an old man facing the end of his life, writes a memoir as a legacy to his son, his only child. The story he tells takes place one freezing day in February 1933, when he was a seventeen-year-old senior in high school and his mother was dying at home of cancer.

Louie works after school delivering flowers. After dropping off lilies at the apartment of a dead girl (whom he views in her coffin), he goes to visit his brother-in-law, a dentist who has an office nearby. The dentist is out, but in the connecting office, in a doctor's examining room, he sees a naked woman lying on a table, apparently a volunteer for one of the doctor's voyeuristic experiments in sexology. She shows no shame, but dresses slowly and asks for Louie's help getting home. She invites him up to her sleazy apartment, has him strip naked, throws his clothes out the window to an accomplice, and flees.

Louie puts on the only clothes he can find, a woman's dress, and goes for help. It is dark and bitter cold and he is overdue at home, where the family is holding a deathwatch. But his brother-in-law is gone, both the dentist's and the doctor's offices locked. A druggist downstairs directs him to a speakeasy where his brother-in-law might be. The bartender there, after interrogating and chastising Louie, gives him a dirty old shirt and tells him to earn carfare by escorting a drunk home to his two little daughters, a further humiliation. Louie must cook the children pork for dinner, which disgusts him because he was raised in an Orthodox Jewish family. He borrows some of the drunk's clothes, takes money for carfare, and goes home. It is very late when he returns, and his father beats him, but Louie is grateful for the beating because it means his mother is still alive.

Clearly this rite of passage is intended to initiate young Louie into "the facts of life" ("Something" 213), as he says, primarily the two taboo subjects of sex and death, which are closely connected in the story. Louie says, "In my time my parents didn't hesitate to speak of death and the dying. What they seldom mentioned was sex. We've got it the other way around" (187). Louie had to face the death of his mother; Louie's son will soon have to face the death of his father.

The story interests me because the adolescent rite of passage is a negative ritual of degradation and shaming. Louie resembles Herzog, the typical Bellow hero who is simultaneously a high-minded intellectual looking for the ultimate meaning of things and a schlemiel led astray by lust. Significantly, in Yiddish, the word for the male genitals and for a fool is the same: "shmuck."

Although the story is told realistically, it has many dreamlike elements: the sudden appearance of a naked woman, the embarrassment over being naked or inappropriately dressed in public, and the nightmare of trying to get home but being prevented by a series of obstacles. It might be useful to think of the story as an Oedipal anxiety dream; that way, the themes of sex, death, and humiliation cohere as aspects of a core fantasy. We could see Louie as feeling guilty for his desires to have sex with the mother and to rebel against the father. Unconsciously, he both fears that his oedipal desires are killing his mother and he wishes her dead. Viewed in this way, the story acts out his penance for his desires through a sexual humiliation which casts his own masculine identity in doubt. As the psychoanalyst Francis Broucek writes, "The entire Oedipal arena is a mine field of potential shame and humiliation. The ultimate repression or abandonment of the child's Oedipal longing may have as much or more to do with shame/humiliation issues as with castration anxiety or guilt" (Broucek 76). Another psychologist, E. Straus, has suggested that one function of shame may be as a possible safeguard against the violation of incest prohibitions (Straus 222).

A dominant figure in the story is the dying mother, who seems a kind, nurturing woman. She resembles the mother in *Herzog*, who also dies of cancer when Herzog is a teenager; both figures are apparently based on Bellow's own mother. She never speaks in the story, but she gave Louie his sheepskin coat, which is stolen by the prostitute, and she gave her son-in-law the dentist the ornamental clock in his office. After he meets the prostitute, Louie feels ashamed in the presence of the clock: "bending my head so that I wouldn't confront the clock with its soundless measured weights revolving" ("Something" 198-99). He can't face the clock, just as he can't face his silent, dying mother. Louie says, "I knew she was dying and didn't allow myself to think about it" (187) and "I was secretive about my family life. The truth is that I didn't want to talk about my mother" (188). Herzog too avoided facing his dying mother; this is a frequent theme in the fiction of Bellow, who himself lost his mother when he was a teenager. Louie seems ashamed of the fact of her dying, but his avoidance could be seen as related to earlier, oedipal guilt which is now intensified. Whatever the reasons, which are unstated, he is in a cycle of denial, guilt, and shame which mutually reinforce one another.

There is a deliberate fusion or confusion between the mother and the other female figures in the story, who dominate the hero. The figure of the dying mother, lying down in bed, is repeated in the recumbent posture of Louie's girlfriend Stephanie, in the dead girl in her coffin, and, finally, in the naked prostitute lying on the doctor's examining table. Immediately after Louie says goodbye to his mother in the morning, he encounters a dead pigeon in the street, shot by Depression hunters. He is careful to deny the event any significance or any connection to him. "This had nothing to do with me. I mention it merely because it happened. I stepped around the blood spots and crossed into the park" (188). The denial shows once again his avoidance of death, of any responsibility for or taint from its presence.

In the next paragraph of the story, he mentions necking with Stephanie in the park:

> To the right of the path, behind the wintry lilac twigs, the crust of the snow was broken. In the dead black night Stephanie and I had necked there, petted, my hands under her raccoon coat, under her sweater, under her skirt, adolescents kissing without restraint. Her coonskin cap had slipped to the back of her head. She opened the musky coat to me to have me closer. (189)

So we see a confluence of three things—the dying mother lying down in bed, the dead pigeon lying in the street, and the girl lying down in the park—images of death and sex associatively connected.

Later, when he views the dead girl in her coffin, he associates her with Stephanie: "a girl older than Stephanie, not so plump" (192). He feels ashamed in the presence of the girl's mother, "ashamed to take money from her within sight of her dead daughter" (193). Once again, he denies any connection to the death, "I didn't figure here, however; this was no death of mine" (193). Louie is being assaulted with images of dead pigeons and dead girls apparently so that he can repeatedly assert his innocence; his shame in the presence of the girl's mother, however, seems to be a displacement of his guilt in relation to his own mother. Guilt implies the power to hurt, whereas shame suggests the opposite, or powerlessness and vulnerability. Nevertheless, the two often work in tandem, one defending against the other (Wurmser 203-04).

When he sees the naked woman on the doctor's table, he associates her with his mother and Stephanie: "Although I tried hard to stop it, my mother's chest mutilated by cancer surgery passed through my mind.

Its gnarled scar tissue. I also called in Stephanie's closed eyes and kissing face—anything to spoil the attraction of this naked young woman" ("Something" 196-97). When she dresses, he notices that this woman, like Stephanie, wears a raccoon coat. Stephanie is further associated with the prostitute through her sexual aggression, fickleness, and hedonism: "She opened the musky coat to me to have me closer" (189) and "She [Stephanie] loved a good time. And when I wouldn't take her downtown to the Oriental Theatre she didn't deny herself the company of other boys. She brought back off-color vaudeville jokes" (201).

The last female figures in the story are the drunk's two little daughters. Since the hero is at this point wearing a dress, they are uncertain if he is a man or a woman. To find out, the younger one spies on him as he pees. "She grinned at me. She was expecting her second teeth. Today all females were making sexual fun of me, and even the infants were looking lewd" (218). So the hero consistently feels shamed by women: tricked, cheated, and made into a sexual laughingstock.

As much as he is shamed by women, Louie is also ridiculed by men. His father beats him, which is another form of humiliation. He calls his father "an intolerant, hasty man. . . . If I were to turn up in this filthy dress, the old man, breaking under his burdens, would come down on me in a blind, Old Testament rage. I never thought of this as cruelty but as archaic right everlasting" (207). Louie's angry, tyrannical father resembles Herzog's father from *Herzog*. Despite his apparent acceptance of his father's abuse, Louie's consorting with a prostitute and arriving home late is clearly a rebellion against his father.

Louie is also mocked by his older brother Albert. In fact, the Bellow hero, such as Joseph in *Dangling Man*, Augie in *The Adventures of Augie March*, Herzog, and Charlie in *Humboldt's Gift*, is often patronized or ridiculed by a more wealthy, worldly wise, tough guy older brother. "'La-di-dah,' my critical, satirical brother Albert called me" (201). "He wore a derby . . . and a camel's hair topcoat and pointed, mafioso shoes. Toward me, Albert was scornful. He said, 'You don't understand fuck-all. You never will'" (203). Louie refuses to go to the police station for help because they would probably call Albert to fetch him. "Albert would love that. He'd say to me, 'Well, aren't you the horny little bastard.' He'd play up to the cops too, and amuse them" (209). Albert's ridicule is sexual mockery, suggesting that Louie is less than a man: "La-di-dah" implies that Louie is a homosexual. And "You don't understand fuck-all. You never will" implies that Louie will remain forever virginal, lacking both knowledge of the world and carnal knowledge.

Albert provides a model of machismo which Louie both envies and hates; it is a gender role which is impossible for him. "Albert might have taught me something if he had trusted me" (202). Other Bellow heroes such as Herzog and Charlie Citrine are eager to associate with tough guys and criminals, as if some of their masculinity will rub off on them. The figure of Albert is repeated in the story by the Greek bartender who interrogates and mocks Louie. Albert wears "mafioso shoes" and the muscular bartender resembles "the kind of man the Organization hired" (215). Albert calls Louie "La-di-dah" and the bartender wonders if Louie in a dress is "a morphodite [sic]" (212). Albert says, "'You don't know fuck-all'" and the bartender says, "'You got a lot to learn, buddy boy'" (215).

Louie feels inadequate when confronted with the bartender, who would have known how to handle the prostitute. "Why didn't I push her down while she was still in her coat, as soon as we entered the room—pull up her clothes, as he would have done? Because he was born to that. While I was not. I wasn't intended for it" (212). Out of guilt, Louie represses his aggression, including sexual aggression, but that makes him feel like less than a man, which in turn makes him feel ashamed. All this is represented by his humiliating situation of wearing a dress. As one psychoanalytic commentator writes, "Instead of overcoming castration anxiety through identification with a respected father, the subject reluctantly might have chosen a feminine ('castrated') identity, which could keep him from competitive interactions with father; but this identity causes him shame" (Miller 101).

Since Louie can identify neither with his tyrannical, Old Testament patriarch nor with his more modern, swaggering, tough guy older brother Albert, there are few acceptable male role models left him. One is his easygoing brother-in-law Philip, who lives with the family and is a sort of substitute, more tolerant older brother for Louie. He describes Philip to the prostitute: "'He's a good guy. He likes to lock the office on Friday and go to the races. He takes me to the fights. Also, at the back of the drugstore there's a poker game'" ("Something" 201). Philip is associated with masculine activities: drinking, going to the fights or the races, and playing poker. He is also a strong man: "The strength of his arms counted when it came to pulling teeth" (194). Nevertheless, Philip has his defects: he is so lazy that he sometimes pees in his office sink rather than make the trek to the bathroom, and he lacks ambition. His wife, Louie's sister Anna, seems to have more ambition and, in that sense, to be more of a man than Philip: "My sister wants him to open a Loop office, but that would be too much of a strain" (201). "Anna had him dressed up as a professional man, but he let the fittings—shirt, tie, buttons—go their own way" (213). Louie feels some contempt for Philip, whom he privately thinks of as "Pussy-Veleerum" (207). As a "pussy," Louie is not an acceptable male role model for Louie either.

The final male figure introduced in the story is the drunk McKern whom Louie must escort home. He is the weakest man in the story, helpless and infantile, and Louie, who feels further degraded by his company, says, "I had little sympathy for McKern" (217). McKern is a caricature of the "shicker goy" (drunken Gentile) whom the Jew typically views with either terror or contempt, a reincarnation of the drunkard Allbee who plagued Asa Leventhal in Bellow's novel *The Victim*. He has no control over his impulses, is a bad father, is uncircumcised (Louie describes with clinical detachment "the short cylinder between his legs ending in a spiral of loose skin" [219]), and, worst of all, he eats pork. When Louie is forced to cook the pork for the children, he feels disgust and nausea: "All that my upbringing held in horror geysered up, my throat filling with it, my guts griping" (219). McKern is a kind of antiself who combines in a single figure all the things of which Louie is most ashamed: he has no self-control, he is less than a man, helpless and infantile, and he is not even a Jew. Louie may have "little sympathy for McKern," but then, as he admits, "For that matter, I had no sympathy for myself" (213).

Why does Louie relate such a shameful story to his son? With the loss of his clothes, Louie suffers a loss of identity as a male and as a Jewish son (the same thing happens to Herzog with his divorce). It is this which most shames him: "Instead of a desirable woman, I had a drunkard in my arms. This disgrace, you see, while my mother was surrendering to death. . . . a deathwatch. I should have been there, not on the far North side" (217). Over fifty years after the event, he still berates himself: "Failed my mother!" (222). His guilt is overpowering, and so he perhaps repeats this shameful story to his son as a way to do penance and to make up for his sense of failure toward his parents. Rather than hiding his shame—the normal impulse—he will counter shame by confession, an act of courage (or bravado or masochism, depending upon your point of view).

Although Louie judges himself severely, the reader is apt to be more tolerant. After all, these "sins" are at least fifty years old, and Louie was a virginal teenager, awkward and shame-prone, inexperienced with both sex and death. One doubts if he had ever seen a naked woman or a dead person before that day. The story thus forestalls our potential criticism and actually gains our sympathy for the hero by making him into his own harshest critic, a tactic Bellow frequently employs in first-person narratives such as *Herzog* and *Humboldt's Gift*. Because his heroes punish themselves so much with shame and guilt, the reader's impulse (at least, this reader's) is to forgive them.

In addition to serving as Louie's confession and penance, the story may serve a reparative function for the narrator, to heal a shattered self and world. According to Helen Merrell Lynd, the shame experience has three main aspects: unexpected exposure, which leads to a sense of confusion ("We are taken by surprise, caught off guard . . . made a fool of" [Lynd 23]); incongruity or inappropriateness, which "violates our previous image of ourselves" (Lynd 34); and a threat to trust, which results in a shattering of trust in oneself, even in one's own body and skill and identity, and in the trusted boundaries or framework of the society and world one has known" (Lynd 46). All of these effects of shame happen to Louie, until he is led not only to doubt his identity but also to distrust the stability of his world: "This was when the measured, reassuring, sleep-inducing turntable of days became a whirlpool, a vortex darkening toward the bottom" ("Something" 221). Through the narrative, he must reclaim his masculine and Jewish identity and renew his sense of his world as meaningful.

Besides its penitential and restorative functions, the story may also serve a pedagogical function, as a way to teach his son "the facts of life"—the facts of sex and death—and as an object lesson to him not to repeat Louie's mistakes but to honor his father and mother, especially his father, who will soon die. In the final lines, he says, "I haven't left a large estate, and this is why I have written this memoir, a sort of addition to your legacy" (222).

Finally, in writing, Louie opens himself up and gives of himself to his son. The narrative is an act of love which proves that, despite the odds, Louie has turned into a "mensch" and is trying to be a better father than his own father was, relating to his son through kind words rather than through angry blows. He hopes his son will be a good man and a good Jewish son.

Bellow's story demonstrates that, for all its sting, shame can still be a hopeful, humanizing emotion. Louie's shame may have its origins in neurosis, in oedipal conflict, and in ambivalence about his own sexual identity. Nevertheless, confessing his shame can perform penitential, reparative, and pedagogical functions and lead finally to love. Writes Carl D. Schneider:

In shame, the self may feel most keenly the pain of its own betrayal of another. But there is more. Shame indicates that the self still values that other. This ambivalence is of the essence of shame. . . . In shame, *the object one is alienated from one also loves still.* (Schneider 28)

Note

1. "Something to Remember Me By" seems partially inspired by *The Adventures of Augie March* and Chicago Depression lore. In *Augie March*, Augie works briefly as a flower delivery boy in Chicago in the 1930s, which may have been a job Bellow actually held. He also mentions a notorious local prostitute of the time who stole her customer's clothes, but she does not appear as a character in the novel or figure in the plot.

Works Cited

Bellow, Saul. *Seize the Day*. 1956; rpt. New York: Viking Penguin, 1986.

_____. "Something to Remember Me By." *Something to Remember Me By: Three Tales*. New York: Signet, 1991.

Broucek, Francis J. *Shame and the Self*. New York: Guilford Press, 1991.

Lynd, Helen Merrell. *On Shame and the Search for Identity*. New York: Harcourt Brace Jovanovich, 1958.

Miller, Susan. *The Shame Experience*. Hillsdale, NJ: The Analytic Press, 1985.

Morrison, Andrew P. *Shame: The Underside of Narcissism*. Hillsdale, NJ: The Analytic Press, 1989.

Piers, Gerhart and Milton P. Singer. *Shame and Guilt: A Psychoanalytic and a Cultural Study*. Springfield, Ill.: Charles C. Thomas, 1953.

Schneider, Carl D. *Shame, Exposure, and Privacy*. Boston: Beacon Press, 1977.

Straus, E. *Phenomenological Psychology*. New York: Garland, 1980.

Wurmser, Leon. *The Mask of Shame*. Baltimore: The Johns Hopkins University Press, 1981.

RESOURCES

1912-1913	Russian authorities convict Abraham Belo of living illegally outside the area in which Jews are required to reside, and fearing that he will be deported to Siberia as punishment, he flees Russia for Canada. After he settles in Lachine, Quebec, he sends in 1913 for his wife Lescha (Liza) Gordin Belo, sons Samuel and Movscha (Maurice), and daughter Zelda (Jane). In their new country, the family name Belo becomes Bellow as a result of a customs official's arbitrary transliteration.
1915	Solomon (Saul) Bellow is born on June 10 to Abraham and Lescha Bellow in Lachine, Quebec, where few Jews reside. His birth date is officially recorded as July 10.
1918	The Bellow family moves to Saint Dominique Street in Montreal, the center of the Jewish ghetto. In this poverty-stricken area, Saul Bellow grows up speaking Yiddish, Hebrew, French, and English.
1923	Following Prohibition in the United States, Bellow's father, who has failed in many enterprises, becomes involved in bootlegging alcohol as a means of supporting his family. Bellow becomes gravely ill with peritonitis and pneumonia and spends half of the year at Royal Victoria Hospital, where he becomes a voracious reader.
1924	The Bellow family moves to Humboldt Park, Chicago, a neighborhood of immigrants.
1930	Bellow collaborates with his friend Sydney J. Harris on a novel.
1933	Bellow graduates from Tuley High School. After a long struggle his mother dies from breast cancer. Bellow enrolls at the University of Chicago.
1934	Bellow's father remarries.
1935	Because of financial problems, Bellow's father cannot pay tuition for the University of Chicago, and Bellow transfers to Northwestern University in Evanston, Illinois.

1936	Bellow publishes in the *Daily Northwestern*.
1937	Bellow graduates with honors from Northwestern University with a B.A. in anthropology. He is awarded a fellowship for graduate study in anthropology at the University of Wisconsin, Madison.
1938	Bellow leaves the University of Wisconsin after two semesters, forsaking graduate school to become a writer; he joins the Works Progress Administration's Federal Writers' Project. Bellow marries Anita Goshkin and teaches courses in English and anthropology at Pestalozzi-Froebel Teachers College in Chicago.
1940	Bellow travels to Mexico City with friend Herbert Passin to meet Leon Trotsky, only to learn on arrival that the Russian revolutionary has been assassinated; they view the bloody corpse.
1941	"Two Morning Monologues" is published by *Partisan Review*.
1942	"The Mexican General" is published by *Partisan Review*.
1943	Bellow works for *Encyclopaedia Britannica*. "Notes of a Dangling Man" is published.
1944	*Dangling Man*, Bellow's first novel, is published. His son Gregory is born.
1945	Bellow joins the Merchant Marine.
1946	Bellow takes a position teaching English at the University of Minnesota, Minneapolis, where he establishes a strong friendship with his colleague Robert Penn Warren.
1947	Bellow travels in Europe. *The Victim* is published.
1948	Bellow receives a Guggenheim Fellowship and travels to Paris, where he resides for two years and works on *The Adventures of Augie March* and other stories.
1949	"Sermon by Dr. Pep" and "Dora" are published. Bellow returns from Europe and resides in Queens, New York.

1950	"The Trip to Galena," a chapter of a novel that is never finished, is published.
1951	"Looking for Mr. Green," "By the Rock Wall," and "Address by Gooley MacDowell to the Hasbeens Club of Chicago" are published. Bellow becomes intrigued by the psychology of Wilhelm Reich and enters treatment with a Reichian analyst, Dr. Chester Raphael.
1952	Bellow receives the National Institute of Arts and Letters Award. He takes a position at Princeton University as a Creative Writing Fellow and assistant to his friend Delmore Schwartz. "Interval in a Lifeboat," an excerpt from *The Adventures of Augie March*, is published. Bellow translates Isaac Bashevis Singer's Yiddish story "Gimpel the Fool" into English; his masterful translation, published in *Partisan Review*, brings Singer's work to the attention of English-language readers.
1953	Bellow teaches at Bard College. *The Adventures of Augie March* is published.
1954	"The Gonzaga Manuscripts" and "The Wrecker" are published. Bellow receives the National Book Award for *The Adventures of Augie March*. He separates from his first wife. His father dies.
1955	Bellow receives a Guggenheim Fellowship. "A Father-to-Be" is published. Bellow's first marriage ends in divorce.
1956	Bellow marries Sondra Tschacbasov. *Seize the Day* is published. Bellow's good friend Isaac Rosenfeld, the inspiration for his fictional characters Zetland and Dahfu, dies.
1957	Bellow's son Adam is born. At the University of Chicago, Bellow meets Philip Roth, who will become a lifelong friend.
1958	"Leaving the Yellow House" is published. Bellow enters therapy with Dr. Paul Meehl (the inspiration for Dr. Edvig in *Herzog*); Meehl also treats Sondra. Bellow receives a Ford Foundation grant.
1959	*Henderson the Rain King* is published. Bellow separates from his second wife. Under the auspices of the U.S. State Department, he lectures in Poland and Yugoslavia.

1960	Bellow receives the Friends of Literature Fiction Award. He founds and coedits the magazine *The Noble Savage*. Bellow and his second wife divorce. Bellow learns that Sondra and his friend Jack Ludwig (the inspiration for Valentine Gersbach in *Herzog*) have been involved in a longtime affair while he and Sondra were married. He enters treatment with Dr. Albert Ellis, the inspiration for Dr. Ellenbogen in *Humboldt's Gift*.
1961	Bellow marries Susan Glassman. "Scenes from Humanitis—A Farce," an early version of *The Last Analysis*, is published.
1962	Bellow takes a position at the University of Chicago and joins the Committee on Social Thought. He receives an honorary doctor of letters degree from Northwestern University.
1963	Bellow receives an honorary doctor of letters degree from Bard College. *Great Jewish Short Stories*, edited by Bellow, is published.
1964	Bellow's son Daniel is born. *Herzog* is published and becomes a surprise best seller. Bellow's play *The Last Analysis* premieres in New York City.
1965	The one-act plays *A Wen* and *Orange Soufflé* are published. Bellow receives the National Book Award for *Herzog*. Gordon Lloyd Harper interviews Bellow at length for *The Paris Review*.
1966	*Under the Weather* (three one-act plays: *Out from Under*, *Orange Soufflé*, and *A Wen*) premieres in London and is later staged on Broadway. Delmore Schwartz dies. Bellow and his third wife separate.
1967	Bellow reports on the Six-Day War as a *Newsday* correspondent. "The Old System" is published.
1968	Bellow receives the Jewish Heritage Award and the Croix de Chevalier des Arts et Lettres. *Mosby's Memoirs, and Other Stories* is published. Bellow and his third wife divorce. An early version of *Mr. Sammler's Planet* is published in *The Atlantic Monthly*.
1969	Bellow consults psychoanalyst Dr. Heinz Kohut, the pioneer of self psychology.

1970	*Mr. Sammler's Planet* is published.
1973	Bellow receives the National Book Award for *Mr. Sammler's Planet*. He visits the Chicago Anthroposophical Society and develops increasing interest in the anthroposophical ideas of Rudolf Steiner.
1974	"Zetland: By a Character Witness" and "Burdens of a Lone Survivor" are published. Bellow marries Alexandra Ionescu Tulcea. He travels to England to discuss Rudolf Steiner's ideas with Owen Barfield, an expert on Steiner.
1975	*Humboldt's Gift* is published. Bellow resides in Israel for three months to interview people for a nonfiction book.
1976	Bellow receives the Pulitzer Prize for *Humboldt's Gift*. *To Jerusalem and Back: A Personal Account* is published. Bellow's former wife Susan Glassman sues him in an alimony dispute. Bellow is awarded the Nobel Prize in Literature.
1977	Bellow receives the Gold Medal for Fiction from the American Academy and Institute of Arts and Letters.
1978	"A Silver Dish" is published. Bellow travels to Romania with his wife to see her mother, who is dying.
1982	*The Dean's December* and "Him with His Foot in His Mouth" are published.
1984	Bellow is named a Commander of the French Legion of Honor. *Him with His Foot in His Mouth, and Other Stories* is published. The Lachine Public Library is renamed in Bellow's honor.
1985	Bellow's former wife Anita dies. His brothers Maurice and Sam die. His fourth wife demands a divorce.
1986	The film adaptation of *Seize the Day*, starring Robin Williams, is released.
1987	*More Die of Heartbreak* is published.

1988	President Ronald Reagan presents Bellow with the Medal of Freedom.
1989	The novellas *A Theft* and *The Bellarosa Connection* are published. Bellow marries Janis Freedman.
1990	"Something to Remember Me By" is published. Bellow begins a strong friendship with British writer Martin Amis.
1992	"Memoirs of a Bootlegger's Son," a chapter of an abandoned novel, is published. Bellow's close friend and colleague Allan Bloom (the inspiration for Ravelstein) dies from complications of AIDS.
1993	Bellow leaves the University of Chicago, where he has been a faculty member for three decades, to accept a position at Boston University.
1994	The nonfiction collection *It All Adds Up: From the Dim Past to the Uncertain Future*, is published. Bellow is hospitalized with a life-threatening illness caused by his eating contaminated fish while staying on the Carribean island of Saint Martin.
1995	"By the St. Lawrence" is published.
1996	Bellow's former wife Susan Glassman dies.
1997	The novella *The Actual* is published.
1999	Bellow's daughter, Naomi Rose, is born.
2000	*Ravelstein* is published.
2001	*Collected Stories* is published.
2003	Bellow's sister, Jane Bellow Kauffman, dies.
2004	Boston University awards Bellow an honorary doctorate.
2005	Bellow dies on April 5 at his Brookline, Massachusetts, home and is buried in Brattleboro, Vermont.
2010	*Saul Bellow: Letters*, edited by Benjamin Taylor, is published.

Works by Saul Bellow _____

Long Fiction
Dangling Man, 1944
The Victim, 1947
The Adventures of Augie March, 1953
Seize the Day, 1956
Henderson the Rain King, 1959
Herzog, 1964
Mr. Sammler's Planet, 1970
Humboldt's Gift, 1975
The Dean's December, 1982
More Die of Heartbreak, 1987
The Bellarosa Connection, 1989
A Theft, 1989
The Actual, 1997
Ravelstein, 2000

Short Fiction
Mosby's Memoirs, and Other Stories, 1968
Him with His Foot in His Mouth, and Other Stories, 1984
Something to Remember Me By: Three Tales, 1991
Collected Stories, 2001

Drama
The Wrecker, pb. 1954
The Last Analysis, pr. 1964
Under the Weather, pr. 1966 (also known as *The Bellow Plays*; includes *Out from Under*, *A Wen*, and *Orange Soufflé*)

Nonfiction
To Jerusalem and Back: A Personal Account, 1976
Conversations with Saul Bellow, 1994 (Gloria L. Cronin and Ben Siegel, editors)
It All Adds Up: From the Dim Past to the Uncertain Future, 1994
Saul Bellow: Letters, 2010 (Benjamin Taylor, editor)

Edited Texts
Great Jewish Short Stories, 1963
Editors: The Best from Five Decades, 2001 (with Keith Botsford)

Bibliography

Amis, Martin. "A Chicago of a Novel." *Atlantic* Oct. 1995: 114-20, 122-27. Rpt. as "Why Augie Has It All." *Guardian Supplement* 4 Aug. 1995: 2-5.

Anand, Tarlochan Singh. *Saul Bellow, the Feminine Mystique.* Jalandhar, India: ABS, 1993.

Assadi, Jamal. *Acting, Rhetoric, and Interpretation in Selected Novels by F. Scott Fitzgerald and Saul Bellow.* New York: Peter Lang, 2006.

Atlas, James. *Bellow: A Biography.* New York: Random House, 2000.

Bach, Gerhard, ed. *The Critical Response to Saul Bellow.* Westport, CT: Greenwood Press, 1995.

Bach, Gerhard, and Gloria L. Cronin, eds. *Small Planets: Saul Bellow and the Art of Short Fiction.* East Lansing: Michigan State University Press, 2000.

Bach, Gerhard, and Jakob J. Köllhofer, eds. *Saul Bellow at Seventy-Five: A Collection of Critical Essays.* Tübingen, Germany: Narr, 1991.

Bakker, Jan. *Fiction as Survival Strategy: A Comparative Study of the Major Works of Ernest Hemingway and Saul Bellow.* Amsterdam: Rodopi, 1983.

Berger, Alan L. *Crisis and Covenant: The Holocaust in American Jewish Fiction.* Albany: State University of New York Press, 1985.

_____. "Holocaust Survivors and Children in *Anya* and *Mr. Sammler's Planet.*" *Modern Language Studies* 16.1 (1986): 81-87.

Bigler, Walter. *Figures of Madness in Saul Bellow's Longer Fiction.* Bern: Peter Lang, 1998.

Bloom, Harold, ed. *Saul Bellow.* New York: Chelsea House, 1986.

_____. *Saul Bellow's "Herzog."* New York: Chelsea House, 1988.

Bradbury, Malcolm. *Saul Bellow.* New York: Methuen, 1982.

Braham, E. Jeanne. *A Sort of Columbus: The American Voyages of Saul Bellow's Fiction.* Athens: University of Georgia Press, 1984.

Campbell, Jeff H. "Bellow's Intimations of Immortality: *Henderson the Rain King.*" *Studies in the Novel* 1.3 (1969): 323-33.

Chavkin, Allan. "Bellow and English Romanticism." *Saul Bellow in the 1980s: A Collection of Critical Essays.* Ed. Gloria L. Cronin and L. H. Goldman. East Lansing: Michigan State University Press, 1989. 67-79.

_____. "Bellow's Alternative to the Wasteland: Romantic Theme and Form in *Herzog.*" *Studies in the Novel* 11.3 (1979): 326-37.

_____. "Fathers and Sons: 'Papa' Hemingway and Saul Bellow." *Papers on Language and Literature* 19.4 (1983): 449-60.

_____. "*Humboldt's Gift* and the Romantic Imagination." *Philological Quarterly* 62.1 (1983): 1-19.

_____. "Ivan Karamazov's Rebellion and Bellow's *The Victim.*" *Papers on Language and Literature* 16.3 (1980): 316-20.

_____. "The Problem of Suffering in the Fiction of Saul Bellow." *Comparative Literature Studies* 21.2 (1984): 161-74.

Chodat, Robert. "Beyond Science and Supermen: Bellow and Mind at Mid-Century." *Texas Studies in Literature and Language* 45.4 (2003): 391-425.

_____. *Worldly Acts and Sentient Things: The Persistence of Agency from Stein to DeLillo*. Ithaca, NY: Cornell University Press, 2008.

Clayton, John J. *Saul Bellow: In Defense of Man*. Bloomington: Indiana University Press, 1968.

Clements, James. "Bottomless Surfaces: Saul Bellow's 'Refreshed Phrenology.'" *Journal of Modern Literature* 33.1 (2009): 75-91.

Clemons, Walter, and Jack Kroll. "America's Master Novelist." *Newsweek* 1 Sept. 1975: 32-34, 39-40.

Codde, Philippe. *The Jewish American Novel*. West Lafayette, IN: Purdue University Press, 2007.

Cohen, Mark R. "'A Recognizable Jewish Type': Saul Bellow's Dr. Tamkin and Valentine Gersbach as Jewish Social History. " *Modern Judaism 3* (Oct. 2007): 350-73.

Cohen, Sarah Blacher. *Saul Bellow's Enigmatic Laughter*. Urbana: University of Illinois Press, 1974.

Cronin, Gloria L. *A Room of His Own: In Search of the Feminine in the Novels of Saul Bellow*. Syracuse, NY: Syracuse University Press, 2000.

Cronin, Gloria L., and Blaine H. Hall. *Saul Bellow: An Annotated Bibliography*. 2d ed. New York: Garland, 1987.

Cronin, Gloria L., and Ben Siegel, eds. *Conversations with Saul Bellow*. Jackson: University Press of Mississippi, 1994.

Detweiler, Robert. *Saul Bellow: A Critical Essay*. Grand Rapids, MI: Eermans, 1967.

Dutton, Robert R. *Saul Bellow*. New York: Twayne, 1971.

Eichelberger, Julia. *Prophets of Recognition: Ideology and the Individual in Novels by Ralph Ellison, Toni Morrison, Saul Bellow, and Eudora Welty*. Baton Rouge: Louisiana State University Press, 1999.

Friedrich, Marianne M. *Character and Narration in the Short Fiction of Saul Bellow*. New York: Peter Lang, 1995.

Fuchs, Daniel. *Saul Bellow: Vision and Revision*. Durham, NC: Duke University Press, 1984.

Galloway, David D. *The Absurd Hero in American Fiction. Updike, Styron, Bellow, Salinger*. Austin: University of Texas Press, 1966.

Glenday, Michael K. *Saul Bellow and the Decline of Humanism*. London: Macmillan, 1990.

Goldman, L. H. *Saul Bellow's Moral Vision: A Critical Study of the Jewish Experience*. New York: Irvington, 1983.

Goldman, L. H., Gloria L. Cronin, and Ada Aharoni. *Saul Bellow: A Mosaic*. New York: Peter Lang, 1992.

Halldorson, Stephanie S. *The Hero in Contemporary American Fiction: The Works of Saul Bellow and Don DeLillo*. New York: Continuum, 2007.

Harris, Mark. *Saul Bellow: Drumlin Woodchuck*. Athens: University of Georgia Press, 1980.

Hollahan, Eugene, ed. *Saul Bellow and the Struggle at the Center*. New York: AMS Press, 1996.

Hyland, Peter. *Saul Bellow*. New York: St. Martin's Press, 1992.

Kegan, Robert. *The Sweeter Welcome: Voices for a Vision of Affirmation—Bellow, Malamud, and Martin Buber*. Needham Heights, MA: Humanitas Press, 1976.

Kramer, Michael P., ed. *New Essays on "Seize the Day."* New York: Cambridge University Press, 1998.

Kulshrestha, Chirantan. *The Saul Bellow Estate*. Calcutta: Writers Workshop Publication, 1976.

_____. *Saul Bellow: The Problem of Affirmation*. New Delhi: Arnold, 1978.

McCadden, Joseph F. *The Flight from Women in the Fiction of Saul Bellow*. Washington, DC: University Press of America, 1981.

McConnell, Frank D. *Four Postwar American Novelists: Bellow, Mailer, Barth, and Pynchon*. Chicago: University of Chicago Press, 1977.

McSweeney, Kerry. "Saul Bellow and the Life to Come." *Critical Quarterly* 18.1 (1976): 67-72.

Majdiak, Daniel. "The Romantic Self and *Henderson the Rain King*." *Bucknell Review* 19.2 (1971): 125-46.

Malin, Irving. *Saul Bellow's Fiction*. Carbondale: Southern Illinois University Press, 1969.

_____, ed. *Saul Bellow and the Critics*. New York: New York University Press, 1967.

Margolies, Edward. *New York and the Literary Imagination: The City in Twentieth Century Fiction and Drama*. Jefferson, NC: McFarland, 2008.

Melbourne, Lucy L. *Double Heart: Explicit and Implicit Texts in Bellow, Camus, and Kafka*. New York: Peter Lang, 1986.

Meyers, Jeffrey. "Bluebeard Bellow." *Kenyon Review* 31.2 (2009): 160-85.

Newman, Judie. *Saul Bellow and History*. New York: St. Martin's Press, 1984.

Opdahl, Keith M. *The Novels of Saul Bellow: An Introduction*. University Park: Pennsylvania State University Press, 1967.

Pifer, Ellen. *Saul Bellow Against the Grain*. Philadelphia: University of Pennsylvania Press, 1990.

Porter, M. Gilbert. *Whence the Power? The Artistry and Humanity of Saul Bellow*. Columbia: University of Missouri Press, 1974.

Pradhan, Ram Prakash. *The Women in the Novels of Saul Bellow*. Delhi: Atlantic, 2006.

Quayum, Mohammed A. *Saul Bellow and American Transcendentalism*. New York: Peter Lang, 2004.

Quayum, Mohammed A., and Sukhbir Singh, eds. *Saul Bellow: The Man and His*

Work. Delhi: B. R. Publications, 2000.

Rodrigues, Eusebio L. "Bellow's Africa." *American Literature* 43.2 (May 1971): 242-56.

_____. *Quest for the Human: An Exploration of Saul Bellow's Fiction*. Lewisburg, PA: Bucknell University Press, 1981.

Rovit, Earl. *Saul Bellow*. Minneapolis: University of Minneapolis Press, 1967.

_____, ed. *Saul Bellow: A Collection of Critical Essays*. Englewood Cliffs, NJ: Prentice Hall, 1975.

Safer, Elaine. "Saul Bellow, Master of the Comic." *Critique* 51.2 (2010): 126-34.

Sandy, Mark. "Webbed with Golden Lines: Saul Bellow's Romanticism." *Romanticism: The Journal of Romantic Culture and Criticism* 14.1 (2008): 57-67.

Scheer-Schaezler, Brigitte. *Saul Bellow*. New York: Frederick Ungar, 1972.

Scott, Nathan A., Jr. *Three American Moralists: Mailer, Bellow, Trilling*. Notre Dame, IN: University of Notre Dame Press, 1973.

Shechner, Mark. *After the Revolution: Studies in the Contemporary Jewish-American Imagination*. Bloomington: Indiana University Press, 1987.

Siegel, Ben. "Saul Bellow and Mr. Sammler: Absurd Seekers of High Qualities." *Saul Bellow: A Collection of Critical Essays*. Ed. Earl Rovit. Englewood Cliffs, NJ: Prentice Hall, 1975. 122-34.

Singh, Sukhbir. "Indian Karma Yogi in Saul Bellow's *Mr. Sammler's Planet*." *Comparative Literature Studies* 44.4 (2007): 434-57.

_____, ed. *Conversations with Saul Bellow: A Collection of Selected Interviews*. Delhi: Academic Foundation, 1993.

Smith, Herbert J. "*Humboldt's Gift* and Rudolf Steiner." *Centennial Review* 22.4 (1978): 479-89.

Tanner, Tony. *Saul Bellow*. London: Oliver & Boyd, 1965.

Trachtenberg, Stanley, ed. *Critical Essays on Saul Bellow*. Boston: G. K. Hall, 1979.

Wasserman, Harriet. *Handsome Is: Adventures with Saul Bellow*. New York: Fromm, 1997.

Weiss, Daniel. "Caliban on Prospero: A Psychoanalytic Study on the Novel *Seize the Day*, by Saul Bellow." *Saul Bellow and the Critics*. Ed. Irving Malin. New York: New York University Press, 1967. 114-41.

Wilson, Jonathan. *"Herzog": The Limits of Ideas*. Boston: Twayne, 1990.

_____. *On Bellow's Planet. Readings from the Dark Side*. Rutherford, NJ: Fairleigh Dickinson University Press, 1985.

Wirth-Nesher, Hana. *Call It English: The Languages of Jewish American Literature*. Princeton, NJ: Princeton University Press, 2006.

Yadav, C. S. *Saul Bellow*. Jaipur: Printwell, 1991.

Yetman, Michael G. "Who Would Not Sing for Humboldt?" *ELH* 48.4 (1981): 935-51.

Zipperstein, Steven J. "Isaac Rosenfeld, Saul Bellow, Friendship and Fate." *New England Review* 30.1 (2009): 10-20.

CRITICAL
INSIGHTS

About the Editor _____

Allan Chavkin is Professor of English at Texas State University-San Marcos. His scholarly work on Saul Bellow spans more than three decades and reflects his interest in understanding Bellow's work in the context of world literature. He has published numerous essays on Bellow's fiction in a variety of books and periodicals, including *Comparative Literature Studies, Philological Quarterly, Papers on Language and Literature, Essays in Literature,* and *Studies in the Novel.* He also has published on the work of other writers, such as Louise Erdrich, Leslie Marmon Silko, William Faulkner, Ernest Hemingway, Wallace Stevens, William Wordsworth, and John Keats. His books include *Conversations with John Gardner, English Romanticism and Modern Fiction: A Collection of Critical Essays, Conversations with Louise Erdrich and Michael Dorris* (with Nancy Feyl Chavkin), *The Chippewa Landscape of Louise Erdrich,* and *Leslie Marmon Silko's "Ceremony": A Casebook.*

Throughout his career, Professor Chavkin has been active in a number of national and international organizations. His research has been supported by grants from the National Endowment for the Humanities, the American Council for Learned Societies, and the American Philosophical Association. He is the recipient of Texas State University's Presidential Award for Scholarship.

About *The Paris Review* _____

The Paris Review is America's preeminent literary quarterly, dedicated to discovering and publishing the best new voices in fiction, nonfiction, and poetry. The magazine was founded in Paris in 1953 by the young American writers Peter Matthiessen and Doc Humes, and edited there and in New York for its first fifty years by George Plimpton. Over the decades, the *Review* has introduced readers to the earliest writings of Jack Kerouac, Philip Roth, T. C. Boyle, V. S. Naipaul, Ha Jin, Ann Patchett, Jay McInerney, Mona Simpson, and Edward P. Jones, and published numerous now-classic works, including Roth's *Goodbye, Columbus,* Donald Barthelme's *Alice,* Jim Carroll's *Basketball Diaries,* and selections from Samuel Beckett's *Molloy* (his first publication in English). The first chapter of Jeffrey Eugenides's *The Virgin Suicides* appeared in the *Review*'s pages, as have stories by Rick Moody, David Foster Wallace, Denis Johnson, Jim Crace, Lorrie Moore, and Jeanette Winterson.

The Paris Review's renowned Writers at Work series of interviews, whose early installments include legendary conversations with E. M. Forster, William Faulkner, and Ernest Hemingway, is one of the landmarks of world literature. The interviews received a George Polk Award and were nominated for a Pulitzer Prize. Among the more than three hundred interviewees are Robert Frost, Marianne Moore, W. H. Auden, Elizabeth Bishop, Susan Sontag, and Toni Morrison. Recent issues feature conversations with Jonathan Franzen, Norman Rush, Louise Erdrich, Joan Didion, Norman Mailer, R. Crumb, Michel Houellebecq, Marilynne Robinson, David Mitchell, Annie Proulx, and Gay Talese. In November 2009, Picador published the final volume of a four-volume series of anthologies of *Paris Review* interviews. The *New York Times* called the Writers at Work series "the most remarkable and extensive interviewing project we possess."

The Paris Review is edited by Lorin Stein, who was named to the post in 2010. The editorial team has published fiction by Lydia Davis, André Aciman, Sam Lipsyte, Damon Galgut, Mohsin Hamid, Uzodinma Iweala, James Lasdun, Padgett Powell, Richard Price, and Sam Shepard. Recent poetry selections include work by Frederick Seidel, Carol Muske-Dukes, John Ashbery, Kay Ryan, Mary Jo Bang, Sharon Olds, Charles Wright, and Mary Karr. Writing published in the magazine has been anthologized in *Best American Short Stories* (2006, 2007, and 2008), *Best American Poetry*, *Best Creative Non-Fiction*, the Pushcart Prize anthology, and *O. Henry Prize Stories*.

The magazine presents three annual awards. The Hadada Award for lifelong contribution to literature has recently been given to Joan Didion, Norman Mailer, Peter Matthiessen, John Ashbery, and, in 2010, Philip Roth. The Plimpton Prize for Fiction, awarded to a debut or emerging writer brought to national attention in the pages of *The Paris Review*, was presented in 2007 to Benjamin Percy, to Jesse Ball in 2008, and to Alistair Morgan in 2009. In 2011, the magazine inaugurated the Terry Southern Prize for Humor.

The Paris Review was a finalist for the 2008 and 2009 National Magazine Awards in fiction and won the 2007 National Magazine Award in photojournalism. The *Los Angeles Times* recently called *The Paris Review* "an American treasure with true international reach," and the *New York Times* designated it "a thing of sober beauty."

Since 1999 *The Paris Review* has been published by The Paris Review Foundation, Inc., a not-for-profit 501(c)(3) organization.

The Paris Review is available in digital form to libraries worldwide in selected academic databases exclusively from EBSCO Publishing. Libraries can contact EBSCO at 1-800-653-2726 for details. For more information on *The Paris Review* or to subscribe, please visit: www.theparisreview.org.

Contributors

Allan Chavkin is Professor of English at Texas State University-San Marcos. He has published many essays on Saul Bellow's fiction and is on the editorial board of the *Saul Bellow Journal*. His books include *Conversations with John Gardner, English Romanticism and Modern Fiction: A Collection of Critical Essays, Conversations with Louise Erdrich and Michael Dorris* (with Nancy Feyl Chavkin), *The Chippewa Landscape of Louise Erdrich*, and *Leslie Marmon Silko's "Ceremony": A Casebook*.

Victoria Aarons is Mitchell Professor of English and Chair of the Department of English at Trinity University, San Antonio, Texas. She is an H. G. Barnard Faculty Fellow and has received the Z. T. Fellowship for excellence in teaching and advising and the Minnie Stevens Piper Award for Excellence in Teaching. She specializes in American Jewish literature and culture and Holocaust studies. Her books include *A Measure of Memory: Storytelling and Identity in American Jewish Fiction* (*Choice* Award for Outstanding Academic Title, 1996) and *What Happened to Abraham? Reinventing the Covenant in American Jewish Fiction* (*Choice* Award for Outstanding Academic Title, 2005). She also has published essays in many scholarly journals.

Natalie Jacoby grew up in Richmond, Virginia, and is a former intern at *The Paris Review*. She currently works for *The New Yorker*.

Andrew M. Gordon is Emeritus Professor of English and Director of the Institute for the Psychological Study of the Arts at the University of Florida. He is the author of *An American Dreamer*, on the fiction of Norman Mailer; *Empire of Dreams*, on the science fiction and fantasy films of Steven Spielberg; and *Screen Saviors: Hollywood Fictions of Whiteness* (with Hernán Vera). He is coeditor (with Peter Rudnytsky) of *Psychoanalyses/Feminisms*. He has also published many essays on Saul Bellow, Philip Roth, Cynthia Ozick, Bernard Malamud, Art Spiegelman, and other Jewish American writers.

Judie Newman is Professor of American Studies at the University of Nottingham. Her recent publications include *Fictions of America: Narratives of Global Empire* and *Public Art, Memorials, and Atlantic Slavery*, edited with Celeste-Marie Bernier. She is also the author of *Saul Bellow and History, John Updike*, and *Nadine Gordimer*, as well as many scholarly articles.

Daniel Fuchs is Professor Emeritus of English at the College of Staten Island, City University of New York. He is the author of *Saul Bellow: Vision and Revision* (selected by *Choice* as an Outstanding Academic Book in 1984) and *The Comic Spirit of Wallace Stevens*, as well as many essays on contemporary American writing. He has been a Senior Fulbright Lecturer in American Literature at the University of Nantes, the University of Vienna, the Free University of Berlin, the Beijing Foreign Studies University, and the Jagiellonian University in Kraków. He has been a fellow at the

Villa Serbelloni, Bellagio; at Yaddo, Saratoga Springs; and at the Wurlitzer Foundation, Taos. His book *The Limits of Ferocity: Sexual Aggression and Modern Literary Rebellion* is forthcoming.

Gloria L. Cronin is Professor of English at Brigham Young University, where she is coeditor of the *Saul Bellow Journal*. She has served as Executive Director of the International Saul Bellow Society since 1991, and she has published widely in the fields of Jewish American and African American literatures. She has published a number of books, including *A Room of His Own: In Search of the Feminine in the Novels of Saul Bellow, Small Planets: Saul Bellow as Short Fiction Writer*, and *Conversations with Saul Bellow*. She is currently coediting two books of essays, one on "Saul Bellow and the comic" and the other on contemporary Jewish American literature.

Jean-François Leroux has published *Modern French Poets* and *The Renaissance of Impasse: From the Age of Carlyle, Emerson, and Melville to the Quiet Revolution in Quebec*. He teaches at the University of Ottawa.

Jonathan Baumbach is a contemporary American novelist, the author of fourteen books of fiction. He has had more than ninety stories published in such places as *Esquire, American Review, TriQuarterly*, and *Partisan Review*, and some of his stories have appeared in *Best American Short Stories, O. Henry Prize Stories*, and *The Best of TriQuarterly*. He is also the author of *The Landscape of Nightmare: Studies in Contemporary American Fiction* and two-time Chairman of the National Society of Film Critics.

Donald Pizer is Pierce Butler Professor of English Emeritus at Tulane University. He is the author of *The Novels of Theodore Dreiser, Realism and Naturalism in Nineteenth-Century American Literature, The Theory and Practice of American Literary Naturalism, The Novels of Frank Norris*, and other books.

Sir Malcolm Stanley Bradbury was an English novelist, screenwriter, literary critic, and academic who published books on Saul Bellow, Evelyn Waugh, and E. M. Forster. He also published editions of classics and handbooks on both modern American and British fiction. His best-known novel is *The History Man*. He died in 2000.

M. Gilbert Porter is Professor of Emeritus at the University of Missouri. He is the author of *Whence the Power? The Artistry and Humanity of Saul Bellow, The Art of Grit: Ken Kesey's Fiction*, and *"One Flew over the Cuckoo's Nest": Rising to Heroism*.

S. Lillian Kremer is Professor Emeritus in the Department of English at Kansas State University. She is the author of *Witness Through the Imagination: The Holocaust in Jewish American Literature* and *Women's Holocaust Writing: Memory and Imagination*.

Nancy Feyl Chavkin is Regents' Professor and Director of the Center for Children and Families at Texas State University-San Marcos. She has published articles on social issues in literature, including such topics as the underclass and family systems theory in Saul Bellow's fiction. Her books include *Conversations with Louise Erdrich* and Michael Dorris (with Allan Chavkin), *Families and Schools in a Pluralistic Society*, and *The Use of Research*. She is the recipient of Texas State University's Presidential Award for Scholarship and the Minnie Stevens Piper Teaching Award for Excellence in Teaching.

Robert F. Kiernan is the author of six books: *Saul Bellow, Gore Vidal, Noel Coward, American Writing Since 1945: A Critical Survey, Carson McCullers and Katherine Anne Porter: A Reference Guide*, and *Frivolity Unbound: Six Masters of the Camp Novel*. He taught at Manhattan College, New York.

Ellen Pifer is Professor of English and Comparative Literature at the University of Delaware. She is the author of *Demon or Doll: Images of the Child in Contemporary Writing and Culture, Saul Bellow Against the Grain* (which received *Choice* magazine's Outstanding Academic Book Award for 1990-91), *Nabokov and the Novel*, and dozens of essays, articles, and chapters on modern and contemporary fiction. She is also editor of *Vladimir Nabokov's "Lolita": A Casebook* and *Critical Essays on John Fowles*. She has published a monograph on Fowles's work and numerous essays and articles on Nabokov. She teaches courses on twentieth-century literature and culture, focusing on the American, English, and Anglophone novel in a global context; she has lectured widely on these topics in Europe, Russia, and the United States.

Sarah Blacher Cohen was a Professor at the University at Albany, State University of New York, where she was a specialist in Jewish American fiction. Her books include *Comic Relief: Humor in Contemporary American Literature, Saul Bellow's Enigmatic Laughter, Cynthia Ozick's Comic Art: From Levity to Liturgy, From Hester Street to Hollywood: The Jewish-American Stage and Screen, Making a Scene: The Contemporary Drama of Jewish-American Women*, and *Jewish Wry: Essays on Jewish Humor*. Her plays include *The Ladies Locker Room, Soul Sisters*, and a musical revue titled *Sophie, Totie & Belle*. She died in 2008.

Eusebio L. Rodrigues was Professor of English at Georgetown University. He is the author of *Quest for the Human: An Exploration of Saul Bellow's Fiction* and the novel *Love and Samsāra*. He has also published articles on William Faulkner, William Gass, Graham Greene, E. M. Forster, and Toni Morrison.

Acknowledgments

"The *Paris Review* Perspective" by Natalie Jacoby. Copyright © 2010 by Natalie Jacoby. Special appreciation goes to Christopher Cox, Nathaniel Rich, and David Wallace-Wells, editors at *The Paris Review.*

"Exhausting Ennui: Bellow, Dostoevsky, and the Literature of Boredom" by Jean-François Leroux. From *College Literature* 35.1 (Winter 2008): 1-15. Copyright © 2008 by *College Literature.* Reprinted with permission of *College Literature.*

"The Double Vision: *The Victim* by Saul Bellow" by Jonathan Baumbach. From *The Landscape of Nightmare: Studies in the Contemporary Novel* (1965) by Jonathan Baumbach. Copyright © 1965 by New York University Press. Reprinted with permission of New York University Press.

"Saul Bellow: *The Adventures of Augie March*" by Donald Pizer. From *Twentieth-Century American Literary Naturalism: An Interpretation* (1982) by Donald Pizer. Copyright © 1982 by Southern Illinois University Press. Reprinted with permission of Southern Illinois University Press.

"'The Hollywood Thread' and the First Draft of Saul Bellow's *Seize the Day*" by Allan Chavkin. From *Studies in the Novel* 14.1 (Spring 1982): 82-94. Copyright © 1982 by the University of North Texas. Reprinted with permission of the University of North Texas.

"The Fifties Novels: *The Adventures of Augie March*, *Seize the Day*, and *Henderson the Rain King*" by Malcolm Bradbury. From *Saul Bellow* (1982) by Malcolm Bradbury. Copyright © 1982 by Methuen & Co. Reprinted with permission of Taylor & Francis Books UK.

"'Weirdly Tranquil' Vision: The Point of View of Moses Herzog" by M. Gilbert Porter. From *Saul Bellow Journal* 8.1 (Winter 1989): 3-11. Copyright © 1989 by *Saul Bellow Journal.* Reprinted with permission of *Saul Bellow Journal.*

"The Holocaust in *Mr. Sammler's Planet*" by S. Lillian Kremer. From *Saul Bellow Journal* 4.1 (Fall/Winter 1985): 19-32. Copyright © 1985 by *Saul Bellow Journal.* Reprinted with permission of *Saul Bellow Journal.*

"'Farcical Martyrs' and 'Deeper Theives' in Bellow's *Humboldt's Gift*" by Allan Chavkin and Nancy Feyl Chavkin. From *Kansas Quarterly* 21.4 (Fall 1989): 77-88. Copyright © 1989 by *Arkansas Review.* Reprinted with permission of *Arkansas Review.*

"*The Dean's December* (1982)" by Robert F. Kiernan. From *Saul Bellow* (1989) by Robert F. Kiernan. Copyright © 1989 by The Continuum International Publishing Group. Reprinted with permission of the publisher, The Continuum International Publishing Group.

"On *Him with His Foot in His Mouth and Other Stories*" by Daniel Fuchs. From *Saul Bellow Journal* 5.1 (Fall/Winter 1986): 3-15. Copyright © 1986 by *Saul Bellow Journal.* Reprinted with permission of *Saul Bellow Journal.*

65, 282-294, 296-297; critical reception, *98*
Mother-son relationships, 46, 65, 77, 141, 169, 181, 325, 330
Motifs. *See* Themes and motifs
Mr. Sammler's Planet (Bellow), xi, 10, 21, 86, 216-222, 224-227, 229; critical reception, 24, 95

Names and naming, 41, 75, 132, 153, 180, 216, 220, 224, 251, 270, 300, 320
Narration and narrators, xiv, 4, 24, 42, 54, 79, 81-82, 84-85, 100, 109, 129, 172, 189, 196, 198, 207, 212, 215, 268, 272, 323, 330
Nausea (Sartre), 4, 110
Nightmares. *See* Dreams and nightmares
Nobel Prize in Literature, 11, 24, 89, 249
Notes from Underground (Dostoevsky), 4, 110, 112, 114-115, 122

"One of Those Days" (Bellow), x, 170-171, 173-174, 176-177, 180-183

Point of view; *Herzog*, xi, 207, 209-210, 212-214; *Seize the Day*, 42, 171; *The Victim*, x, 142; *What Kind of Day Did You Have?*, 16
Post-traumatic stress disorder, 11
Psychoanalysis, 37, 39-40, 44-45, 64, 94
Pulitzer Prize, 11, 24

Raresh, Valeria (*The Dean's December*), 65, 98, 250, 255, 257, 264
Ravelstein (Bellow), xiv-15, 25, 57, 65, 300-304, 306-309; critical reception, 101
Reflections and mirrors, xi, 61, 120, 209, 211

Reichian psychotherapy, 37, 45, 94, 185
Romans à clef, xiv-15, 301
Rose, Billy (*The Bellarosa Connection*), 16, 80-82, 100

Sammler, Artur (*Mr. Sammler's Planet*), 10-11, 86, 216, 220, 222, 227, 229, 284, 322
Sammler, Shula (*Mr. Sammler's Planet*), 11, 220
Seize the Day (Bellow), viii, x-xi, 6, 29, 42, 45-46, 48-49, 63, 191, 193, 321; critical reception, 92, 172; first draft, 170-172, 174-183; and psychoanalysis, 41, 43
Self psychology, 40, 48
Shame, 49, 321-323, 325-326, 328, 330
Siddhartha (Hesse), 119
"Silver Dish, A" (Bellow), xiii, 267, 277
"Something to Remember Me By" (Bellow), xv, 321-331
Suffering, 5, 43-44, 50, 65, 73, 75, 82, 129, 145, 149, 164, 174, 184, 193, 197, 210, 220, 223-224, 246, 316

"Take Pity" (Malamud), 73-74
Tamkin, Dr. (*Seize the Day*), 7, 42-43, 46-47, 49, 170, 172, 178, 185, 192, 194
Theft, A (Bellow), 40, 65, 99
Themes and motifs; aging, xiii, 8, 101, 177, 181, 216, 267; anthropology, 57, 94, 198, 274; anti-Semitism, 5, 22, 59, 75, 90, 132, 143-144, 220, 228; automobiles, xii, 158, 231-232, 234-245; boredom, ix, 99, 109-110, 117; Catholicism, 42, 170, 221; death and dying, 8, 11-12, 15-16, 44, 46, 59, 62, 78, 84, 93-94, 121, 131-132, 135, 140, 150, 161, 176, 181, 184, 187, 194, 200, 202, 205-206, 212, 216,

218, 221, 223-224, 239, 250, 253,
256, 258, 264, 267, 277, 289-291,
306, 308, 310, 323, 325-326, 330;
domes, 175, 251, 264; doubles, 59-
60, 62, 113, 119, 133, 136, 144-145,
194, 300; dreams and nightmares, 60-
61, 72, 83, 86, 114; driving, xii, 231-
232, 234-245; family relationships, 7,
41-43, 46, 49, 65, 77, 92, 141, 169,
176, 178, 180-182, 240, 268, 277,
283, 288, 325, 327, 330-331; guilt,
ix, 4, 44, 46, 58, 129-130, 132, 135,
140, 143, 181, 234, 322, 326, 330;
Holocaust, ix, xi, 10, 16, 23, 59, 61,
70, 96, 100, 216, 218, 221, 229;
hope, 150, 191, 317; idolatry, 291-
292; illness and disease, 5, 15, 142,
223, 275, 304, 323, 325-326;
infidelity, 9, 12, 39, 135, 241, 269;
Jewish identity, 15, 42, 81, 83-84, 86,
100, 144, 241, 275, 308, 331; love, 8,
43, 49, 65, 99-101, 116, 129, 137,
155, 160, 165-167, 181, 255, 269,
277, 285, 288-289; marriage, 4, 178,
258, 274, 300; memory, 16, 63, 69,
83, 86, 100, 213, 217, 225, 297, 301;
psychoanalysis, 37, 39-40, 45, 64, 94
; reflections and mirrors, xi, 61, 120,
209, 211; shame, 49, 321-323, 325-
326, 328, 330; suffering, 5, 43-44,
50, 65, 73, 75, 82, 129, 145, 149,
164, 174, 184, 193, 197, 210, 220,

223-224, 246, 316; water, 7, 44, 56,
140, 171, 194, 201-202, 211
To Jerusalem and Back (Bellow), 24, 63,
229; critical reception, 97
Trachtenberg, Kenneth (*More Die of
Heartbreak*), xiv, 99, 282, 284

Victim, The (Bellow), ix, 4-5, 22, 58, 62,
127-129, 131-132, 134-140, 142-143,
145-146, 188; critical reception, 90
Vilitzer, Harold (*More Die of
Heartbreak*), 15, 287, 289

Water imagery, 7, 44, 56, 140, 171, 194,
201-202, 211
What Kind of Day Did You Have?
(Bellow), xiii, 16, 267-268, 270-272,
301
Wilhelm, Tommy (*Seize the Day*), viii,
7, 29, 42, 44, 46, 48, 172, 180, 321;
Bellow on, 50
Winter Notes on Summer Impressions
(Dostoevsky), 112, 118
Women. *See* Female characters
Wulpy, Victor (*What Kind of Day Did
You Have?*), xiii, 267-269, 271, 301

Yiddish expressions, 72, 92, 103, 149,
187, 216, 224, 305, 324

"Zetland: By a Character Witness"
(Bellow), xiii, 38, 267, 276